Sunset

BEST HOME PLANS

Sloping Lots

Three-story hillside home is designed for efficient use of space. Particularly well suited for recreation, it features a generous view-side deck and spacious living and recreation rooms. See plan H-966-1B on page 218.

Sunset Publishing Corporation ■ Menlo Park, California

A Dream Come True

Planning and building a house is one of life's most creative and rewarding challenges. Whether you're seriously considering building a new home or you're just dreaming about it, this book offers a wealth of inspiration and information to help you get started.

On the following pages, you'll learn how to plan and manage a home-building project—and how to ensure its success. Then you'll discover more than 200 proven home plans, designed for families just like yours by architects and professional designers. Peruse the pages and study the floor plans; you're sure to find a home that's just right for you. When you're ready to order blueprints, you can simply call or mail in your order, and you'll receive the plans within days.

Enjoy the adventure!

SUNSET BOOKS
President and Publisher: Susan J. Maruyama
Director, Finance & Business Affairs: Gary Loebner
Director, Manufacturing & Sales Service: Lorinda Reichert
Western Regional Sales Director: Richard A. Smeby
Eastern Regional Sales Director: Richard M. Miller
Editorial Director: Kenneth Winchester
Coordinating Editor: Linda J. Selden
Contributing Editor: Don Vandervort

SUNSET PUBLISHING CORPORATION
Chairman: Robert L. Miller
President/Chief Executive Officer: Robin Wolaner
Chief Financial Officer: James E. Mitchell
Circulation Director: Robert I. Gursha
Editor, Sunset Magazine: William R. Marken

Photographers: Mark Englund/HomeStyles: 4, 5; Philip Harvey: 10 top, back cover; Stephen Marley: 11 top left and right; Russ Widstrand: 10 bottom; Tom Wyatt: 11 bottom.

Cover: Pictured is plan CDG-4005 on page 125. Cover design by Naganuma Design & Direction. Photography by Mark Englund/HomeStyles.

First printing August 1994

ISBN 0-376-01134-3.
Library of Congress Catalog Card Number: 94-66502.
Printed in the United States.

Contents

Taking advantage of a slope, the garages of this rustic charmer tuck under the main floor. See plan C-8339 on page 105.

Designs for Sloping Sites

Hillsides and sloping lots make special demands on house design. If you've been searching for plans that take advantage of such a site, you're sure to appreciate the home plans presented here. These proven designs, created by some of America's foremost architects and designers, pay special attention to sloping sites. They feature multiple levels, decks, and other architectural features particularly suited to slopes and hillsides. We have also included some best-selling flat-lot plans that, with the addition of an optional daylight basement, can be built on a sloping lot.

You'll discover all styles: classic traditional homes, striking contemporary houses, country charmers, affordable starters, even rustic vacation homes. And you'll find homes designed for all types of slopes.

The two keys to success in building are capable project management and good design. The next few pages will walk you through some of the most important aspects of project management: you'll find an overview of the building process, directions for selecting the right plan and getting the most from it, and methods for successfully working with a builder and other professionals.

The balance of the book presents professionally designed stock plans. Once you find a plan that will work for you—perhaps with a few modifications made later to personalize it for your family—you can order construction blueprints for a fraction of the cost of a custom design, a savings of many thousands of dollars (see pages 12–15 for information on how to order).

Two-story contemporary is perfectly suited to its sloping lot. The step-down formal living and dining rooms to the left of the entry feature soaring 13-foot ceilings. The spacious kitchen, eating area, and family room overlook a patio at the rear. On the upper floor are three bedrooms, one an elegant master suite. See plan R-2167-D on page 217.

Raised deck that projects over a gentle slope extends this compact home's family room outdoors. An optional daylight basement foundation plan is offered to accommodate a steeper site. See plan P-7758-2 on page 81.

Nestled into a hillside, this luxurious home provides multilevel living centered around a dramatic two-story foyer. The master suite is on the main floor; above are two more bedrooms, a bath, and a bonus room. The garage is under the main level. See plan R-4043 on page 222.

Classic home greets guests with a wide, covered porch and, inside, a two-story entry foyer. The living room and study feature high ceilings. On the second floor are a large master suite and two additional bedrooms. See plan CDG-4002 on page 172.

The Art of Building

As you embark on your home-building project, think of it as a trip—clearly not a vacation but rather an interesting, adventurous, at times difficult expedition. Meticulous planning will make your journey not only far more enjoyable but also much more successful. By careful planning, you can avoid—or at least minimize—some of the pitfalls along the way.

Start with realistic expectations of the road ahead. To do this, you'll want to gain an understanding of the basic house-building process, settle on a design that will work for you and your family, and make sure your project is actually doable. By taking those initial steps, you can gain a clear idea of how much time, money, and energy you'll need to invest to make your dream come true.

The Building Process

Your role in planning and managing a house-building project can be divided into two parts: prebuilding preparation and construction management.

■ **Prebuilding preparation.** This is where you should focus most of your attention. In the hands of a qualified contractor whose expertise you can rely on, the actual building process should go fairly smoothly. But during most of the prebuilding stage, you're generally on your own. Your job will be to launch the project and develop a talented team that can help you bring your new home to fruition.

When you work with stock plans, the prebuilding process usually goes as follows:

First, you research the general area where you want to live, selecting one or more possible home sites (unless you already own a suitable lot). Then you choose a basic house design, with the idea that it may require some modification. Finally, you analyze the site, the design, and your budget to determine if the project is actually attainable.

If you decide that it is, you purchase the land and order blueprints. If you want to modify them, you consult an architect, designer, or contractor. Once the plans are finalized, you request bids from contractors and arrange any necessary construction financing.

After selecting a builder and signing a contract, you (or your contractor) then file the plans with the building department. When the plans are approved, often several weeks—or even months—later, you're ready to begin construction.

■ **Construction management.** Unless you intend to act as your own contractor, your role during the building process is mostly one of quality control and time management. Even so, it's important to know the sequence of events and something about construction methods so you can discuss progress with your builder and prepare for any important decisions you may need to make along the way.

Decision-making is critical. Once construction begins, the builder must usually plunge ahead, keeping his carpenters and subcontractors progressing steadily. If you haven't made a key decision—which model bathtub or sink to install, for example—it can bring construction to a frustrating and expensive halt.

Usually, you'll make such decisions before the onset of building, but, inevitably, some issue or another will arise during construction. Being knowledgeable about the building process will help you anticipate and circumvent potential logjams.

Selecting a House Plan

Searching for the right plan can be a fun, interactive family experience—one of the most exciting parts of a house-building project. Gather the family around as you peruse the home plans in this book. Study the size, location, and configuration of each room; traffic patterns both inside the house and to the outdoors; exterior style; and how you'll use the available space. Discuss the pros and cons of the various plans.

Browse through pictures of homes in magazines to stimulate ideas. Clip the photos you like so you can think about your favorite options. When you visit the homes of friends, note special features that appeal to you. Also, look carefully at the homes in your neighborhood, noting their style and how they fit the site.

Mark those plans that most closely suit your ideals. Then, to narrow down your choices, critique each plan, using the following information as a guide.

■ **Overall size and budget.** How large a house do you want? Will the house you're considering fit your family's requirements? Look at the overall square footage and room sizes. If you have a hard time visualizing room sizes, measure some of the rooms in your present home and compare.

It's often better for the house to be a little too big than a little too small, but remember that every extra square foot will cost more money to build and maintain.

■ **Number and type of rooms.** Beyond thinking about the number of bedrooms and baths you want, consider your family's life-style and how you use space. Do you want both a family room and a living room? Do you need a formal dining space? Will you require some extra rooms, or "swing spaces," that can serve multiple purposes, such as a home office–guest room combination?

■ **Room placement and traffic patterns.** What are your preferences for locations of formal living areas, master bedroom, and children's rooms? Do you prefer a kitchen that's open to family areas or one that's private and out of the way? How much do you use exterior spaces and how should they relate to the interior?

Once you make those determinations, look carefully at the floor plan of the house you're considering to see if it meets your needs and if the traffic flow will be convenient for your family.

■ **Architectural style.** Have you always wanted to live in a Victorian farmhouse? Now is your chance to create a house that matches your idea of "home" (taking into account, of course, styles in your neighborhood). But don't let your preference for one particular architectural style dictate your home's floor plan. If the floor plan doesn't work for your family, keep looking.

■ **Site considerations.** Most people choose a site before selecting a plan—or at least they've zeroed in on the basic type of land where they'll situate their house. It sounds elementary, but choose a house that will fit the site.

When figuring the "footprint" of a house, you must know about any restrictions that will affect your home's height or proximity to the property lines. Call the local building department (look under city or county listings in the phone book) and get a very clear description of any restrictions, such as setbacks, height limits, and lot coverage, that will affect what you can build on the site (see "Working with City Hall," at right).

When you visit potential sites, note trees, rock outcroppings, slopes, views, winds, sun, neighboring homes, and other factors. All will impact on how your house works on a particular site.

Once you've narrowed down the choice of sites, consult an architect or building designer (see page 8) to help you evaluate how some potential houses will work on the sites you have in mind.

Working with City Hall

For any building project, even a minor one, it's essential to be familiar with building codes and other restrictions that can affect your project.

■ **Building codes,** generally implemented by the city or county building department, set the standards for safe, lasting construction. Codes specify minimum construction techniques and materials for foundations, framing, electrical wiring, plumbing, insulation, and all other aspects of a building. Although codes are adopted and enforced locally, most regional codes conform to the standards set by the national Uniform Building Code, Standard Building Code, or Basic Building Code. In some cases, local codes set more restrictive standards than national ones.

■ **Building permits** are required for home-building projects nearly everywhere. If you work with a contractor, the builder's firm should handle all necessary permits.

More than one permit may be needed; for example, one will cover the foundation, another the electrical wiring, and still another the heating equipment installation. Each will probably involve a fee and require inspections by building officials before work can proceed. (Inspections benefit *you,* as they ensure that the job is being done satisfactorily.) Permit fees are generally a percentage (1 to 1.5 percent) of the project's estimated value, often calculated on square footage.

It's important to file for the necessary permits. Failure to do so can result in fines or legal action against you. You can even be forced to undo the work performed. At the very least, your negligence may come back to haunt you later when you're ready to sell your house.

■ **Zoning ordinances,** particular to your community, restrict setbacks (how near to property lines you may build), your house's allowable height, lot coverage factors (how much of your property you can cover with structures), and other factors that impact design and building. If your plans don't conform to zoning ordinances, you can try to obtain a variance, an exception to the rules. But this legal work can be expensive and time-consuming. Even if you prove that your project won't negatively affect your neighbors, the building department can still refuse to grant the variance.

■ **Deeds and covenants** attach to the lot. Deeds set out property lines and easements; covenants may establish architectural standards in a neighborhood. Since both can seriously impact your project, make sure you have complete information on any deeds or covenants before you turn over a spadeful of soil.

Is Your Project Doable?

Before you purchase land, make sure your project is doable. Although it's too early at this stage to pinpoint costs, making a few phone calls will help you determine whether your project is realistic. You'll be able to learn if you can afford to build the house, how long it will take, and what obstacles may stand in your way.

To get a ballpark estimate of cost, multiply a house's total square footage (of livable space) by the local average cost per square foot for new construction. (To obtain local averages, call a contractor, an architect, a realtor, or the local chapter of the National Association of Home Builders.) Some contractors may even be willing to give you a preliminary bid. Once you know approximate costs, speak to your lender to explore financing.

It's a good idea to discuss your project with several contractors (see page 8). They may be aware of problems in your area that could limit your options—bedrock that makes digging basements difficult, for example. These conversations are actually the first step in developing a list of contractors from which you'll choose the one who will build your home.

Recruiting Your Home Team

A home-building project will interject you and your family into the building business, an area that may be unfamiliar territory. Among the people you'll be working with are architects, designers, landscapers, contractors, and subcontractors.

Design Help

A qualified architect or designer can help you modify and personalize your home plan, taking into account your family's needs and budget and the house's style. In fact, you may want to consider consulting such a person while you're selecting a plan to help you articulate your needs.

Design professionals are capable of handling any or all aspects of the design process. For example, they can review your house plans, suggest options, and then provide rough sketches of the options on tracing paper. Many architects will even secure needed permits and negotiate with contractors or subcontractors, as well as oversee the quality of the work.

Of course, you don't necessarily need an architect or designer to implement minor changes in a plan; although most contractors aren't trained in design, some can help you with modifications.

An open-ended, hourly-fee arrangement that you work out with your architect or designer allows for flexibility, but it often turns out to be more costly than working on a flat-fee basis. On a flat fee, you agree to pay a specific amount of money for a certain amount of work.

To find architects and designers, contact such trade associations as the American Institute of Architects (AIA), American Institute of Building Designers (AIBD), American Society of Landscape Architects (ASLA), and American Society of Interior Designers (ASID). Although many professionals choose not to belong to trade associations, those who do have met the standards of their respective associations. For phone numbers of local branches, check the Yellow Pages.

■ **Architects** are licensed by the state and have degrees. They're trained in all facets of building design and construction. Although some can handle interior design and structural engineering, others hire specialists for those tasks.

■ **Building designers** are generally unlicensed but may be accredited by the American Institute of Building Designers. Their backgrounds are varied: some may be unlicensed architects in apprenticeship; others are interior designers or contractors with design skills.

■ **Draftspersons** offer an economical route to making simple changes on your drawings. Like building designers, these people may be unlicensed architect apprentices, engineers, or members of related trades. Most are accomplished at drawing up plans.

■ **Interior designers,** as their job title suggests, design interiors. They work with you to choose room finishes, furnishings, appliances, and decorative elements. Part of their expertise is in arranging furnishings to create a workable space plan. Some interior designers are employed by architectural firms; others work independently. Financial arrangements vary, depending on the designer's preference.

Related professionals are kitchen and bathroom designers, who concentrate on fixtures, cabinetry, appliances, materials, and space planning for the kitchen and bath.

■ **Landscape architects, designers, and contractors** design outdoor areas. Landscape architects are state-licensed to practice landscape design. A landscape designer usually has a landscape architect's education and training but does not have a state license. Licensed landscape contractors specialize in garden construction, though some also have design skills and experience.

■ **Soils specialists and structural engineers** may be needed for projects where unstable soils or uncommon wind loads or seismic forces must be taken into account. Any structural changes to a house require the expertise of a structural engineer to verify that the house won't fall down.

Services of these specialists can be expensive, but they're imperative in certain conditions to ensure a safe, sturdy structure. Your building department will probably let you know if their services are required.

General Contractors

To build your house, hire a licensed general contractor. Most states require a contractor to be licensed and insured for worker's compensation in order to contract a building project and hire other subcontractors. State licensing ensures that contractors have met minimum training standards and have a specified level of experience. Licensing does not guarantee, however, that they're good at what they do.

When contractors hire subcontractors, they're responsible for overseeing the quality of work and materials of the subcontractors and for paying them.

■ **Finding a contractor.** How do you find a good contractor? Start by getting referrals from people you know who have built or remodeled their home. Nothing beats a personal recommendation. The best contractors are usually busily moving from one satisfied client to another prospect, advertised only by word of mouth.

You can also ask local real estate brokers and lenders or even your building inspector for names of qualified builders. Experienced lumber dealers are another good source of names.

In the Yellow Pages, look under "Contractors–Building, General"; or call the local chapter of the National Association of Home Builders.

■ **Choosing a contractor.** Once you have a list of names of prospective builders, call several of them. On the telephone, ask first whether they handle your type of job and can work within your schedule. If they can, arrange a meeting with each one and ask them to be prepared with references of former clients and photos of previous jobs. Better still, meet them at one of their current work sites so you can get a glimpse of the quality of their work and how organized and thorough they are.

Take your plan to the meeting and discuss it enough to request a rough estimate (some builders will comply, while others will be reluctant to offer a ballpark estimate, preferring to give you a hard bid based on complete drawings). Don't hesitate to probe for advice or suggestions that might make building your house less expensive.

Be especially aware of each contractor's personality and how well you communicate. Good chemistry between you and your builder is a key ingredient for success.

Narrow down the candidates to three or four. Ask each for a firm bid, based on the exact same set of plans and specifications. For the bids to be accurate, your plans need to be complete and the specifications as precise as possible, calling out particular appliances, fixtures, floorings, roofing material, and so forth. (Some of these are specified in a stock-plan set; others are not.)

Call the contractors' references and ask about the quality of their work, their relationship with their clients, their promptness, and their readiness to follow up on problems. Visit former clients to check the contractor's work firsthand.

Be sure your final candidates are licensed, bonded, and insured for worker's compensation, public liability, and property damage. Also, try to determine how financially solvent they are (you can call their bank and credit references). Avoid contractors who are operating hand-to-mouth.

Don't automatically hire the contractor with the lowest bid if you don't think you'll get along well or if you have any doubts about the quality of the person's work. Instead, look for both the most reasonable bid and the contractor with the best credentials, references, terms, and compatibility with your family.

A word about bonds: You can request a performance bond that guarantees that your job will be finished by your contractor. If the job isn't completed, the bonding company will cover the cost of hiring another contractor to finish it. Bonds cost from 2 to 6 percent of the value of the project.

Your Building Contract

A building contract (see below) binds and protects both you and your contractor. It isn't just a legal document. It's also a list of the expectations of both parties. The best way to minimize the possibility of misunderstandings and costly changes later on is to write down every possible detail. Whether the contract is a standard form or one composed by you, have an attorney look it over before both you and the contractor sign it.

The contract should clearly specify all the work that needs to be done, including particular materials and work descriptions, the time schedule, and method of payment. It should be keyed to the working drawings.

A Sample Building Contract

Project and participants. Give a general description of the project, its address, and the names and addresses of both you and the builder.

Construction materials. Identify all construction materials by brand name, quality markings (species, grades, etc.), and model numbers where applicable. Avoid the clause "or equal," which allows the builder to substitute other materials for your choices. For materials you can't specify now, set down a budget figure.

Time schedule. Include both start and completion dates and specify that work will be "continuous." Although a contractor cannot be responsible for delays caused by strikes and material shortages, your builder should assume responsibility for completing the project within a reasonable period of time.

Work to be performed. State all work you expect the contractor to perform, from initial grading to finished painting.

Method and schedule of payment. Specify how and when payments are to be made. Typical installment agreements specify installment payments as particular phases of work are completed. Final payment is withheld until the job receives its final inspection and is cleared of all liens.

Waiver of liens. Protect yourself with a waiver of liens signed by the general contractor, the subcontractors, and all major suppliers. That way, subcontractors who are not paid for materials or services cannot place a lien on your property.

Personalizing Stock Plans

The beauty of buying stock plans for your new home is that they offer tested, well-conceived design at an affordable price. And stock plans dramatically reduce the time it takes to design a house, since the plans are ready when you are.

Because they were not created specifically for your family, stock plans may not reflect your personal taste. But it's not difficult to make revisions in stock plans that will turn your home into an expression of your family's personality. You'll surely want to add personal touches and choose your own finishes.

Ideally, the modifications you implement will be fairly minor. The more extensive the changes, the more expensive the plans. Major changes take valuable design time, and those that affect a house's structure may require a structural engineer's approval.

If you anticipate wholesale changes, such as moving a number of bearing walls or changing the roofline significantly, you may be better off selecting another plan. On the other hand, reconfiguring or changing the sizes of some rooms can probably be handled fairly easily.

Some structural changes may even be necessary to comply with local codes. Your area may have specific requirements for snow loads, energy codes, seismic or wind resistance, and so forth. Those types of modifications are likely to require the services of an architect or structural engineer.

Plan Modifications

Before you pencil in any changes, live with your plans for a while. Study them carefully—at your building site, if possible. Try to picture the finished house: how rooms will interrelate, where the sun will enter and at what angle, what the view will be from each window. Think about traffic patterns, access to rooms, room sizes, window and door locations, natural light, and kitchen and bathroom layouts.

Typical changes might involve adding windows or skylights to bring in natural light or capture a view. Or you may want to widen a hallway or doorway for roomier access, extend a room, eliminate doors, or change window and door sizes. Perhaps you'd like to shorten a room, stealing the gained space for a large closet. Look closely at the kitchen; it's not difficult to reconfigure the layout if it makes the space more convenient for you.

Above all, take your time—this is your home and it should reflect your taste and needs. Make your changes now, during the planning stage. Once construction begins, it will take crowbars, hammers, saws, new materials, and, most significantly, time to alter the plans. Because changes are not part of your building contract, you can count on them being expensive extras once construction begins.

Specifying Finishes

One way to personalize a house without changing its structure is to substitute your favorite finishes for those specified on the plan.

Would you prefer a stuccoed exterior rather than the wood siding shown on the plan? In most cases, this is a relatively easy change. Do you like the look of a wood shingle roof rather than the composition shingles shown on the plan? This, too, is easy. Perhaps you would like to change the windows from sliders to casements, or upgrade to high-efficiency glazing. No problem. Many of those kinds of changes can be worked out with your contractor.

Inside, you may want hardwood where vinyl flooring is shown. In fact, you can—and should—choose types, colors, and styles of floorings, wall coverings, tile, plumbing fixtures, door hardware, cabinetry, appliances, lighting fixtures, and other interior details, for it's these materials that will personalize your home. For help in making selections, consult an architect or interior designer (see page 8).

Each material you select should be spelled out clearly and precisely in your building contract.

Finishing touches can transform a house built from stock plans into an expression of your family's taste and style. Clockwise, from far left: Colorful tilework and custom cabinetry enliven a bathroom (Design: Osburn Design); highly organized closet system maximizes storage space (Architect: David Jeremiah Hurley); low-level deck expands living space to outdoor areas (Landscape architects: The Runa Group, Inc.); built-ins convert the corner of a guest room into a home office (Design: Lynn Williams of The French Connection); French country cabinetry lends style and old-world charm to a kitchen (Design: Garry Bishop/Showcase Kitchens).

What the Plans Include

Complete construction blueprints are available for every house shown in this book. Clear and concise, these detailed blueprints are designed by licensed architects or members of the American Institute of Building Designers (AIBD). Each plan is designed to meet standards set down by nationally recognized building codes (the Uniform Building Code, Standard Building Code, or Basic Building Code) at the time and for the area where they were drawn.

Remember, however, that every state, county, and municipality has its own codes, zoning requirements, ordinances, and building regulations. Modifications may be necessary to comply with such local requirements as snow loads, energy codes, seismic zones, and flood areas.

Although blueprint sets vary depending on the size and complexity of the house and on the individual designer's style, each set may include the elements described below and shown at right.

■ **Exterior elevations** show the front, rear, and sides of the house, including exterior materials, details, and measurements.

■ **Foundation plans** include drawings for a full, partial, or daylight basement, crawlspace, pole, pier, or slab foundation. All necessary notations and dimensions are included. (Foundation options will vary for each plan. If the plan you choose doesn't have the type of foundation you desire, a generic conversion diagram is available.)

■ **Detailed floor plans** show the placement of interior walls and the dimensions of rooms, doors, windows, stairways, and similar elements for each level of the house.

■ **Cross sections** show details of the house as though it were cut in slices from the roof to the foundation. The cross sections give the home's construction, insulation, flooring, and roofing details.

■ **Interior elevations** show the specific details of cabinets (kitchen, bathroom, and utility room), fireplaces, built-in units, and other special interior features.

■ **Roof details** give the layout of rafters, dormers, gables, and other roof elements, including clerestory windows and skylights. These details may be shown on the elevation sheet or on a separate diagram.

■ **Schematic electrical layouts** show the suggested locations for switches, fixtures, and outlets. These details may be shown on the floor plan or on a separate diagram.

■ **General specifications** provide instructions and information regarding excavation and grading, masonry and concrete work, carpentry and woodwork, thermal and moisture protection, drywall, tile, flooring, glazing, and caulking and sealants.

Other Helpful Building Aids

In addition to the construction information on every set of plans, you can buy the following guides.

■ **Reproducible blueprints** are helpful if you'll be making changes to the stock plan you've chosen. These blueprints are original line drawings produced on erasable, reproducible paper for the purpose of modification. When alterations are complete, working copies can be made.

■ **Itemized materials list** details the quantity, type, and size of materials needed to build your home. (This list is extremely helpful in obtaining an accurate construction bid. It's not intended for use to order materials.)

■ **Mirror-reverse plans** are useful if you want to build your home in the reverse of the plan that's shown. Because the lettering and dimensions read backwards, be sure to buy at least one regular-reading set of blueprints.

■ **Description of materials** gives the type and quality of materials suggested for the home. This form may be required for obtaining FHA or VA financing.

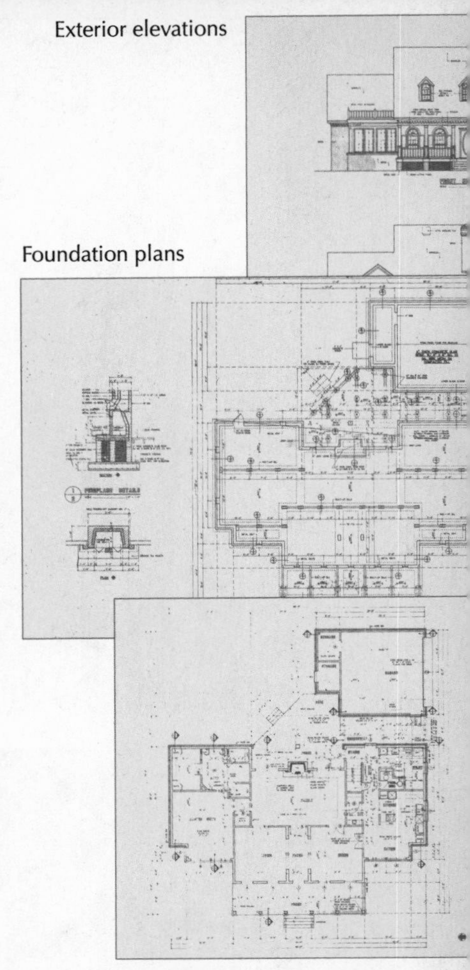

Detailed floor plans

■ **How-to diagrams** for plumbing, wiring, solar heating, framing and foundation conversions show how to plumb, wire, install a solar heating system, convert plans with 2 by 4 exterior walls to 2 by 6 construction (or vice versa), and adapt a plan for a basement, crawlspace, or slab foundation. These diagrams are not specific to any one plan.

NOTE: Due to regional variations, local availability of materials, local codes, methods of installation, and individual preferences, detailed heating, plumbing, and electrical specifications are not included on plans. The duct work, venting, and other details will vary, depending on the heating and cooling system you use and the type of energy that operates it. These details and specifications are easily obtained from your builder or local supplier.

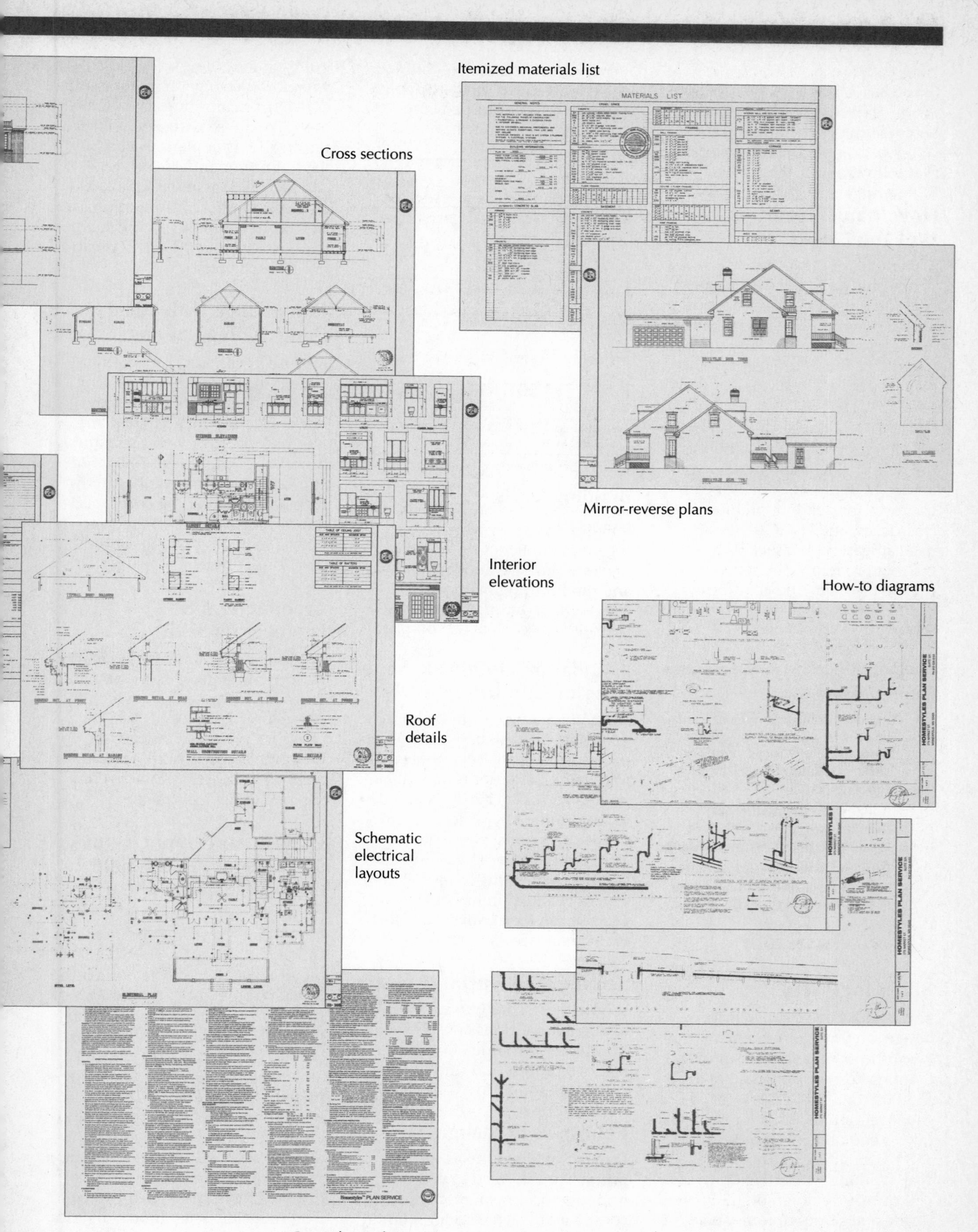
Itemized materials list
MATERIALS LIST
Cross sections
Mirror-reverse plans
Interior
elevations
How-to diagrams
Roof
details
Schematic
electrical
layouts
HOMESTYLES PLAN SERVICE
General specifications

Before You Order

Once you've chosen the one or two house plans that work best for you, you're ready to order blueprints. Before filling in the form on the facing page, note the information that follows.

How Many Blueprints Will You Need?

A single set of blueprints will allow you to study a home design in detail. You'll need more for obtaining bids and permits, as well as some to use as reference at the building site. If you'll be modifying your home plan, order a reproducible set (see page 12).

Figure you'll need at least one set each for yourself, your builder, the building department, and your lender. In addition, some subcontractors—foundation, plumber, electrician, and HVAC—may also need at least partial sets. If they do, ask them to return the sets when they're finished. The chart below can help you calculate how many sets you're likely to need.

Blueprint Checklist

____Owner's set(s)

____Builder usually requires at least three sets: one for legal documentation, one for inspections, and a minimum of one set for subcontractors.

____Building department requires at least one set. Check with your local department before ordering.

____Lending institution usually needs one set for a conventional mortgage, three sets for FHA or VA loans.

____TOTAL SETS NEEDED

Blueprint Prices

The cost of having an architect design a new custom home typically runs from 5 to 15 percent of the building cost, or from $5,000 to $15,000 for a $100,000 home. A single set of blueprints for the plans in this book ranges from $250 to $535, depending on the house's size. Working with these drawings, you can save enough on design fees to add a deck, a swimming pool, or a luxurious kitchen.

Pricing is based on "total finished living space." Garages, porches, decks, and unfinished basements are not included.

Price Code (Size)	1 Set	4 Sets	7 Sets	Reproducible Set
A (under 1,500 sq. ft.)	$250	$295	$325	$425
B (1,500-1,999 sq. ft.)	$285	$330	$360	$460
C (2,000-2,499 sq. ft.)	$320	$365	$395	$495
D (2,500-2,999 sq. ft.)	$355	$400	$430	$530
E (3,000-3,499 sq. ft.)	$390	$435	$465	$565
F (3,500-3,999 sq. ft.)	$425	$470	$500	$600
G (4,000 sq. ft. and up)	$460	$505	$535	$635

Building Costs

Building costs vary widely, depending on a number of factors, including local material and labor costs and the finishing materials you select. For help estimating costs, see "Is Your Project Doable?" on page 7.

Foundation Options & Exterior Construction

Depending on your site and climate, your home will be built with a slab, pier, pole, crawlspace, or basement foundation. Exterior walls will be framed with either 2 by 4s or 2 by 6s, determined by structural and insulation standards in your area. Most contractors can easily adapt a home to meet the foundation and/or wall requirements for your area. Or ask for a conversion how-to diagram (see page 12).

Service & Blueprint Delivery

Service representatives are available to answer questions and assist you in placing your order. Every effort is made to process and ship orders within 48 hours.

Returns & Exchanges

Each set of blueprints is specially printed and shipped to you in response to your specific order; consequently, requests for refunds cannot be honored. However, if the prints you order cannot be used, you may exchange them for another plan from any Sunset home plan book. For an exchange, you must return all sets of plans within 30 days. A nonrefundable service charge will be assessed for all exchanges; for more information, call the toll-free number on the facing page. Note: Reproducible sets cannot be exchanged.

Compliance with Local Codes & Regulations

Because of climatic, geographic, and political variations, building codes and regulations vary from one area to another. These plans are authorized for your use expressly conditioned on your obligation and agreement to comply strictly with all local building codes, ordinances, regulations, and requirements, including permits and inspections at time of construction.

Architectural & Engineering Seals

With increased concern about energy costs and safety, many cities and states now require that an architect or engineer review and "seal" a blueprint prior to construction. To find out whether this is a requirement in your area, contact your local building department.

License Agreement, Copy Restrictions & Copyright

When you purchase your blueprints, you are granted the right to use those documents to construct a single unit. All the plans in this publication are protected under the Federal Copyright Act, Title XVII of the United States Code and Chapter 37 of the Code of Federal Regulations. Each designer retains title and ownership of the original documents. The blueprints licensed to you cannot be used by or resold to any other person, copied, or reproduced by any means. The copying restrictions do not apply to reproducible blueprints. When you buy a reproducible set, you may modify and reproduce it for your own use.

Blueprint Order Form

Complete this order form in just three easy steps. Then mail in your order or, for faster service, call toll-free.

1. Blueprints & Accessories

BLUEPRINT CHART

Price Code	1 Set	4 Sets	7 Sets	Reproducible Set*
A	$250	$295	$325	$425
B	$285	$330	$360	$460
C	$320	$365	$395	$495
D	$355	$400	$430	$530
E	$390	$435	$465	$565
F	$425	$470	$500	$600
G	$460	$505	$535	$635

Prices subject to change

*A reproducible set is produced on erasable paper for the purpose of modification. It is only available for plans with prefixes AG, AGH, AH, AHP, APS, AX, B, C, CAR, CPS, DD, DW, E, EOF, FB, GL, GML, GSA, H, HFL, J, K, KLF, LMB, LRD, M, NW, OH, PH, PI, PM, S, SDG, THD, UDG, V.

Mirror-Reverse Sets: $40 surcharge. From the total number of sets you ordered above, choose the number you want to be reversed. *Note: All writing on mirror-reverse plans is backwards. Order at least one regular-reading set.*

Itemized Materials List: One set $40; each additional set $10. Details the quantity, type, and size of materials needed to build your home.

Description of Materials: Sold in a set of two for $40 (for use in obtaining FHA or VA financing).

Typical How-To Diagrams: One set $12.50; two sets $23; three sets $30; four sets $35. General guides on plumbing, wiring, and solar heating, plus information on how to convert from one foundation or exterior framing to another. *Note: These diagrams are not specific to any one plan.*

2. Sales Tax & Shipping

Determine your subtotal and add appropriate local state sales tax, plus shipping and handling (see chart below).

SHIPPING & HANDLING

	1–3 Sets	4–6 Sets/ Reproducible Set	7 or More Sets
U.S. Regular (4–6 working days)	$12.50	$15.00	$17.50
U.S. Express (2–3 working days)	$25.00	$27.50	$30.00
Canada Regular (2–3 weeks)	$12.50	$15.00	$17.50
Canada Express (4–6 working days)	$25.00	$30.00	$35.00
Overseas/Airmail (7–10 working days)	$50.00	$60.00	$70.00

3. Customer Information

Choose the method of payment you prefer. Include check, money order, or credit card information, complete name and address portion, and mail to:

Sunset/HomeStyles Plan Service
P.O. Box 50670
Minneapolis, MN 55405

FOR FASTER SERVICE
CALL 1-800-547-5570

SS10

COMPLETE THIS FORM

Plan Number ______________ **Price Code** _____

Foundation ______________________________
(Review your plan carefully for foundation options—basement, pole, pier, crawlspace, or slab. Many plans offer several options; others offer only one.)

Number of Sets: $__________ (See chart at left)
- ☐ One Set
- ☐ Four Sets
- ☐ Seven Sets
- ☐ One Reproducible Set

Additional Sets ______ $__________ ($35 each)

Mirror-Reverse Sets ______ $__________ ($40 surcharge)

Itemized Materials List $__________
Only available for plans with prefixes AH, AHP, APS*, AX, B*, C, CAR, CDG*, CPS, DD*, DW, E, FB, GSA, H, HFL, I, J, K, LMB*, LRD, N, NW*, P, PH, R, S, SD*, THD, U, UDG, VL.*Not available on all plans. Please call before ordering.

Description of Materials $__________
Only available for plans with prefixes AHP, C, DW, H, HFL, J, K, KY, LMB, N, P, PH, VL.

Typical How-To Diagrams $__________
☐ Plumbing ☐ Wiring ☐ Solar Heating ☐ Foundation & Framing Conversion

SUBTOTAL $__________

SALES TAX $__________

SHIPPING & HANDLING $__________

GRAND TOTAL $__________

☐ Check/money order enclosed (in U.S. funds)

☐ VISA ☐ MasterCard ☐ AmEx ☐ Discover

Credit Card # ______________________ **Exp. Date** ______

Signature ______________________________

Name ______________________________

Address ______________________________

City ____________ **State** ___ **Country** ________

Zip ________ **Daytime Phone** (____)__________

☐ Please check if you are a contractor.

Mail form to: Sunset/HomeStyles Plan Service
P.O. Box 50670
Minneapolis, MN 55405

Or Fax to: (612) 338-1626

FOR FASTER SERVICE
CALL 1-800-547-5570

SS10

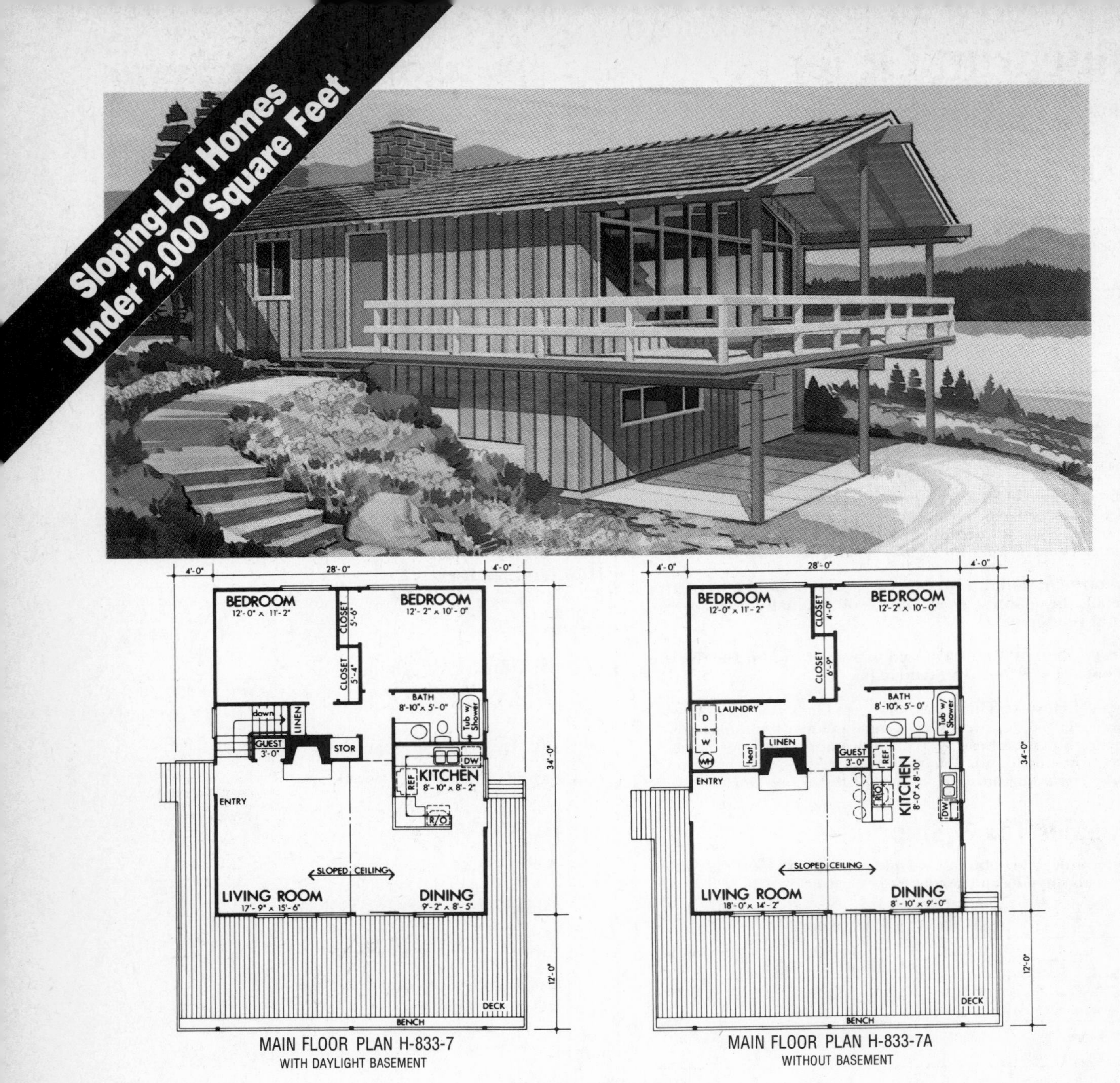

MAIN FLOOR PLAN H-833-7
WITH DAYLIGHT BASEMENT

MAIN FLOOR PLAN H-833-7A
WITHOUT BASEMENT

An Owner-Builder Special

- Everything you need for a leisure or retirement retreat is neatly packaged in just 952 square feet.
- The basic rectangular design features a unique wraparound deck, which is entirely covered by the projecting roof-line.
- Vaulted ceilings and a central fireplace visually enhance the cozy living/dining room.
- The daylight-basement option is suitable for building on a sloping lot.

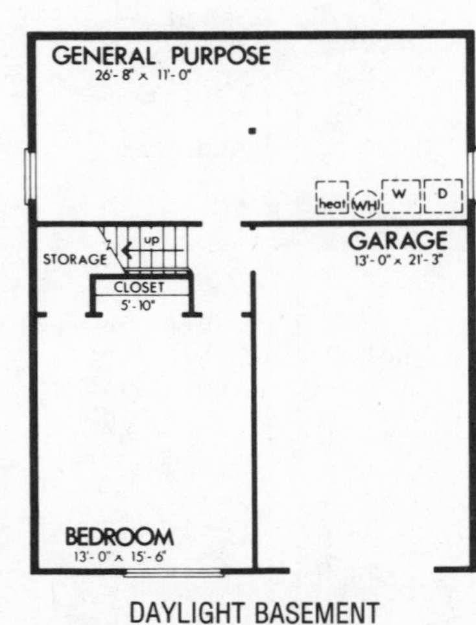

DAYLIGHT BASEMENT

Plans H-833-7 & -7A	
Bedrooms: 2-3	**Baths:** 1
Living Area:	
Main floor	952 sq. ft.
Optional daylight basement	676 sq. ft.
Total Living Area:	**952/1,628 sq. ft.**
Garage	276 sq. ft.
Exterior Wall Framing:	2x6
Foundation Options:	**Plan #**
Daylight basement	H-833-7
Crawlspace	H-833-7A
(Typical foundation & framing conversion diagram available—see order form.)	
BLUEPRINT PRICE CODE:	**A/B**

PRICES AND DETAILS ON PAGES 12-15

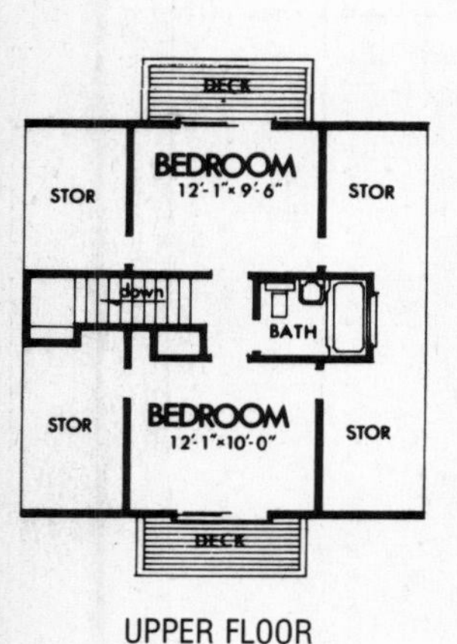

UPPER FLOOR

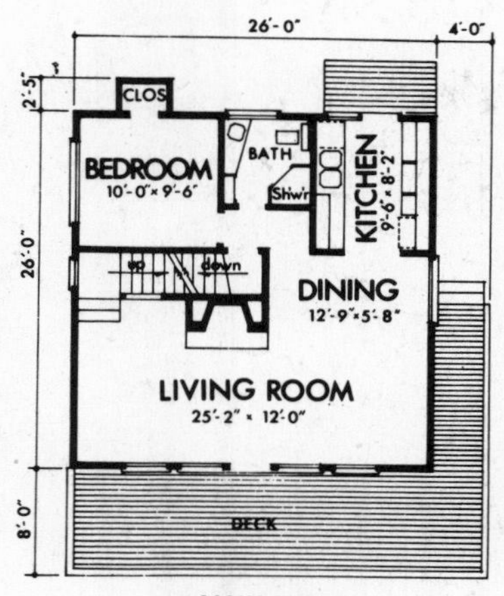

MAIN FLOOR
PLAN H-720-11

MAIN FLOOR
PLAN H-720-10

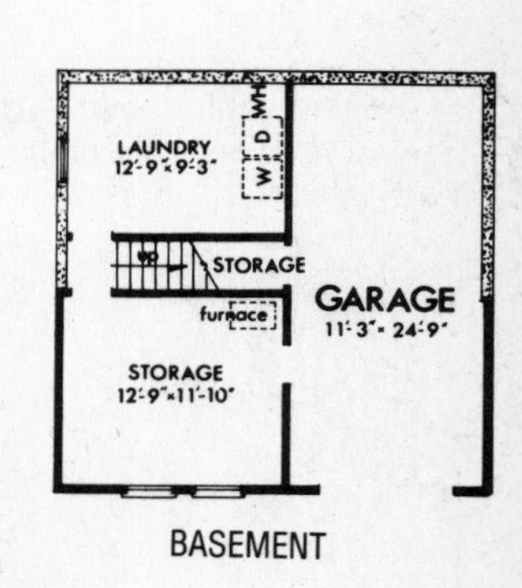

BASEMENT

Chalet with Variations

- Attractive chalet offers several main level variations, with second floor and basement layouts identical.
- All versions feature well-arranged kitchen, attached dining area, and large living room.
- Second-floor amenities include private decks off each bedroom and storage space in every corner!

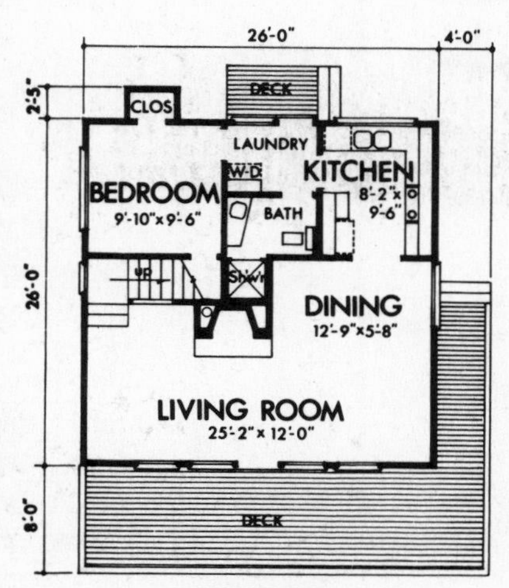

MAIN FLOOR
PLAN H-720-12A
WITHOUT BASEMENT

Plans H-720-10, -11 & -12A

Bedrooms: 3-4	**Baths:** 2
Space:	
Upper floor:	328 sq. ft.
Main floor:	686 sq. ft.
Total living area:	1,014 sq. ft.
Basement:	approx. 686 sq. ft.
Garage: (incl. in basement)	278 sq. ft.
Exterior Wall Framing:	2x4

Foundation options:
Daylight basement
(Plans H-720-10 or -11).
Crawlspace (Plan H-720-12A)
(Foundation & framing conversion diagram available — see order form.)

Blueprint Price Code:

Without basement:	A
With basement:	B

TO ORDER THIS BLUEPRINT, CALL TOLL-FREE 1-800-547-5570 Plans H-720-10, -11 & -12A *PRICES AND DETAILS ON PAGES 12-15*

Casual Flexibility

- This beautifully designed vacation or year-round home is spacious and flexible.
- The interior is brightened by an abundance of windows.
- The open, vaulted living room boasts a central fireplace that makes a great conversation place or a cozy spot for spending cold winter evenings.
- The kitchen opens to the dining room and the scenery beyond through the dramatic window wall with half-round transom.
- The sleeping room and loft upstairs can easily accommodate several guests or could be used as multi-purpose space.

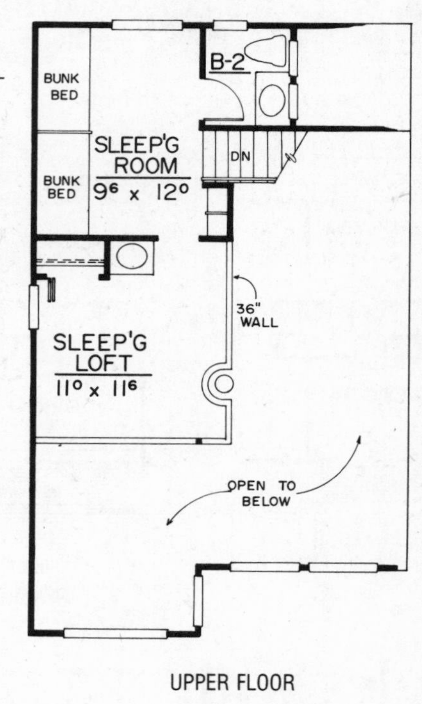

UPPER FLOOR

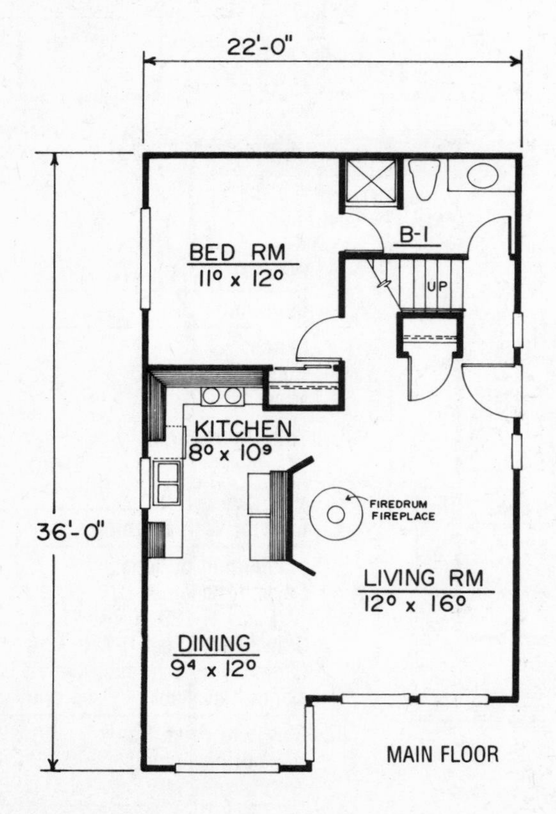

MAIN FLOOR

Plan I-1032-A	
Bedrooms: 2-3	**Baths:** 1½
Living Area:	
Upper floor	288 sq. ft.
Main floor	744 sq. ft.
Total Living Area:	**1,032 sq. ft.**
Exterior Wall Framing:	2x6
Foundation Options:	
Crawlspace	
(Typical foundation & framing conversion diagram available—see order form.)	
BLUEPRINT PRICE CODE:	**A**

TO ORDER THIS BLUEPRINT, CALL TOLL-FREE 1-800-547-5570

Plan I-1032-A

PRICES AND DETAILS ON PAGES 12-15

High Ceilings, Large Spaces!

- This affordable home is filled with large spaces that are further enhanced by high ceilings and lots of windows.
- The charming exterior is complemented by a combination of lap siding and brick, a covered front porch with a column and a sidelighted entry door.
- Inside, the first area to come into view is the huge family room, which features a vaulted ceiling and a space-saving corner fireplace. Sliding glass doors open up the room to the backyard.
- The family room flows into the spacious breakfast room and kitchen. A picture window or an optional bay window brightens the breakfast room, while the kitchen offers a window above the sink and a convenient laundry closet that hides the clutter.
- The master suite leaves out nothing. A tray ceiling in the sleeping area gives way to the vaulted master bath, which is accented with a plant shelf above the entrance. A roomy walk-in closet is also included. The two smaller bedrooms share a hall bath.
- The optional basement doubles the home's size, providing ample expansion space.

Plan FB-1070

Bedrooms: 3	**Baths:** 2
Living Area:	
Main floor	1,070 sq. ft.
Total Living Area:	**1,070 sq. ft.**
Daylight basement	1,070 sq. ft.
Garage	484 sq. ft.
Exterior Wall Framing:	2x4
Foundation Options:	
Daylight basement	
Crawlspace	
Slab	

(All plans can be built with your choice of foundation and framing. A generic conversion diagram is available. See order form.)

BLUEPRINT PRICE CODE: A

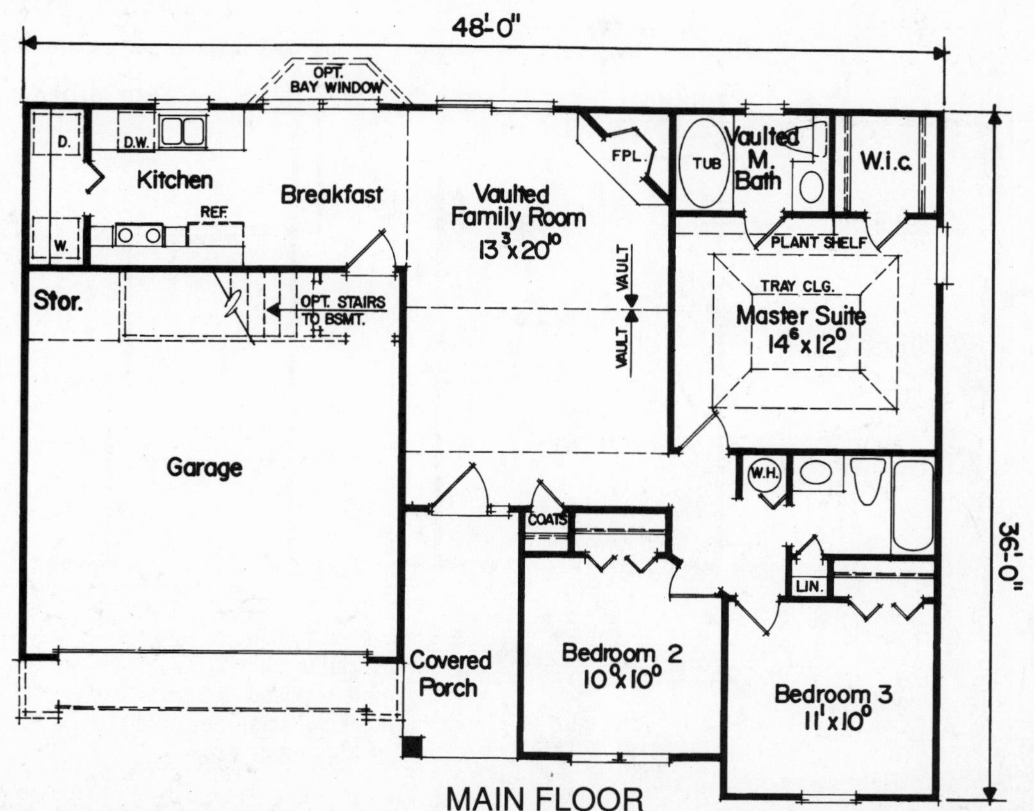

MAIN FLOOR

Versatile A-Frame

Perfect as a weekend retreat or outdoor-sports headquarters, this 882 sq. ft. A-Frame is completely equipped to serve as either a full time or retirement home, especially if built with the daylight basement that includes a large bedroom, bath, shop and garage.

Sliding glass doors open from the wide wood entry deck into the great room and dining area, brightened with six skylights and warmed with a wood-burning stove. Another skylight is located over the work area of the corridor kitchen. The adjacent utility room has a door opening onto a rear-entry porch.

The master bedroom has a large wardrobe closet and a bump-out window seat. Stairs next to the bathroom lead up to a loft which can be used as a study, craft room or additional sleeping space. From the loft, an open railing overlooks the great room.

This multi-level A-Frame has diagonal board siding on the end walls and a boxed chimney to add a custom touch and accent the roof lines. Only 26′ wide, the house can be built on a small lot.

Main floor:	720 sq. ft.
Loft:	162 sq. ft.
Total living area: (Not counting basement or garage)	882 sq. ft.

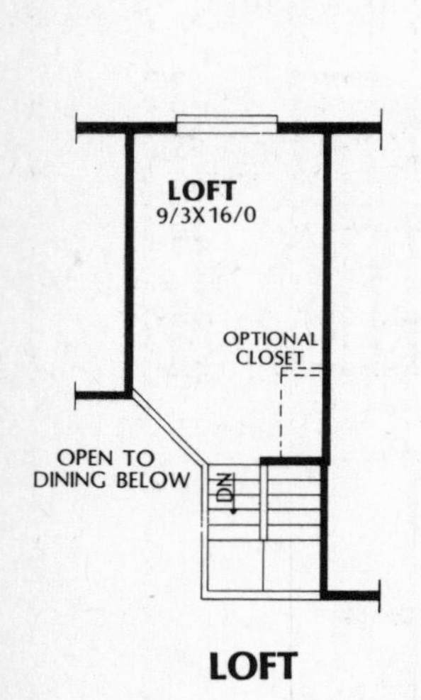

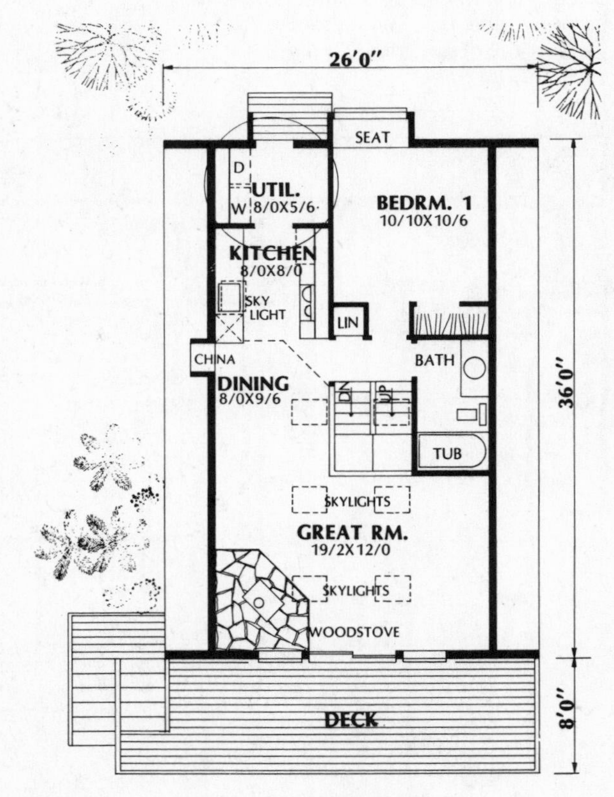

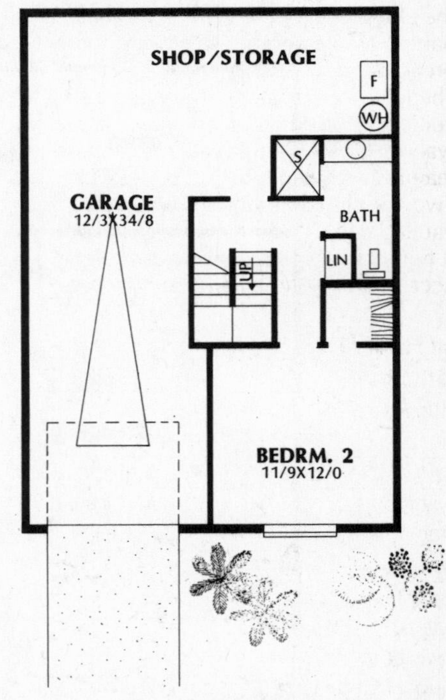

PLAN P-527-2A
WITHOUT BASEMENT
(CRAWLSPACE FOUNDATION)

PLAN P-527-2D
WITH DAYLIGHT BASEMENT
MAIN FLOOR 720 SQ. FT.
LOFT 162 SQ. FT.

BASEMENT
FINISHED AREA 322 SQ. FT.

Blueprint Price Code A

Plans P-527-2A & P-527-2D

TO ORDER THIS BLUEPRINT, CALL TOLL-FREE 1-800-547-5570

PRICES AND DETAILS ON PAGES 12-15

Extra-Special Ranch-Style

- Repeating gables, wood siding and brick adorn the exterior of this ranch-style home, which offers numerous extras inside.
- The entry leads directly into the vaulted family room, an ideal entertainment area accented by a corner fireplace and a French door to the backyard.
- A serving bar joins the family room to the efficient kitchen, with its walk-in pantry, ample counter space and sunny breakfast room.
- The luxurious master suite boasts a tray ceiling, a large bank of windows and a walk-in closet. The private master bath features a garden tub.
- Two additional bedrooms, one with a vaulted ceiling, share another full bath.
- A two-car garage provides convenient access to the kitchen and laundry area.

Plan FB-1104	
Bedrooms: 3	**Baths:** 2
Living Area:	
Main floor	1,104 sq. ft.
Total Living Area:	**1,104 sq. ft.**
Daylight basement	1,104 sq. ft.
Garage	400 sq. ft.
Exterior Wall Framing:	2x4
Foundation Options:	
Daylight basement	
Crawlspace	
(Typical foundation & framing conversion diagram available—see order form.)	
BLUEPRINT PRICE CODE:	**A**

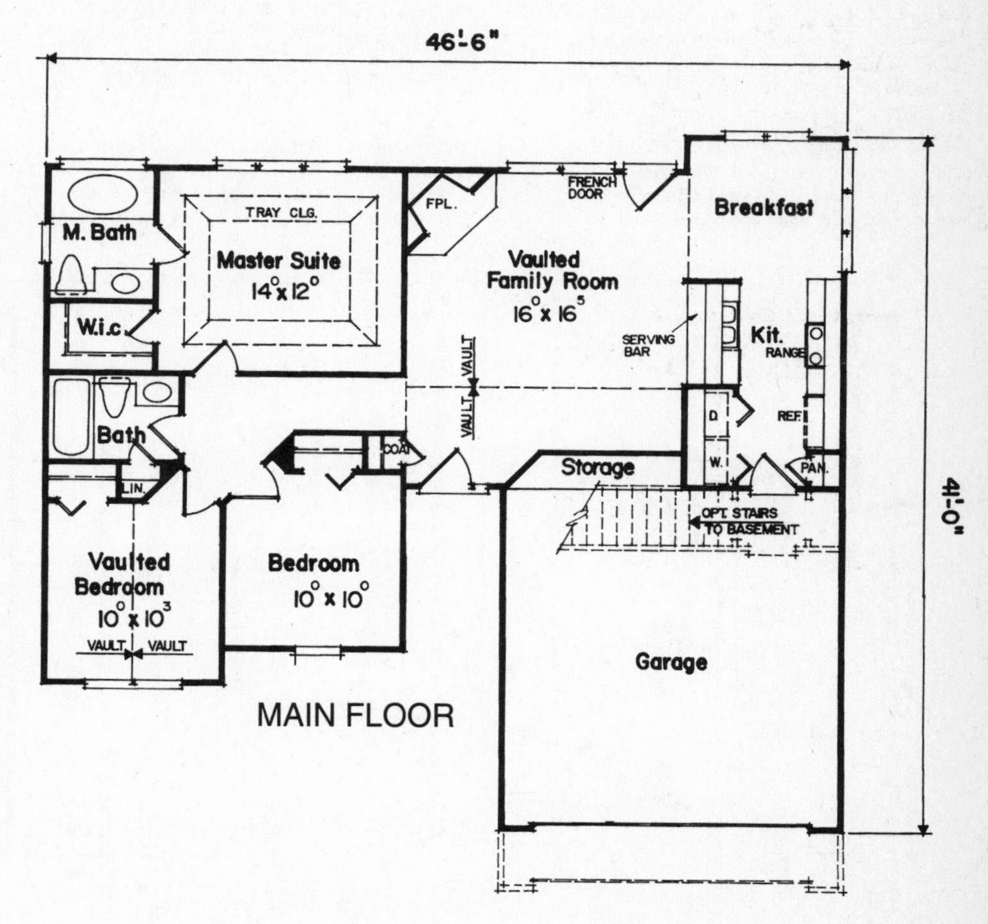

MAIN FLOOR

Compact, Easy to Build

This compact vacation or retirement home is economical and easy to construct. Only 24′ x 46′ for the daylight basement version, it nonetheless contains all the necessities and some of the luxuries one desires in a three-bedroom home. The non-basement version measures 24′ x 44′.

Overall width for both versions including deck and carport is 50′.

One luxury is the separate, private bath adjoining the master bedroom; another is the double "His & Hers" wardrobe closets for the same room. The other two bedrooms are equipped with good-sized closets and share a second bathroom. Even if you choose the basement version, the convenience of first floor laundry facilities is yours.

The open stairway to the basement adds 3′ to the visual size of the living room. A pre-fab fireplace is located to allow enjoyment of a cozy hearth and a beautiful view from the same chair.

The plans are so completely detailed that a handyman amateur might frame this building (with the help of a few friends). Why not try it? (Be sure to order a materials list, too!).

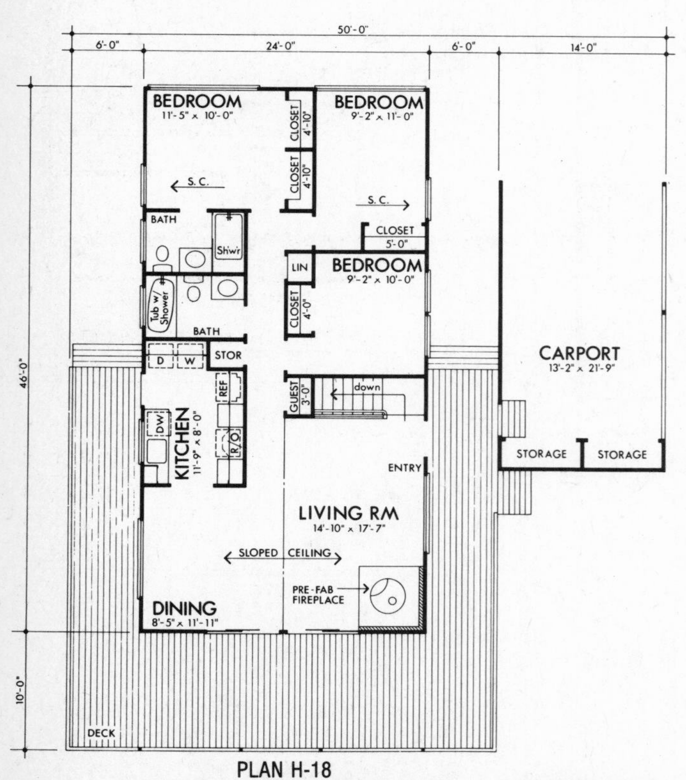

PLAN H-18
WITH DAYLIGHT BASEMENT
1104 SQUARE FEET

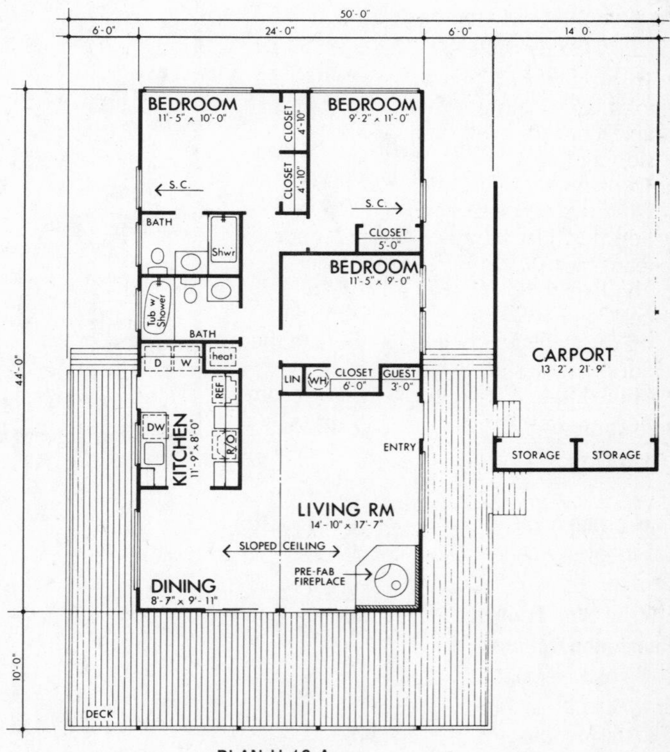

PLAN H-18-A
WITH CRAWLSPACE
1056 SQUARE FEET

Total living area: 1,104 sq. ft.
(Not counting basement or carport)

Blueprint Price Code A

Plans H-18 & H-18-A

PRICES AND DETAILS ON PAGES 12-15

UPPER FLOOR
PLANS H-946-1A & -1B

Plans H-946-1A & -1B (Two Bedrooms)

Bedrooms: 2	**Baths:** 2
Living Area:	
Upper floor	381 sq. ft.
Main floor	814 sq. ft.
Total Living Area:	**1,195 sq. ft.**
Basement	approx. 814 sq. ft.
Garage	315 sq. ft.
Exterior Wall Framing:	2x6

Foundation Options:
Daylight basement (Plan H-946-1B)
Crawlspace (Plan H-946-1A)
(Typical foundation & framing conversion diagram available—see order form.)

BLUEPRINT PRICE CODE: A

Narrow-Lot Solar Design

- This design offers your choice of foundation and number of bedrooms, and it can be built on a narrow, sloping lot.
- The passive-solar dining room has windows on three sides and a slate floor for heat storage. A French door leads to a rear deck.
- The living room features a sloped ceiling, a woodstove in ceiling-high masonry, and sliding glass doors to the adjoining deck.
- The kitchen is open to the dining room but separated from the living room by a 7½-ft.-high wall.
- The upper-level variations include a choice of one or two bedrooms. Clerestory windows above the balcony railing add drama to both versions.

MAIN FLOOR

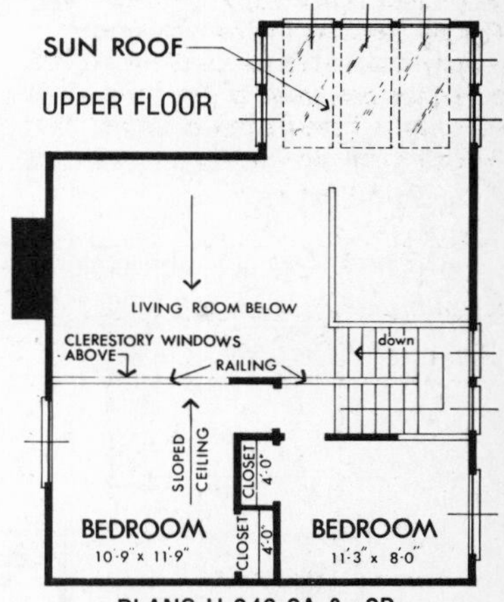

PLANS H-946-2A & -2B

Plans H-946-2A & -2B (Three Bedrooms)

Bedrooms: 3	**Baths:** 2
Living Area:	
Upper floor	290 sq. ft.
Main floor	814 sq. ft.
Total Living Area:	**1,104 sq. ft.**
Basement	approx. 814 sq. ft.
Garage	315 sq. ft.
Exterior Wall Framing:	2x6

Foundation Options:
Daylight basement (Plan H-946-2B)
Crawlspace (Plan H-946-2A)
(Typical foundation & framing conversion diagram available—see order form.)

BLUEPRINT PRICE CODE: A

PRICES AND DETAILS ON PAGES 12-15

The Simple & Economical Housing Solution

- This compact plan could serve as a second home or a primary residence for a small family.
- Spacious Great Room features woodstove and a large adjoining deck.
- Efficient kitchen is close to storage and laundry area.
- Large, overlooking loft offers infinite possibilities, such as extra sleeping quarters, a home office, art studio, or recreation room.
- Clerestory window arrangement and sloped-ceilings top the loft for added light.

Plan H-963-2A

Bedrooms: 1	**Baths:** 1
Space:	
Loft:	432 sq. ft.
Main floor:	728 sq. ft.
Total living area:	1,160 sq. ft.
Lower level/garage:	728 sq. ft.
Exterior Wall Framing:	2x4

Foundation options:
Slab.
(Foundation & framing conversion diagram available — see order form.)

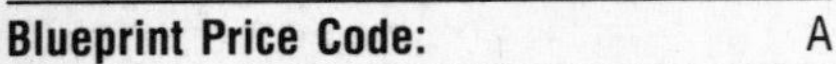

Blueprint Price Code: A

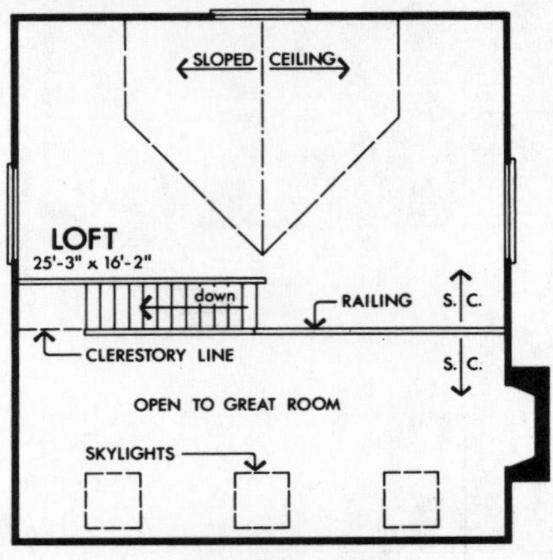

LOFT

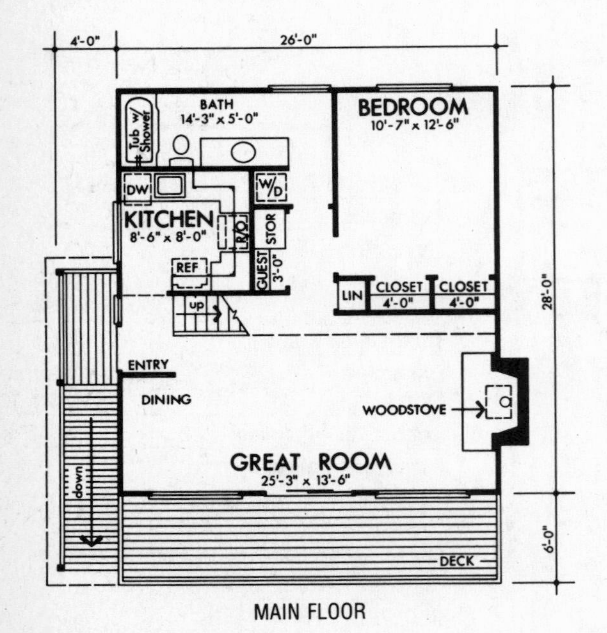

MAIN FLOOR

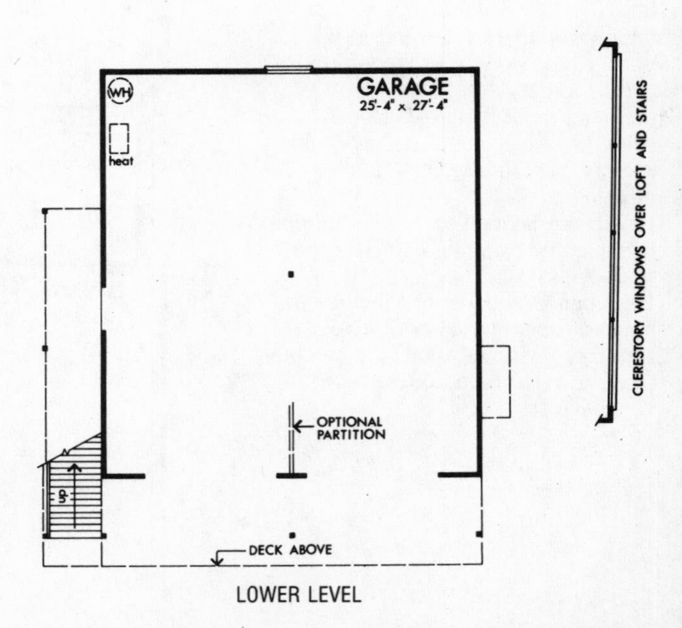

LOWER LEVEL

Plan H-963-2A

PRICES AND DETAILS ON PAGES 12-15

A-Frame Offers Options

In this versatile A-frame, the main floor is the same in all versions, and includes one bedroom. The upper floor gives you a choice of one large bedroom or two smaller ones.

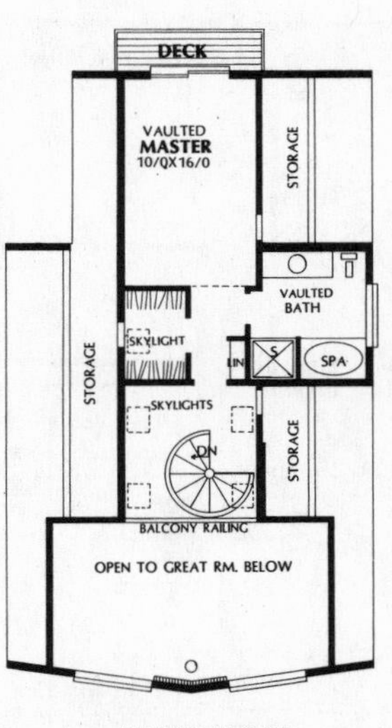

UPPER FLOOR
PLAN P-530-5A
WITH CRAWLSPACE

PLAN P-530-5D
WITH BASEMENT

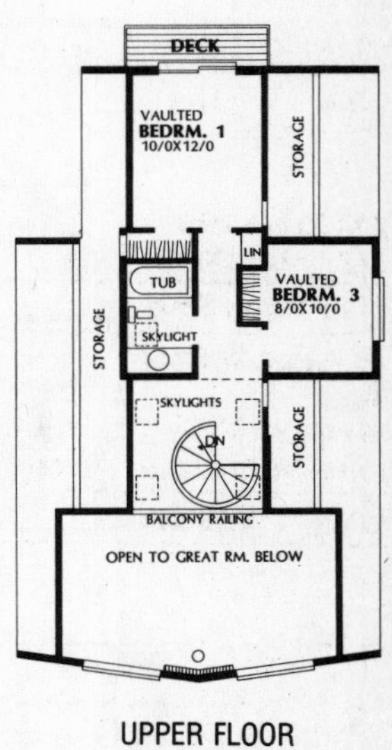

UPPER FLOOR
PLAN P-530-2A
WITH CRAWLSPACE

PLAN P-530-2D
WITH BASEMENT

Upper floor:	400 sq. ft.
Main floor:	761 sq. ft.
Total living area: (Not counting basement or garage)	1,161 sq. ft.
Basement:	938 sq. ft.
Total living area with daylight basement:	2,099 sq. ft.

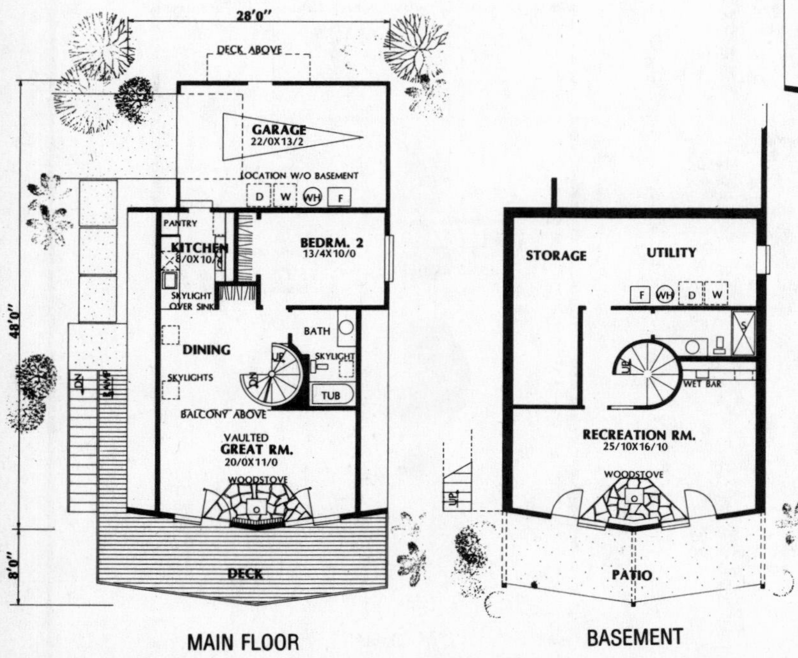

MAIN FLOOR

BASEMENT

Blueprint Price Code C With Basement
Blueprint Price Code A Without Basement

TO ORDER THIS BLUEPRINT, CALL TOLL-FREE 1-800-547-5570

Plans P-530-2A/2D & -5A/5D

PRICES AND DETAILS ON PAGES 12-15

Floating Sunspace

- Designed to take advantage of narrow or 'left-over' lots, this compact home is intended for the economy-minded small family. Even so, it still includes an entry hall and a spacious sun room, features not often found in plans of this size.
- Both the living and dining rooms are spacious and flow together to create a great space for parties or family gatherings.
- The optional daylight basement provides an additional bedroom as well as a garage and storage space.

Plans H-951-1A & -1B

Bedrooms: 2-3	**Baths:** 1-2
Space:	
Main floor	1,075 sq. ft.
Sun room	100 sq. ft.
Total Living Area	**1,175 sq. ft.**
Basement	662 sq. ft.
Garage	311 sq. ft.
Exterior Wall Framing	2x6

Foundation options:
Daylight Basement
Crawlspace
(Foundation & framing conversion diagram available—see order form.)

Blueprint Price Code:

Without Basement	**A**
With Basement	**B**

4'-0" 28'-0" 6'-0" 42'-0"
BEDROOM 11'-9"x13'-5"
CLOSET 4'-0"
BEDROOM 12'-5"x10'-0"
CLOSET 5'-8"
BATH
down
CLOSET 6'-0"
GUEST 3'-0"
STOR
LINEN
R/O
KITCHEN 9'-0"x8'-0"
ENTRY
SLOPED CEILING
REF
DW
S.C.
S.C.
DECK
DINING 13'-3"x9'-0"
WOOD STOVE
THERMAL STORAGE FLOOR
LIVING ROOM 13'-3"x17'-0"

PLAN H-951-1B
WITH BASEMENT

PASSIVE SUN ROOM
13'-5"x7'-8"

BEDROOM
LIN
CLOSET 6'-6"
WH
D
W
STOR
GUEST 3'-0"
heat
LAUNDRY
ENTRY
SLOPED CEILING

PLAN H-951-1A
WITHOUT BASEMENT
(CRAWLSPACE FOUNDATION)

TOP OF CLOSETS
CLERESTORY WINDOWS OVER HALLWAY
CLERESTORY WINDOW AT CORNER OF LIVING ROOM

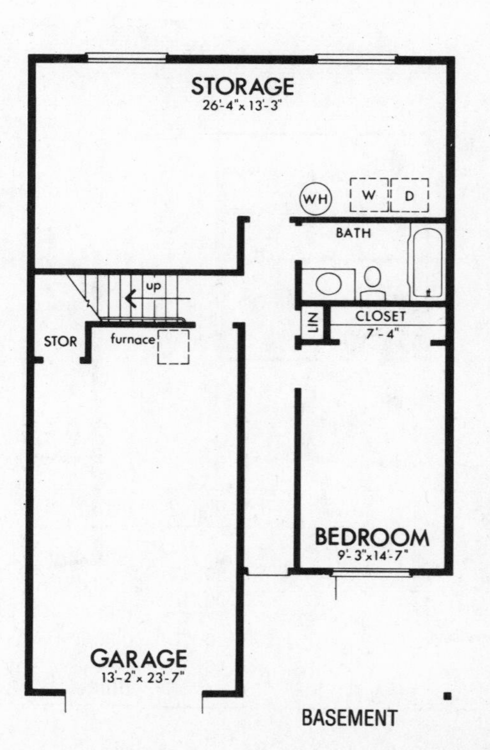

BASEMENT

Multi-Level Design

- This open and attractive design features multi-level construction and efficient use of living space.
- Elevated den and high ceilings with exposed rafters enhance the spacious feeling of the living room.
- Washer/dryer and kitchen are separated from the dining area by an eating counter.
- Third level comprises the master bedroom and bath.
- Garage and storage space are combined in the basement level.

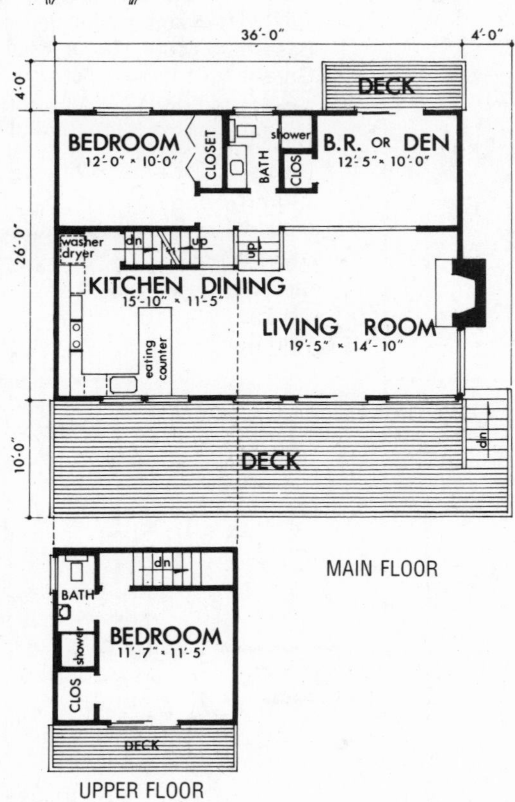

MAIN FLOOR

UPPER FLOOR

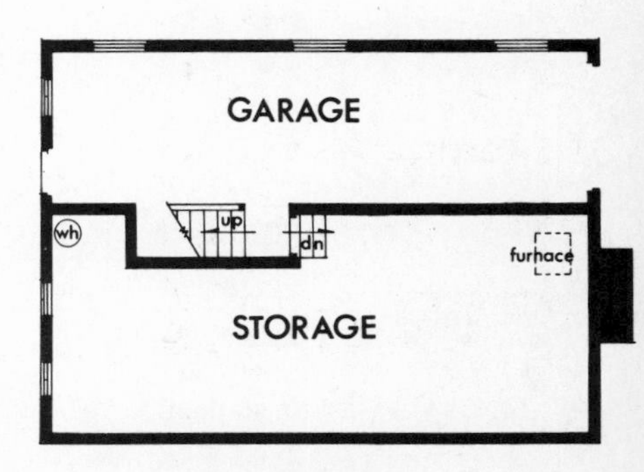

BASEMENT

Plan H-863-2

Bedrooms: 2-3	**Baths:** 2
Space:	
Upper floor:	252 sq. ft.
Main floor:	936 sq. ft.
Total living area:	1,188 sq. ft.
Basement: (includes garage)	approx. 936 sq. ft.

Exterior Wall Framing:	2x4

Foundation options:
Daylight basement only.
(Foundation & framing conversion diagram available — see order form.)

Blueprint Price Code:	A

PRICES AND DETAILS ON PAGES 12-15

Simple and Economical Chalet

- This home away from home is relatively simple to construct; it is also an enjoyable reason to spend your weekends in the mountains or at the beach.
- The main level is largely devoted to open living space, other than the kitchen and master bedroom, which could also be used as a study or hobby room.
- Second-floor bedrooms are larger and share a full bath and large storage areas.

BEDROOM 13'-7" x 10'-0"
SLOPED CEILING
STORAGE
CLOSET 4'-10"
CLOSET 4'-10"
STORAGE
Tub w/ Shower
BATH
down
CLOSET 5'-7"
STORAGE
S. C.
CLOSET 7'-5"
STORAGE
BEDROOM 13'-7" x 11'-5"
DECK

UPPER FLOOR

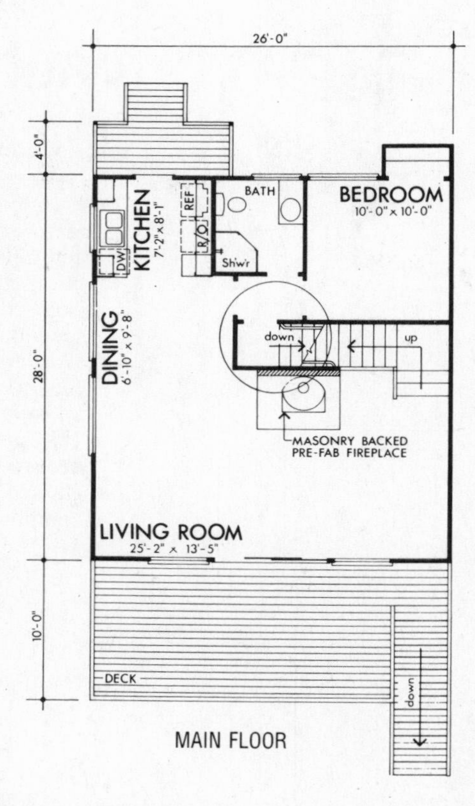

MAIN FLOOR

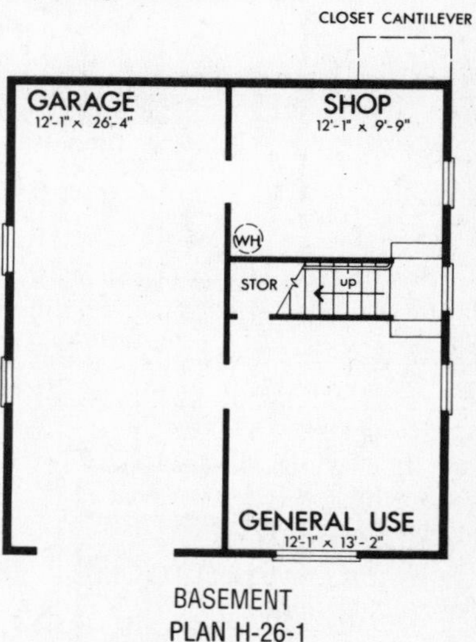

BASEMENT
PLAN H-26-1
DAYLIGHT BASEMENT

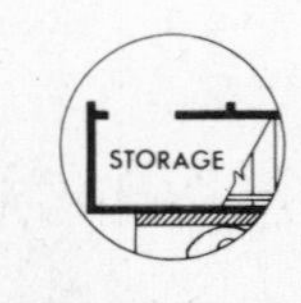

PLAN H-26-1A
WITHOUT BASEMENT

Plans H-26-1 & -1A

Bedrooms: 3	**Baths:** 2	**Exterior Wall Framing:**	2x4
Space:		**Foundation options:**	
Upper floor:	476 sq. ft.	Daylight basement (Plan H-26-1).	
Main floor:	728 sq. ft.	Crawlspace (Plan H-26-1A).	
Total living area:	1,204 sq. ft.	(Foundation & framing conversion diagram available — see order form.)	
Basement:	410 sq. ft.		
Garage:	318 sq. ft.	**Blueprint Price Code:**	A

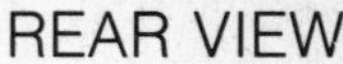

Easy Living

- Large, beautiful living area with sloped ceiling and fireplace lies five steps below entry and sleeping areas.
- Attached dining room and kitchen separated by eating bar.
- Convenient main floor laundry near kitchen and side entrance.
- Secluded master suite includes personal bath and private access to sun deck.

Plans H-925-1 & -1A

Bedrooms: 3	**Baths:** 2
Space:	
Upper floor:	288 sq. ft.
Main floor:	951 sq. ft.
Total living area:	1,239 sq. ft.
Basement:	approx. 951 sq. ft.
Garage:	266 sq. ft.
Exterior Wall Framing:	2x4

Foundation options:
Daylight basement (Plan H-925-1).
Crawlspace (Plan H-925-1A).
(Foundation & framing conversion diagram available — see order form.)

Blueprint Price Code: A

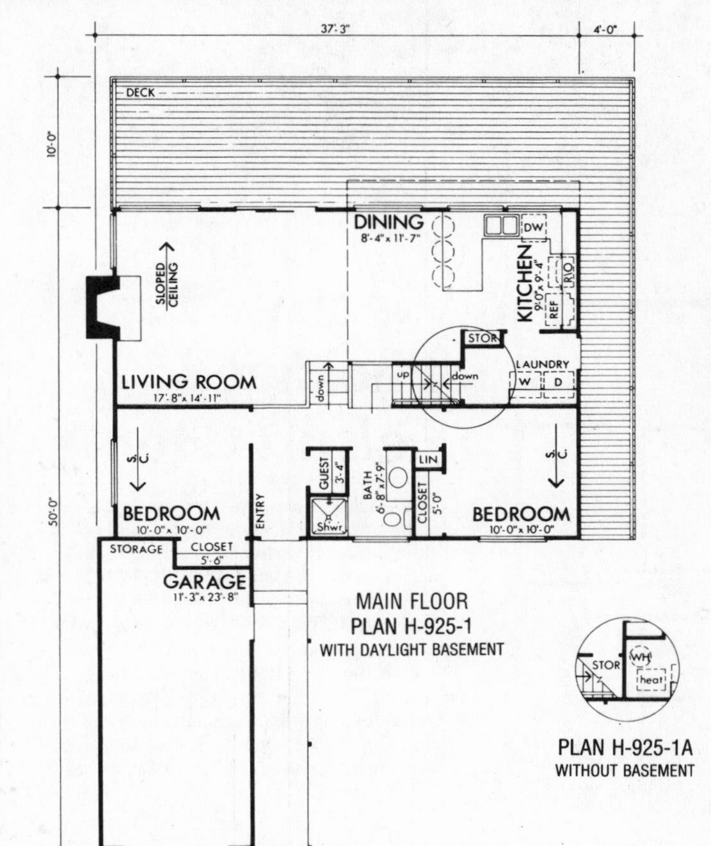

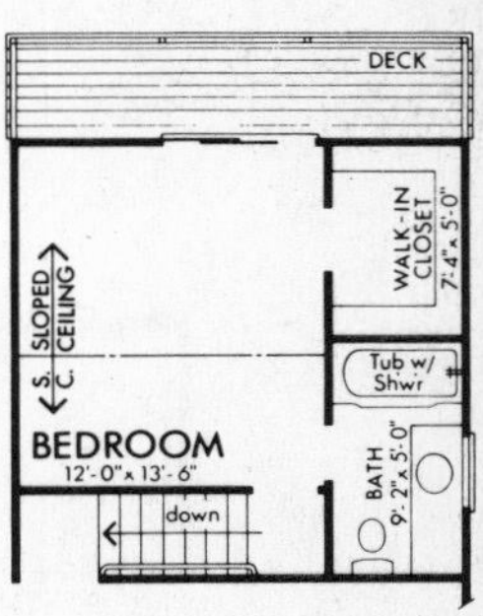

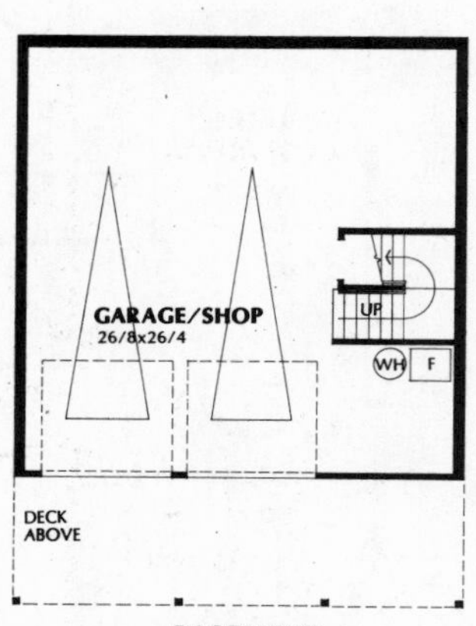

BASEMENT
PLAN P-520-D
WITH DAYLIGHT BASEMENT

Neatly Packaged Leisure Home

This pitched-roof two-story contemporary leisure home is accented with solid wood siding, placed vertically and diagonally, and it neatly packages three bedrooms and a generous amount of living space into a 1,271 sq. ft. plan that covers a minimum of ground space.

Half the main floor is devoted to the vaulted Great Room, which is warmed by a woodstove and opens out through sliding glass doors to a wide deck. The U-shaped kitchen adjacent to the Great Room has a window looking onto the deck and a circular window in the front wall. The master bedroom, a full bath and the utility room complete the 823 sq. ft. first floor.

Stairs next to the entry door lead down to the daylight basement, double garage and workroom, or up to the second floor. An open railing overlooking the Great Room and clerestory windows add natural light and enhance the open feeling of the home. The two bedrooms share another full bathroom.

Main floor:	823 sq. ft.
Upper floor:	448 sq. ft.
Total living area: (Not counting basement or garage)	1,271 sq. ft.

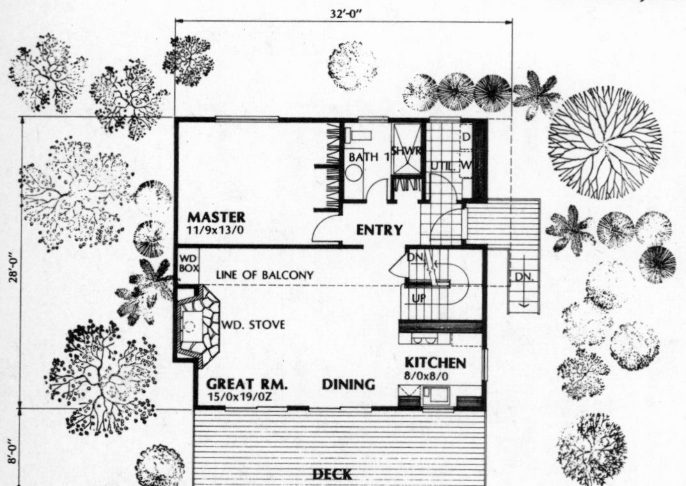

MAIN FLOOR

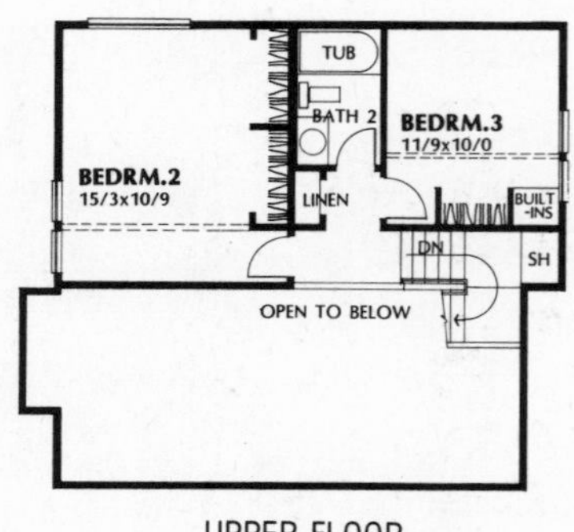

UPPER FLOOR

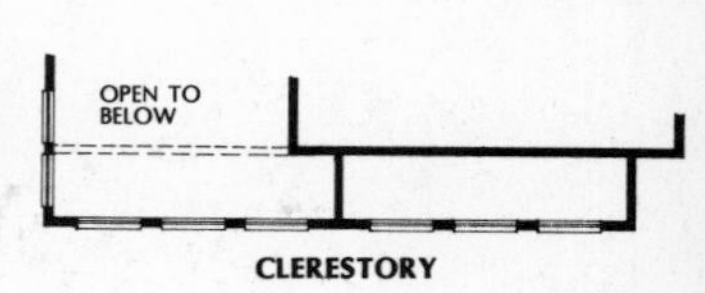

Blueprint Price Code A

Plan P-520-D

TO ORDER THIS BLUEPRINT, CALL TOLL-FREE 1-800-547-5570

PRICES AND DETAILS ON PAGES 12-15

Eye-Catching Details

- This handsome home features an eye-catching exterior and an exciting floor plan that maximizes square footage.
- A covered porch leads into a vaulted foyer with an angled coat closet. Straight ahead, the vaulted Great Room combines with the dining room and kitchen to create one huge, well-integrated living and entertaining area.
- The Great Room includes a fireplace and access to the backyard. The vaulted, galley-style kitchen is bordered by the vaulted dining room on one side and a breakfast area with a laundry closet on the other.
- The isolated master suite boasts a tray ceiling and a vaulted bath with a garden tub, a separate shower, a vanity with knee space and a walk-in closet.
- The two remaining bedrooms are located on the opposite side of the home and share a full bath. A plant shelf is an attention-getting detail found here.

Plan FB-1289

Bedrooms: 3	**Baths:** 2
Living Area:	
Main floor	1,289 sq. ft.
Total Living Area:	**1,289 sq. ft.**
Daylight basement	1,289 sq. ft.
Garage	430 sq. ft.
Exterior Wall Framing:	2x4

Foundation Options:
Daylight basement
Crawlspace
Slab
(Typical foundation & framing conversion diagram available – see order form.)

BLUEPRINT PRICE CODE: A

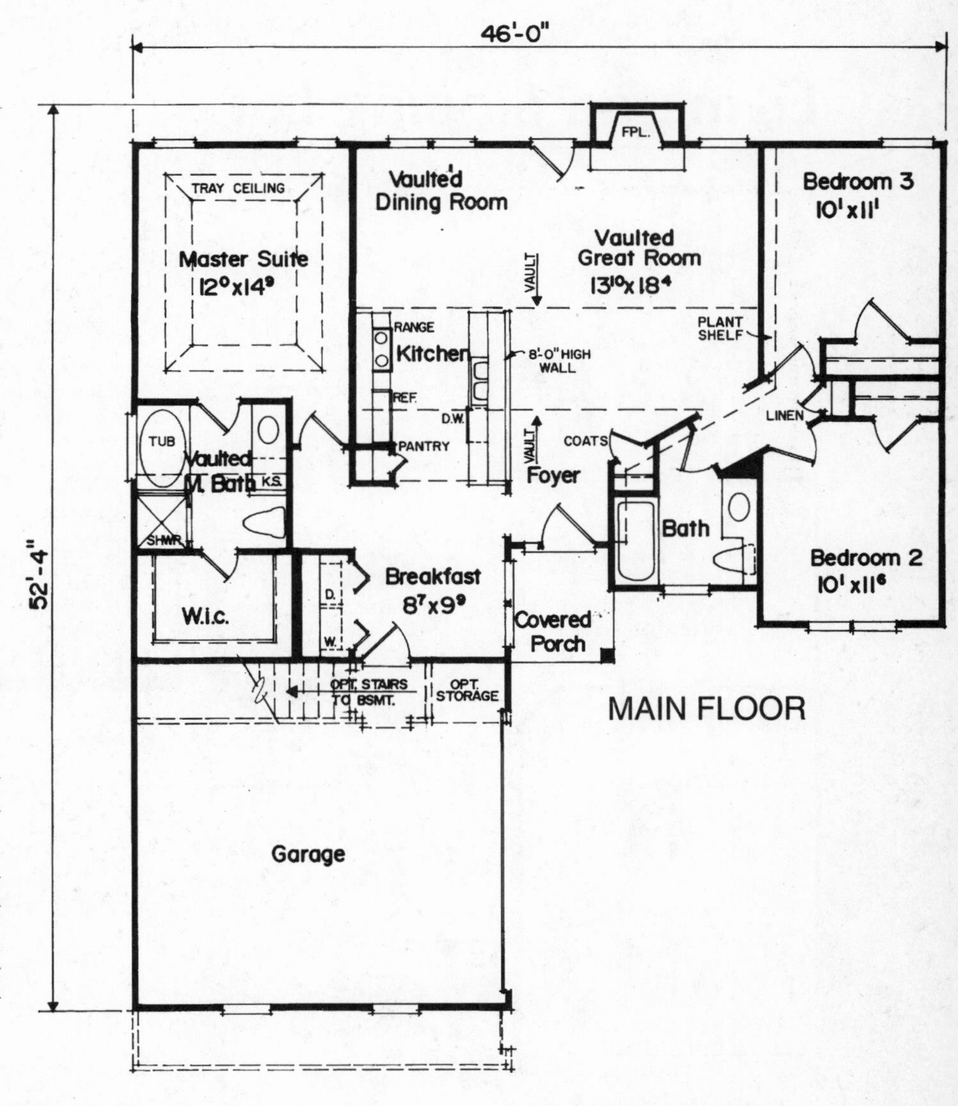

Easy Living on Sloping Lot

Main floor:	696 sq. ft.
Lower floor:	603 sq. ft.
Total living area: (Not counting garage)	1,299 sq. ft.

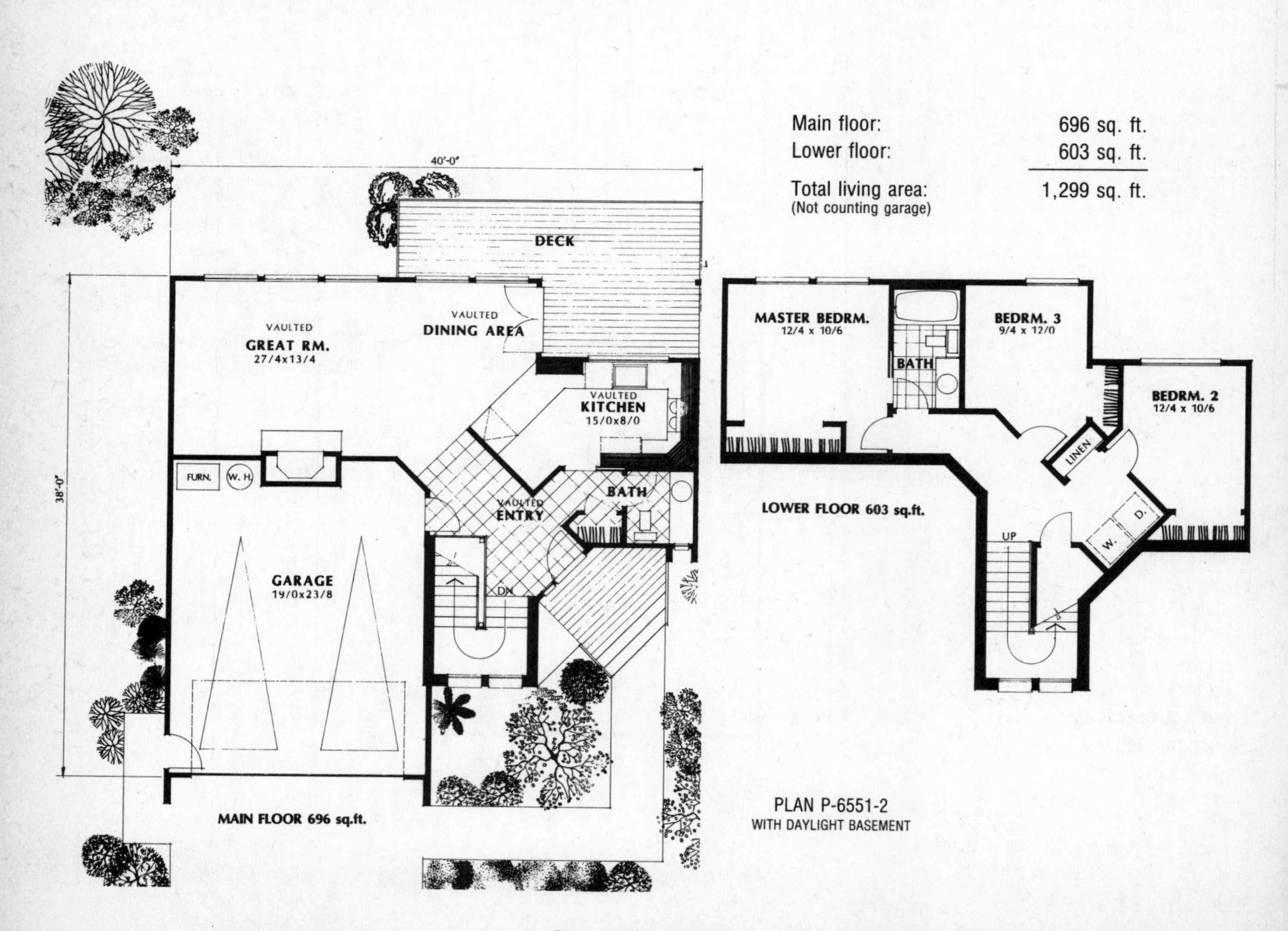

PLAN P-6551-2
WITH DAYLIGHT BASEMENT

Blueprint Price Code A

Plan P-6551-2

TO ORDER THIS BLUEPRINT, CALL TOLL-FREE 1-800-547-5570

PRICES AND DETAILS ON PAGES 12-15

A Chalet for Today

- This new, up-to-date chalet design is ideal for recreational living, whether year-round or part-time. The home's rustic appeal and soaring windows are ideally suited to scenic sites.
- The living and dining rooms are combined to take advantage of the dramatic cathedral ceiling, the view through the spectacular windows and the rugged stone fireplace.
- A quaint balcony adds to the warm country feeling of the living area, which is further expanded by a wrap-around deck. The open, peninsula kitchen includes a breakfast bar that connects it to the living area.
- The first-floor study or den is an added feature rarely found in a home of this size and style.
- A convenient main-floor laundry is adjacent to two bedrooms and a full bath.
- The master bedroom retreat takes up the entire second floor. Cathedral ceilings, sweeping views from the balcony and a private bath with spa tub are highlights here.
- The optional basement plan calls for a tuck-under garage, a large family room, plus utility and storage space.

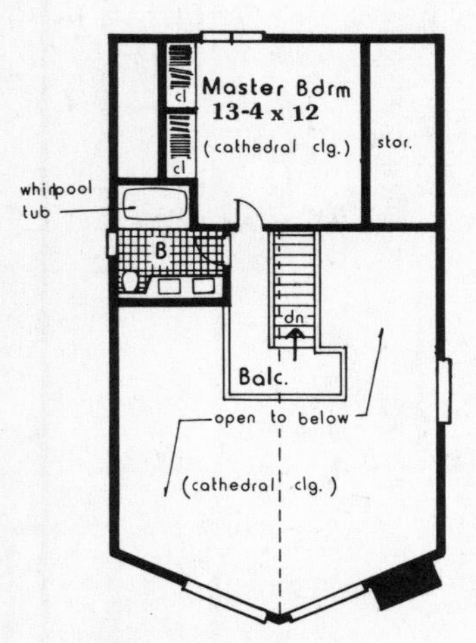

UPPER FLOOR

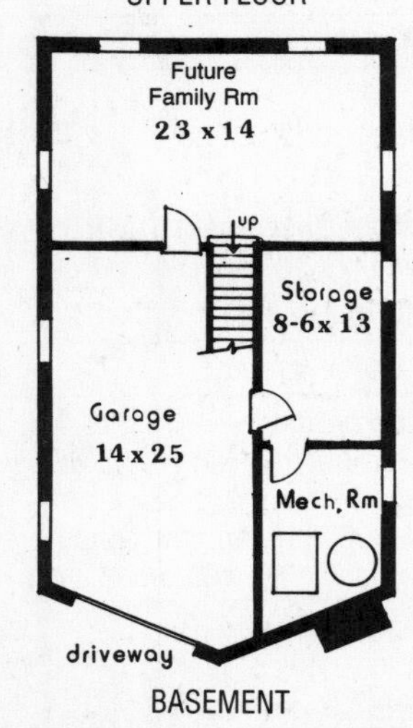

BASEMENT

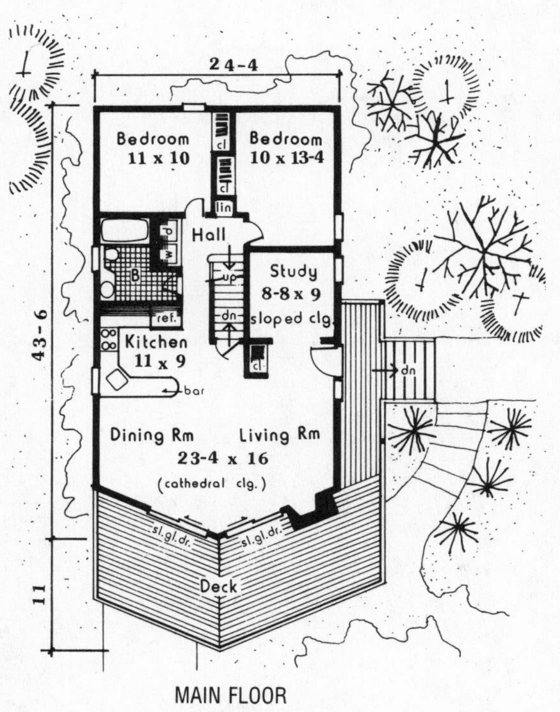

MAIN FLOOR

Plan AHP-9340

Bedrooms: 3-4	**Baths:** 2
Living Area:	
Upper floor	332 sq. ft.
Main floor	974 sq. ft.
Total Living Area:	**1,306 sq. ft.**
Basement	624 sq. ft.
Garage	350 sq. ft.
Exterior Wall Framing:	2x4 or 2x6

Foundation Options:

Daylight basement
Standard basement
Crawlspace
Slab
(Typical foundation & framing conversion diagram available—see order form.)

BLUEPRINT PRICE CODE: A

Handsome Chalet Design Features View

- Roomy floor plan will make this chalet something you'll yearn for all year long.
- Massive fireplace in living room is a pleasant welcome after a day in the cold outdoors.
- Open kitchen has two entrances for smoother traffic.
- Generous laundry facilities and large bath are unexpected frills you'll appreciate.
- Upper floor bedrooms feature sloped ceilings and plenty of storage space.
- Optional basement plan affords more storage and general use space.

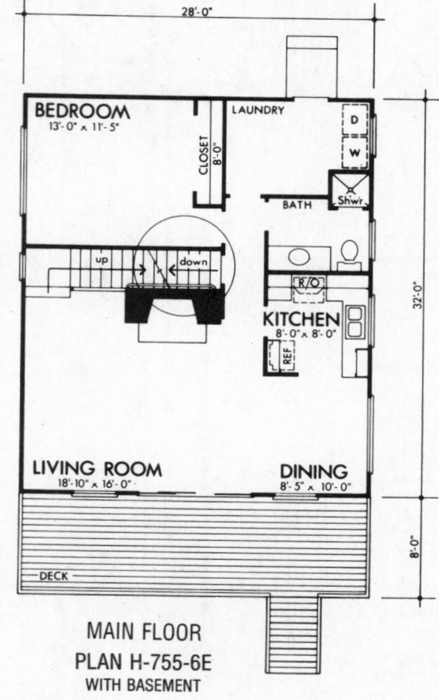

MAIN FLOOR
PLAN H-755-6E
WITH BASEMENT

DECK
STORAGE
BEDROOM
13'-7" x 11'-5"
STORAGE
CLOSET
5'-0"
BATH
down
CLOSET
4'-0"
Tub w/ Shower
SLOPED CEILING
STORAGE
BEDROOM
11'-7" x 11'-5"
STORAGE
DECK

UPPER FLOOR

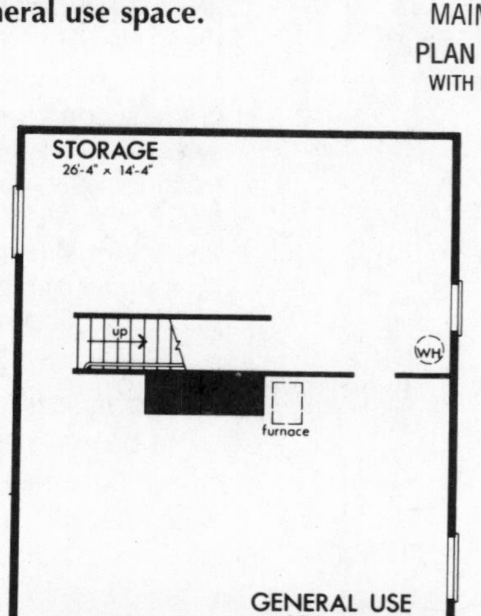

BASEMENT

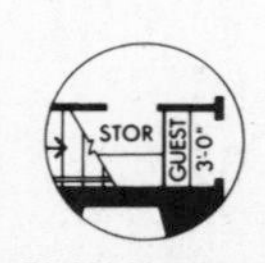

PLAN H-755-5E
WITHOUT BASEMENT

WATER HEATER & FURNACE LOCATED IN LAUNDRY RM.

Plans H-755-5E & -6E

Bedrooms: 3	**Baths:** 2
Space:	
Upper floor:	454 sq. ft.
Main floor:	896 sq. ft.
Total without basement:	1,350 sq. ft.
Basement:	896 sq. ft.
Total with basement:	2,246 sq. ft.
Exterior Wall Framing:	2x4

Foundation options:
Daylight basement (Plan H-755-6E).
Crawlspace (Plan H-755-5E).
(Foundation & framing conversion diagram available — see order form.)

Blueprint Price Code:	
Without basement:	A
With basement:	C

PRICES AND DETAILS ON PAGES 12-15

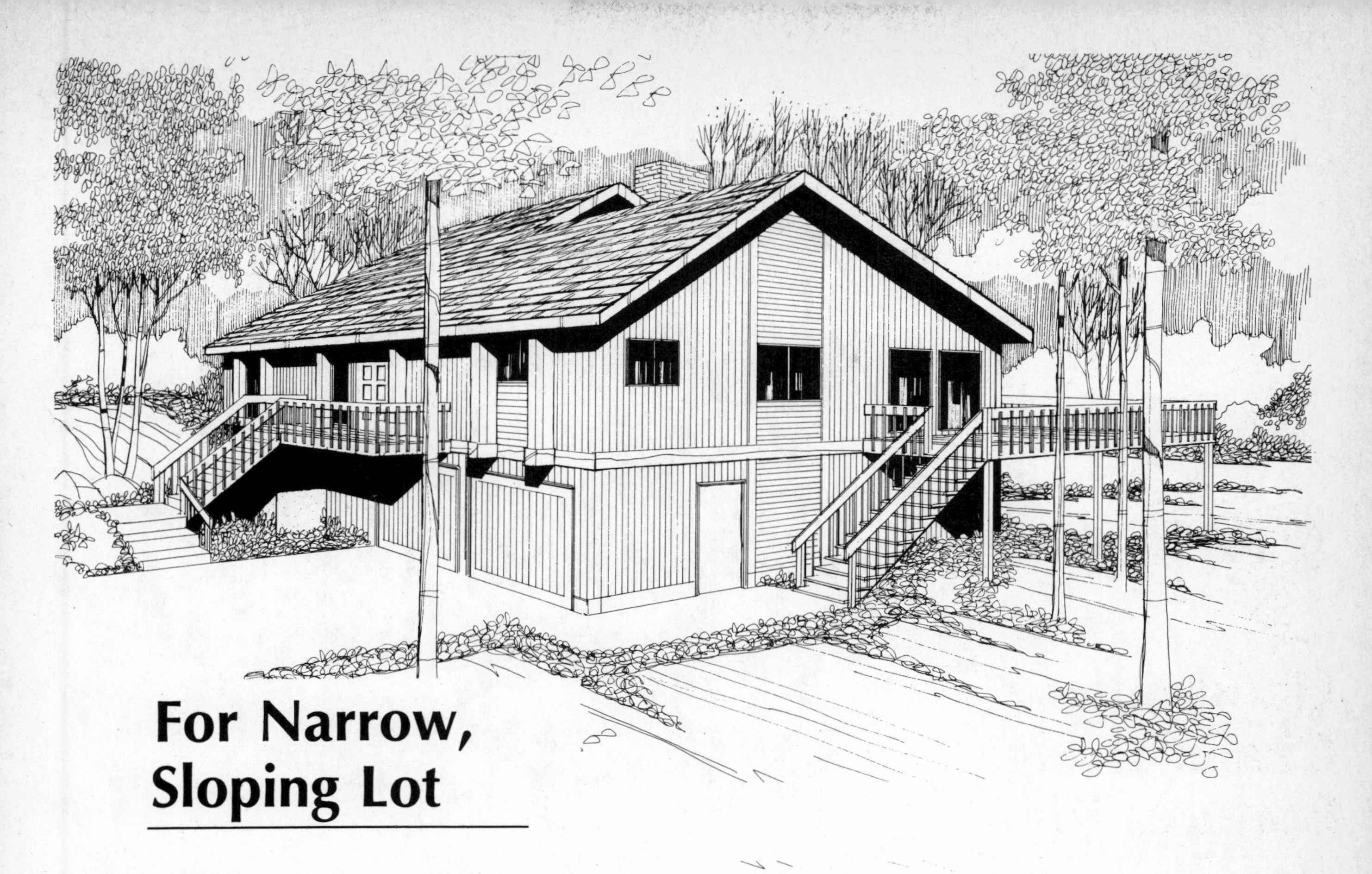

For Narrow, Sloping Lot

Main floor: 1,352 sq. ft.
Basement level: 319 sq. ft.

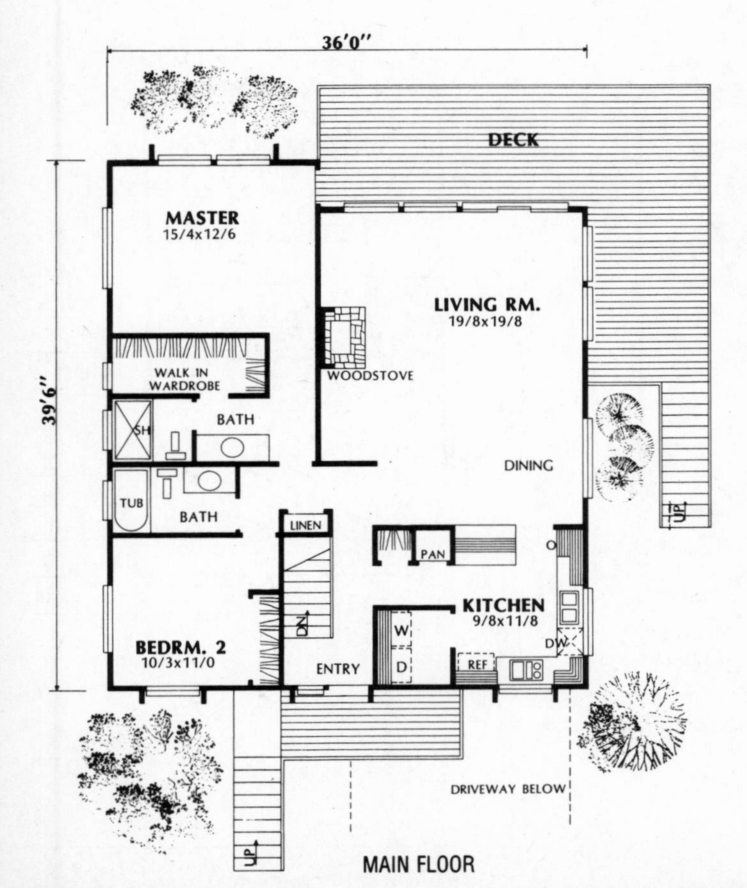

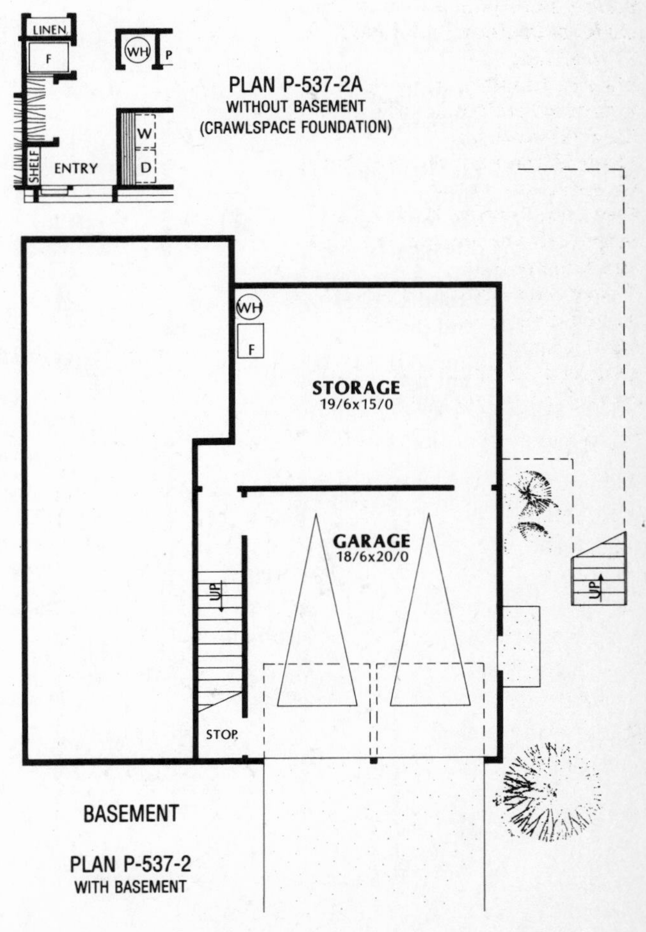

Blueprint Price Code A

Plans P-537-2 & P-537-2A

PRICES AND DETAILS ON PAGES 12-15

Windowed Great Room

- This attractive, open design can function as a cabin, mountain retreat or permanent residence.
- The main level of the home is entered via a split-landing, wraparound deck.
- The kitchen and Great Room merge to form a large family activity area; an open balcony loft above offers an elevated view of the massive front window wall.
- Two quiet main-floor bedrooms share a hall bath.
- A third sleeping room upstairs could be split into two smaller bedrooms.

Plan I-1354-B	
Bedrooms: 2+	**Baths:** 2
Living Area:	
Upper floor	366 sq. ft.
Main floor	988 sq. ft.
Total Living Area:	**1,354 sq. ft.**
Daylight basement	658 sq. ft.
Tuck-under garage	260 sq. ft.
Exterior Wall Framing:	2x6
Foundation Options:	
Daylight basement	
(All plans can be built with your choice of foundation and framing. A generic conversion diagram is available. See order form.)	
BLUEPRINT PRICE CODE:	**A**

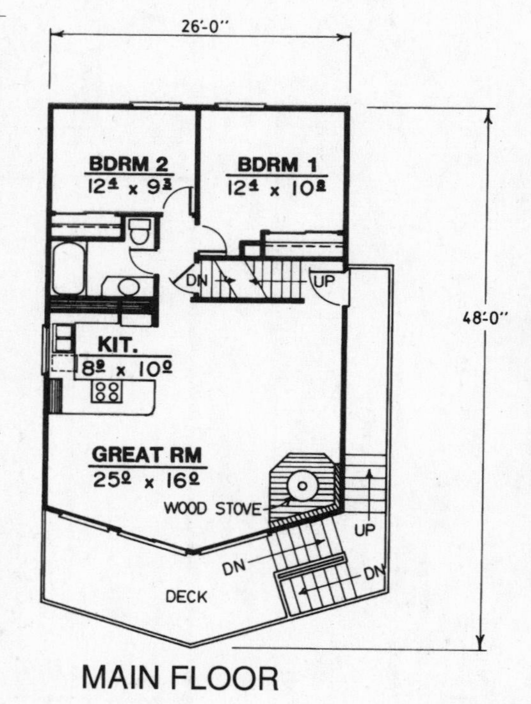

MAIN FLOOR

26'-0"
SLEEP'G LOFT
24^{0} x 13^{0}
UP
LOFT
16^{0} x 6^{0}
OPEN TO BELOW
40'-0"

UPPER FLOOR

Vaulted Design for Narrow Lot

- Vaulted living spaces add to the spacious feel of this narrow-lot home.
- The focal point is a large fireplace flanked by windows that give views of a lovely patio and the yard beyond.
- The dining room offers access to a secluded courtyard, while the bayed kitchen overlooks a front garden.
- The master suite features a sitting room with sliders to the patio. The master bath leads to a large walk-in closet.
- The two remaining bedrooms share the hall bath.

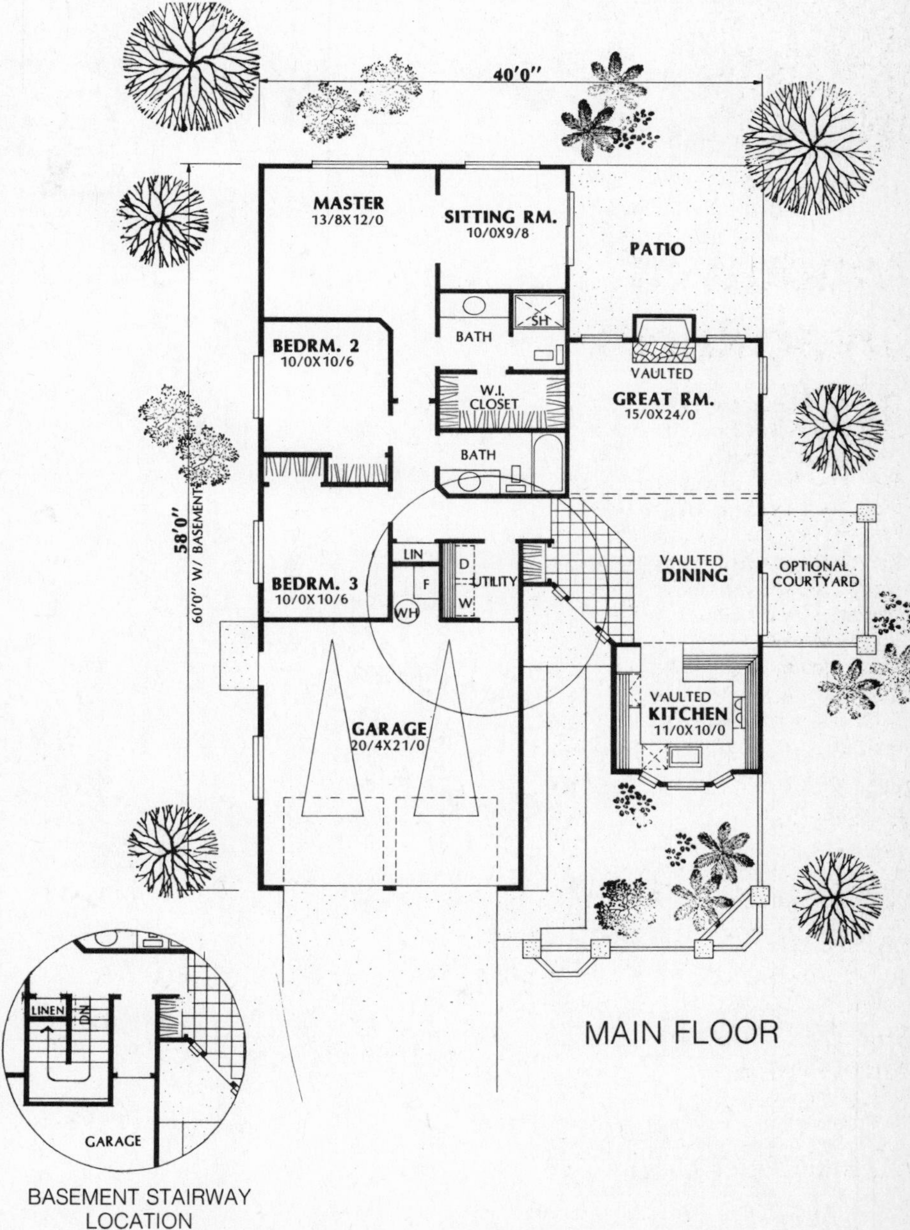

Plans P-6588-2A & -2D

Bedrooms: 3	**Baths:** 2
Living Area:	
Main floor (non-basement version)	1,362 sq. ft.
Main floor (basement version)	1,403 sq. ft.
Total Living Area:	**1,362/1,403 sq. ft.**
Daylight basement	1,303 sq. ft.
Garage	427 sq. ft.
Exterior Wall Framing:	2x6
Foundation Options:	**Plan #**
Daylight basement	P-6588-2D
Crawlspace	P-6588-2A
(Typical foundation & framing conversion diagram available—see order form.)	
BLUEPRINT PRICE CODE:	**A**

Garden Home

- This thoroughly modern plan exhibits beautiful traditional touches in its exterior design.
- A gracious courtyard-like area leads visitors to a side door with a vaulted entry.
- A delightful kitchen/nook area is just to the right of the entry, and includes abundant window space and a convenient utility room.
- The vaulted living and dining areas join together to create an impressive space for entertaining and family living.
- The master suite boasts a large closet and a private bath.
- The daylight-basement option adds almost 1,500 square feet of space to the home.

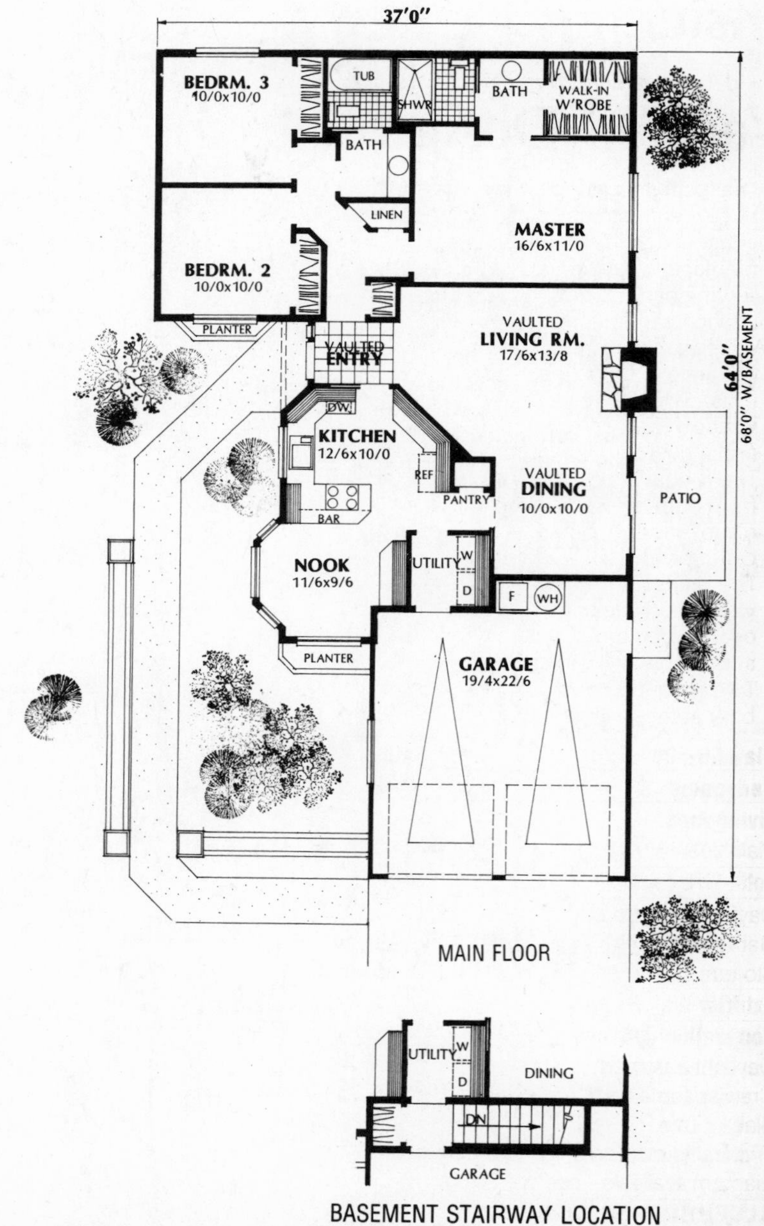

Plans P-6598-2A & -2D	
Bedrooms: 3	**Baths:** 2
Living Area:	
Main floor (without basement)	1,375 sq. ft.
Main floor (with basement)	1,470 sq. ft.
Total Living Area:	**1,375/1,470 sq. ft.**
Daylight basement	1,470 sq. ft.
Garage	435 sq. ft.
Exterior Wall Framing:	2x4
Foundation Options:	**Plan #**
Daylight basement	P-6598-2D
Crawlspace	P-6598-2A
(Typical foundation & framing conversion diagram available—see order form.)	
BLUEPRINT PRICE CODE:	**A**

Distinctive Inside and Out

- A decorative columned entry, shuttered windows and a facade of stucco and stone offer a distinct look to this economical one-story home.
- The focal point of the interior is the huge, central family room. The room is enhanced with a dramatic corner fireplace, a vaulted ceiling and a neat serving bar that extends from the kitchen and includes a wet bar.
- A decorative plant shelf adorns the entrance to the adjoining breakfast room, which features a lovely bay window. The kitchen offers a pantry and a pass-through to the serving bar.
- The formal dining room is easy to reach from both the kitchen and the family room, and is highlighted by a raised ceiling and a tall window.
- The secluded master suite boasts a vaulted private bath with dual sinks, an oval garden tub, a separate toilet room and a large walk-in closet.
- Two more bedrooms share a second bath at the other end of the home.

Plan FB-5001-SAVA

Bedrooms: 3	**Baths:** 2
Living Area:	
Main floor	1,429 sq. ft.
Total Living Area:	**1,429 sq. ft.**
Daylight basement	1,429 sq. ft.
Garage	250 sq. ft.
Storage	14 sq. ft.
Exterior Wall Framing:	2x4

Foundation Options:
Daylight basement
Crawlspace
Slab
(Typical foundation & framing conversion diagram available—see order form.)

BLUEPRINT PRICE CODE: **A**

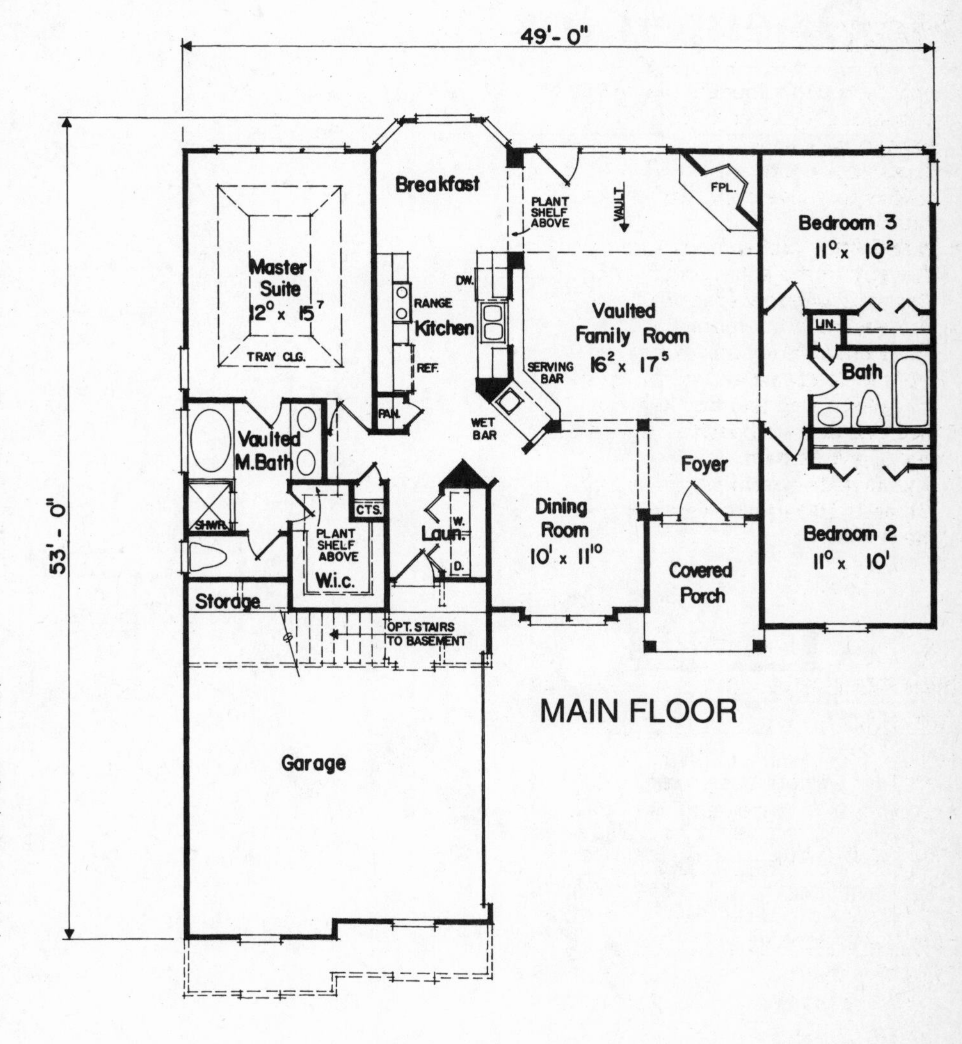

Oriented for Scenic Rear View

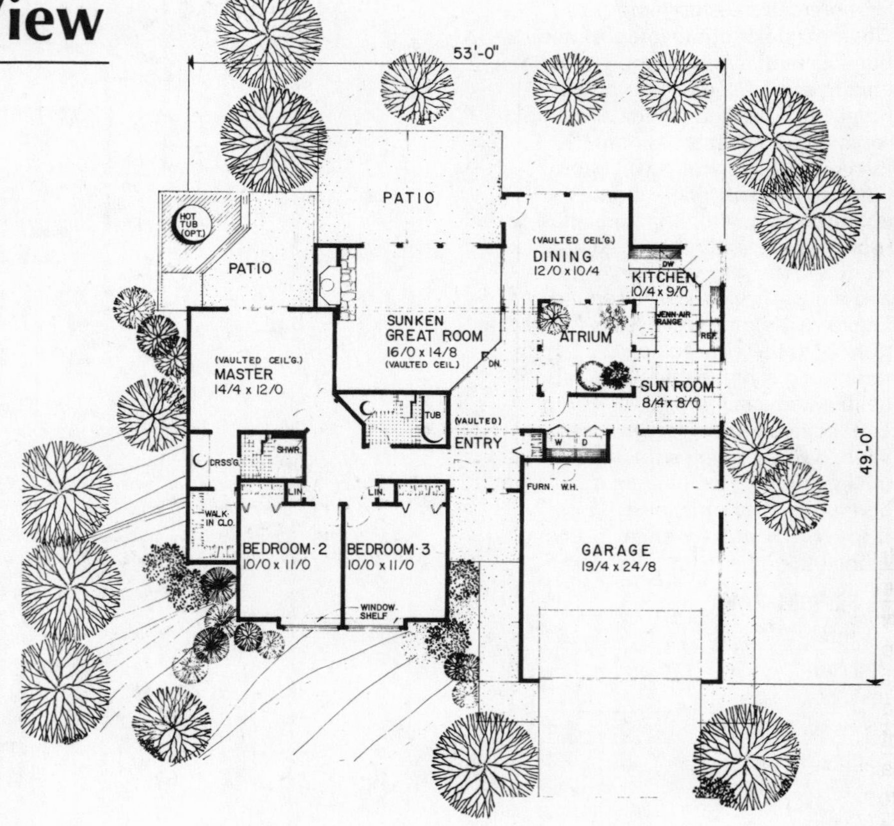

SUN ROOM

DN

W D

PLAN P-6533-2D
WITH DAYLIGHT BASEMENT

Main floor: 1,484 sq. ft.
(Not counting garage)

Basement level: 1,484 sq. ft.

PLAN P-6533-2A
WITHOUT BASEMENT
(CRAWLSPACE FOUNDATION)

Total living area: 1,399 sq. ft.
(Not counting garage)

Blueprint Price Code A

Plans P-6533-2A & -2D

TO ORDER THIS BLUEPRINT, CALL TOLL-FREE 1-800-547-5570

PRICES AND DETAILS ON PAGES 12-15

Vacation Home with Views

- The octagonal shape and window-filled walls of this home create a powerful interior packed with panoramic views.
- Straight back from the angled entry, the Great Room is brightened by expansive windows and sliding glass doors to a huge wraparound deck. An impressive spiral staircase at the center of the floor plan lends even more character.
- The walk-through kitchen offers a handy pantry. A nice storage closet and a coat closet are located between the entry and the two-car garage.
- The main-floor bedroom is conveniently located near a full bath.
- The upper-floor master suite is a sanctuary, featuring lots of glass, a walk-in closet, a private bath and access to concealed storage rooms.
- The optional daylight basement offers an extra bedroom, a full bath, a laundry area and a large recreation room.

Plans H-964-1A & -1B	
Bedrooms: 2+	**Baths:** 2-3
Living Area:	
Upper floor	346 sq. ft.
Main floor	1,067 sq. ft.
Daylight basement	1,045 sq. ft.
Total Living Area:	**1,413/2,458 sq. ft.**
Garage	512 sq. ft.
Storage (upper floor)	134 sq. ft.
Exterior Wall Framing:	2x6
Foundation Options:	**Plan #**
Daylight basement	H-964-1B
Crawlspace	H-964-1A

(All plans can be built with your choice of foundation and framing. A generic conversion diagram is available. See order form.)

BLUEPRINT PRICE CODE:	**A/C**

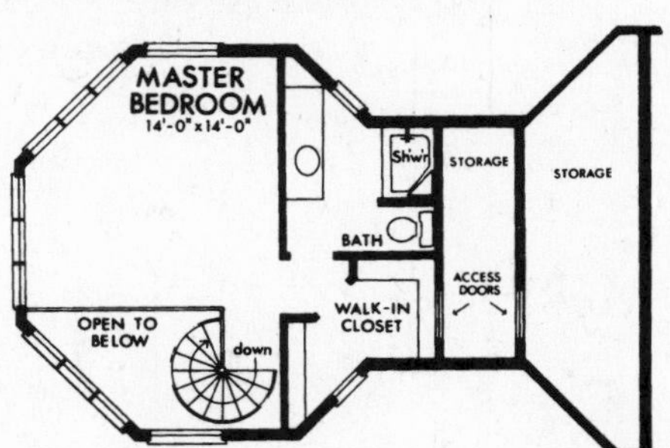

UPPER FLOOR

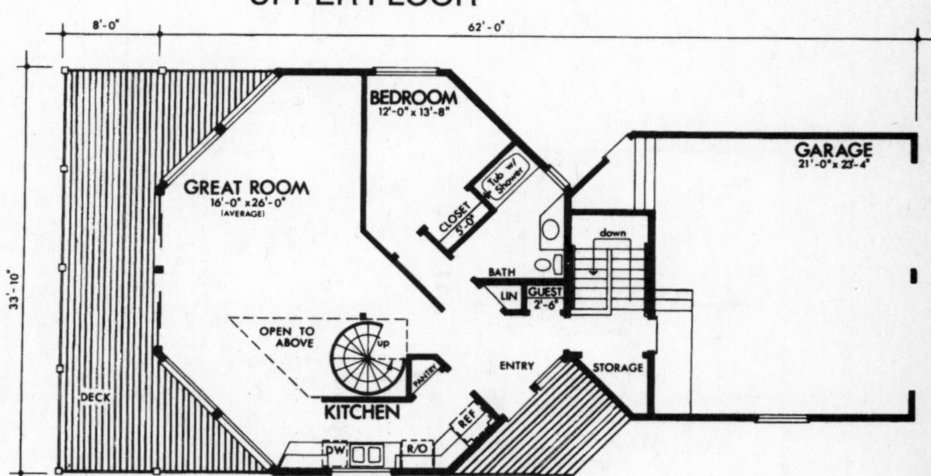

MAIN FLOOR

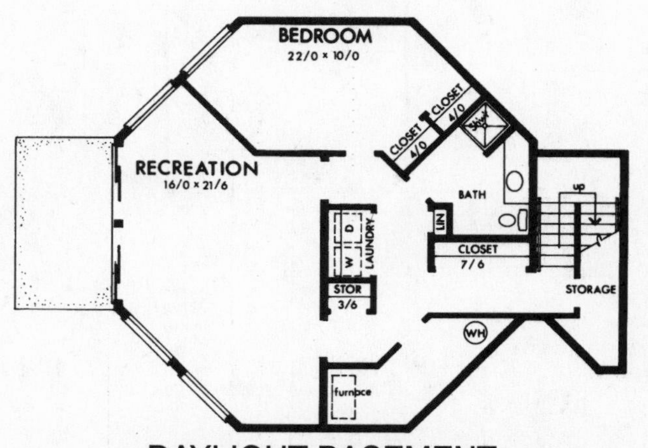

DAYLIGHT BASEMENT

(Alternate, included in blueprints)

49'0"

51'0"

PATIO

VAULTED MASTER 12/8x13/0

VAULTED DRESSING

8'0" WALL

SKYLIGHT

SHWR

TUB

LIN

VAULTED GREAT RM. 25/4x16/0

EXPOSED BEAMS

VAULTED DINING RM.

CEILING LINE

BAR

PANTRY

VAULTED ENTRY

SKYLIGHT

UTIL.

W

D

KITCHEN 10/8x11/4

DW

WH

F

BEDRM. 2 10/4x10/4

BEDRM. 3 10/4x10/2

GARAGE 19/4x22/8

ENTRY

KITCHEN

DN

GARAGE

PLAN P-6584-4D
WITH DAYLIGHT BASEMENT

Main floor	1,458 sq. ft.
Lower floor	1,413 sq. ft.

PLAN P-6584-4A
WITHOUT BASEMENT

Total living area: 1,415 sq. ft.
(Not counting garage)

Distinctive Contemporary Offers Two Exterior Designs

An open-arbor entry porch, boxed chimney, horizontal board siding and semihipped rooflines lend a custom look to the exterior of this contemporary ranch home. And the home's 1,415 sq. ft. interior is equally distinctive.

The front entry hall, which separates the spacious, open living area from the comfortably sized bedroom wing, has a vaulted ceiling with skylight for a dramatic first impression. The great room also has a vaulted ceiling, plus a long window wall (with sliding-glass door off the dining area opening onto a partly covered patio) and large fireplace.

There's an efficient U-shaped kitchen with pantry storage and an adjacent utility room. (In the daylight basement version, the utility room is replaced by stairs, and the entry to the garage is relocated.) A large master bedroom suite also has a vaulted ceiling with a skylight in the wardrobe/dressing area.

Blueprint Price Code A

Plans P-6584-4A & 4D

PRICES AND DETAILS ON PAGES 12-15

Two-Bedroom Country Cottage

A covered veranda and screened rear porch provide extra living spaces in this modest-sized ranch design. The large all-purpose family room has a built-in fireplace and bright dining corner.

Two roomy bedrooms and two full baths make up the sleeping wing.

An efficient galley kitchen is adjacent to utility room (with pantry) and side-entry garage.

Total living area: 1,420 sq. ft.
(Not counting basement or garage)

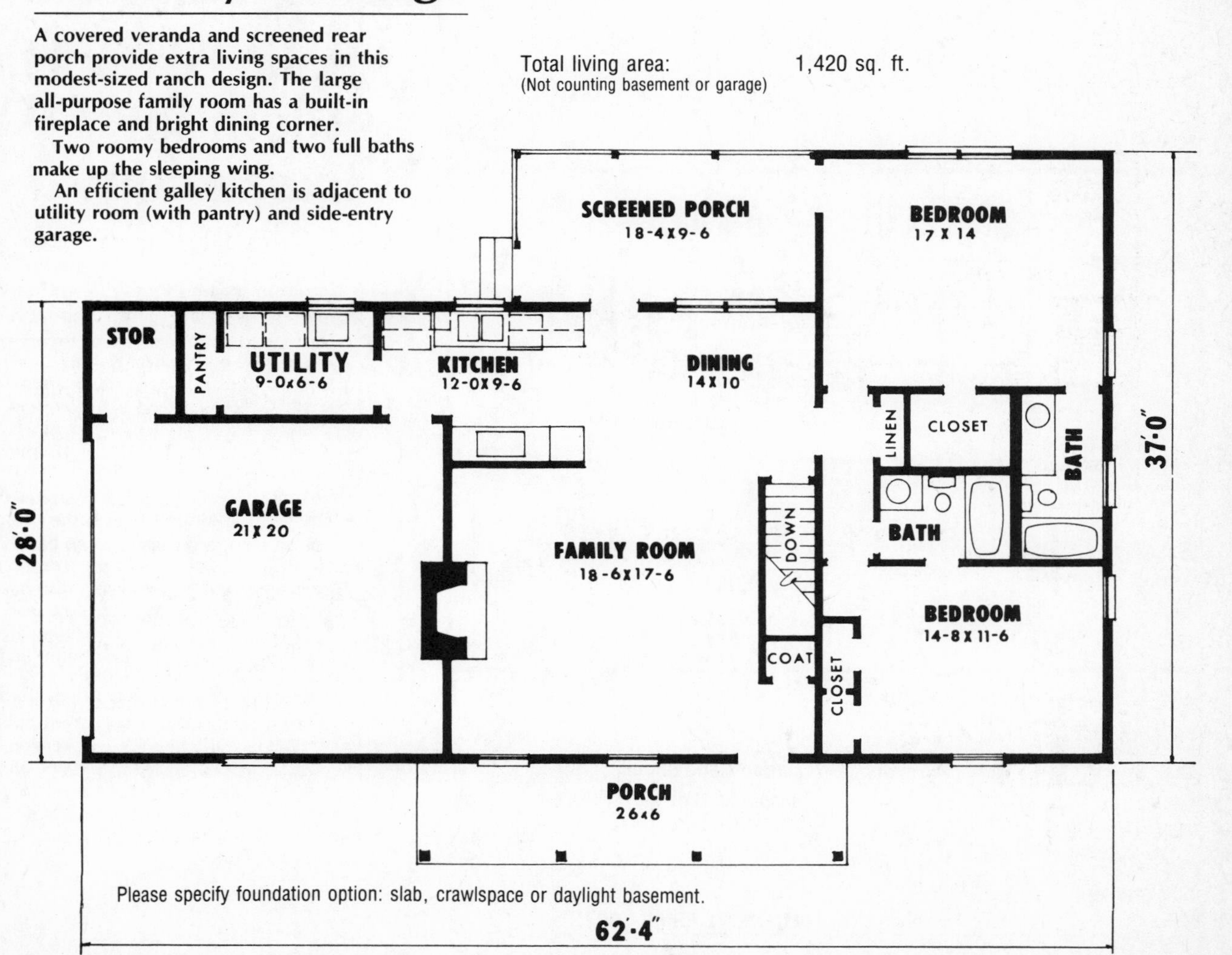

Please specify foundation option: slab, crawlspace or daylight basement.

Blueprint Price Code A

Plan C-7520

TO ORDER THIS BLUEPRINT, CALL TOLL-FREE 1-800-547-5570

PRICES AND DETAILS ON PAGES 12-15

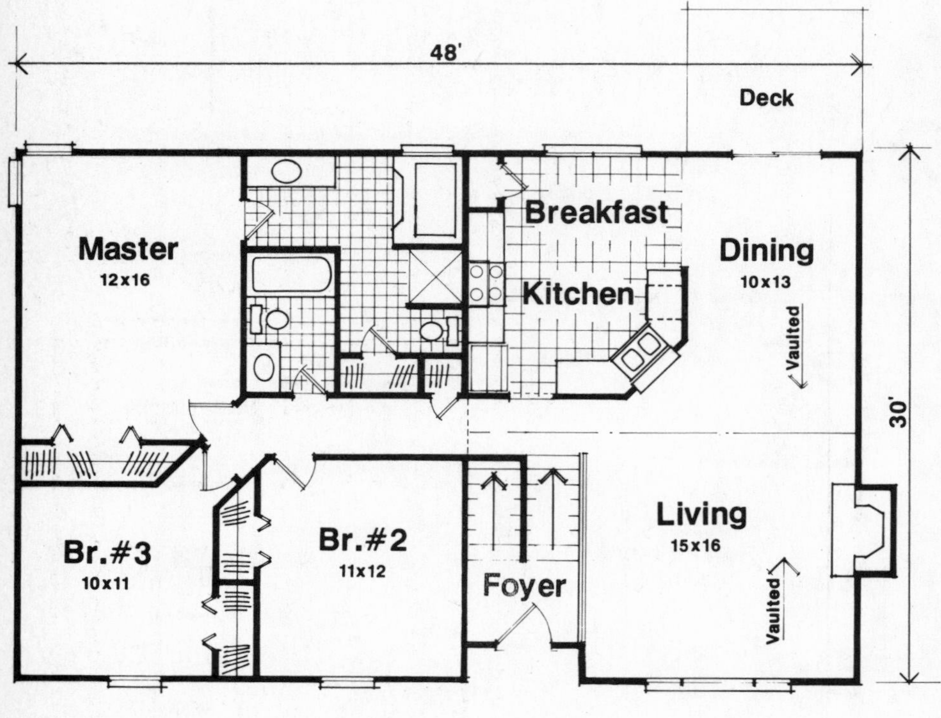

Split-Foyer Has Room for Expansion

- This popular split-foyer design provides space for expansion with the inclusion of an unfinished family room in the lower level. The garage and laundry room also share the lower level.
- A vaulted ceiling highlights both the living room and the dining room; the living room also offers a warming fireplace and a view to the backyard deck, which is accessible through the dining room.
- The roomy kitchen features an angled countertop, a pantry and an eat-in kitchen.
- Secluded to the rear, the spacious master suite features two closets, a corner window and a generous bath with a step-up tub and separate shower.
- The two additional bedrooms share a second full bath.

Plan APS-1410

Bedrooms: 3	**Baths:** 2
Living Area:	
Main floor	1,428 sq. ft.
Total Living Area:	**1,428 sq. ft.**
Daylight basement	458 sq. ft.
Garage	480 sq. ft.

Exterior Wall Framing:	2x4
Foundation Options:	
Daylight basement	
(Typical foundation & framing conversion diagram available—see order form.)	
BLUEPRINT PRICE CODE:	**A**

Loft Lookout

- Unique lakeside living is possible with this getaway home that can be built on posts.
- Inside, a large living and dining space with a dramatic cathedral ceiling is surrounded by an expansive deck.
- A nice-sized kitchen, two baths and three bedrooms complete the main floor.
- The versatile loft could be used as a rec room, a lookout station or extra sleeping space.

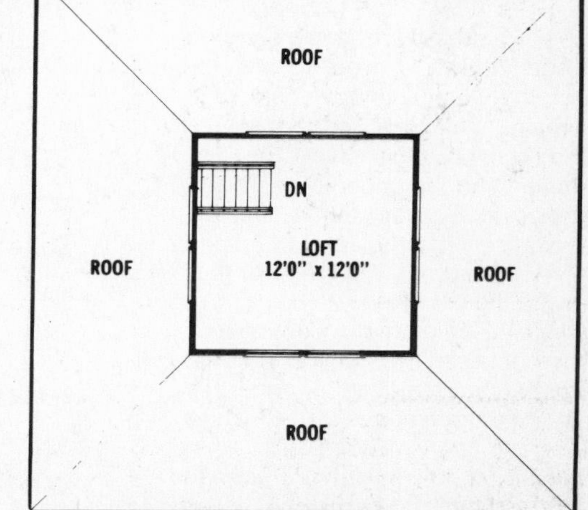

Plan PH-1440

Bedrooms: 3	**Baths:** 2
Space:	
Upper floor	144 sq. ft.
Main floor	1,296 sq. ft.
Total Living Area	**1,440 sq. ft.**
Exterior Wall Framing	2x6
Foundation options:	
Crawlspace	
Pole	
Slab	
(Foundation & framing conversion diagram available—see order form.)	
Blueprint Price Code	**A**

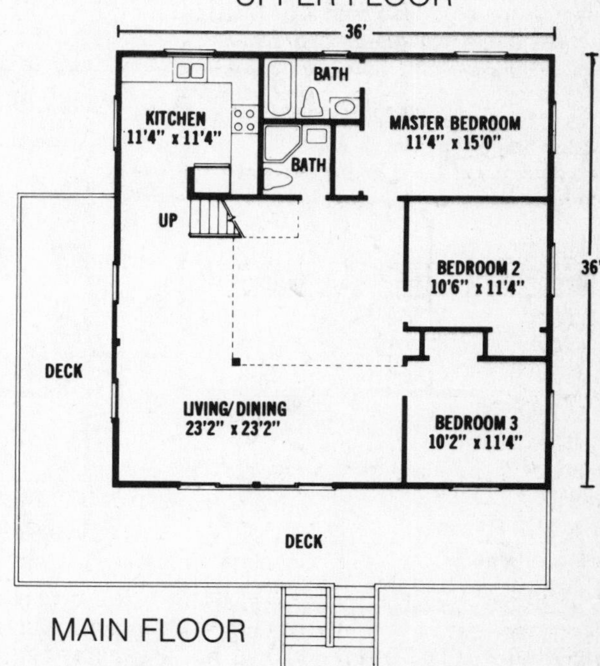

Authentic Charm

- A covered front porch, decorative trim and shuttered windows lend authentic charm to this space-efficient home.
- The main living areas are oriented around stairways that access the basement and the upper floor. The spacious family room shows off a dramatic central fireplace and an array of glass, including a French door that opens to the backyard.
- The nice-sized kitchen is conveniently nestled between the sunny breakfast room and the formal dining room. The breakfast room features a 10-ft vaulted ceiling and two walls of glass.
- A laundry closet is neatly positioned to one side of the breakfast room, where it is handy from both the kitchen and the garage entrance. A half-bath is nearby.
- Upstairs, the deluxe master bedroom offers a huge walk-in closet and a 9-ft. tray ceiling. The luxurious master bath hosts a 13-ft. vaulted ceiling, an oval spa tub and a separate shower.
- Two more good-sized bedrooms and a hall bath complete the upper floor.

Plan FB-5013-LYNW	
Bedrooms: 3	**Baths:** 2½
Living Area:	
Upper floor	681 sq. ft.
Main floor	771 sq. ft.
Total Living Area:	**1,452 sq. ft.**
Daylight basement	771 sq. ft.
Garage	420 sq. ft.
Storage	20 sq. ft.
Exterior Wall Framing:	2x4
Foundation Options:	
Daylight basement	

(All plans can be built with your choice of foundation and framing. A generic conversion diagram is available. See order form.)

BLUEPRINT PRICE CODE: A

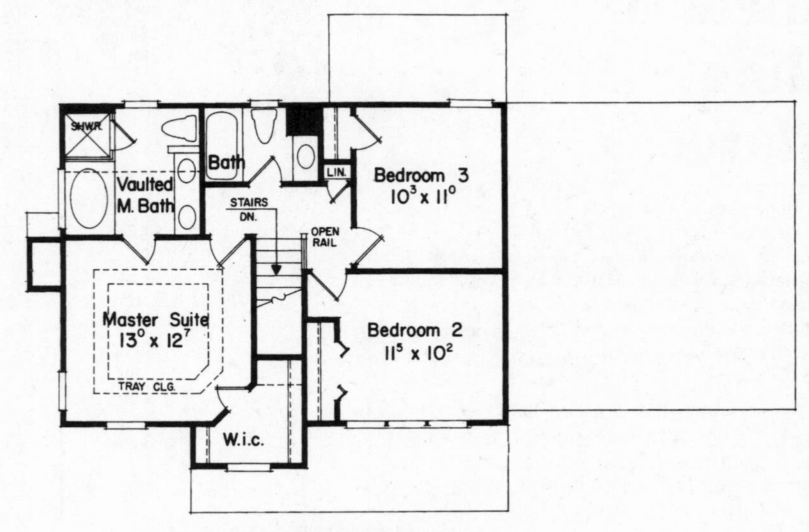

UPPER FLOOR

53'-4"
Vaulted Breakfast
D.
Laund.
W.
FRENCH DOOR
Pwdr.
D.W.
Family Room
13⁰ x 19⁵
STAIRS DN.
Kitchen
RANGE
REF.
CTS.
PAN.
FPL.
Garage
34'-0"
Stor.
Dining Room
12⁰ x 10⁰
OPEN RAIL
STAIRS UP
Foyer
Covered Porch

MAIN FLOOR

Cathedral Ceiling Featured

The open floor plan of this modified A-Frame design virtually eliminates wasted hall space. The centrally located Great Room features a 15'4" cathedral ceiling with exposed wood beams and large areas of fixed glass on both front and rear. Living and dining areas are visually separated by a massive stone fireplace.

The isolated master suite features a walk-in closet and sliding glass doors opening onto the front deck.

A walk-thru utility room provides easy access from the carport and outside storage area to the compact kitchen. On the opposite side of the Great Room are two additional bedrooms and a second full bath. All this takes up only 1,454 square feet of heated living area. A full length deck and vertical wood siding with stone accents on the corners provide a rustic yet contemporary exterior.

Total living area: 1,454 sq. ft.
(Not counting basement or garage)

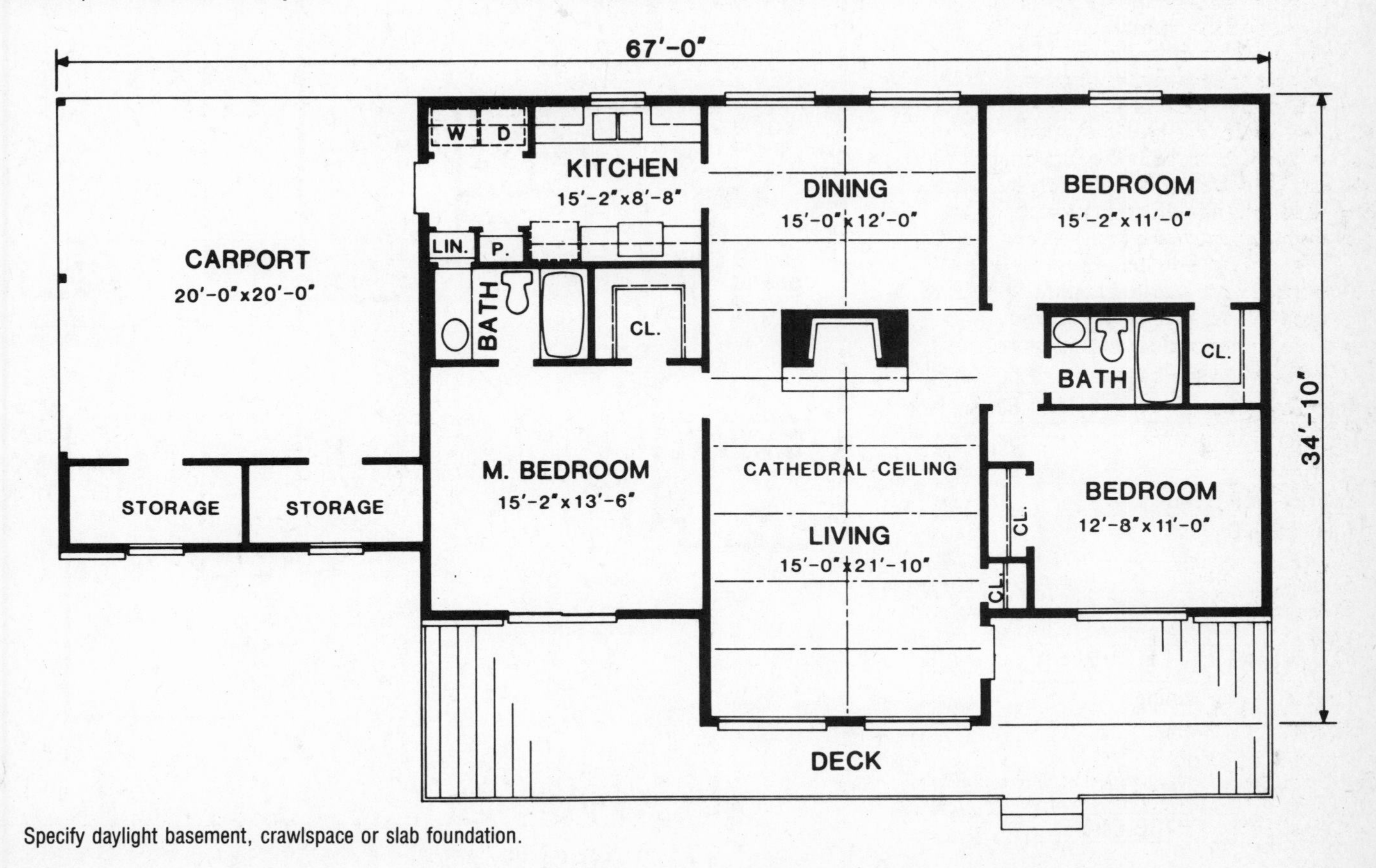

Specify daylight basement, crawlspace or slab foundation.

Blueprint Price Code A

Plan C-7360

TO ORDER THIS BLUEPRINT, CALL TOLL-FREE 1-800-547-5570

PRICES AND DETAILS ON PAGES 12-15

Big on Luxury

- This modestly sized home is big on luxuries and is well suited to a small or narrow lot.
- The tiled entry leads to the living room, where a 13-ft.-high vaulted ceiling and a boxed-out window add an extra-spacious feel. The adjoining dining area has a half-wall opening to the hall, further expanding the area.
- The kitchen features a spacious eating bar that overlooks the family room. Sliding glass doors in the family room open to a backyard patio for extended entertainment space.
- The master bedroom offers generous closet space and a private bath with a dual-sink vanity. Two additional bedrooms share another full bath.

Plans P-7699-2A & -2D	
Bedrooms: 3	**Baths:** 2
Living Area:	
Main floor (crawlspace version)	1,460 sq. ft.
Main floor (basement version)	1,509 sq. ft.
Total Living Area:	**1,460/1,509 sq. ft.**
Daylight basement	1,530 sq. ft.
Garage	383 sq. ft.
Exterior Wall Framing:	2x4
Foundation Options:	**Plan #**
Daylight basement	P-7699-2D
Crawlspace	P-7699-2A

(All plans can be built with your choice of foundation and framing. A generic conversion diagram is available. See order form.)

BLUEPRINT PRICE CODE:	A/B

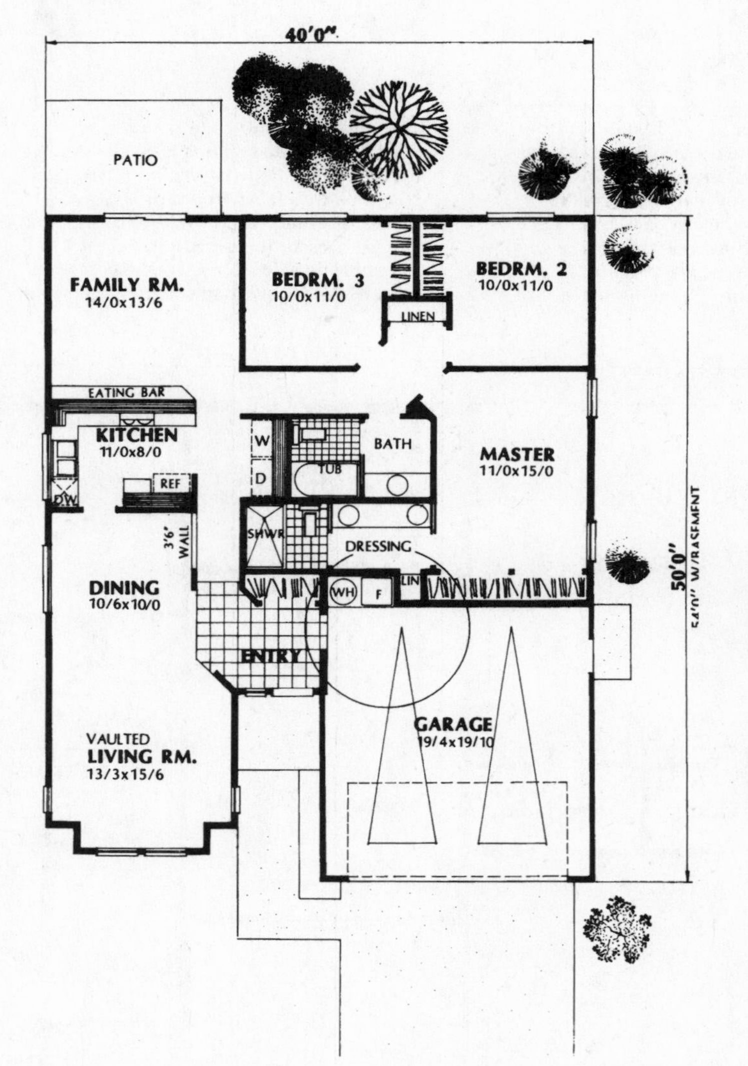

MAIN FLOOR

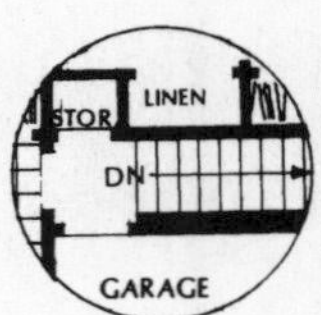

BASEMENT STAIRWAY LOCATION

TO ORDER THIS BLUEPRINT, CALL TOLL-FREE 1-800-547-5570

Plans P-7699-2A & -2D

PRICES AND DETAILS ON PAGES 12-15

Contemporary Blends with Site

The striking contemporary silhouette of this home paradoxically blends with the rustic setting. Perhaps it is the way the shed rooflines repeat the spreading limbs of the surrounding evergreens, or the way the foundation conforms to the grade much as do the rocks in the foreground. Whatever the reason, the home "belongs."

Aesthetics aside, one must examine the floor plan to determine genuine livability. From the weather-protected entry there is access to any part of the house without annoying cross traffic. Kitchen, dining and living room, the active "waking-hours" section of the residence, are enlarged and enhanced by the convenient outdoor deck. Laundry and bath are located inconspicuously along the hall leading to the main floor bedroom. A huge linen closet is convenient to this area. The additional bedrooms are located upstairs on the 517 sq. ft. second level. A romantic feature of the second floor is the balcony overlooking the living area.

Plans including a full basement are available at your option. A large double garage completes the plan and is an important adjunct, especially if the home is built without a basement, because it can provide much needed storage space.

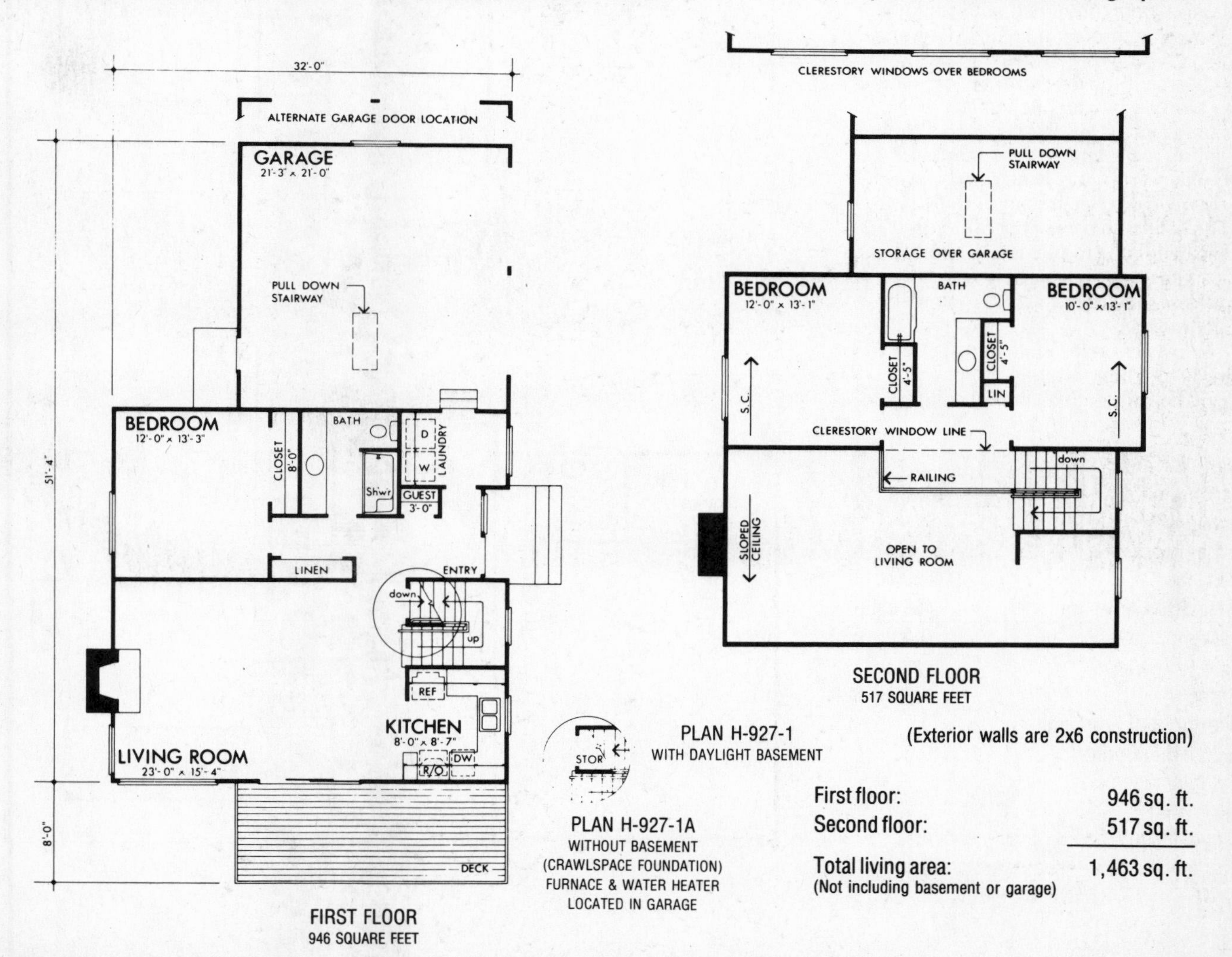

(Exterior walls are 2x6 construction)

First floor:	946 sq. ft.
Second floor:	517 sq. ft.
Total living area:	1,463 sq. ft.

(Not including basement or garage)

Blueprint Price Code A

TO ORDER THIS BLUEPRINT, CALL TOLL-FREE 1-800-547-5570

Plans H-927-1 & -1A

PRICES AND DETAILS ON PAGES 12-15

Pleasantly Peaceful

- You'll enjoy relaxing on the covered front porch of this pleasant two-story traditional home.
- Off the open foyer is an oversized family room, drenched with sunlight streaming through a French door and windows on three sides. A nice fireplace also adds warmth.
- A neatly arranged kitchen is conveniently nestled between a formal dining room and a sunny, casual breakfast room. A pantry and a powder room adjoin the breakfast room.
- The stairway to the upper floor is located in the family room. Closets and a sizable laundry room isolate the master suite from the two secondary bedrooms.
- The master bedroom features a tray ceiling, a huge walk-in closet and a private bath with a vaulted ceiling and a separate tub and shower.

Plan FB-1466	
Bedrooms: 3	**Baths:** 2½
Living Area:	
Upper floor	703 sq. ft.
Main floor	763 sq. ft.
Total Living Area:	**1,466 sq. ft.**
Daylight basement	763 sq. ft.
Garage	426 sq. ft.
Storage	72 sq. ft.
Exterior Wall Framing:	2x4
Foundation Options:	
Daylight basement	
Crawlspace	
(Typical foundation & framing conversion diagram available—see order form.)	
BLUEPRINT PRICE CODE:	**A**

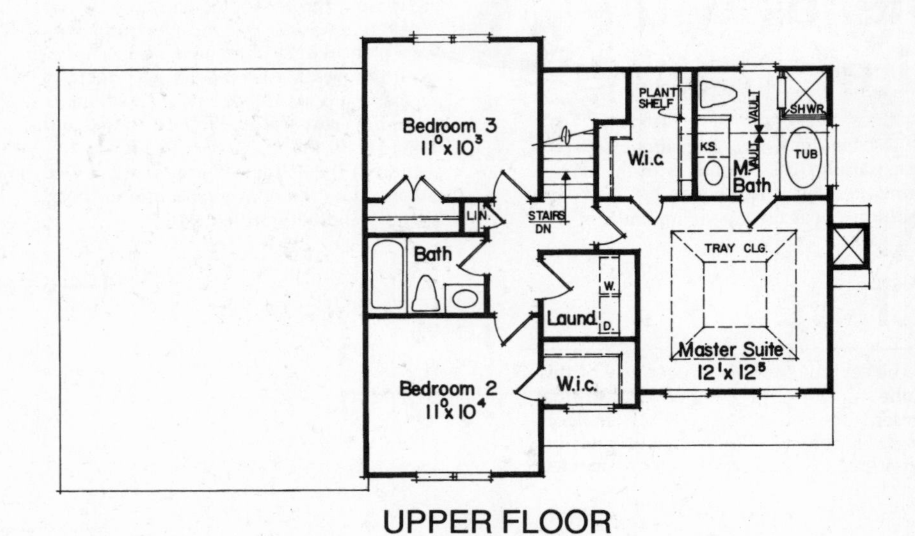

UPPER FLOOR

52'-4"
Storage
PAN.
Breakfast
Powder
STAIRS UP
FRENCH DOOR
D.W.
RANGE
Kitchen
STAIRS DN
REF.
COATS
Family Room
15⁰x19⁸
FPL.
Garage
30'-0"
Dining Room
11⁰x11⁸
Covered Porch

MAIN FLOOR

TO ORDER THIS BLUEPRINT, CALL TOLL-FREE 1-800-547-5570

Plan FB-1466

PRICES AND DETAILS ON PAGES 12-15

All-Season Chalet

A guided tour from the front entry of this home takes you into the central hallway that serves as the hub of traffic to the main floor level. From here, convenience extends in every direction and each room is connected in a step-saving manner. Besides the master bedroom with twin closets, a full bathroom with stall shower is placed adjacent to a common wall that also serves the laundry equipment.

The living room and dining area are connected to allow for the expandable use of the dining table should the need arise for additional seating. The kitchen is open ended onto the dining area and has all the modern conveniences and built-in details.

A raised deck flanks the gable end of the living zone and extends outward for a distance of 8′.

A full basement is reached via a stairway connecting with the central hallway. The basement provides ample storage plus room for the central heating system. Another interesting feature is the garage placed under the home where the owner may not only store his automobile but such things as a boat and trailer and other sporting equipment.

First floor:	1,008 sq. ft.
Second floor:	462 sq. ft.
Total living area: (Not counting basement or garage)	1,470 sq. ft.

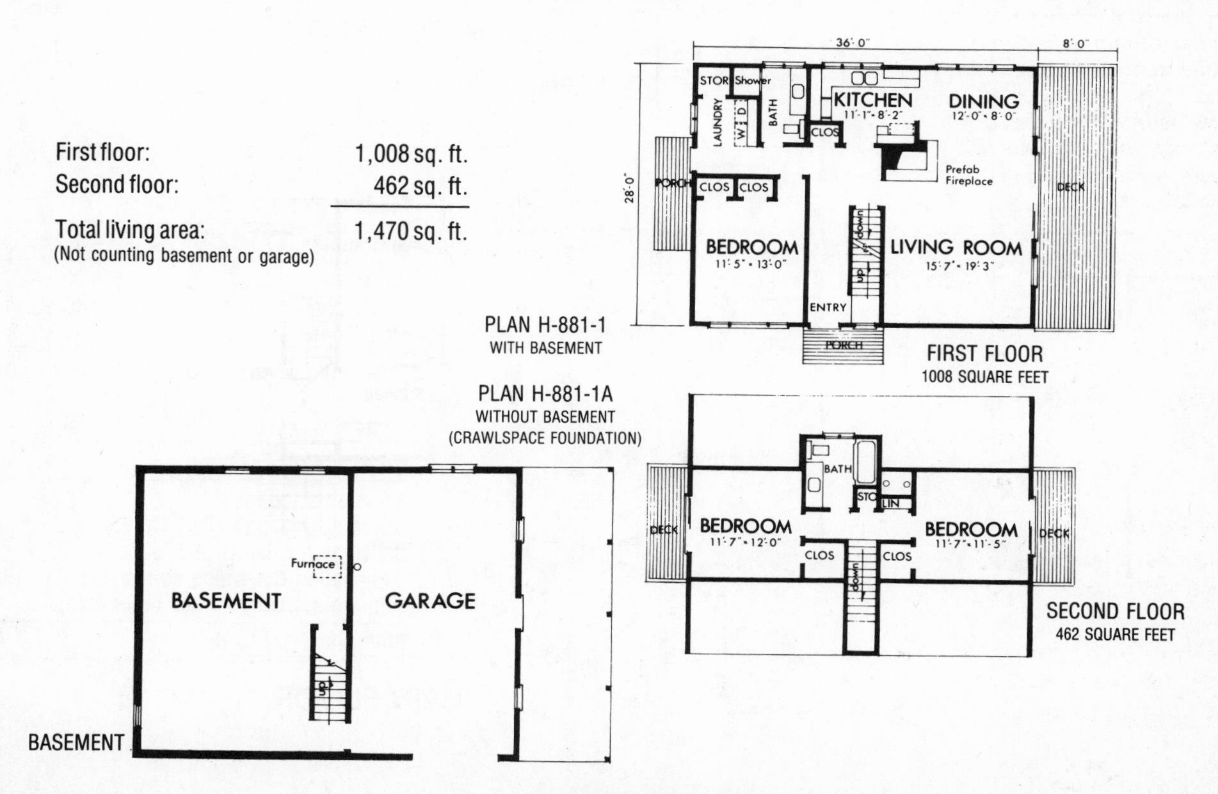

Blueprint Price Code A

Plans H-881-1 & -1A

Eye-Catching Prow-Shaped Chalet

- Steep pitched roof lines and wide cornices give this chalet a distinct alpine appearance.
- Prowed shape, large windows, and 10′ deck provide view and enhancement of indoor/outdoor living.
- Functional division of living and sleeping areas by hallway and first floor full bath.
- Laundry facilities conveniently located near bedroom wing.
- U-shaped kitchen and spacious dining/living areas make the main floor perfect for entertaining.

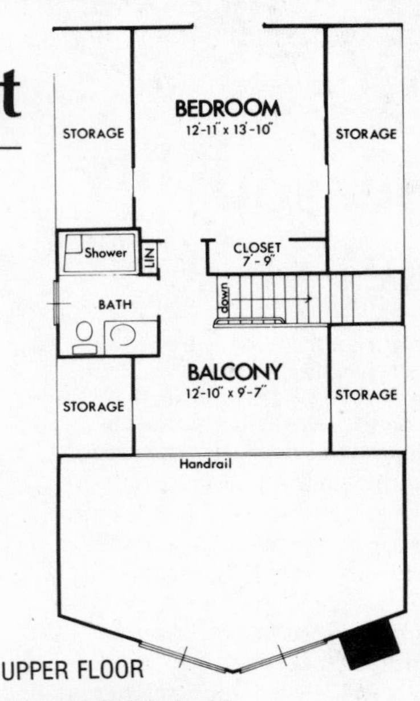

UPPER FLOOR

Plans H-886-3 & -3A

Bedrooms: 3 **Baths:** 2

Space:
Upper floor: 486 sq. ft.
Main floor: 994 sq. ft.

Total without basement: 1,480 sq. ft.
Basement: approx. 715 sq. ft.
Garage: 279 sq. ft.

Exterior Wall Framing: 2x6

Foundation options:
Daylight basement (Plan H-886-3).
Crawlspace (Plan H-886-3A).
(Foundation & framing conversion diagram available — see order form.)

Blueprint Price Code: A

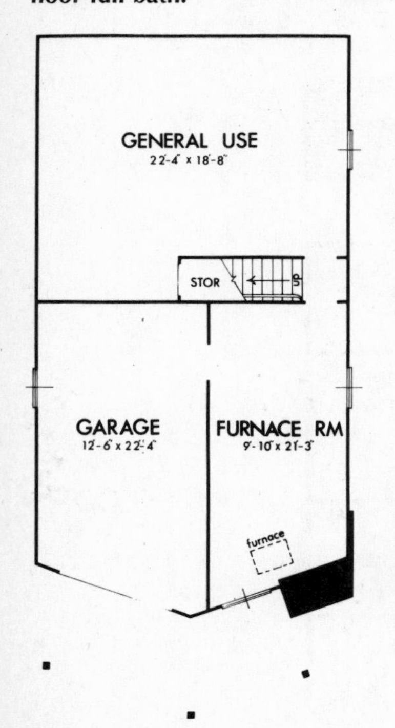

BASEMENT

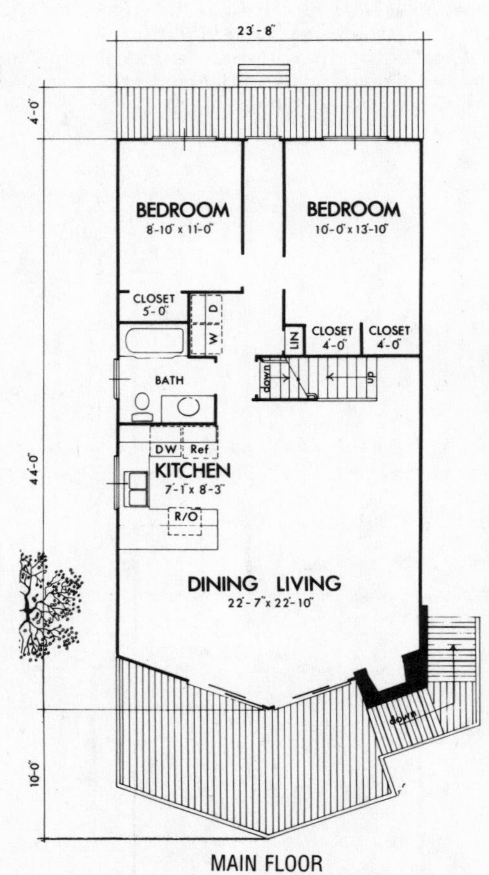

MAIN FLOOR

Plans H-886-3 & -3A

PRICES AND DETAILS ON PAGES 12-15

TRADITIONAL

CONTEMPORARY

Split-Level with Flexibility

- Choose a contemporary or a traditional facade for this roomy split-level plan. Both options are included in the blueprints.
- A covered entry opens into the Great Room, which boasts a vaulted ceiling, a fireplace and access to a rear deck.
- The open kitchen offers a snack counter and a handy pantry. It also has a view of the Great Room as well as a window overlooking the charming plant shelf.
- The master bedroom features built-in shelves, a walk-in closet and a private bath. Two more bedrooms share another full bath.
- The bonus space on the lower level is ideal as a playroom, study, office or entertainment area. A convenient half-bath is nearby.

Plan B-8321	
Bedrooms: 2+	**Baths:** 2½
Living Area:	
Main floor	1,096 sq. ft.
Lower floor	400 sq. ft.
Total Living Area:	**1,496 sq. ft.**
Partial basement	405 sq. ft.
Garage	400 sq. ft.
Exterior Wall Framing:	2x4
Foundation Options:	
Partial basement	
(All plans can be built with your choice of foundation and framing. A generic conversion diagram is available. See order form.)	
BLUEPRINT PRICE CODE:	**A**

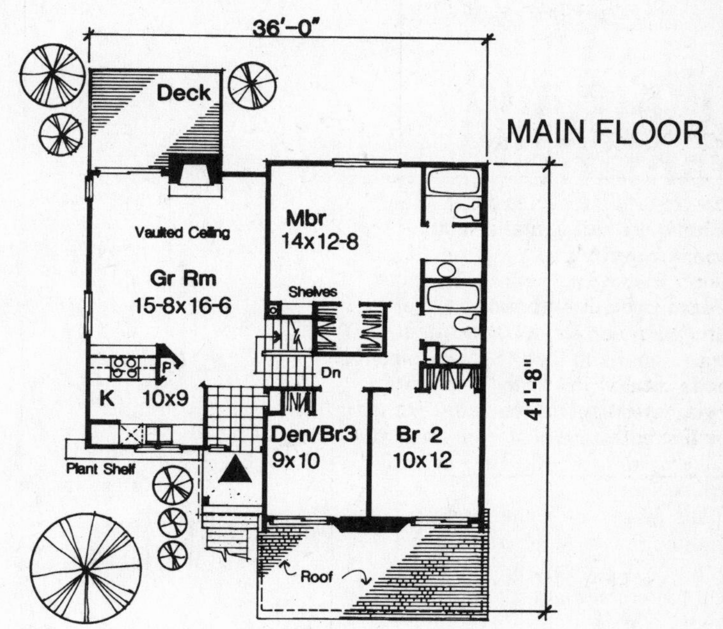

MAIN FLOOR

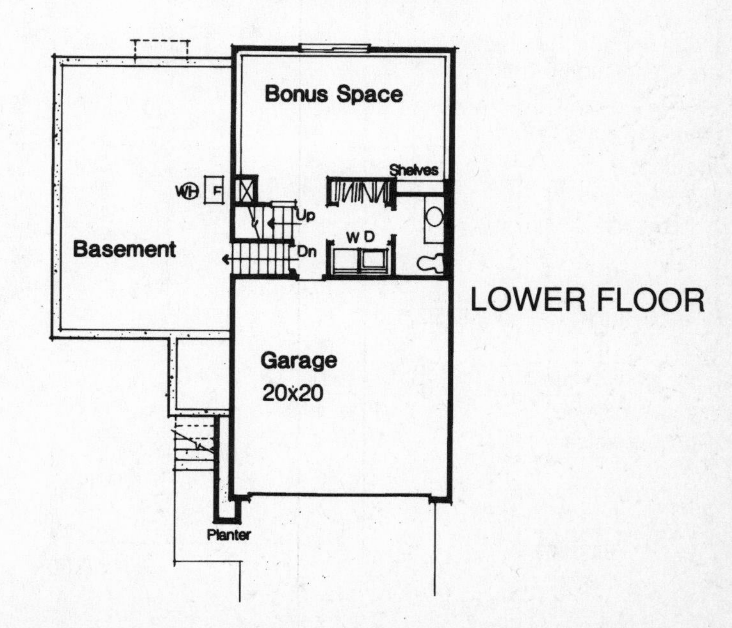

LOWER FLOOR

Unique and Dramatic

- This home's unique interior and dramatic exterior make it perfect for a sloping, scenic lot.
- An expansive and impressive Great Room, warmed by a woodstove, flows into an island kitchen that's completely open in design.
- The passive-solar sun room is designed to collect and store heat from the sun, while providing a good view of the surroundings.
- Upstairs, you'll see a glamorous, skylighted master suite with a private bath and a huge walk-in closet.
- A skylighted hall bath serves the bright second bedroom.
- The daylight basement adds a sunny sitting room, a third bedroom and a large recreation room.

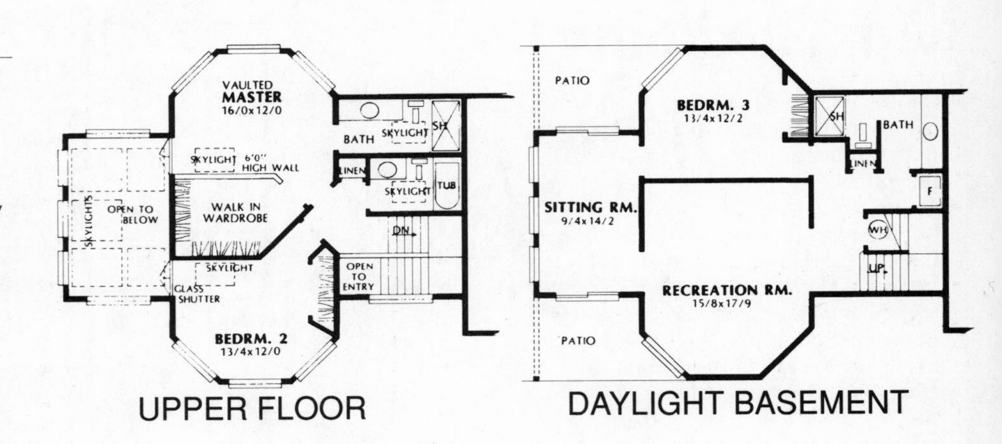

Plans P-536-2A & -2D

Bedrooms: 2+	**Baths:** 2½-3½
Living Area:	
Upper floor	642 sq. ft.
Main floor	863 sq. ft.
Daylight basement	863 sq. ft.
Total Living Area:	**1,505/2,368 sq. ft.**
Garage	445 sq. ft.
Exterior Wall Framing:	2x6
Foundation Options:	**Plan #**
Daylight basement	P-536-2D
Crawlspace	P-536-2A

(All plans can be built with your choice of foundation and framing. A generic conversion diagram is available. See order form.)

BLUEPRINT PRICE CODE:	**B/C**

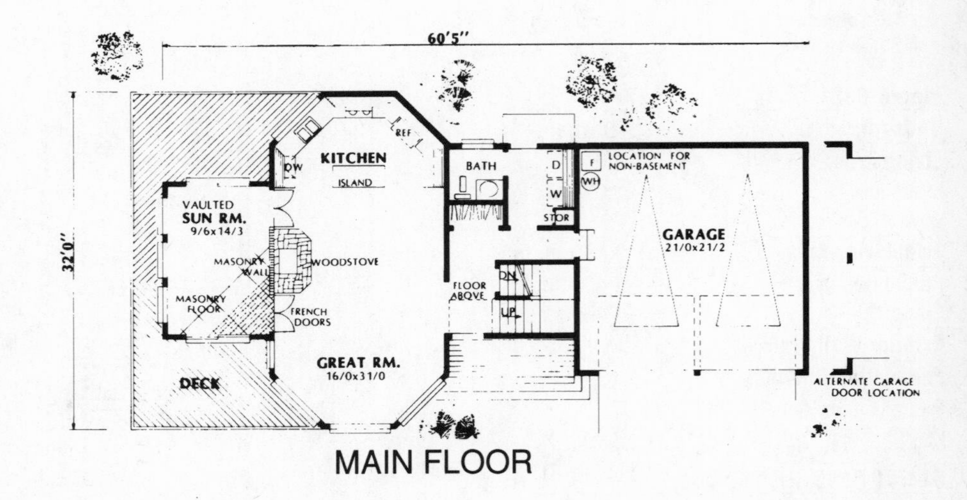

Quality Design for a Narrow, Sloping Lot

Multi-pitched rooflines, custom window treatments and beveled board siding add a distinctive facade to this two-level home of only 1,516 sq. ft. Its slim 34′ width allows it to fit nicely on a narrow lot while offering ample indoor and outdoor living areas.

The enclosed entry courtyard is a pleasant area for al fresco breakfasts or spill-over entertaining. The wide, high-ceilinged entry hall opens directly into the sweeping Great Room and dining area. This room is warmed by a large fireplace and has a door to a large wood deck. Also off the entry hall is the morning room with a vaulted ceiling and a matching arched window overlooking the courtyard. A half-bath and utility room is on the other side of the entry.

An open-railed stairway leads from the entry to the bedrooms on the second level. The master suite has a high dormer with peaked windows, a walk-in closet and a private bathroom. The larger of the other bedrooms could be used as a den, and it also overlooks the morning room and entry hall. If additional room is required, this plan is available with a daylight basement.

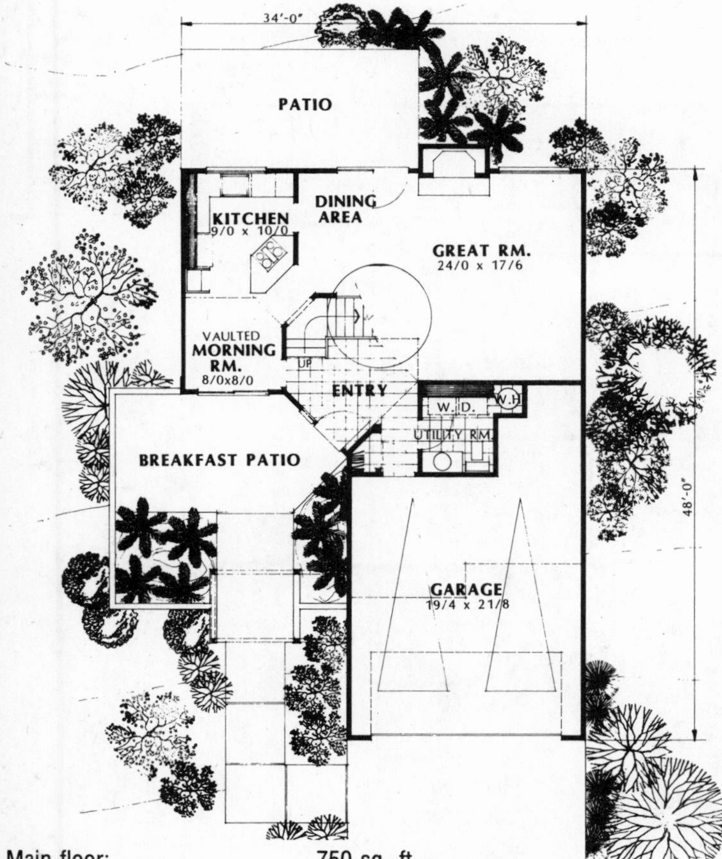

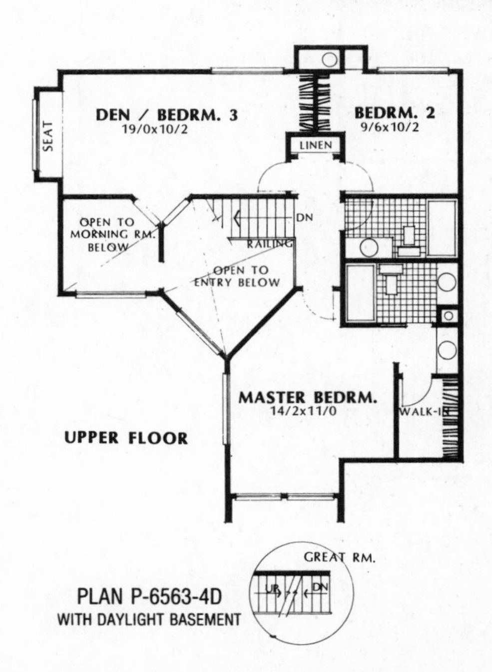

Main floor:	750 sq. ft.
Upper floor:	766 sq. ft.
Total living area:	1,516 sq. ft.
Basement level:	809 sq. ft.

PLAN P-6563-4A
WITHOUT BASEMENT

PLAN P-6563-4D
WITH DAYLIGHT BASEMENT

Blueprint Price Code B

TO ORDER THIS BLUEPRINT, CALL TOLL-FREE 1-800-547-5570

Plans P-6563-4A & -4D

PRICES AND DETAILS ON PAGES 12-15

Vaulted Master Suite Upstairs

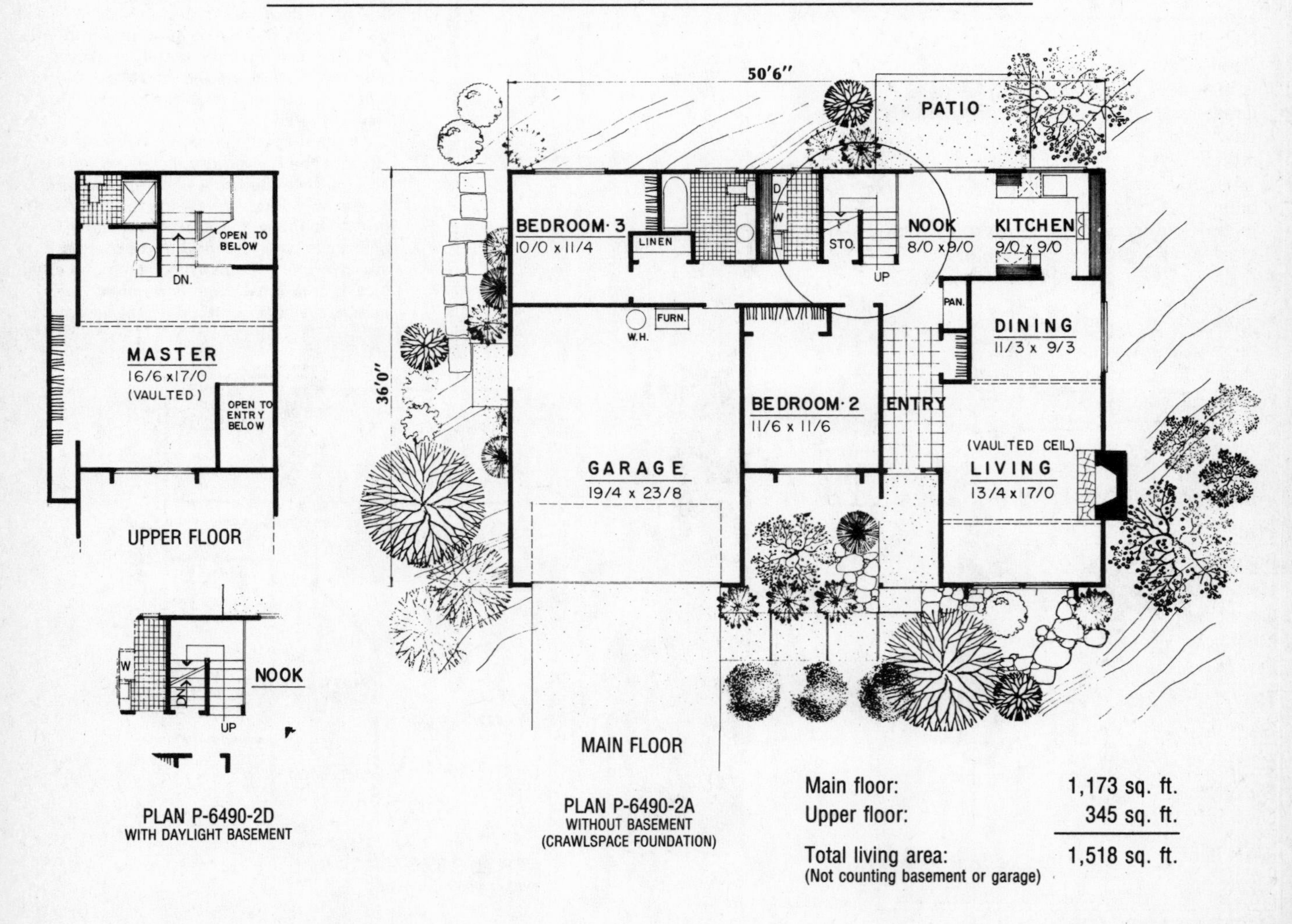

PLAN P-6490-2D
WITH DAYLIGHT BASEMENT

PLAN P-6490-2A
WITHOUT BASEMENT
(CRAWLSPACE FOUNDATION)

Main floor:	1,173 sq. ft.
Upper floor:	345 sq. ft.
Total living area: (Not counting basement or garage)	1,518 sq. ft.

Blueprint Price Code B

Plans P-6490-2A & -2D

TO ORDER THIS BLUEPRINT, CALL TOLL-FREE 1-800-547-5570

PRICES AND DETAILS ON PAGES 12-15

REAR VIEW

For Vacation or Year-Round Casual Living

- More than 500 square feet of deck area across the rear sets the theme of casual outdoor living for this compact plan.
- The living/dining/kitchen combination is included in one huge, 15′ x 39′ Great Room, which is several steps down from the entry level for an even more dramatic effect.
- Two large downstairs bedrooms share a bath. Upstairs, a hideaway bedroom includes a private bath, a walk-in closet and a romantic private deck.
- A utility room is conveniently placed in the garage entry area.
- The optional basement features a large recreation room with a fireplace and sliders to a patio underneath the rear deck.
- A fourth bedroom and a third bath in the basement would be ideal for guests.
- At the front of the basement is a large area that could be used for a hobby room or a children's play area.

Plans H-877-1 & -1A	
Bedrooms: 3-4	**Baths:** 2-3
Living Area:	
Upper floor	320 sq. ft.
Main floor	1,200 sq. ft.
Daylight basement	1,200 sq. ft.
Total Living Area:	**1,520/2,720 sq. ft.**
Garage	155 sq. ft.
Exterior Wall Framing:	2x6
Foundation Options:	**Plan #**
Daylight basement	H-877-1
Crawlspace	H-877-1A
(Typical foundation & framing conversion diagram available—see order form.)	
BLUEPRINT PRICE CODE:	**B/D**

UPPER FLOOR

BASEMENT STAIRWAY LOCATION

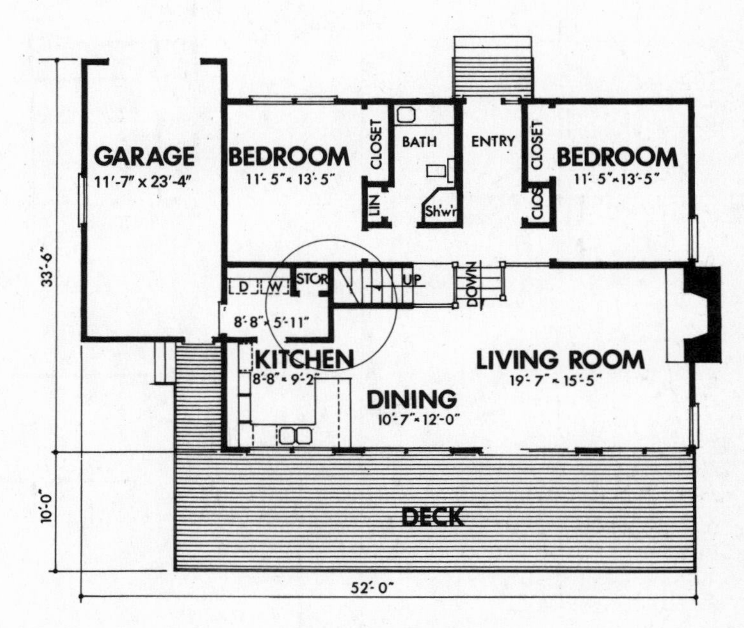

MAIN FLOOR

Rustic Styling, Comfortable Interior

- Front-to-back split level with large decks lends itself to steep sloping site, particularly in a scenic area.
- Compact, space-efficient design makes for economical construction.
- Great Room design concept utilizes the entire 36′ width of home for the kitchen/dining/living area.
- Two bedrooms and a bath are up three steps, on the entry level.
- Upper level bedroom includes a compact bath and a private deck.

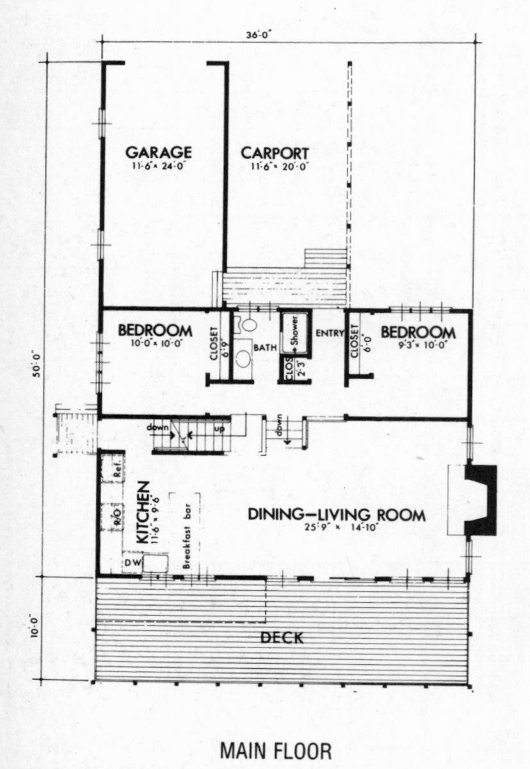

MAIN FLOOR

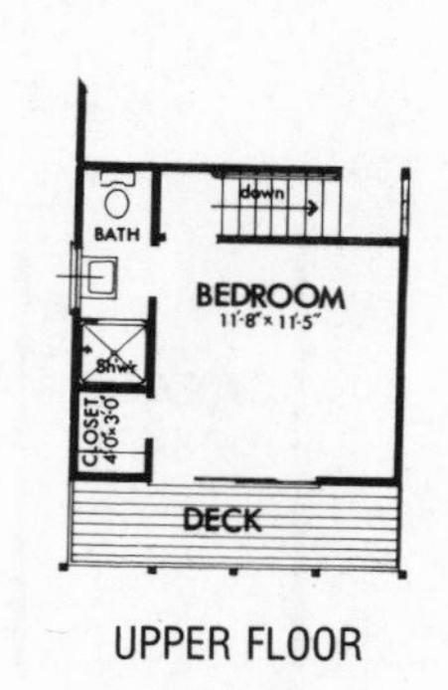

UPPER FLOOR

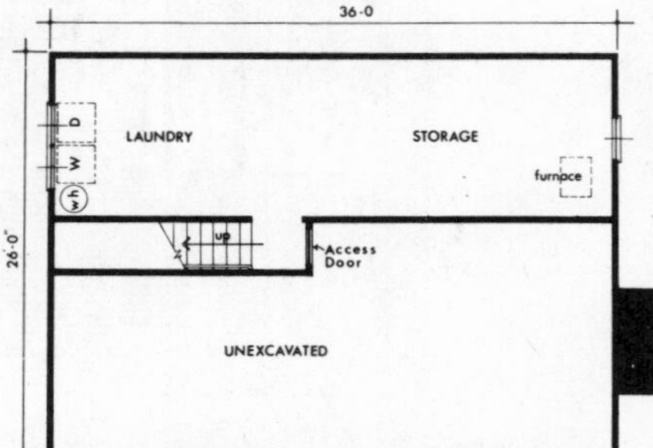

BASEMENT

Plan H-25-C

Bedrooms: 3	**Baths:** 2
Space:	
Upper floor:	222 sq. ft.
Main floor:	936 sq. ft.
Basement:	365 sq. ft.
Total living area:	1,523 sq. ft.
Garage:	276 sq. ft.
Exterior Wall Framing:	2x4

Foundation options:
Daylight basement only.
(Foundation & framing conversion diagram available — see order form.)

Blueprint Price Code: B

PRICES AND DETAILS ON PAGES 12-15

Economical Design

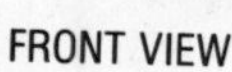

FRONT VIEW

REAR VIEW

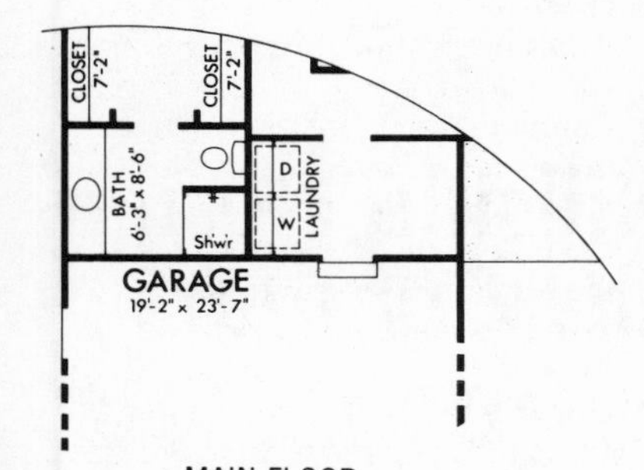

MAIN FLOOR
PLAN H-868-1A
WITHOUT BASEMENT

- **Uninterrupted glass and a full, rear deck afford a sweeping view of the outdoors.**
- **Rear orientation provides a seclusion from street and neighbors.**
- **Open, flexible family living areas allow for efficient traffic flow.**
- **Optional daylight basement plan offers recreation room, additional bedroom and third bath.**

Plans H-868-1 & -1A

Bedrooms: 3-4	**Baths:** 2-3
Space:	
Main floor:	1,525 sq. ft.
Total living area:	1,525 sq. ft.
Basement:	1,420 sq. ft.
Garage:	426 sq. ft.
Exterior Wall Framing:	2x4

Foundation options:
Daylight basement (Plan H-868-1).
Crawlspace (Plan H-868-1A).
(Foundation & framing conversion diagram available — see order form.)

Blueprint Price Code:

Without basement	B
With basement	D

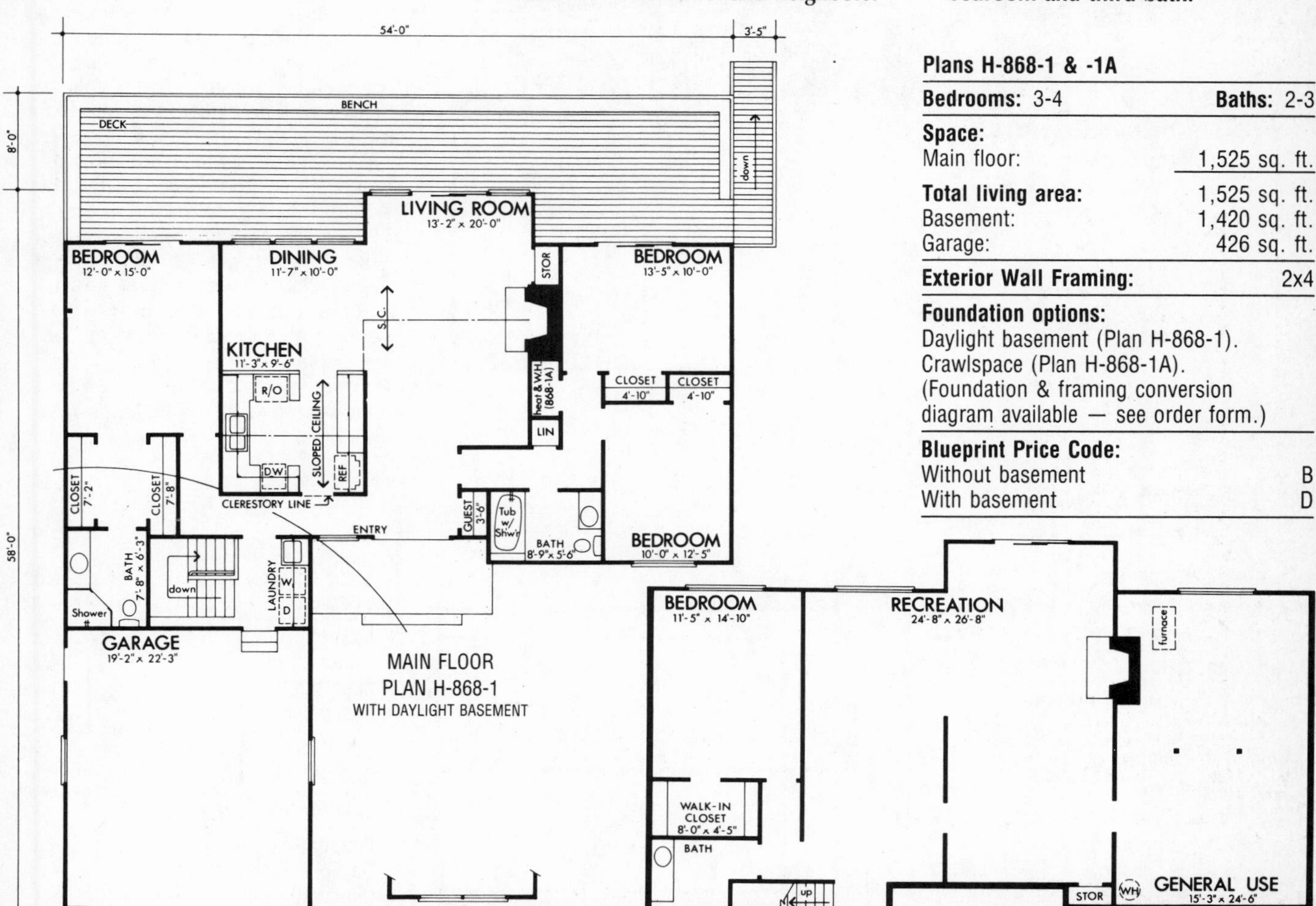

MAIN FLOOR
PLAN H-868-1
WITH DAYLIGHT BASEMENT

DAYLIGHT BASEMENT

FRONT VIEW

Hillside Design Fits Contours

- The daylight-basement version of this popular plan is perfect for a scenic, sloping lot.
- A large, wraparound deck embraces the rear-oriented living areas, accessed through sliding glass doors.
- The spectacular living room boasts a corner fireplace, a sloped ceiling and outdoor views to the side and rear.
- The secluded master suite upstairs offers a walk-in closet, a private bath and sliders to a sun deck.
- The daylight basement (not shown) includes a fourth bedroom with private bath and walk-in closet, as well as a recreation room with fireplace and sliders to a rear patio.
- The standard basement (not shown) includes a recreation room with fireplace and a room for hobbies or child's play.
- Both basements also have a large unfinished area below the main-floor bedrooms.

REAR VIEW

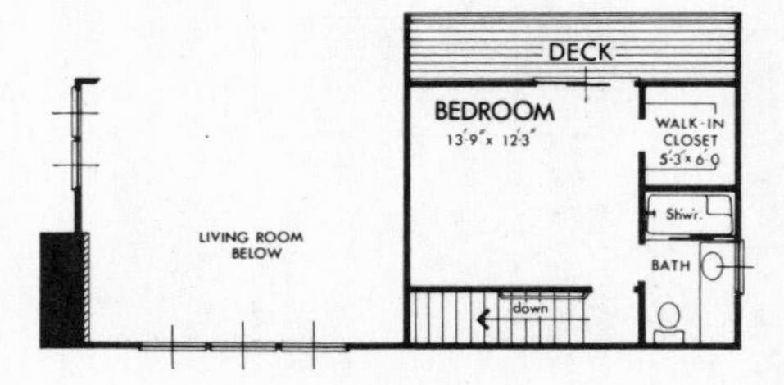

UPPER FLOOR

Plans H-877-4, -4A & -4B	
Bedrooms: 3-4	**Baths:** 2-3
Living Area:	
Upper floor	333 sq. ft.
Main floor	1,200 sq. ft.
Basement (finished portion)	591 sq. ft.
Total Living Area:	**1,533/2,124 sq. ft.**
Basement (unfinished portion)	493 sq. ft.
Garage	480 sq. ft.
Exterior Wall Framing:	2x6
Foundation Options:	**Plan #**
Daylight basement	H-877-4B
Standard basement	H-877-4
Crawlspace	H-877-4A
(Typical foundation & framing conversion diagram available—see order form.)	
BLUEPRINT PRICE CODE:	**B/C**

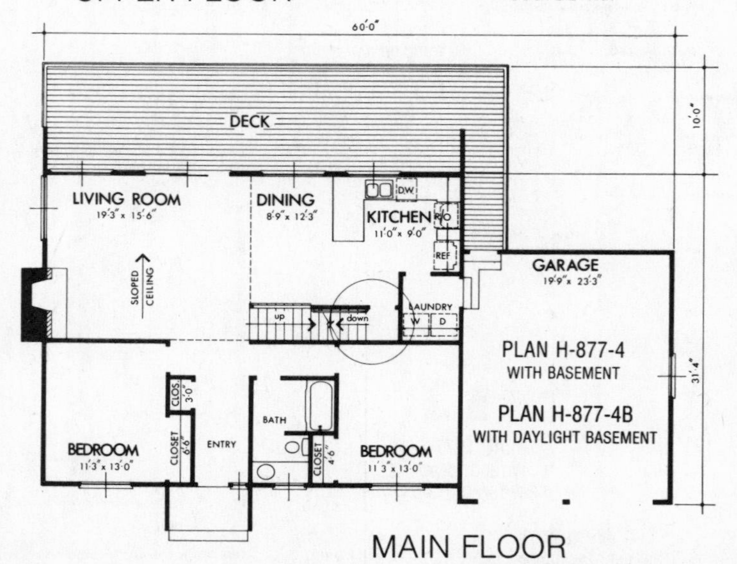

MAIN FLOOR

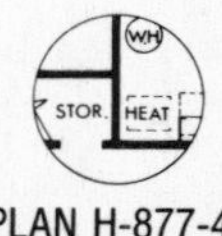

PLAN H-877-4A
WITHOUT BASEMENT

 TO ORDER THIS BLUEPRINT, CALL TOLL-FREE 1-800-547-5570

Plans H-877-4, -4A & -4B

PRICES AND DETAILS ON PAGES 12-15

Vaulted Living Room Featured

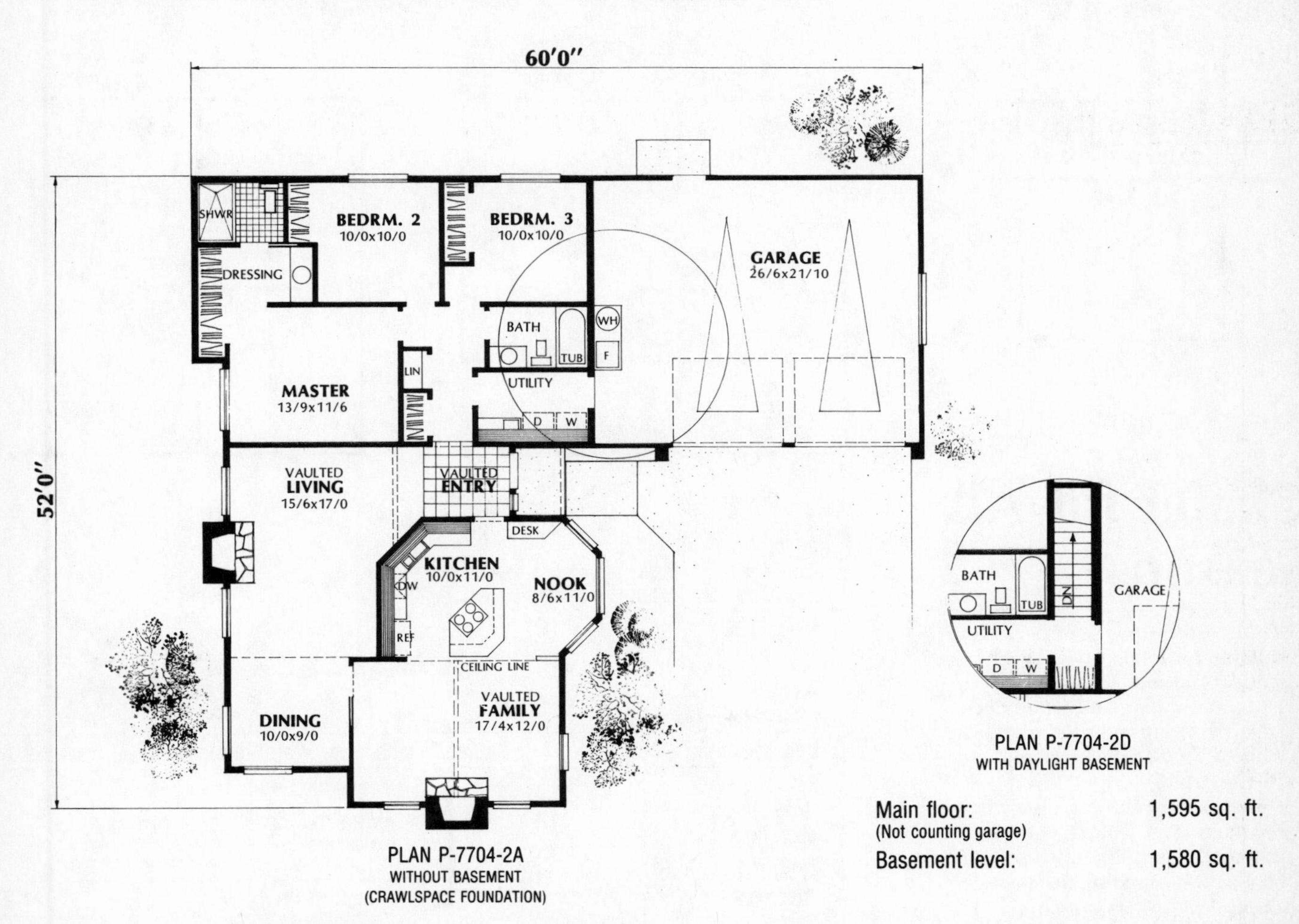

PLAN P-7704-2A
WITHOUT BASEMENT
(CRAWLSPACE FOUNDATION)

PLAN P-7704-2D
WITH DAYLIGHT BASEMENT

Main floor: (Not counting garage)	1,595 sq. ft.
Basement level:	1,580 sq. ft.

Total living area: (Not counting garage)	1,535 sq. ft.

Blueprint Price Code B

TO ORDER THIS BLUEPRINT, CALL TOLL-FREE 1-800-547-5570

Plans P-7704-2A & -2D

PRICES AND DETAILS ON PAGES 12-15

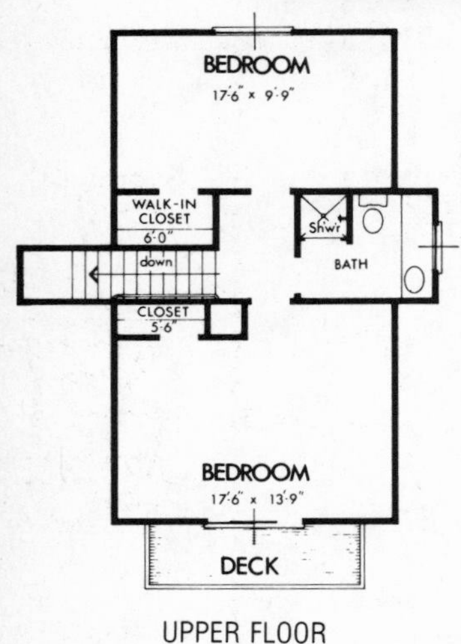

UPPER FLOOR

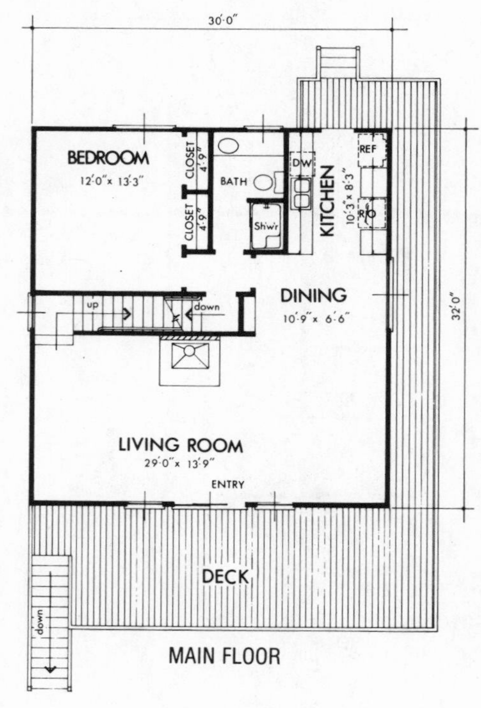

MAIN FLOOR

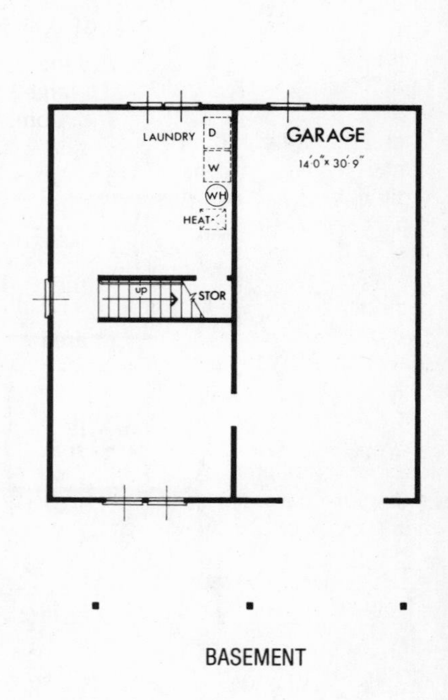

BASEMENT

Chalet for All Seasons

- Rustic exterior makes this design suitable for a lakefront, beach, or wooded setting.
- Patterned railing and wood deck edge the front and side main level, while a smaller deck assumes a balcony role.
- Designed for relaxed, leisure living, the main level features a large L-shaped Great Room warmed by a central free-standing fireplace.
- Upper level offers a second bath and added sleeping accommodations.

Plan H-858-2

Bedrooms: 3	**Baths:** 2
Space:	
Upper floor:	576 sq. ft.
Main floor:	960 sq. ft.
Total living area:	1,536 sq. ft.
Basement:	530 sq. ft.
Garage:	430 sq. ft.

Exterior Wall Framing:	2x6
Foundation options: Daylight basement. (Foundation & framing conversion diagram available — see order form.)	
Blueprint Price Code:	B

TO ORDER THIS BLUEPRINT, CALL TOLL-FREE 1-800-547-5570

Plan H-858-2

PRICES AND DETAILS ON PAGES 12-15

One-Story with Impact

- Striking gables, a brick facade and an elegant sidelighted entry door with a half-round transom give this one-story lots of impact.
- The interior spaces are just as impressive, beginning with the raised ceiling in the foyer. To the left of the foyer, decorative columns and a large picture window grace the dining room.
- The wonderful family living spaces center around a vaulted Great Room, which also has decorative columns separating it from the main hall. A fireplace framed by a window on one side and a French door on the other provides a stunning focal point.
- The open kitchen and breakfast area features a built-in desk and a pass-through above the sink.
- The master suite is superb, with its elegant tray ceiling and vaulted spa bath with a plant shelf.
- Two more bedrooms and a full bath are at the other end of the home.

Plan FB-1553	
Bedrooms: 3	**Baths:** 2
Living Area:	
Main floor	1,553 sq. ft.
Total Living Area:	**1,553 sq. ft.**
Daylight basement	1,553 sq. ft.
Garage	410 sq. ft.
Exterior Wall Framing:	2x4
Foundation Options:	
Daylight basement	
Crawlspace	
Slab	
(Typical foundation & framing conversion diagram available—see order form.)	
BLUEPRINT PRICE CODE:	**B**

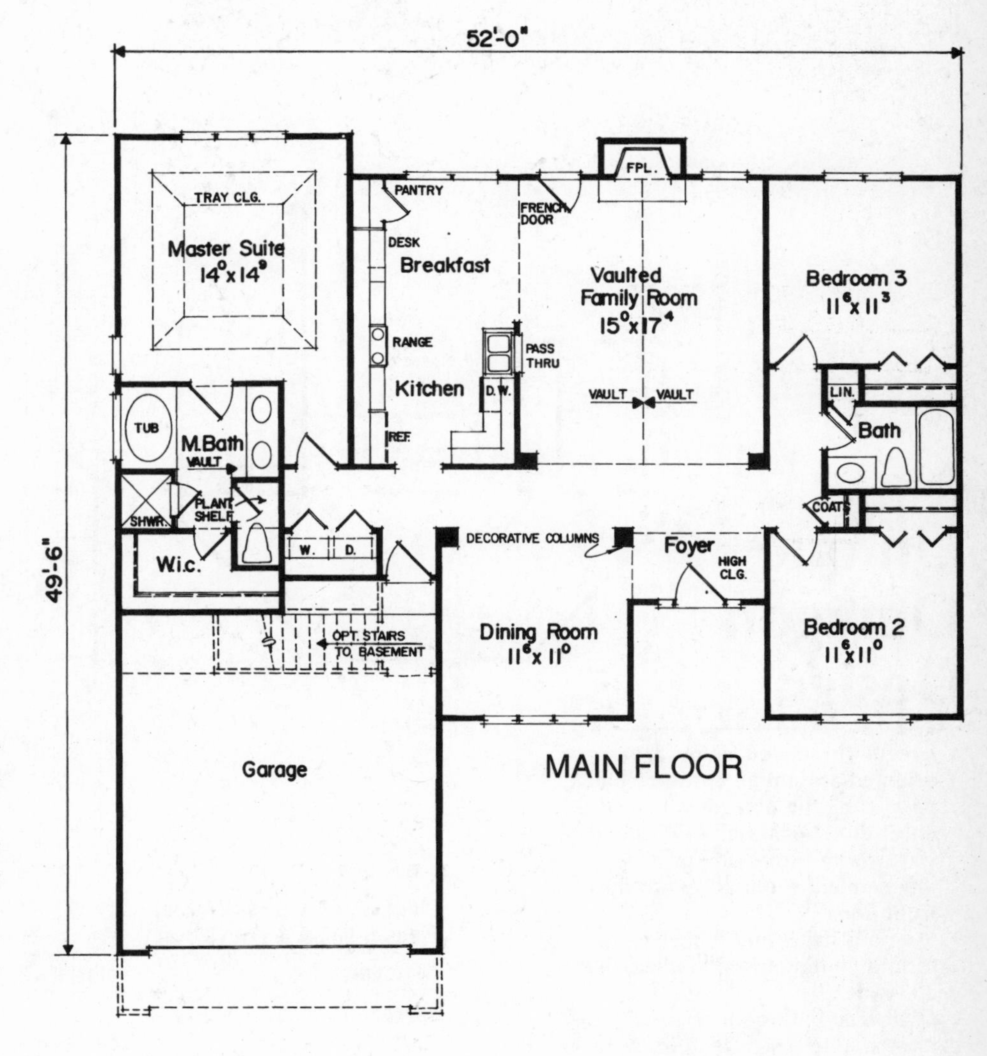

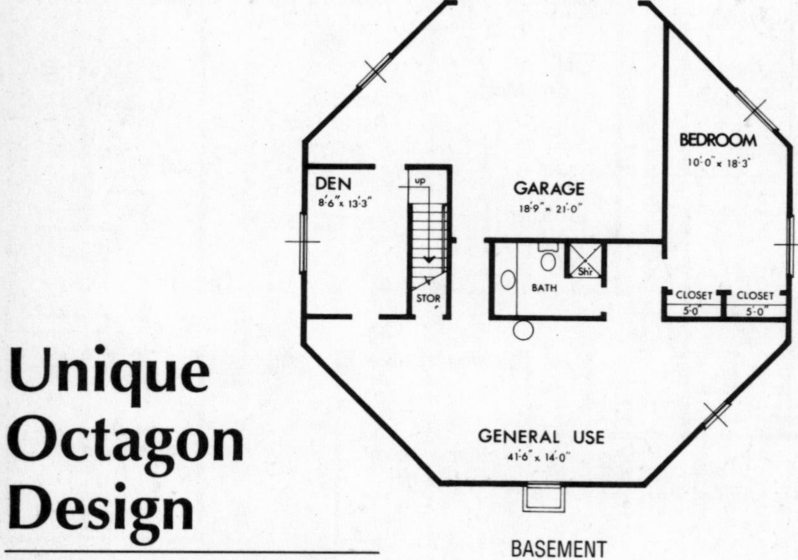

BASEMENT

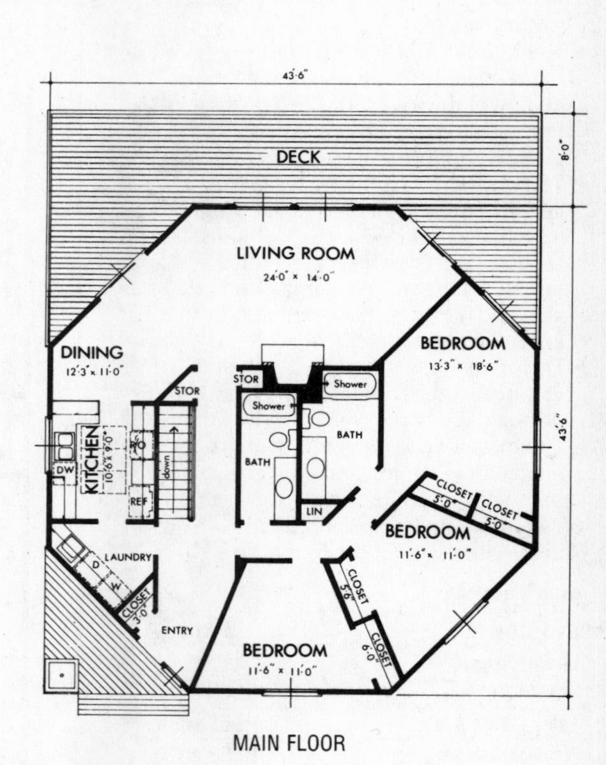

MAIN FLOOR

1/16" = 1'

Unique Octagon Design

- Irregularly shaped rooms are oriented around an entrance hall paralleling the octagonal exterior.
- Short directional hallways eliminate cross-room traffic and provide independent room access to the front door.
- Spacious living and dining rooms form a continuous area more than 38' wide.
- Oversized bathroom serves a large master suite which features a deck view and dual closets.
- This plan is also available with a stucco exterior (Plans H-942-2, with daylight basement, and H-942-2A, without basement).

Plans H-942-1 & -1A (Wood)
Plans H-942-2 & -2A (Stucco)

Bedrooms: 3-4	**Baths:** 2-3
Space:	
Main floor:	1,564 sq. ft.
Basement:	approx. 1,170 sq. ft.
Total with basement:	2,734 sq. ft.
Garage:	394 sq. ft.
Exterior Wall Framing:	2x6

Foundation options:
Daylight basement (Plans H-942-1 & -2).
Crawlspace (Plans H-942-1A & -2A).
(Foundation & framing conversion diagram available — see order form.)

Blueprint Price Code:

Without basement:	B
With basement:	D

Plans H-942-1/1A & -2/2A

PRICES AND DETAILS ON PAGES 12-15

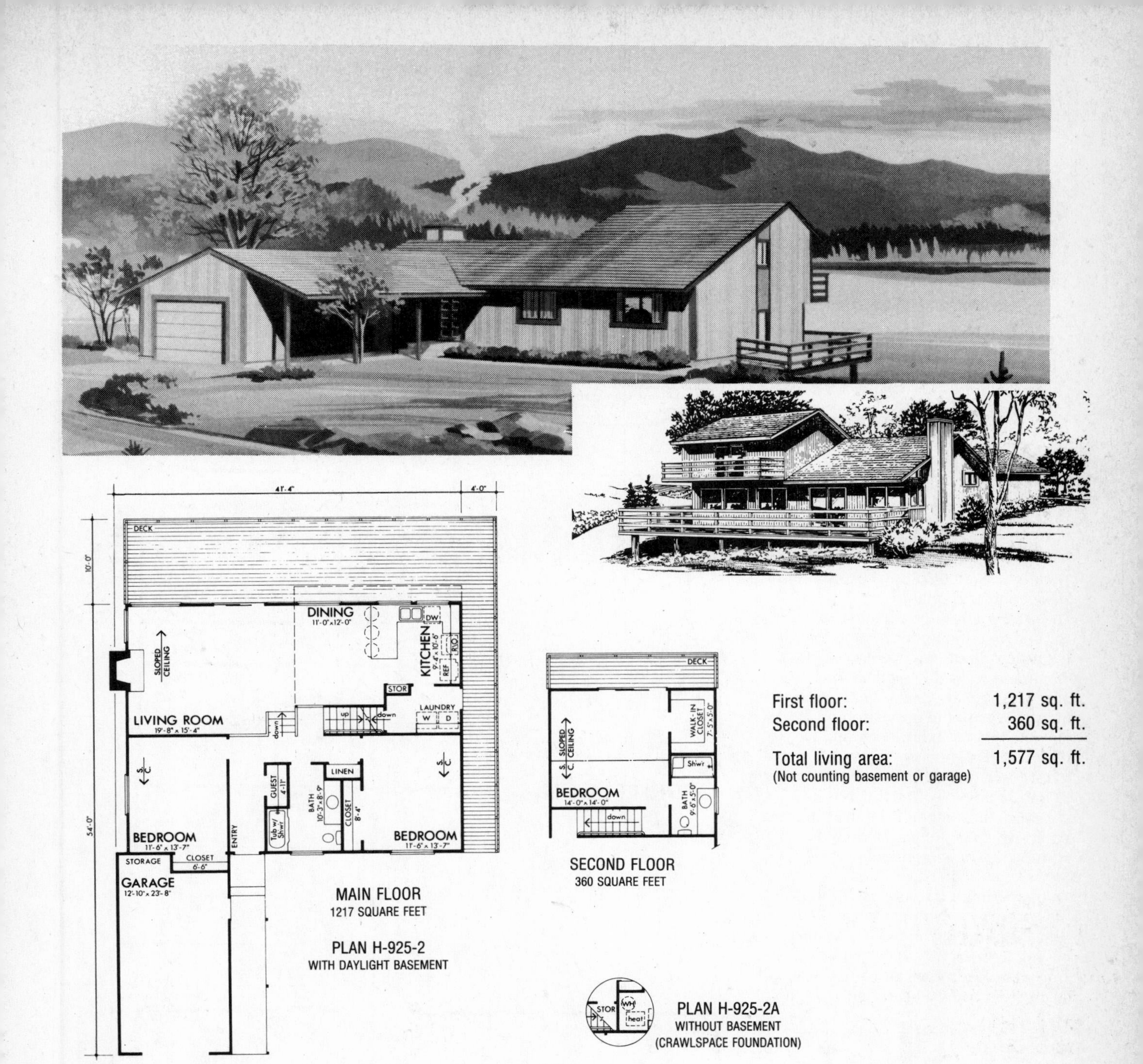

Economical and Convenient

In an effort to merge the financial possibilities and the space requirements of the greatest number of families, the designers of this home restricted themselves to just over 1,200 sq. ft. of ground cover (exclusive of garage), and still managed to develop a superior three-bedroom design.

From a covered walkway, one approaches a centralized entry hall which effectively distributes traffic throughout the home without causing interruptions. Two main floor bedrooms and bath as well as the stairway to the second floor master suite are immediately accessible to the entry. Directly forward and four steps down finds one in the main living area, consisting of a large living room with vaulted ceiling and a dining-kitchen combination with conventional ceiling height. All these rooms have direct access to an outdoor living deck of over 400 sq. ft. Thus, though modest and unassuming from the street side, this home evolves into eye-popping expansion and luxury toward the rear.

To ease homemaking chores, whether this is to be a permanent or vacation home, the working equipment, including laundry space, is all on the main floor. Yet the homemaker remains part of the family scene because there is only a breakfast counter separating the work space from the living area.

Tucked away upstairs, in complete privacy, one finds a master bedroom suite equipped with separate bath, walk-in wardrobe and a romantic private deck.

The plan is available with or without a basement and is best suited to a lot that slopes gently down from the road.

Blueprint Price Code B

Plans H-925-2 & -2A

Luxury and Livability

- Big on style, this modest-sized home features a quaint Colonial exerior and an open interior plan.
- The covered front porch leads to a vaulted foyer that opens to the formal living and dining rooms. A coat closet, an attractive display niche and a powder room are centrally located, as is the stairway to the upper floor.
- The kitchen, breakfast nook and family room are designed so that each room has its own definition yet also functions as part of a whole. The angled sink separates the kitchen from the breakfast nook, which is outlined by bay windows. The large family room includes a fireplace.
- The upper floor has a hard-to-miss master suite, featuring a tray ceiling in the large sleeping area and a vaulted ceiling in the spa bath.
- Two more bedrooms and a balcony hall add to this home's luxury and livability.

Plan FB-1600	
Bedrooms: 3	**Baths:** 2½
Living Area:	
Upper floor	772 sq. ft.
Main floor	828 sq. ft.
Total Living Area:	**1,600 sq. ft.**
Daylight basement	828 sq. ft.
Garage	473 sq. ft.
Exterior Wall Framing:	2x4
Foundation Options:	
Daylight basement	
Crawlspace	
Slab	
(Typical foundation & framing conversion diagram available—see order form.)	
BLUEPRINT PRICE CODE:	**B**

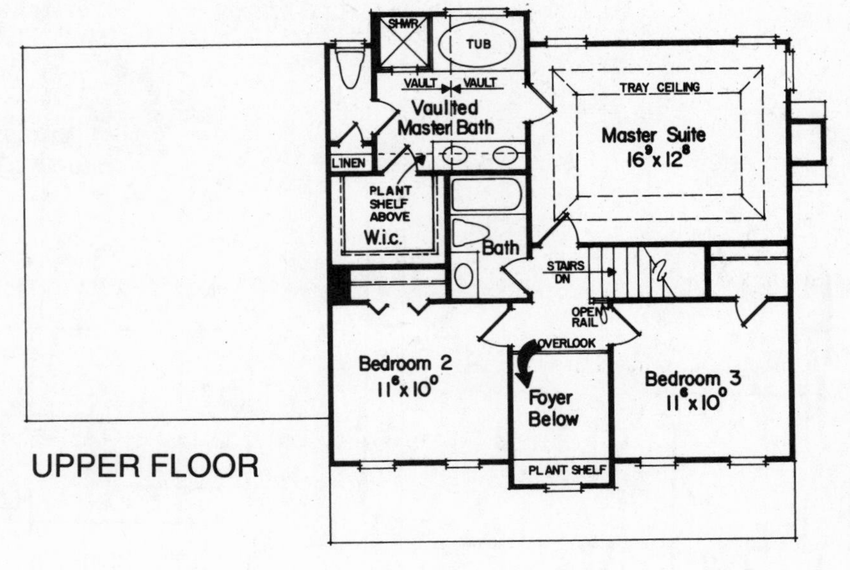

UPPER FLOOR

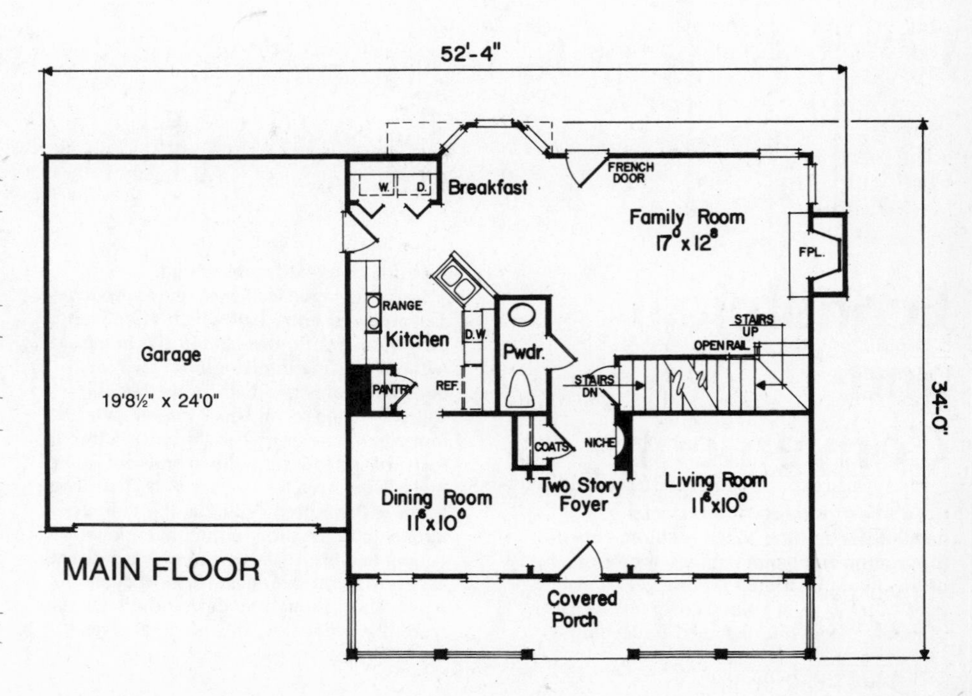

MAIN FLOOR

TO ORDER THIS BLUEPRINT, CALL TOLL-FREE 1-800-547-5570

Plan FB-1600

PRICES AND DETAILS ON PAGES 12-15

Covered Wraparound Deck Featured

- A covered deck spans this home from the main entrance to the kitchen door.
- An over-sized fireplace is the focal point of the living room, which merges into an expandable dining area.
- The kitchen is tucked into one corner, but open counter space allows visual contact with living areas beyond.
- Two good-sized main-floor bedrooms are furnished with sufficient closet space.
- The basement level adds a third bedroom in an additional 673 sq. ft. of living space.

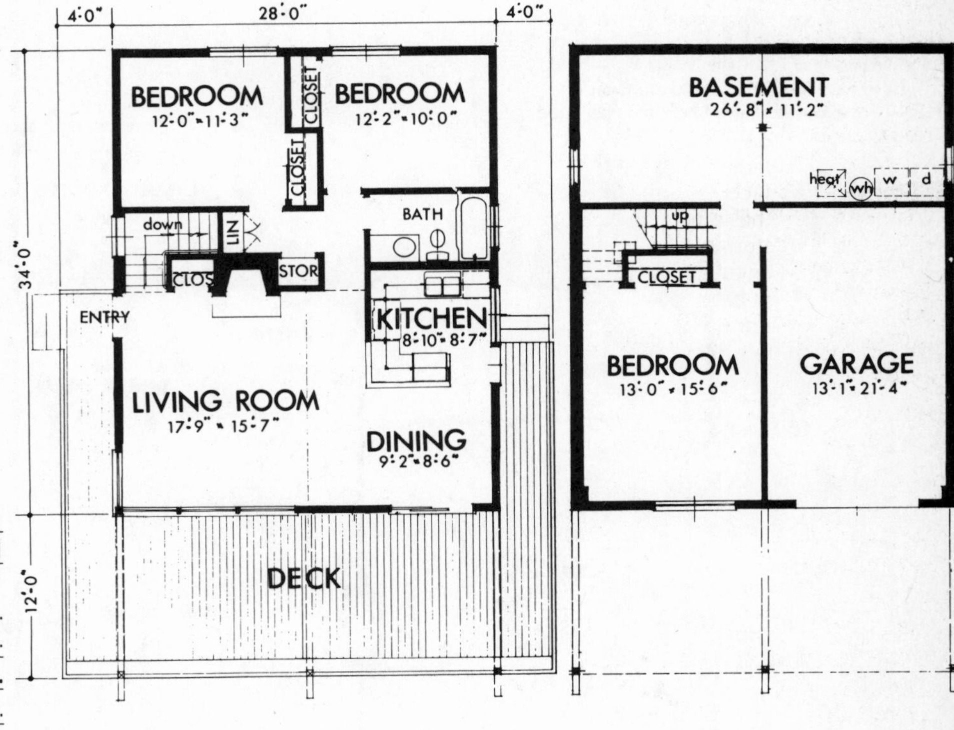

MAIN FLOOR

DAYLIGHT BASEMENT

Plan H-806-2

Bedrooms: 3	**Baths:** 1
Living Area:	
Main floor	952 sq. ft.
Daylight basement	673 sq. ft.
Total Living Area:	**1,625 sq. ft.**
Garage	279 sq. ft.
Exterior Wall Framing:	2x6

Foundation Options:

Daylight basement
(Typical foundation & framing conversion diagram available—see order form.)

BLUEPRINT PRICE CODE: **B**

Designed for Relaxed Living

Wood post and railing, shutters and covered porch give a relaxed look to this country home. A fireplace lends extra appeal to the large living room. A country kitchen with center work bar is located between the breakfast room and separate dining room.

All three bedrooms are located on one side of the house. Each bedroom has good closet space.

Total living area: 1,627 sq. ft.
(Not counting basement or garage)

Specify daylight basement, crawlspace or slab foundation.

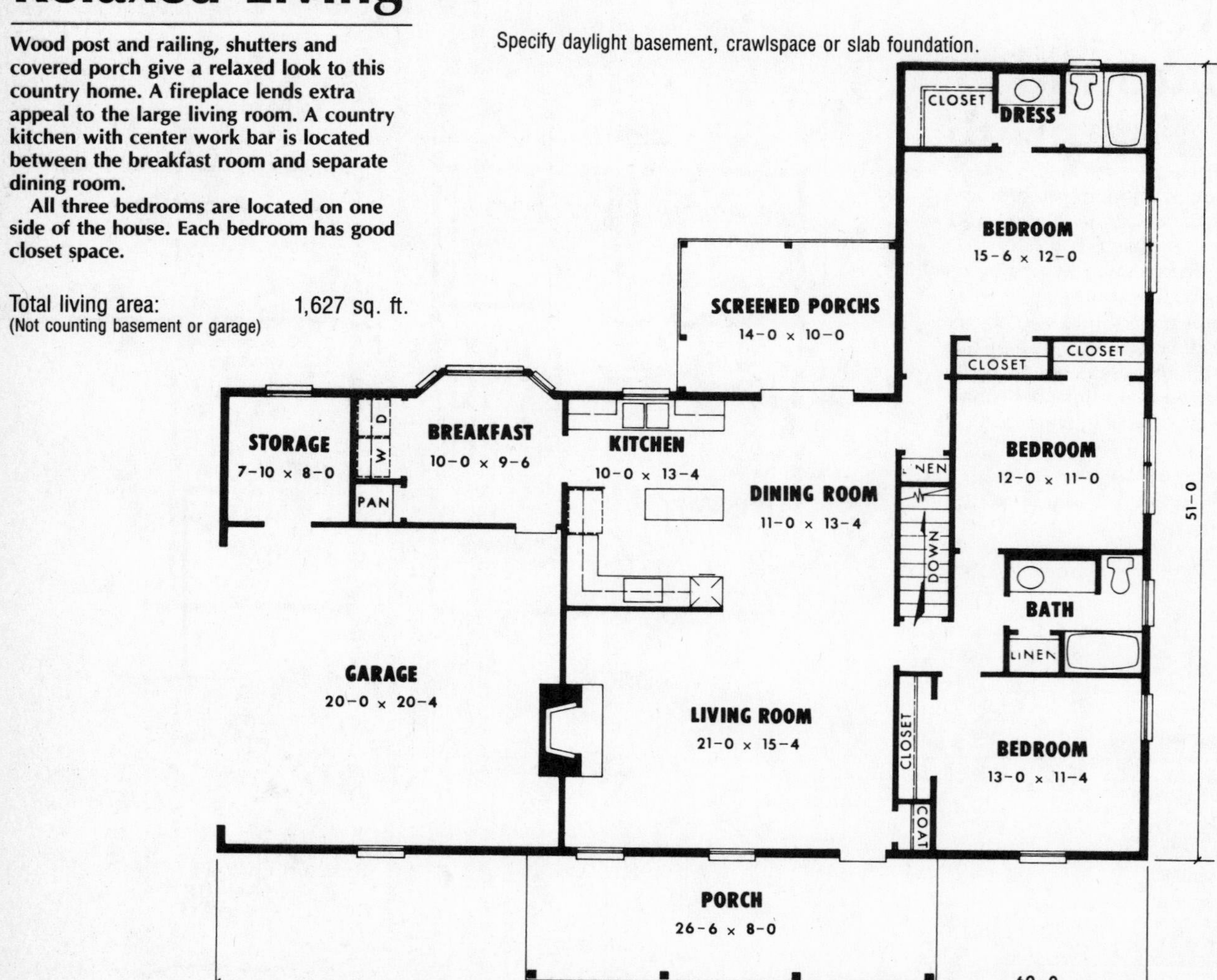

Blueprint Price Code B

Plan C-7549

PRICES AND DETAILS ON PAGES 12-15

Indoor/Outdoor Pleasure

- For a scenic lake or mountain lot, this spectacular design takes full advantage of the views.
- A three-sided wraparound deck makes indoor/outdoor living a pleasure.
- The sunken living room—with a 19-ft. cathedral ceiling, a skylight, a beautiful fireplace and glass galore—is the heart of the floor plan.
- Both the formal dining room and the kitchen overlook the living room and the surrounding deck beyond.
- The main-floor master bedroom has a 12-ft. cathedral ceiling and private access to the deck and hall bath.
- Upstairs, two more bedrooms share a skylighted bath and flank a dramatic balcony sitting area that views to the living room below.

Plan AX-98607	
Bedrooms: 3	**Baths:** 2
Living Area:	
Upper floor	531 sq. ft.
Main floor	1,098 sq. ft.
Total Living Area:	**1,629 sq. ft.**
Standard basement	894 sq. ft.
Garage	327 sq. ft.
Exterior Wall Framing:	2x4
Foundation Options:	
Standard basement	
Slab	

(All plans can be built with your choice of foundation and framing. A generic conversion diagram is available. See order form.)

BLUEPRINT PRICE CODE: B

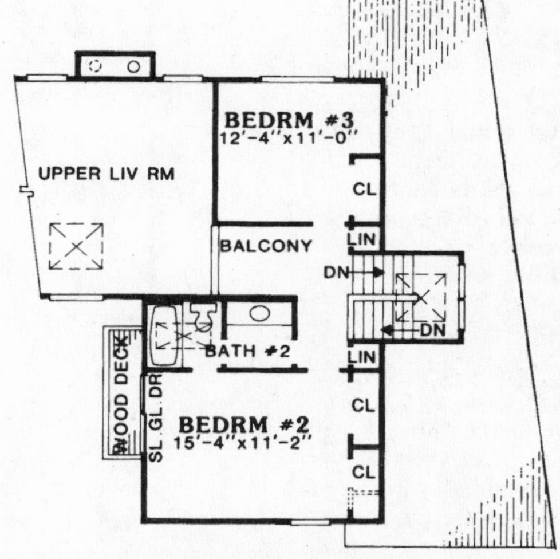

UPPER FLOOR

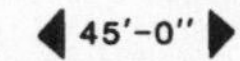

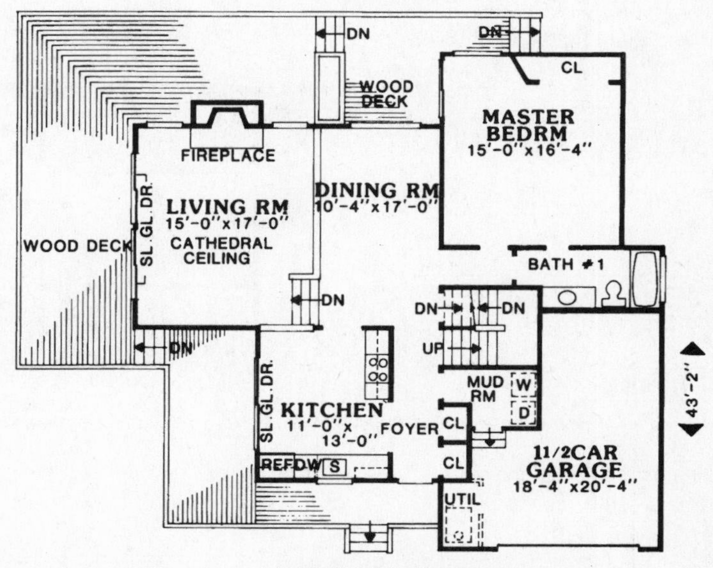

MAIN FLOOR

Expandable Living Spaces!

- Expandable spaces make this attractive two-story a great choice for growing families. The formal dining room or the living room could be easily converted into a library or den, while the optional bonus room above the garage provides a host of possible uses.
- The nice-sized family room offers an inviting fireplace and access to the backyard. The sunny breakfast room is just a few steps away and adjoins an efficient L-shaped kitchen.
- The upper floor features a balcony hall that overlooks the two-story-high foyer. The master suite is dignified by a tray ceiling in the sleeping area and a vaulted ceiling in the private bath with a corner spa tub. The large walk-in closet includes a handy linen closet and sports a decorative plant shelf.
- A convenient laundry closet, two bedrooms and a full bath complete the upper floor.

Plan FB-1631

Bedrooms: 3+	**Baths:** 2½
Living Area:	
Upper floor	787 sq. ft.
Main floor	844 sq. ft.
Bonus room	340 sq. ft.
Total Living Area:	**1,971 sq. ft.**
Daylight basement	844 sq. ft.
Garage	460 sq. ft.
Exterior Wall Framing:	2x4
Foundation Options:	
Daylight basement	
(Typical foundation & framing conversion diagram available—see order form.)	
BLUEPRINT PRICE CODE:	B

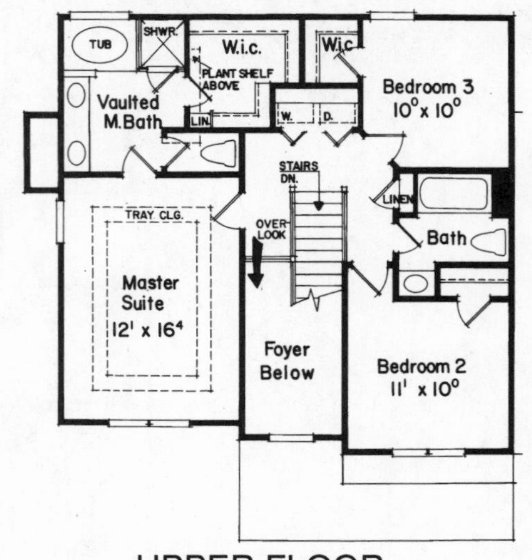

UPPER FLOOR

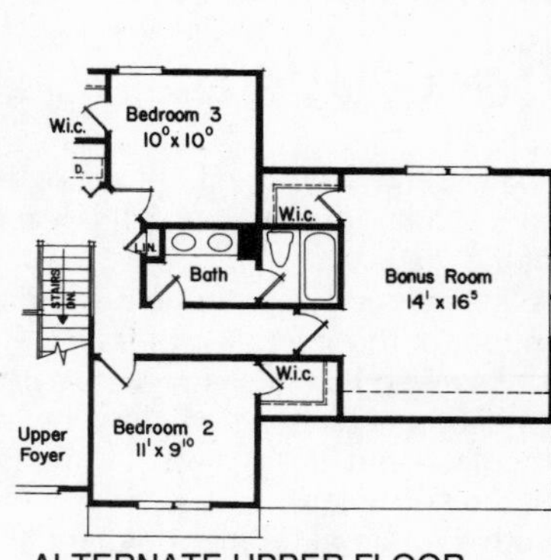

ALTERNATE UPPER FLOOR

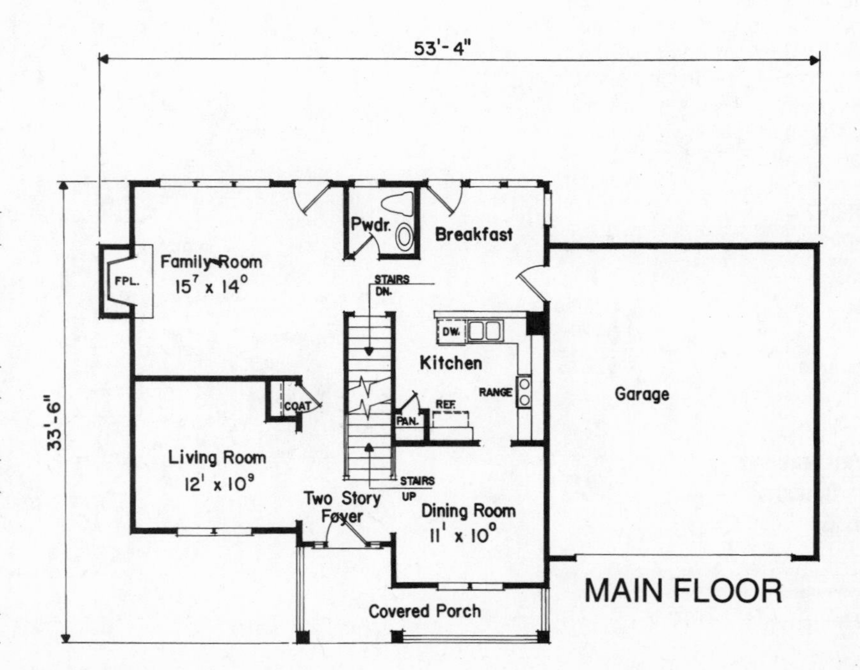

MAIN FLOOR

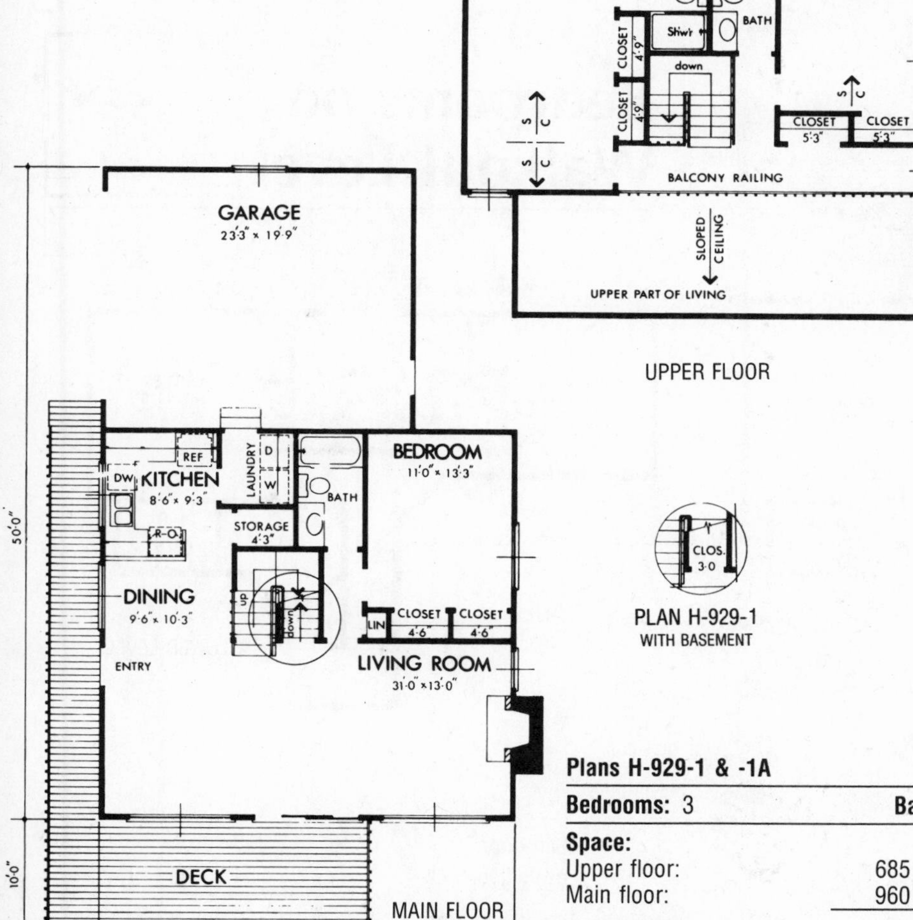

Contemporary Retreat

- Main floor plan revolves around an open, centrally located stairway.
- Spaciousness prevails throughout entire home with open kitchen and combination dining/living room.
- Living room features a great-sized fireplace and access to two-sided deck.
- Separate baths accommodate each bedroom.
- Upstairs hallway reveals an open balcony railing to oversee activities below.

Plans H-929-1 & -1A

Bedrooms: 3	**Baths:** 3
Space:	
Upper floor:	685 sq. ft.
Main floor:	960 sq. ft.
Total living area:	1,645 sq. ft.
Basement:	approx. 960 sq. ft.
Garage:	459 sq. ft.

Exterior Wall Framing:	2x6
Foundation options:	
Daylight basement (Plan H-929-1). Crawlspace (Plan H-929-1A). (Foundation & framing conversion diagram available — see order form.)	
Blueprint Price Code:	B

Bedrooms on Walkout Level

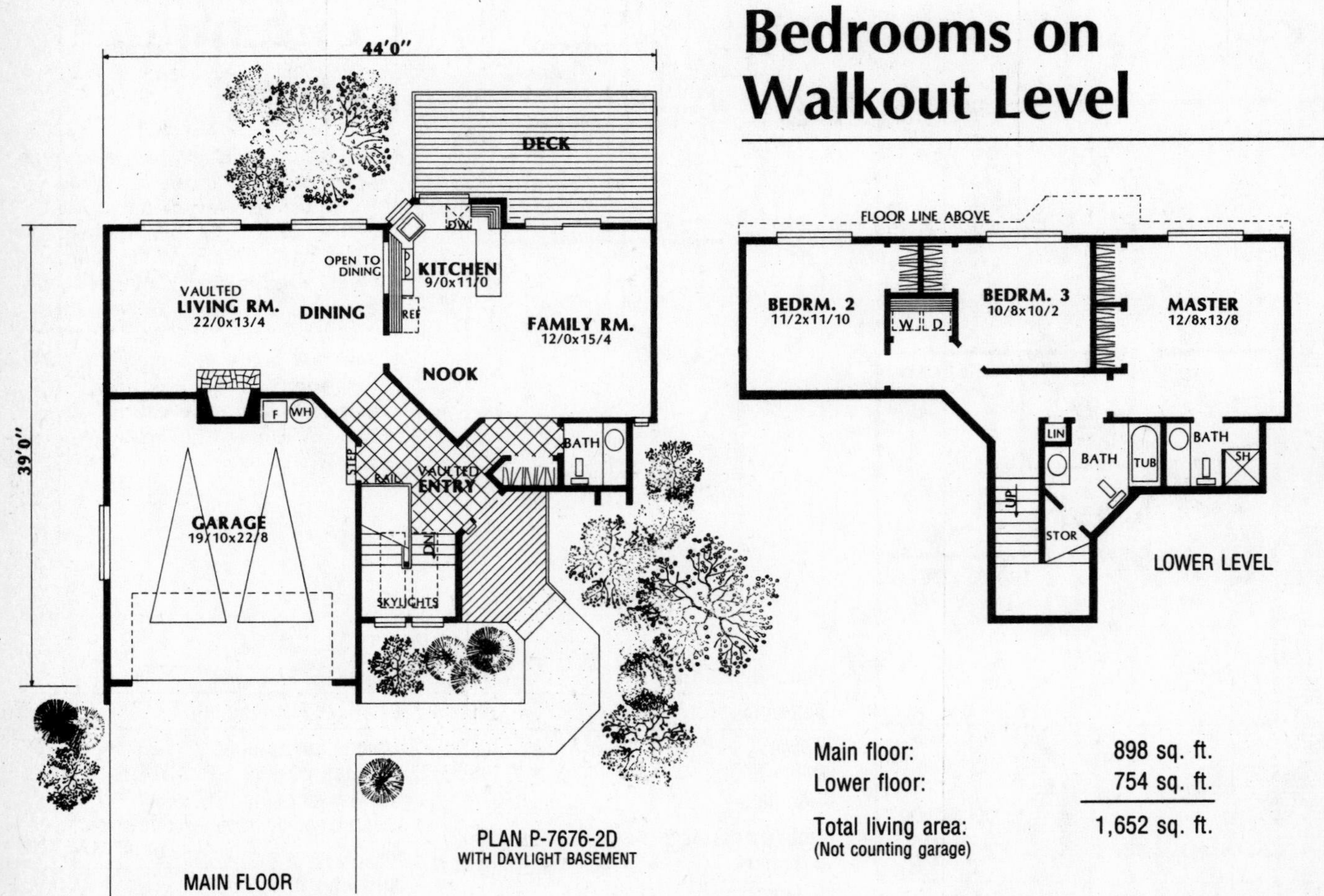

Main floor:	898 sq. ft.
Lower floor:	754 sq. ft.
Total living area: (Not counting garage)	1,652 sq. ft.

Blueprint Price Code B

Plan P-7676-2D

PRICES AND DETAILS ON PAGES 12-15

Gracious Indoor/ Outdoor Living

- A clean design makes this plan adaptable to almost any climate or setting.
- Perfect for a scenic, hillside lot, the structure and wrap-around deck offers a spanning view.
- Kitchen is flanked by family and dining rooms, allowing easy entrance from both.
- Foundation options include a daylight basement on concrete slab (H-2083-1), a wood-framed lower level (H-2083-1B), and a crawlspace (H-2083-1A).

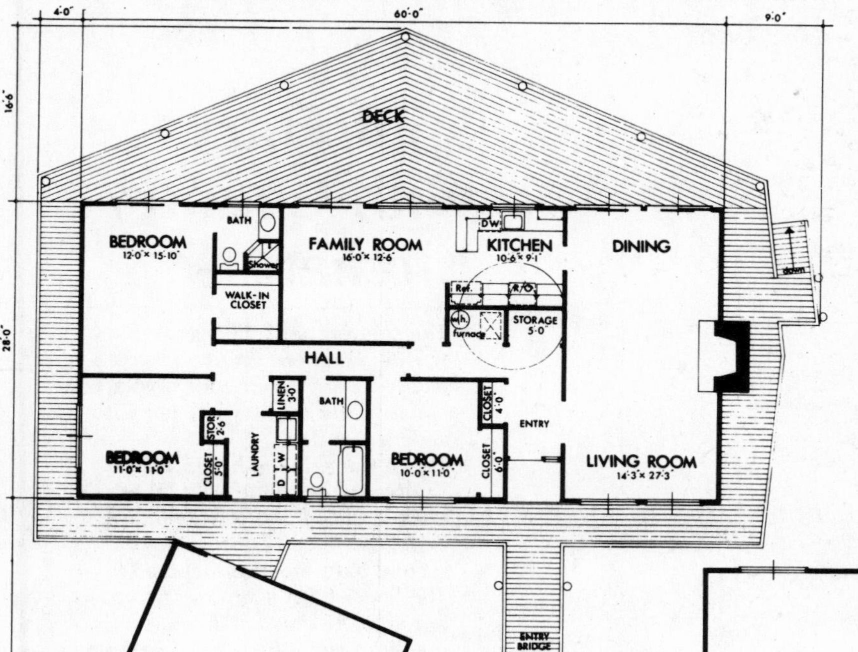

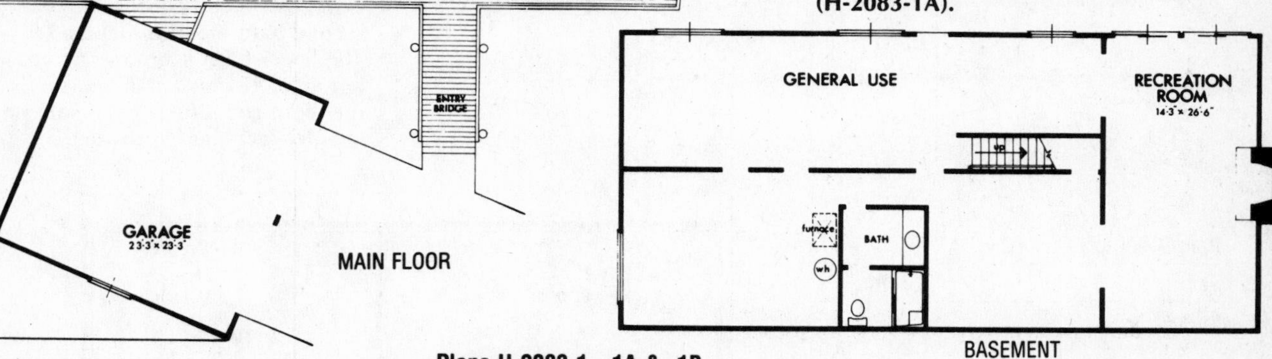

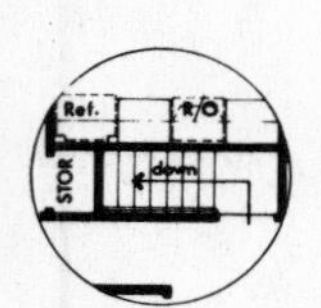

PLAN H-2083-1
WITH DAYLIGHT BASEMENT
(ON CONCRETE SLAB)

PLAN H-2083-1B
(WITH WOOD-FRAMED LOWER LEVEL)

Plans H-2083-1, -1A & -1B

Bedrooms: 3 **Baths:** 2-3

Space:

Main floor:	1,660 sq. ft.
Basement:	1,660 sq. ft.
Total living area: with basement:	3,320 sq. ft.
Garage:	541 sq. ft.

Exterior Wall Framing: 2x4

Foundation options:
Daylight basement (Plan H-2083-1 or -1B).
Crawlspace (Plan H-2083-1A).
(Foundation & framing conversion diagram available — see order form.)

Blueprint Price Code:

Without basement:	B
With basement:	E

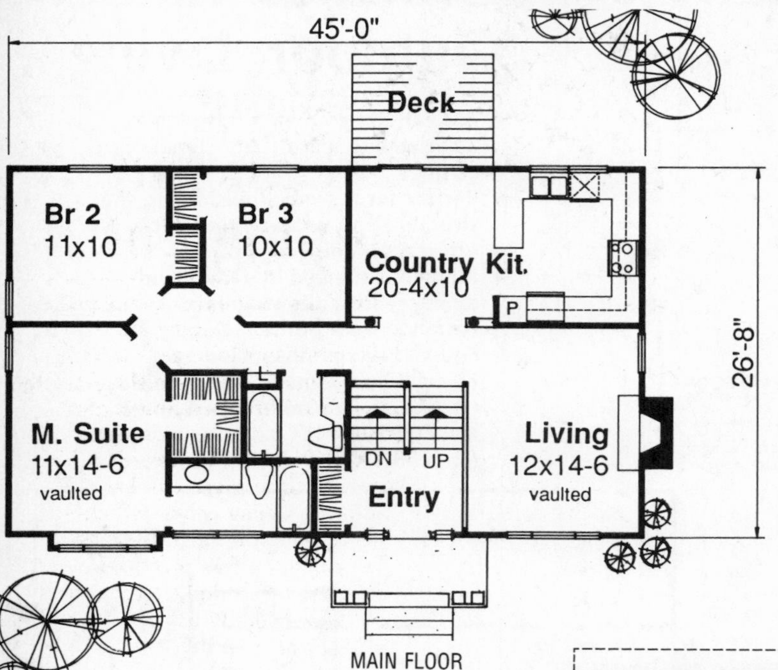

Split Entry with Country Kitchen

- The split entry of this updated traditional opens up to a large vaulted living room with fireplace and a lovely country kitchen with sliders to a deck.
- Down the hall you'll find the vaulted master suite with large walk-in closet and private bath.
- Two additional bedrooms and a second bath are also included.
- The lower level is unfinished and left up to the owner to choose its function; room for a third bath and laundry facilities is provided.

Plan B-90012

Bedrooms: 3	**Baths:** 2-3
Space:	
Main/upper level:	1,203 sq. ft.
Basement:	460 sq. ft.
Total living area:	1,663 sq. ft.
Garage:	509 sq. ft.
Exterior Wall Framing:	2x4
Foundation options: Daylight basement. (Foundation & framing conversion diagram available — see order form.)	
Blueprint Price Code:	B

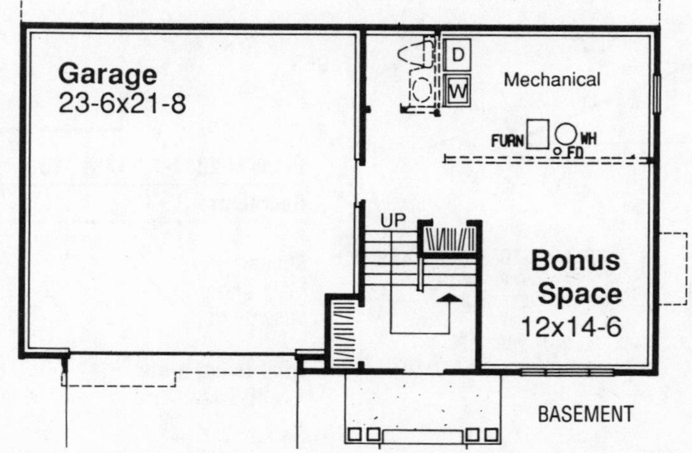

Exciting Design for Sloping Lot

- This design offers an exciting floor plan for a side-sloping lot.
- The vaulted foyer opens to the living room which is highlighted by a cheerful fireplace and is also vaulted.
- A half-wall with overhead arch separates the foyer and hallway from the dining room without interrupting the flow of space.
- The kitchen offers plenty of counter and cabinet space, and adjoins a brightly lit vaulted nook with a pantry in the corner.
- Separated from the rest of the household, the upper level master suite is a true haven from the day's worries, with its relaxing whirlpool tub, dual vanities and roomy closet.
- The lower level includes two bedrooms, a bath plus a large area which can be finished as a recreation room, plus a utility and storage area.

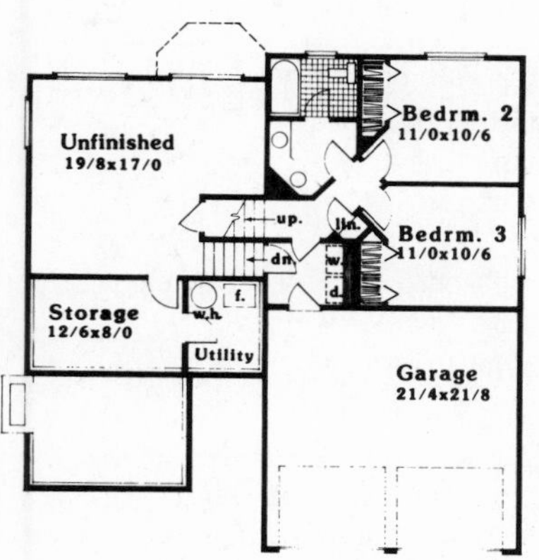

UPPER FLOOR

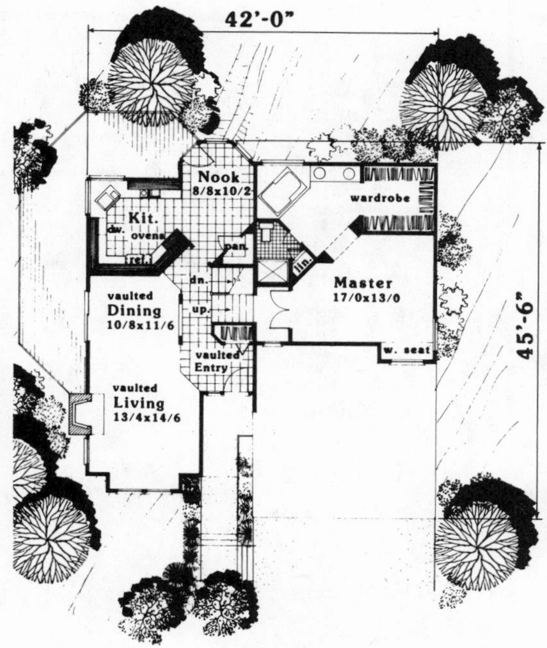

MAIN FLOOR

Plan R-4033

Bedrooms: 3	**Baths:** 2
Space:	
Upper two levels:	1,185 sq. ft.
Lower level:	480 sq. ft.
Total living area:	1,665 sq. ft.
Bonus area:	334 sq. ft.
Garage:	462 sq. ft.
Storage:	100 sq. ft.
Exterior Wall Framing:	2x6

Foundation options:
Daylight basement only.
(Foundation & framing conversion diagram available — see order form.)

Blueprint Price Code: B

Plan C-8160

Bedrooms: 3	**Baths:** 2

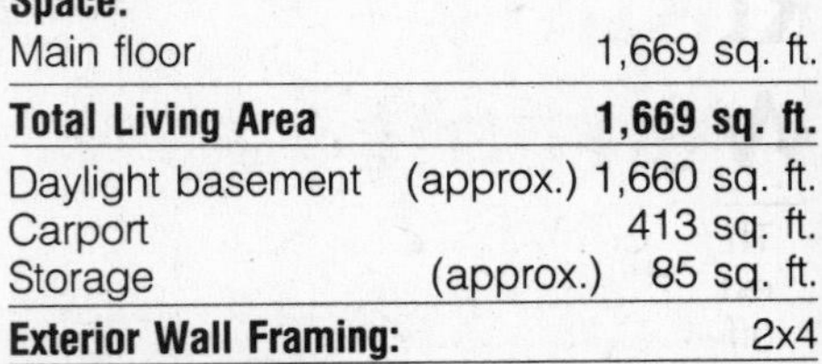

Space:	
Main floor	1,669 sq. ft.
Total Living Area	**1,669 sq. ft.**
Daylight basement	(approx.) 1,660 sq. ft.
Carport	413 sq. ft.
Storage	(approx.) 85 sq. ft.
Exterior Wall Framing:	2x4

Foundation Options:
Daylight basement
Crawlspace
Slab
(Foundation & framing conversion diagram available—see order form.)

Blueprint Price Code	**B**

Comfortable, Open Plan

- A central Great Room features a cathedral ceiling and is visually separated from the dining area by a huge fireplace.
- A wing on the left includes two secondary bedrooms which share a bath.
- In the right wing, you'll find a spacious master bedroom with private bath and walk-in closet.
- The kitchen is roomy and well-planned, with a utility room in the garage entry area.
- A house-spanning front deck adds an extra welcoming touch to the plan.

Rustic Welcome

- This rustic design boasts an appealing exterior with a covered front porch that offers guests a friendly welcome.
- The side-entry garage gives the front of the home an extra-appealing and uncluttered look.
- Inside, the centrally located Great Room features a cathedral ceiling with exposed wood beams. A massive fireplace separates the living area from the large dining area, which offers access to a nice backyard patio.
- The master suite features a walk-in closet and a compartmentalized bath.
- The galley kitchen lies between the formal dining room and the breakfast room, which features a bay window and a convenient pantry.
- A large utility room and a storage room complete the garage area.
- On the opposite side of the Great Room are two additional bedrooms with oversized closets and a second full bath.
- The optional daylight basement offers expanded living space. The stairway (not shown) would be located along the wall between the dining room and the back bedroom.

Plan C-8460

Bedrooms: 3	**Baths:** 2
Living Area:	
Main floor	1,670 sq. ft.
Total Living Area:	**1,670 sq. ft.**
Daylight basement	1,600 sq. ft.
Garage	427 sq. ft.
Exterior Wall Framing:	2x4

Foundation Options:
Daylight basement
Crawlspace
Slab
(Typical foundation & framing conversion diagram available—see order form.)

BLUEPRINT PRICE CODE: **B**

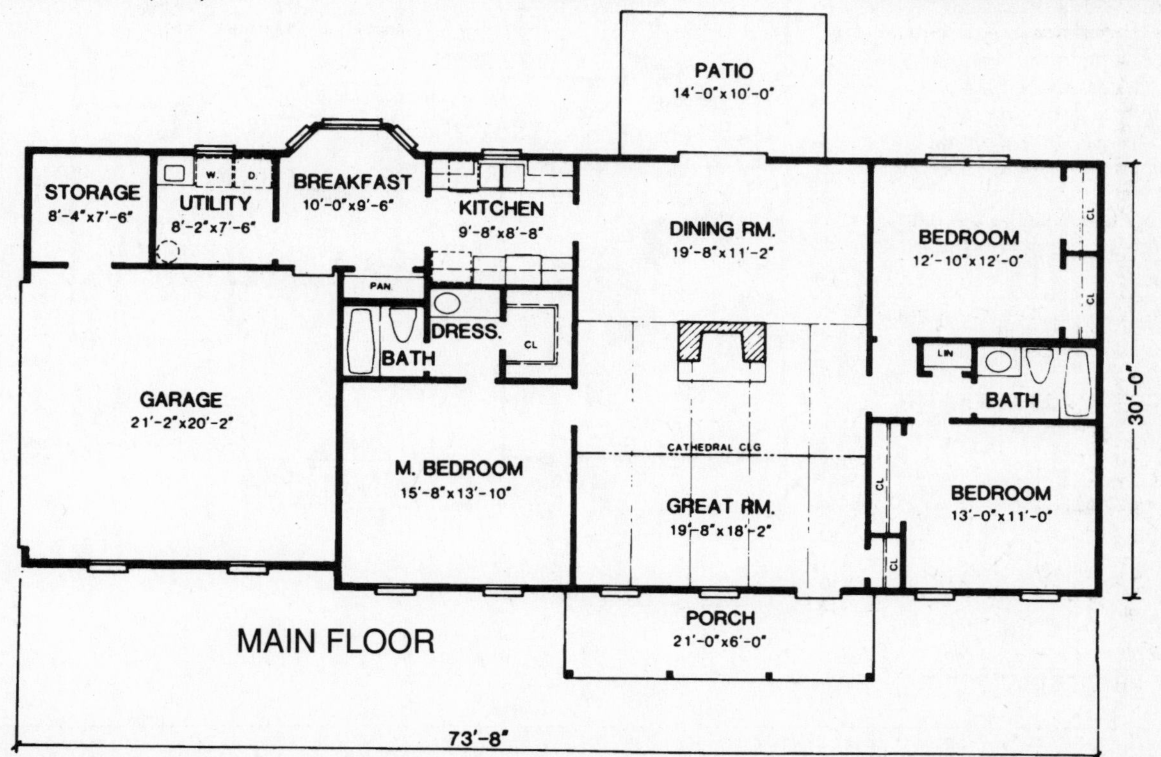

Smashing Master Suite!

- Corniced gables accented with arched louvers and a covered front porch with striking columns take this one-story design beyond the ordinary.
- The vaulted foyer leads directly into the family room, which also has a vaulted ceiling, plus a central fireplace framed by a window and a French door.
- The angled serving bar/snack counter connects the family room to the sunny dining room and kitchen. The adjoining breakfast room has easy access to the garage, the optional basement and the laundry room with a plant shelf.
- The master suite is simply smashing, with a tray ceiling in the sleeping area and private access to the backyard. The vaulted bath has all of today's finest amenities, while a vaulted sitting area with an angled wall and an optional fireplace is a special bonus.
- Two more bedrooms and a full bath round out this wonderful one-story.

Plan FB-1671	
Bedrooms: 3	**Baths:** 2
Living Area:	
Main floor	1,671 sq. ft.
Total Living Area:	**1,671 sq. ft.**
Daylight basement	1,671 sq. ft.
Garage	240 sq. ft.
Exterior Wall Framing:	2x4
Foundation Options:	
Daylight basement	
Crawlspace	
(Typical foundation & framing conversion diagram available—see order form.)	
BLUEPRINT PRICE CODE:	**B**

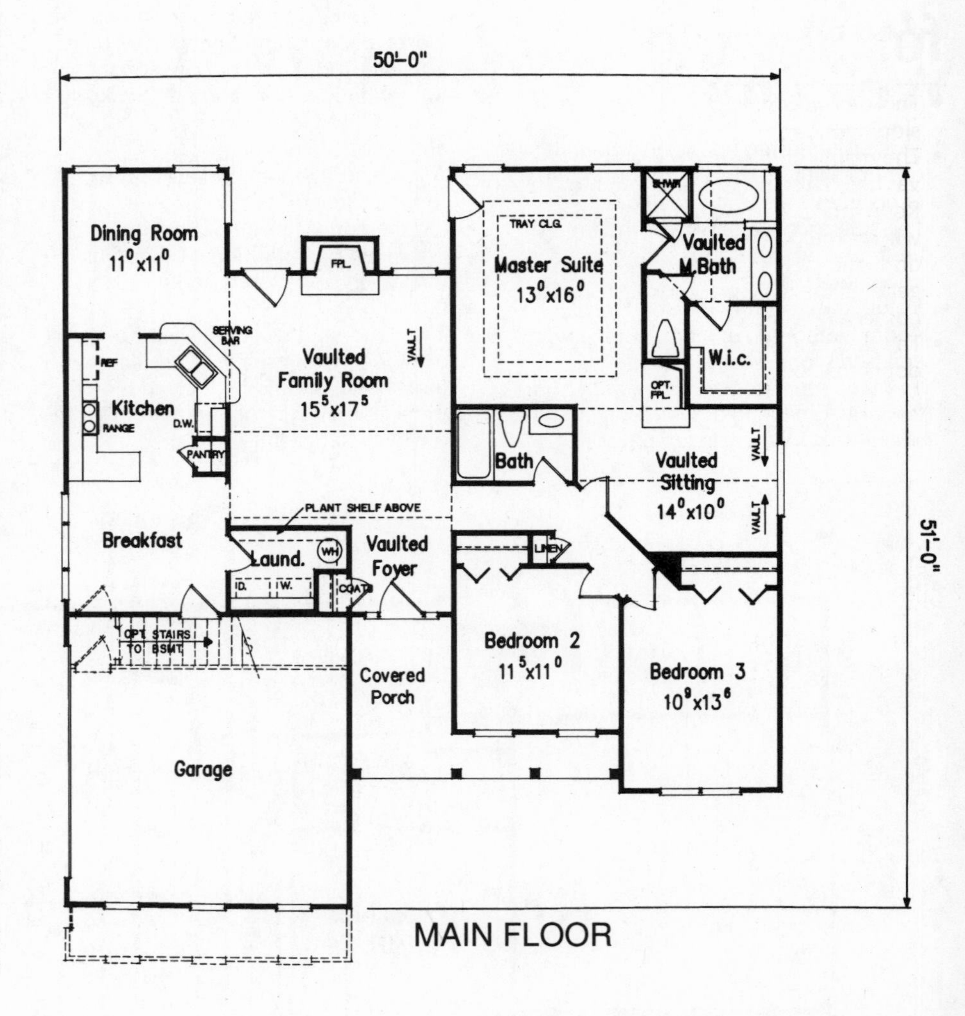

MAIN FLOOR

Plan FB-1671

PRICES AND DETAILS ON PAGES 12-15

Smart Design for Sloping Lot

- This design is perfect for a narrow, sloping lot.
- The main entry opens to a spacious, vaulted living area. A comfortable Great Room and a sunny dining area merge with corner windows that create a dramatic boxed bay. Another attention-getter is the cozy woodstove in the corner of the beautiful Great Room.
- The dining area offers sliding glass doors that extend family activities or entertaining to the adjoining deck.
- The dining area flows into the kitchen, which features a vaulted ceiling and a windowed sink that overlooks the deck.
- Two bedrooms are located at the back of the home, each with a private, skylighted bath. The master bedroom also has a walk-in wardrobe, a lovely window seat and deck access.
- A vaulted, skylighted hall leads to the stairway to the basement, where there are a third bedroom and another full bathroom. A very large shop/storage area and a two-car garage are also included. An extra bonus is the carport/storage area below the deck.

Plan P-529-2D	
Bedrooms: 3	**Baths:** 3
Living Area:	
Main floor	1,076 sq. ft.
Daylight basement	597 sq. ft.
Total Living Area:	**1,673 sq. ft.**
Tuck-under garage	425 sq. ft.
Exterior Wall Framing:	2x6
Foundation Options:	
Daylight basement	
BLUEPRINT PRICE CODE:	**B**

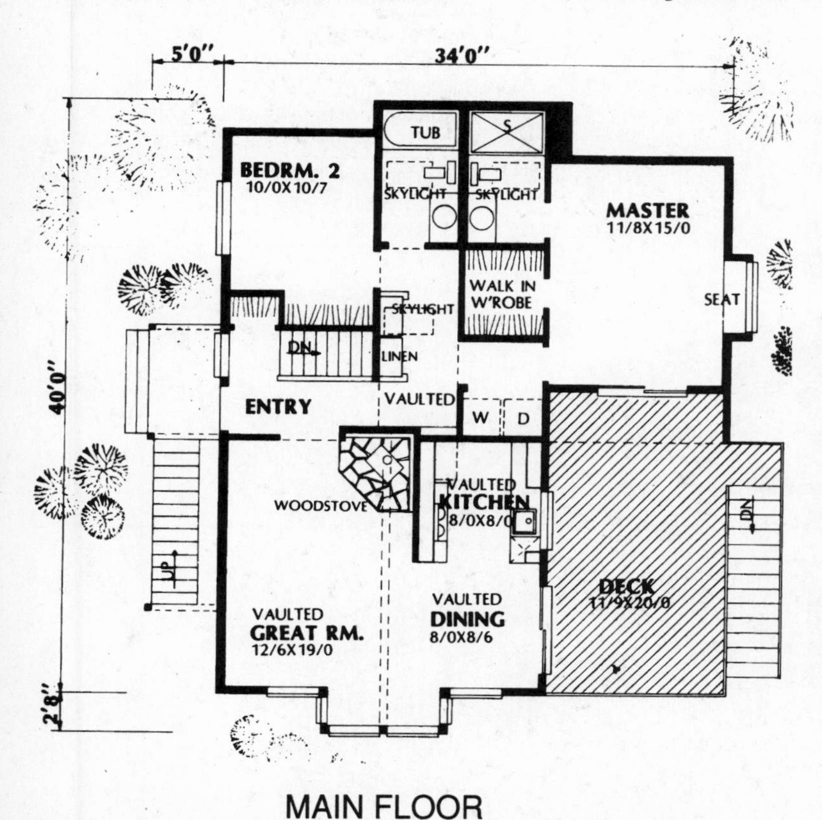

MAIN FLOOR

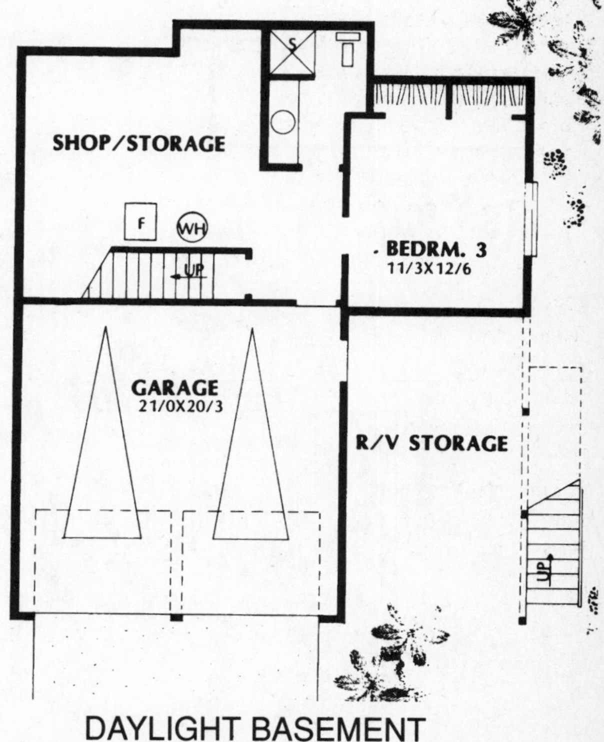

DAYLIGHT BASEMENT

FRONT VIEW

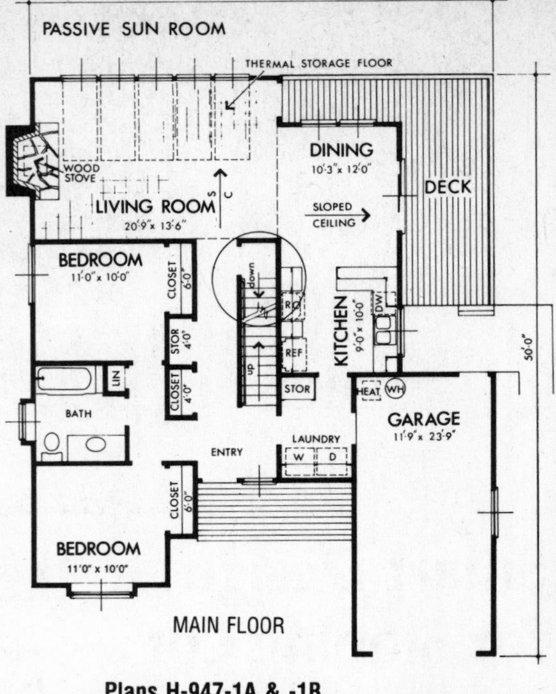

MAIN FLOOR

Sunny Family Living

- Pleasant-looking and unassuming from the front, this plan breaks into striking, sun-catching angles at the rear.
- The living room sun roof gathers passive solar heat, which is stored in the tile floor and the two-story high masonry backdrop to the wood stove.
- A 516-square-foot master suite with private bath and balcony makes up the second floor.
- The main floor offers two more bedrooms and a full bath.

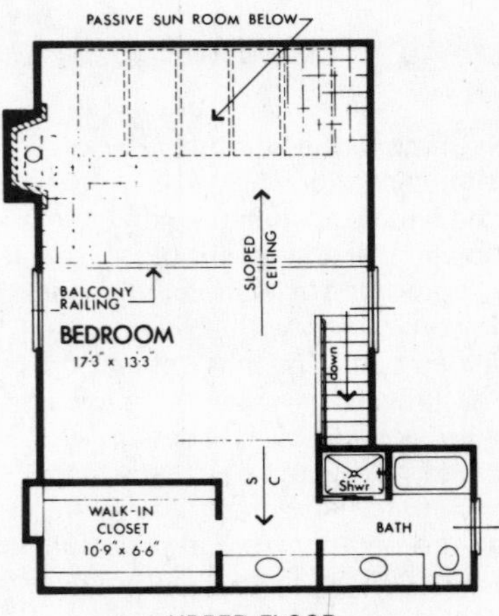

UPPER FLOOR

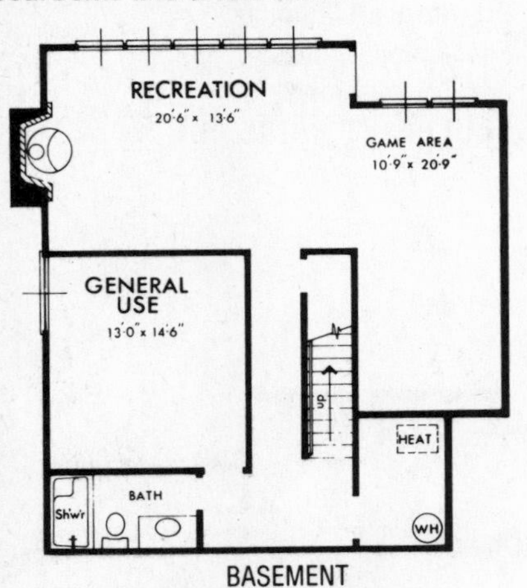

BASEMENT

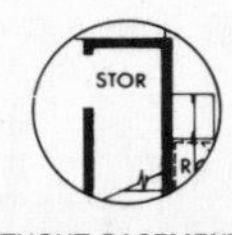

WITHOUT BASEMENT (CRAWLSPACE FOUNDATION)

Plans H-947-1A & -1B

Bedrooms: 3	**Baths:** 2-3
Space:	
Upper floor:	516 sq. ft.
Main floor:	1,162 sq. ft.
Total without basement:	1,678 sq. ft.
Daylight basement:	966 sq. ft.
Total with basement:	2,644 sq. ft.
Garage:	279 sq. ft.
Exterior Wall Framing:	2x6

Foundation options:
Daylight basement (H-947-1B).
Crawlspace (H-947-1A).
(Foundation & framing conversion diagram available — see order form.)

Blueprint Price Code:

Without basement:	B
With basement:	D

REAR VIEW

Photo by Mark Englund/HomeStyles

Sunny and Sensational

- All of the living spaces in this spectacular home revolve around a sensational kitchen with an adjoining bay-windowed nook.
- The vaulted entry is strategically positioned to allow easy access to the bedroom wing, the kitchen and the vaulted living room. The latter offers a fireplace framed by picture windows. The open dining room is outlined by a dropped ceiling and has a pocket door closing it off from the family room.
- The spacious family room is further enlarged by a cathedral ceiling, a large picture window and sliders leading to a deck or patio.
- The sunny kitchen and nook are joined by a large island with a cooktop and a serving counter. In addition to its appealing bay windows, the nook offers a practical desk that is handy to the entry and the kitchen.
- The utility room is convenient to the bedrooms, plus provides an easy passageway between the garage and the kitchen.
- The master bedroom has a private bath, while the two remaining bedrooms share a full bath.

Plans P-7758-2A & - 2D

Bedrooms: 3	**Baths:** 2
Living Area:	
Main floor (crawlspace version)	1,535 sq. ft.
Main floor (basement version)	1,595 sq. ft.
Total Living Area:	**1,535/1,595 sq. ft.**
Daylight basement	1,580 sq. ft.
Garage	579 sq. ft.
Exterior Wall Framing:	2x4
Foundation Options:	**Plan #**
Daylight basement	P-7758-2D
Crawlspace	P-7758-2A

(Typical foundation & framing conversion diagram available—see order form.)

BLUEPRINT PRICE CODE: B

Five-Bedroom Chalet

Realizing that there are situations that require the maximum number of bedrooms, we have created this modest-sized home containing five bedrooms. One of these, especially the one over the garage, would serve very well as a private den, card room or library. The plan is available with or without basement.

This is an excellent example of the classic chalet. Close study will reveal how hall space has been kept at an absolute minimum. As a result, a modest first floor area of 952 sq. ft. and a compact second floor plan of 767 sq. ft. make the five bedrooms possible.

Also notice the abundance of storage space and built-ins with many other conveniences. Plumbing is provided in two complete bathrooms, and a washer and dryer has been tucked into one corner of the central hall on the main floor.

A clever technique has been used in the design of the staircase as it progresses halfway up to a landing midway between the two floors. From here it branches in two directions to a bedroom over the garage and to a hallway common to other rooms.

First floor:	952 sq. ft.
Second floor:	767 sq. ft.
Total living area: (Not counting basement or garage)	1,719 sq. ft.

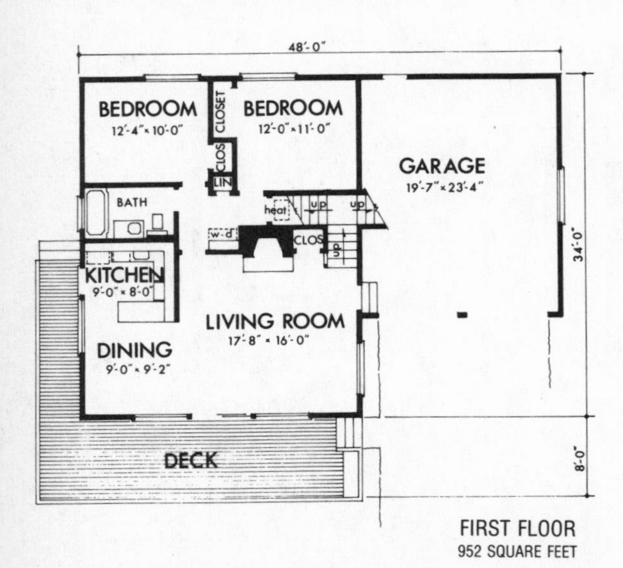

FIRST FLOOR
952 SQUARE FEET

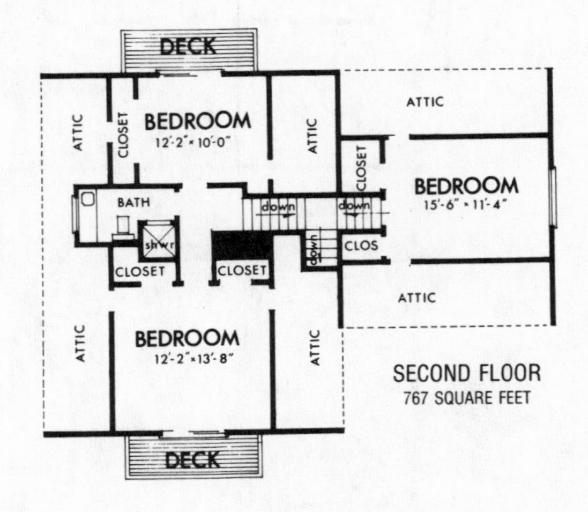

SECOND FLOOR
767 SQUARE FEET

PLAN H-804-2
WITH BASEMENT
PLAN H-804-2A
WITHOUT BASEMENT
(CRAWLSPACE FOUNDATION)

Blueprint Price Code B

Plans H-804-2 & -2A

TO ORDER THIS BLUEPRINT, CALL TOLL-FREE 1-800-547-5570

PRICES AND DETAILS ON PAGES 12-15

Panoramic View Embraces Outdoors

- This geometric design takes full advantage of scenic sites.
- Living area faces a glass-filled wall and wrap-around deck.
- Open dining/living room arrangement is complemented by vaulted ceilings, an overhead balcony, and a 5-ft-wide fireplace.
- 12′ deep main deck offers generous space for outdoor dining and entertaining.

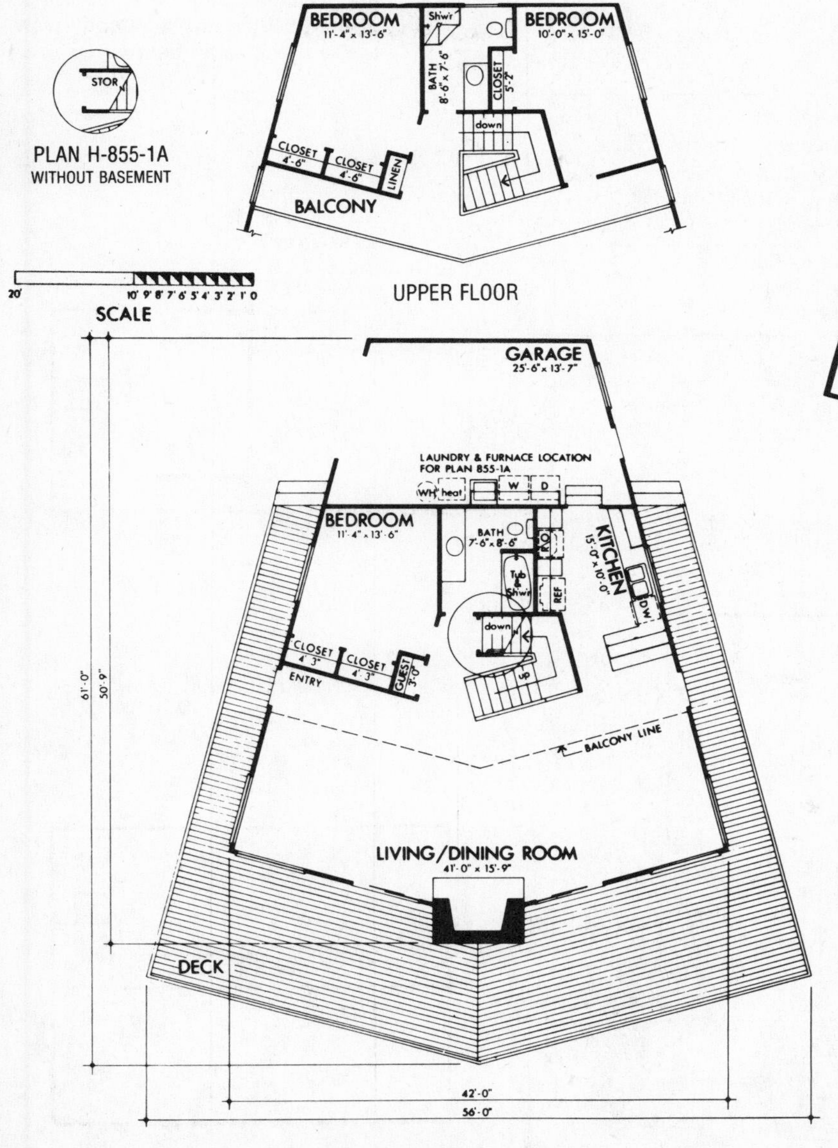

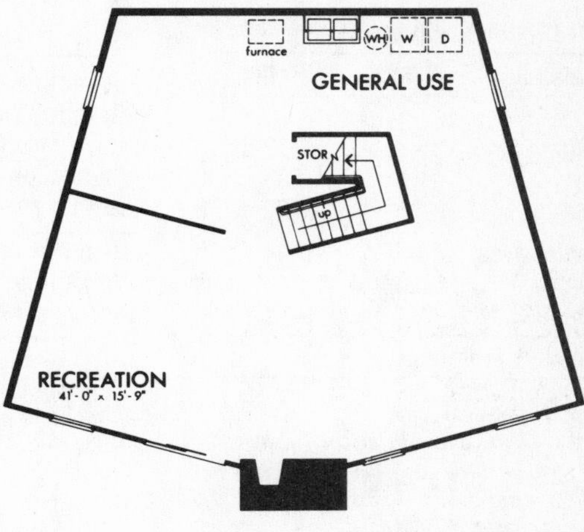

Plans H-855-1 & -1A

Bedrooms: 3	**Baths:** 2
Space:	
Upper floor:	625 sq. ft.
Main floor:	1,108 sq. ft.
Total living area:	1,733 sq. ft.
Basement:	approx. 1,108 sq. ft.
Garage:	346 sq. ft.
Exterior Wall Framing:	2x6
Foundation options:	
Daylight basement (Plan H-855-1).	
Crawlspace (Plan H-855-1A).	
(Foundation & framing conversion diagram available — see order form.)	
Blueprint Price Code:	
Without basement	B
With basement	D

REAR VIEW

Solar Flair

- Full window walls and a sun room with glass roof act as passive energy collectors in this popular floor plan.
- Expansive living room features wood stove and vaulted ceilings.
- Dining room shares a breakfast counter with the merging kitchen.
- Convenient laundry room is positioned near kitchen and garage entrance.
- Second level is devoted entirely to the private master suite, featuring vaulted ceiling and a balcony view to the living room below.

Plans H-877-5A & -5B

Bedrooms: 3-4	**Baths:** 2-3
Space:	
Upper floor:	382 sq. ft.
Main floor:	1,200 sq. ft.
Sun room:	162 sq. ft.
Total living area:	1,744 sq. ft.
Basement:	approx. 1,200 sq. ft.
Garage:	457 sq. ft.
Exterior Wall Framing:	2x6

Foundation options:
Daylight basement (Plan H-877-5B).
Crawlspace (Plan H-877-5A).
(Foundation & framing conversion diagram available — see order form.)

Blueprint Price Code:	
Without basement:	B
With basement:	D

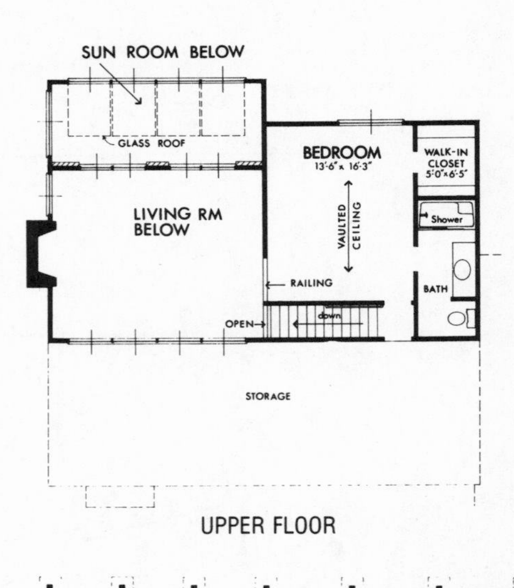

UPPER FLOOR

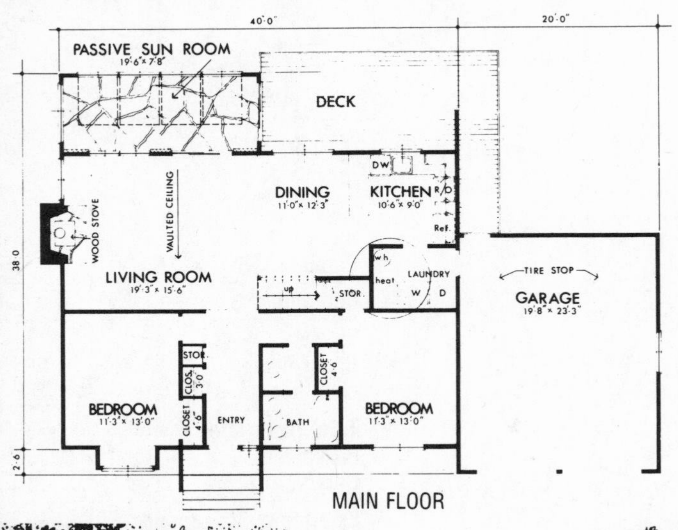

MAIN FLOOR

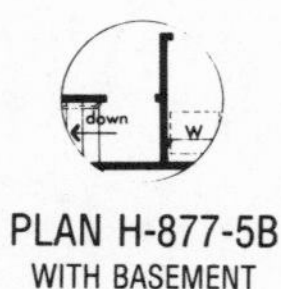

PLAN H-877-5B
WITH BASEMENT

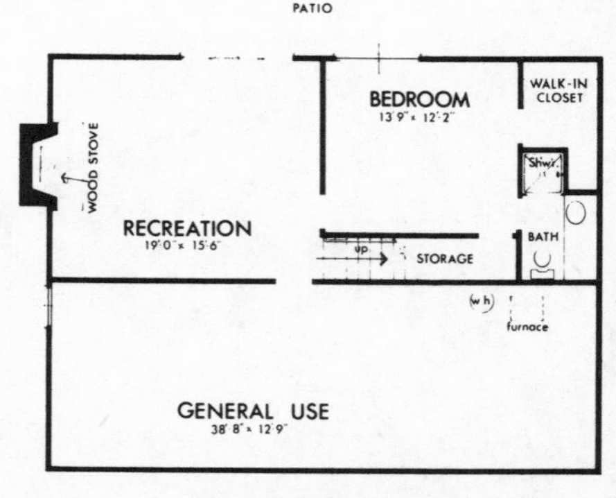

BASEMENT

FRONT VIEW

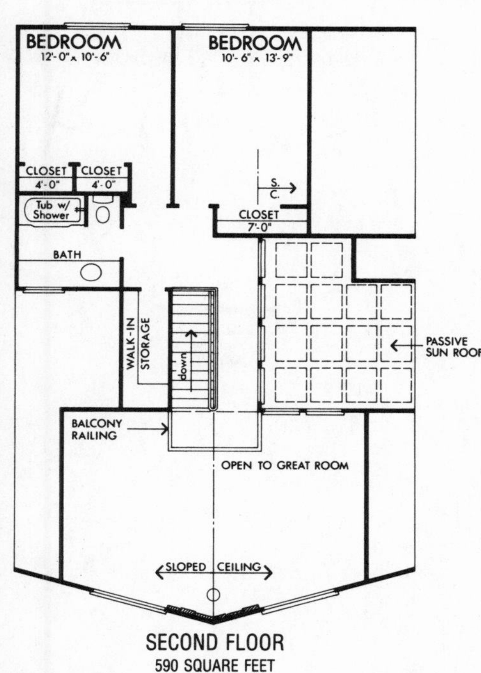

SECOND FLOOR
590 SQUARE FEET

First floor:	1,074 sq. ft.
Passive sun room:	136 sq. ft.
Second floor:	590 sq. ft.
Total living area: (Not counting basement or garage)	1,800 sq. ft.

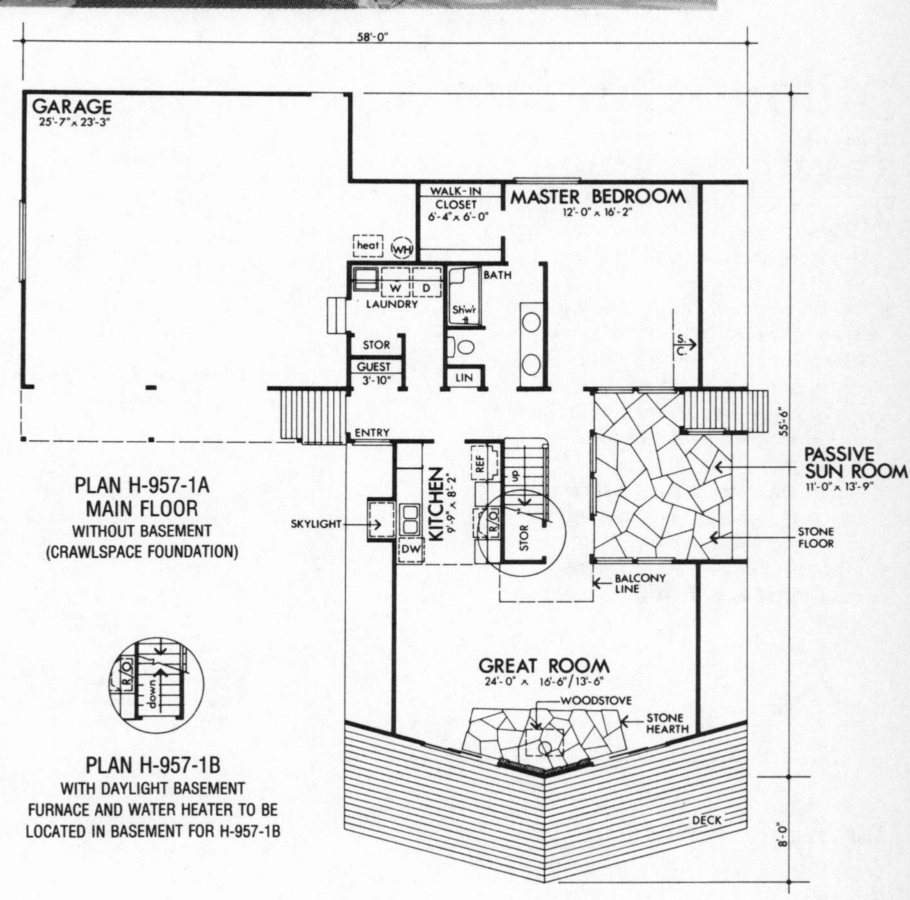

PLAN H-957-1A
MAIN FLOOR
WITHOUT BASEMENT
(CRAWLSPACE FOUNDATION)

PLAN H-957-1B
WITH DAYLIGHT BASEMENT
FURNACE AND WATER HEATER TO BE
LOCATED IN BASEMENT FOR H-957-1B

A Truly Livable Retreat

For a number of years the A-Frame idea has enjoyed great acceptance and popularity, especially in recreational areas. Too often, however, hopeful expectations have led to disappointment because economic necessity resulted in small and restricted buildings. Not so with this plan. Without ignoring the need for economy, the designers allowed themselves enough freedom to create a truly livable and practical home with a main floor of 1,210 sq. ft., exclusive of the garage area. The second floor has 590 sq. ft., and includes two bedrooms, a bath and ample storage space.

Take special note of the multi-use passive sun room. Its primary purpose is to collect, store and redistribute the sun's heat, not only saving a considerable amount of money but contributing an important function of keeping out dampness and cold when the owners are elsewhere. Otherwise the room might serve as a delightful breakfast room, a lovely arboretum, an indoor exercise room or any of many other functions limited only by the occupants' ingenuity.

A truly livable retreat, whether for weekend relaxation or on a daily basis as a primary residence, this passive solar A-Frame is completely equipped for the requirements of today's active living.

Exterior walls are framed with 2x6 studs.

Blueprint Price Code B

TO ORDER THIS BLUEPRINT, CALL TOLL-FREE 1-800-547-5570

Plans H-957-1A & -1B

PRICES AND DETAILS ON PAGES 12-15

Indoor-Outdoor Living

- Attention-getting pentagonal-shaped home is ideal for full-time or vacation living.
- Huge, two-story high living/dining area takes up half of the main floor, ideal for family gatherings.
- Compact, but functional kitchen features breakfast bar and adjacent laundry room that can also serve as a pantry and/or mudroom.
- Open stairway leads to second-floor balcony hallway overlooking the main level living area.
- Upper level has room for two additional bedrooms and a second bath.

Plans H-855-2 & -2A

Bedrooms: 3 — **Baths:** 2

Space:

Upper floor:	660 sq. ft.
Main floor:	1,174 sq. ft.
Total living area:	1,834 sq. ft.
Basement:	approx. 1,174 sq. ft.
Garage:	277 sq. ft.

Exterior Wall Framing: 2x4

Foundation options:
Daylight basement (Plan H-855-2).
Crawlspace (Plan H-855-2A).
(Foundation & framing conversion diagram available — see order form.)

Blueprint Price Code:

Without basement	B
With basement	E

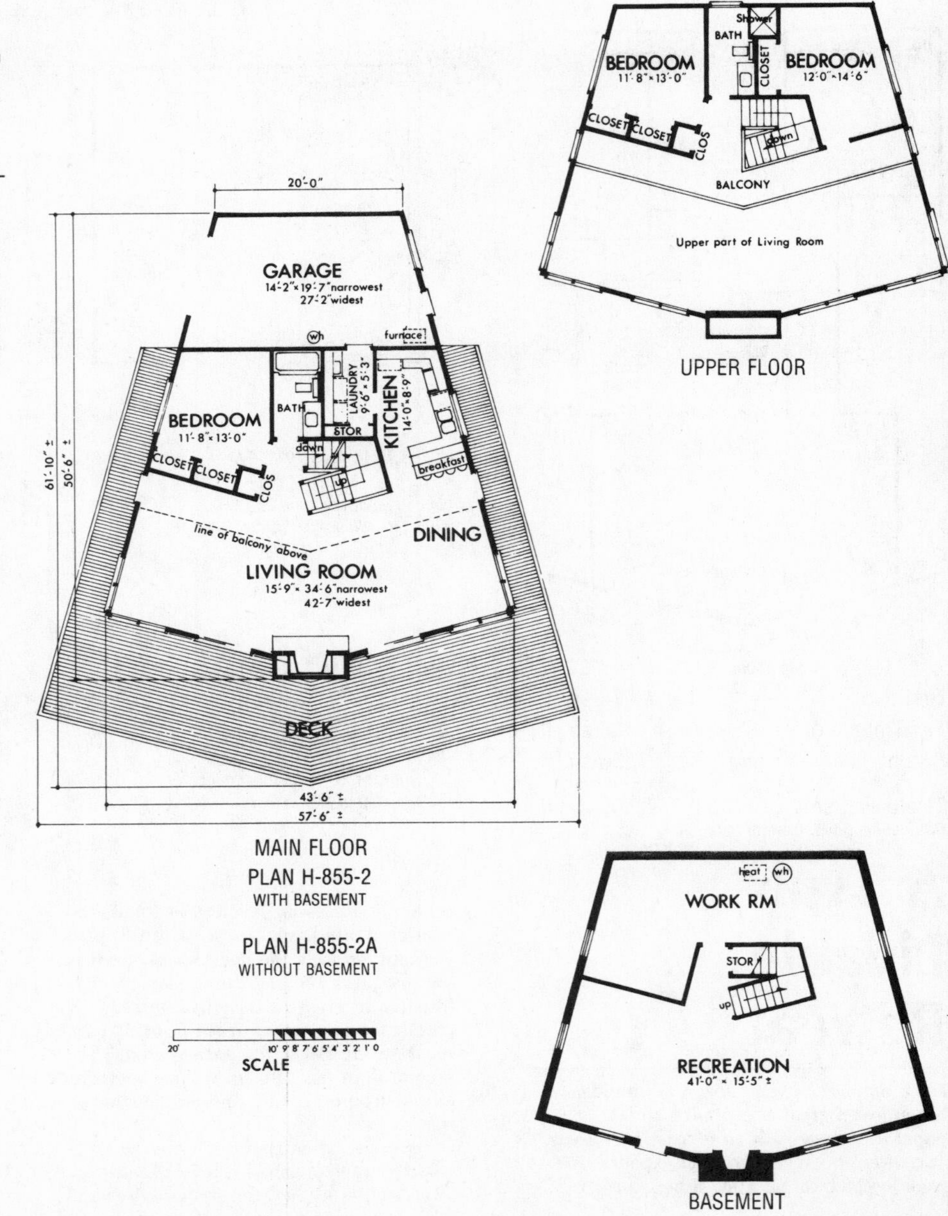

Country Styling for Up-to-Date Living

- Nearly surrounded by a covered wood porch, this traditional 1,860 square-foot farm-styled home is modernized for today's active, up-to-date family.
- Inside, the efficient floor plan promotes easy mobility with a minimum of cross-traffic.
- The spacious living and dining area is warmed by a fireplace with a stone hearth; the U-shaped country kitchen is centrally located between these areas and the nook and family room with wood stove on the other side.
- Sliding glass doors lead out to both the rear patio and the deck that adjoins the dining and living rooms.
- The large master bedroom with corner window, dressing area and private bath and two other bedrooms with a second shared bath are found on the upper level.

Plans P-7677-2A & -2D

Bedrooms: 3	**Baths:** 2 ½
Space:	
Upper floor	825 sq. ft.
Main floor	1,035 sq. ft.
Total Living Area	**1,860 sq. ft.**
Basement	1,014 sq. ft.
Garage	466 sq. ft.
Exterior Wall Framing	2x6
Foundation options:	Plan #
Daylight Basement	P-7677-2D
Crawlspace	P-7677-2A
(Foundation & framing conversion diagram available—see order form.)	
Blueprint Price Code	B

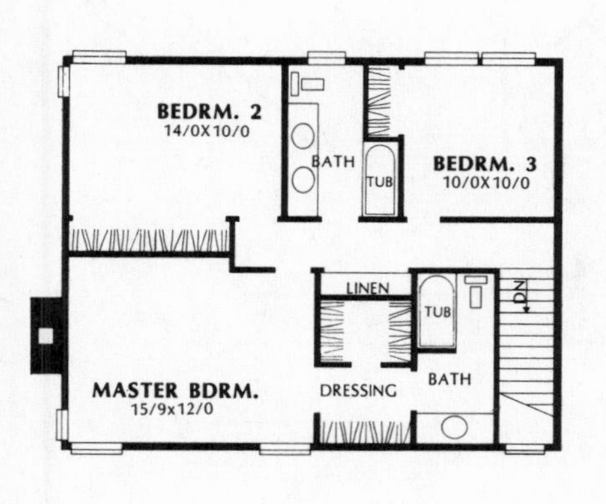

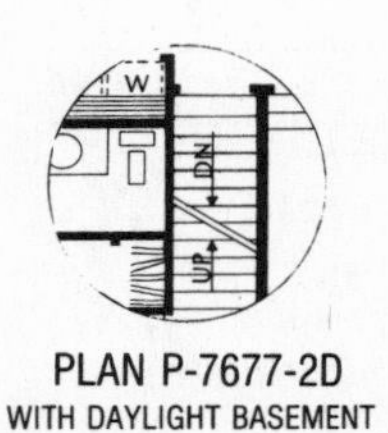

PLAN P-7677-2D
WITH DAYLIGHT BASEMENT

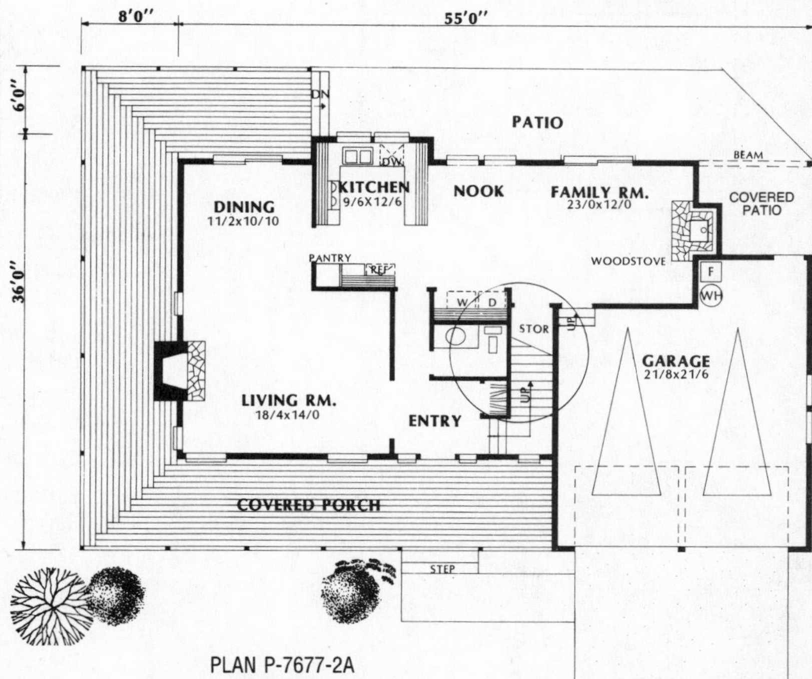

PLAN P-7677-2A
(CRAWLSPACE)

Spacious Octagon

- Highly functional main floor plan makes traffic easy and minimizes wasted hall space.
- Double-sized entry opens to spacious octagonal living room with central fireplace and access to all rooms.
- U-shaped kitchen and attached dining area allow for both informal and formal occasions.
- Contiguous bedrooms each have independent deck entrances.
- Exciting deck borders entire home.

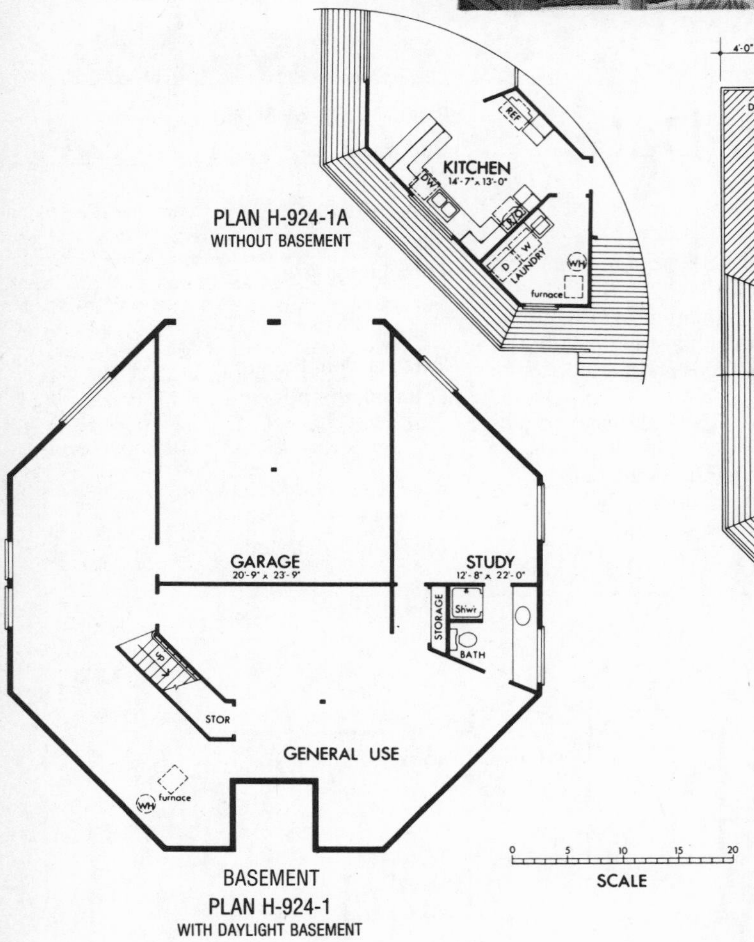

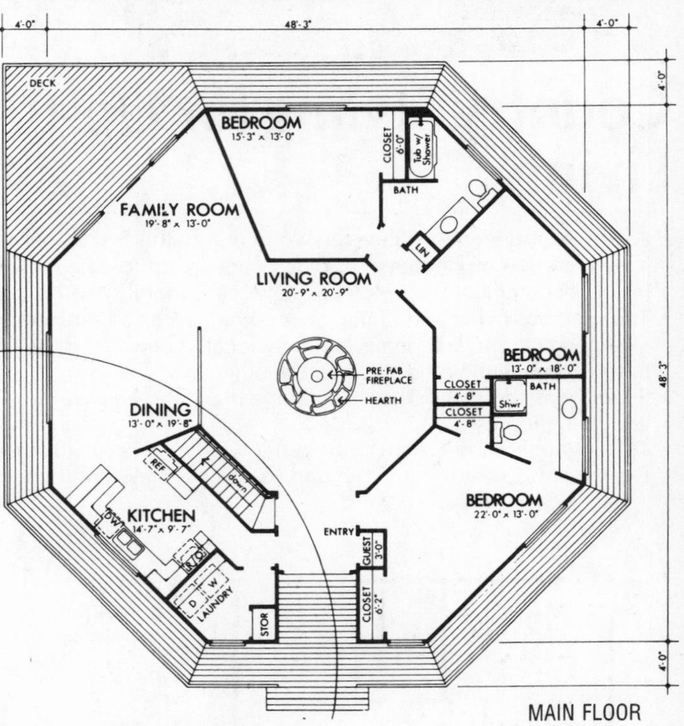

Plans H-924-1 & -1A

Bedrooms: 3-4	**Baths:** 2-3
Space:	
Main floor:	1,888 sq. ft.
Total without basement:	1,888 sq. ft.
Basement:	1,395 sq. ft.
Total with basement:	3,283 sq. ft.
Garage:	493 sq. ft.
Exterior Wall Framing:	2x4

Foundation options:
Daylight basement (Plan H-924-1).
Crawlspace (Plan H-924-1A).
(Foundation & framing conversion diagram available — see order form.)

Blueprint Price Code:

Without basement:	B
With basement:	E

Photo by Mark Englund/HomeStyles

**NOTE:
The above photographed home may have been modified by the homeowner. Please refer to floor plan and/or drawn elevation shown for actual blueprint details.

Exciting, Economical Design

Exciting but economical, this 1,895 sq. ft., three-bedroom house is arranged carefully for maximum use and enjoyment on two floors, and is only 42 feet wide to minimize lot size requirements. The multi-paned bay windows of the living room and an upstairs bedroom add contrast to the hip rooflines and lead you to the sheltered front entry porch.

The open, vaulted foyer is brightened by a skylight as it sorts traffic to the downstairs living areas or to the upper bedroom level. A few steps to the right puts you in the vaulted living room and the adjoining dining area. Sliding doors in the dining area and the nook, and a pass-through window in the U-shaped kitchen, make the patio a perfect place for outdoor activities and meals.

A large fireplace warms the spacious family room, which has a corner wet bar for efficient entertaining. A utility room leading to the garage and a powder room complete the 1,020 sq. ft. main floor.

An open stairway in the foyer leads to the 875 sq. ft. upper level. The master bedroom has a large walk-in wardrobe, twin vanity, shower and bathroom. The front bedroom has a seat in the bay window and the third bedroom has a built-in seat overlooking the vaulted living room. A full bath with twin vanity serves these bedrooms.

The daylight basement version of the plan adds 925 sq. ft. of living space.

Main floor:	1,020 sq. ft.
Upper floor:	875 sq. ft.
Total living area:	1,895 sq. ft.
(Not counting basement or garage)	

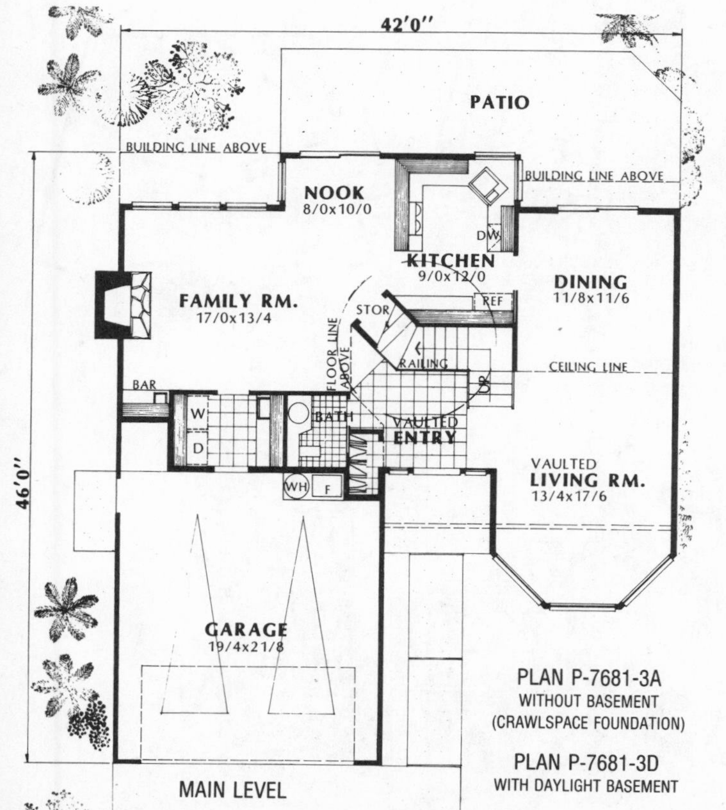

PLAN P-7681-3A
WITHOUT BASEMENT
(CRAWLSPACE FOUNDATION)

PLAN P-7681-3D
WITH DAYLIGHT BASEMENT

PLAN P-7681-3D
BASEMENT LEVEL: 925 sq. ft.

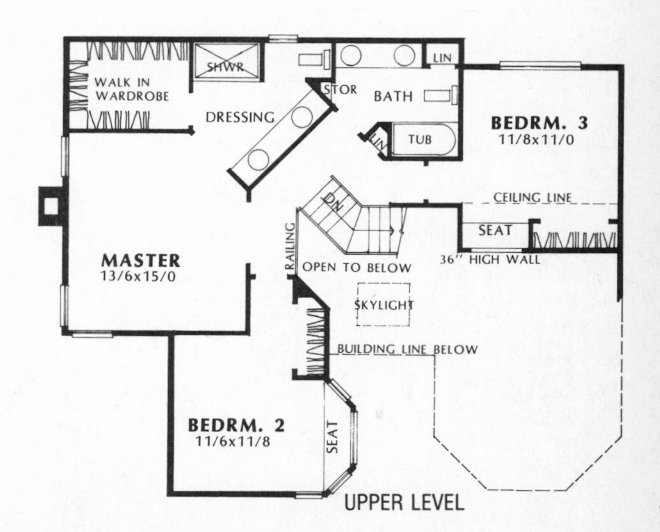

Blueprint Price Code B

TO ORDER THIS BLUEPRINT, CALL TOLL-FREE 1-800-547-5570

Plans P-7681-3A & 3D

PRICES AND DETAILS
ON PAGES 12-15

Photo by Carren Strock

Proven Plan Features Passive Sun Room

- A passive sun room, energy-efficient wood stove, and a panorama of windows make this design highly economical.
- Open living/dining room features attractive balcony railing, stone hearth, and adjoining sun room with durable stone floor.
- Well-equipped kitchen is separated from dining area by a convenient breakfast bar.
- Second level sleeping areas border a hallway and balcony.
- Optional basement plan provides extra space for entertaining or work.

Plans H-855-3A & -3B

Bedrooms: 3	**Baths:** 2-3
Space:	
Upper floor:	586 sq. ft.
Main floor:	1,192 sq. ft.
Sun room:	132 sq. ft.
Total living area:	1,910 sq. ft.
Basement:	approx. 1,192 sq. ft.
Garage:	520 sq. ft.
Exterior Wall Framing:	2x6

Foundation options:
Daylight basement (Plan H-855-3B).
Crawlspace (Plan H-855-3A).
(Foundation & framing conversion diagram available — see order form.)

Blueprint Price Code:

Without basement	B
With basement	E

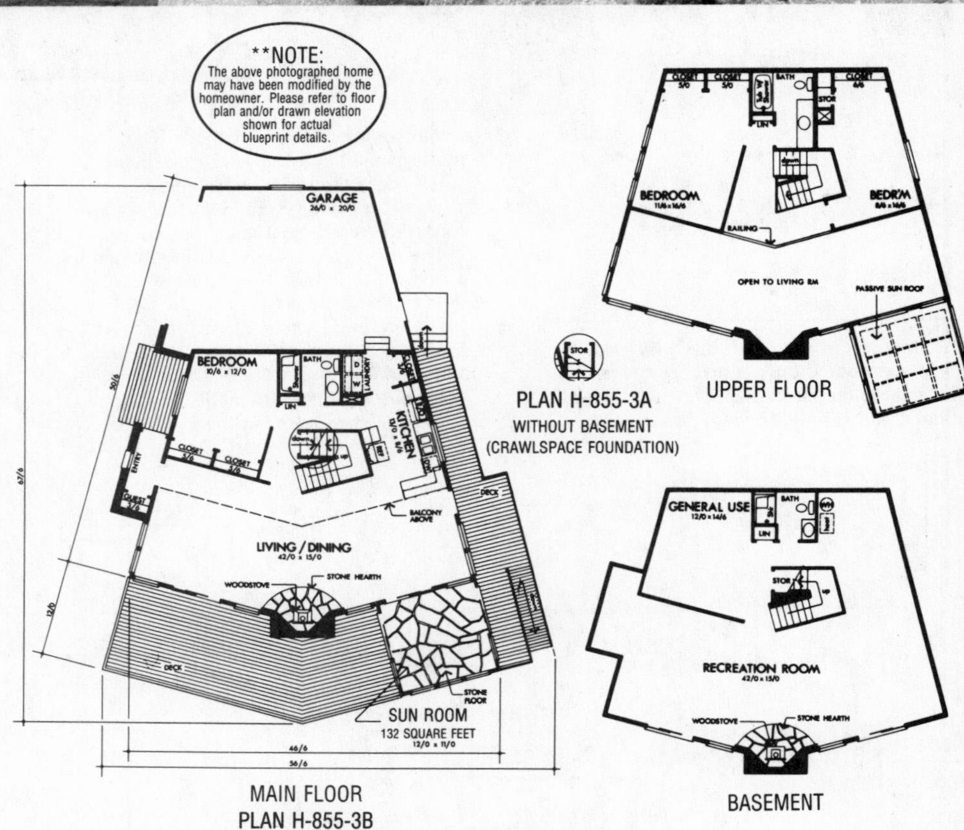

Soaring Design Lifts the Human Spirit

- Suitable for level or sloping lots, this versatile design can be expanded or finished as time and budget allow.
- Surrounding deck accessible from all main living areas.
- Great living room enhanced by vaulted ceilings, second-floor balcony, skylights and dramatic window wall.
- Rear entrance has convenient access to full bath and laundry room.
- Two additional bedrooms on upper level share second bath and balcony room.

Photo by Bob Hallinen

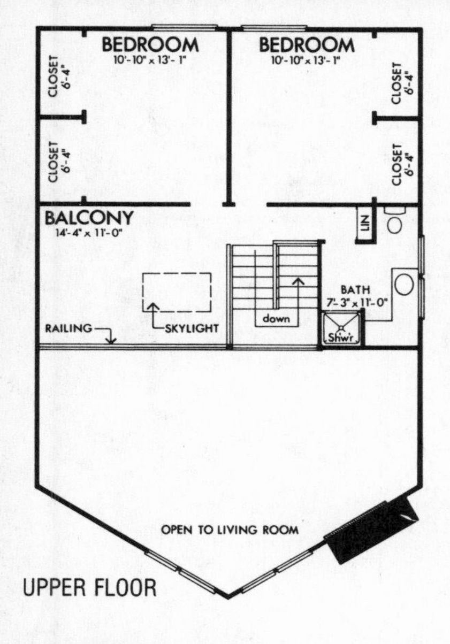

Plans H-930-1 & -1A

Bedrooms: 3	**Baths:** 2
Space:	
Upper floor:	710 sq. ft.
Main floor:	1,210 sq. ft.
Total living area:	1,920 sq. ft.
Basement:	605 sq. ft.
Garage/shop:	605 sq. ft.
Exterior Wall Framing:	2x6

Foundation options:
Daylight basement (Plan H-930-1).
Crawlspace (Plan H-930-1A).
(Foundation & framing conversion diagram available — see order form.)

Blueprint Price Code:

Without basement:	B
With basement:	D

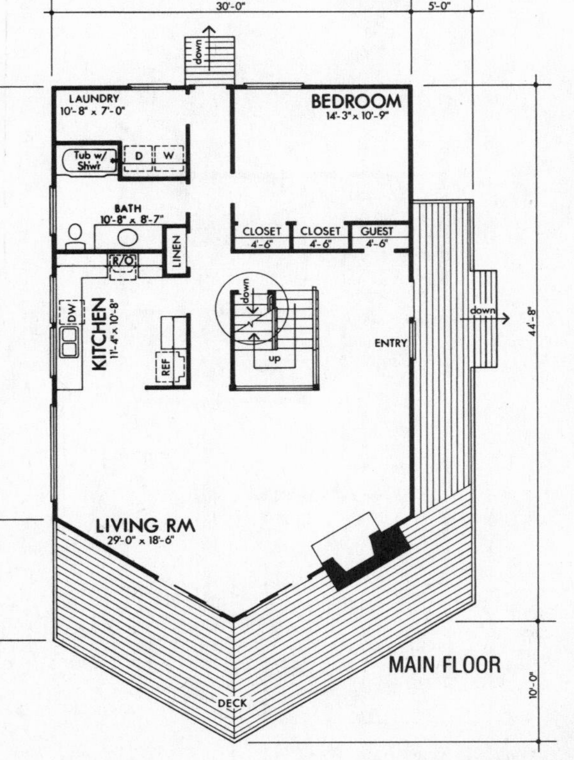

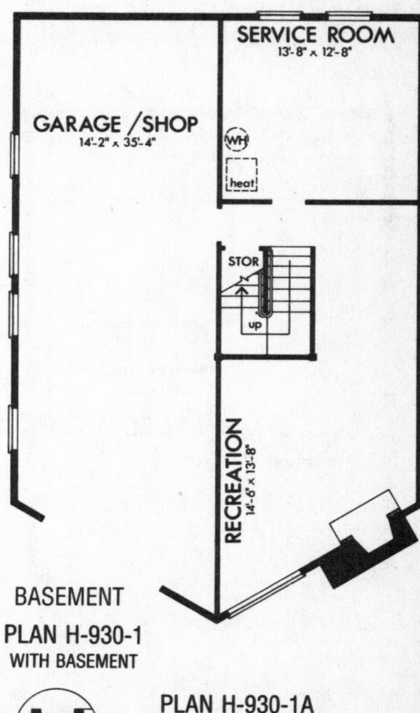

Decked Out for Fun

- Spacious deck surrounds this comfortable cabin/chalet.
- Sliding glass doors and windows blanket the living-dining area, indulged with raised hearth and a breathtaking view.
- Dining area and compact kitchen separated by breakfast bar.
- Master bedroom, laundry room and bath complete first floor; two additional bedrooms located on second floor.
- Upper level also features impressive balcony room with exposed beams.

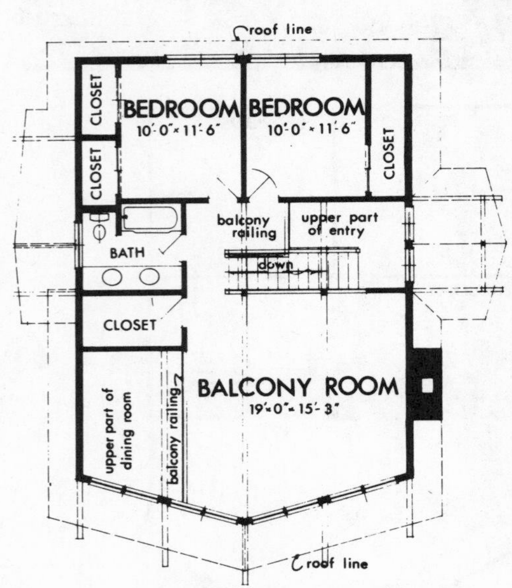

UPPER FLOOR

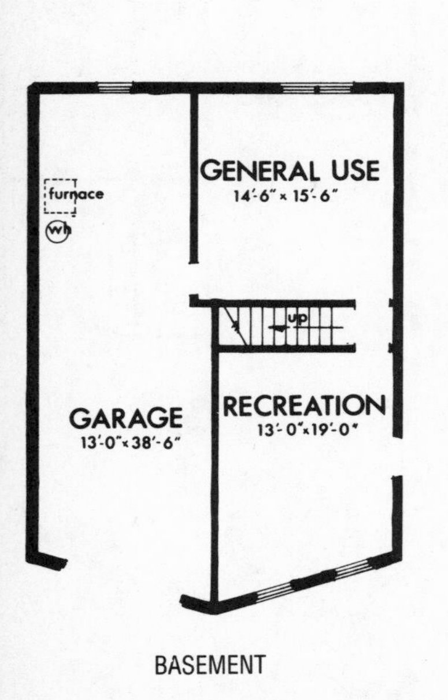

BASEMENT

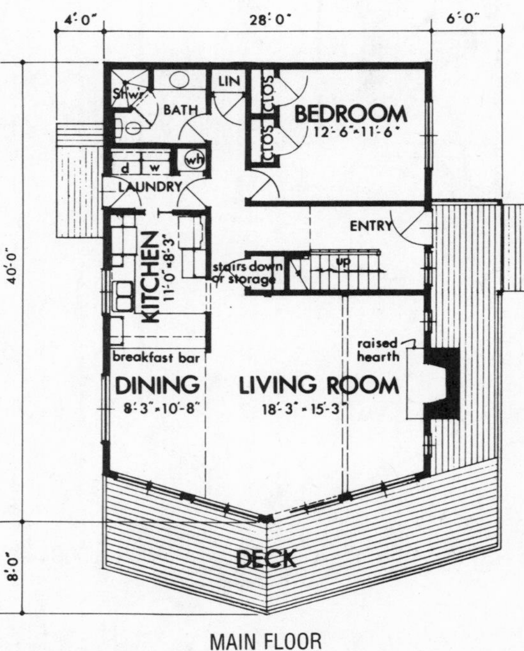

MAIN FLOOR

Plans H-919-1 & -1A

Bedrooms: 3	**Baths:** 2
Space:	
Upper floor:	869 sq. ft.
Main floor:	1,064 sq. ft.
Total living area:	1,933 sq. ft.
Basement:	475 sq. ft.
Garage:	501 sq. ft.
Exterior Wall Framing:	2x6

Foundation options:
Daylight basement (Plan H-919-1).
Crawlspace (Plan H-919-1A).
(Foundation & framing conversion diagram available — see order form.)

Blueprint Price Code:	
Without basement:	B
With basement:	C

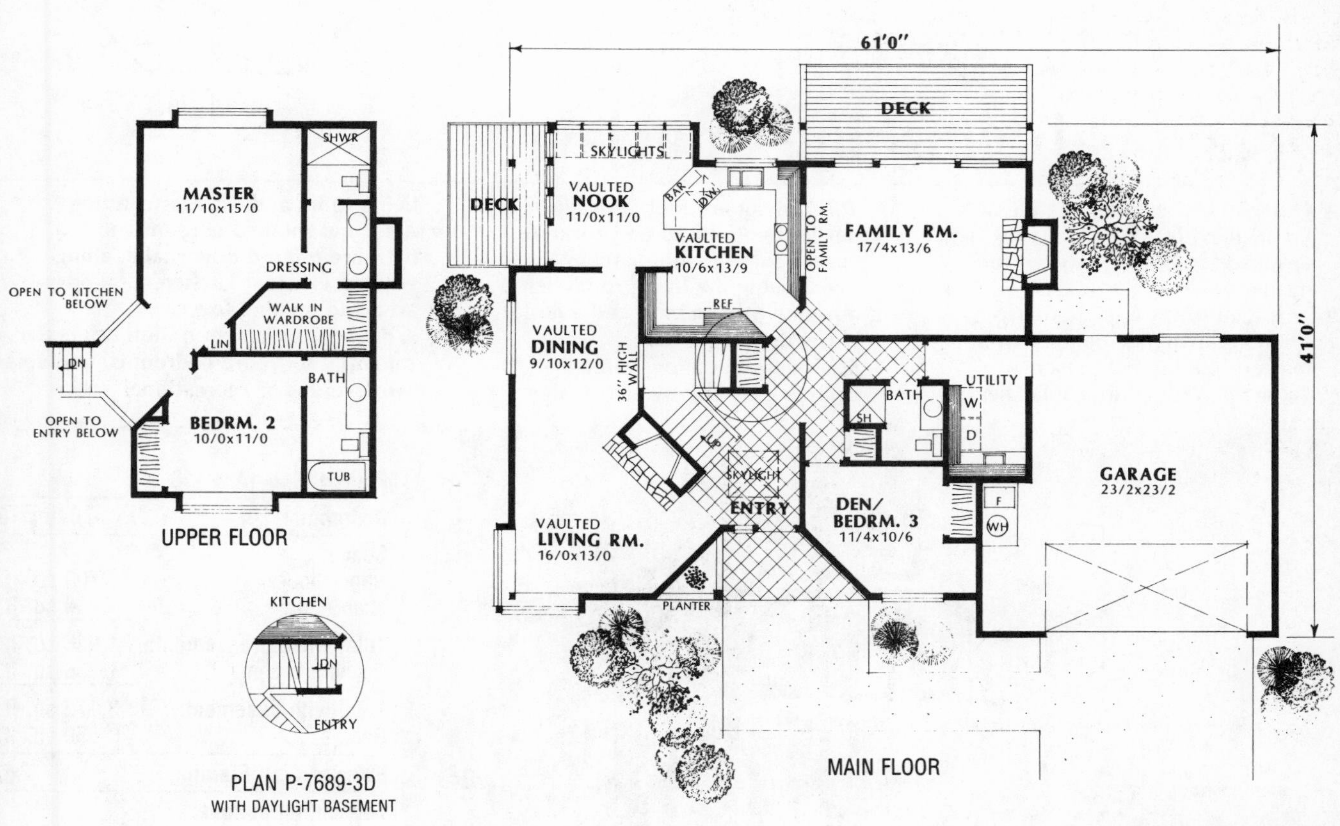

PLAN P-7689-3D
WITH DAYLIGHT BASEMENT

PLAN P-7689-3A
WITHOUT BASEMENT
(CRAWLSPACE FOUNDATION)

Main floor:	1,358 sq. ft.
Upper floor:	576 sq. ft.
Total living area: (Not counting basement or garage)	1,934 sq. ft.
Basement level:	1,358 sq. ft.

Blueprint Price Code B

TO ORDER THIS BLUEPRINT, CALL TOLL-FREE 1-800-547-5570

Plans P-7689-3A & -3D

PRICES AND DETAILS ON PAGES 12-15

FRONT VIEW

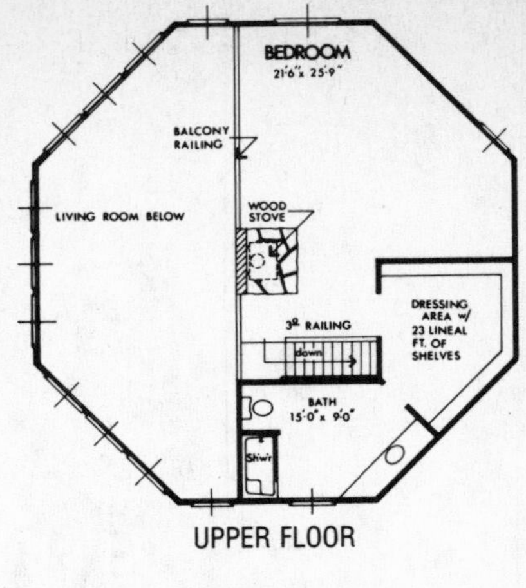

UPPER FLOOR

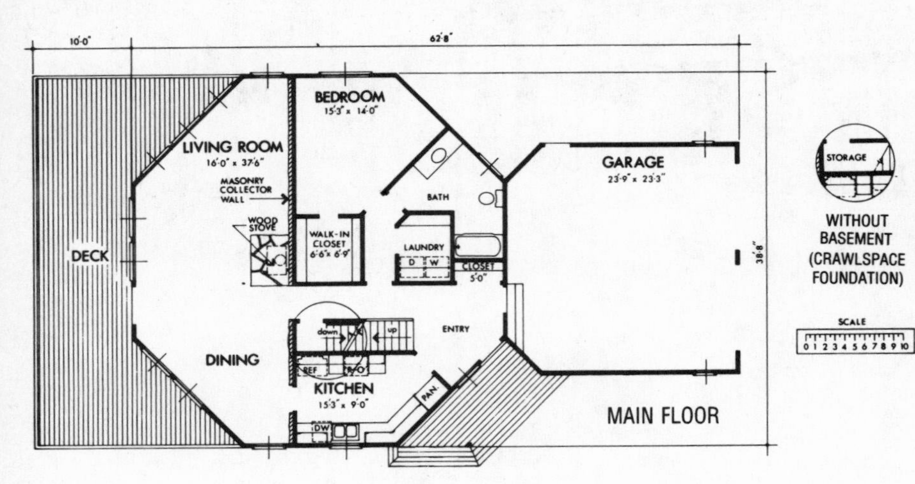

MAIN FLOOR

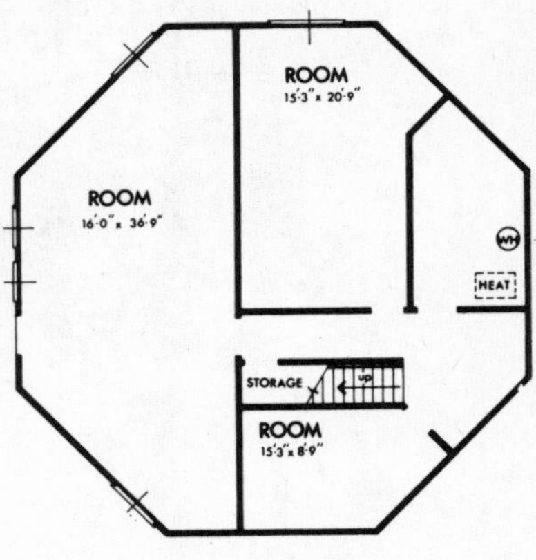

BASEMENT

Octagonal Sunshine Special

- Octagon homes offer the ultimate for taking advantage of a view, and are fascinating designs even for more ordinary settings.
- This plan offers a huge, house-spanning living/dining area with loads of glass and a masonry collector wall to store solar heat.
- The 700-square-foot upper level is devoted entirely to an enormous master suite, with a balcony overlooking the living room below, a roomy private bath and a large closet/dressing area.
- Scissor-trusses allow vaulted ceilings over the two-story-high living room and the master suite.
- A second roomy bedroom and full bath are offered downstairs, along with an efficient kitchen, a laundry area and inviting foyer.
- A daylight basement option offers the potential for more bedrooms, hobbies, work rooms or recreational space.

REAR VIEW

Plans H-948-1A & -1B

Bedrooms: 2-4 **Baths:** 2

Space:

Upper floor:	700 sq. ft.
Main floor:	1,236 sq. ft.
Total without basement:	1,936 sq. ft.
Daylight basement:	1,236 sq. ft.
Total with basement:	3,172 sq. ft.
Garage:	550 sq. ft.
Exterior Wall Framing:	2x6

Foundation options:
Daylight basement (H-948-1B).
Crawlspace (H-948-1A).
(Foundation & framing conversion diagram available — see order form.)

Blueprint Price Code:

Without basement:	B
With basement:	E

Ideal for Formal Entertaining

This lovely 1,940 sq. ft. French Provincial design features a formal foyer flanked by the living room on one side and the dining room on the other. A family room with a raised-hearth fireplace and double doors to the patio, and the L-shaped island kitchen with breakfast bay and open counter to the family room, allow for more casual living.

Adjacent to the breakfast bay is a utility room with outside entrance.

The master suite includes one double closet and a compartmentalized bath with walk-in closet, step-up garden tub, double vanity and linen closet. Two front bedrooms and a second full bath with linen closet complete the design. A recessed entry and circular porch add to the formal exterior.

Total living area: 1,940 sq. ft.
(Not counting basement or garage)

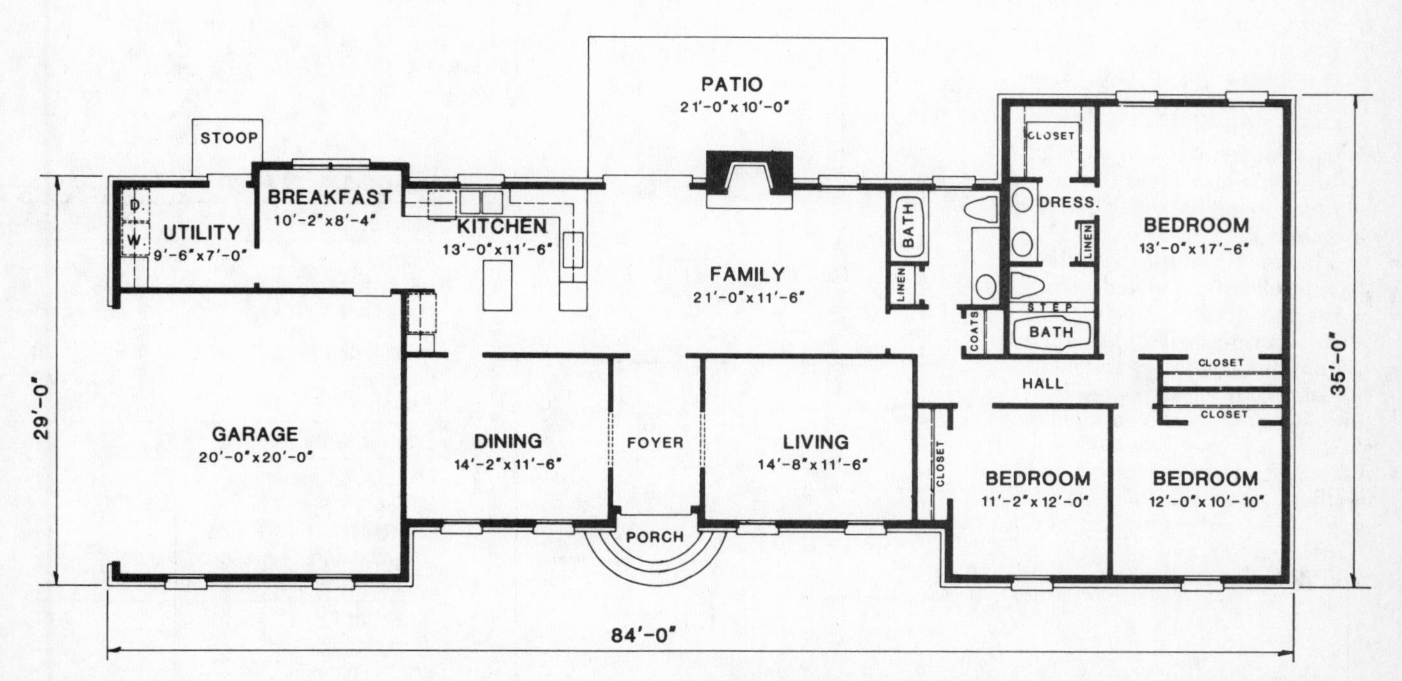

Specify daylight basement, crawlspace or slab foundation when ordering.

Blueprint Price Code B

Plan C-8103

TO ORDER THIS BLUEPRINT, CALL TOLL-FREE 1-800-547-5570

PRICES AND DETAILS ON PAGES 12-15

Excellent Family Design

- Long sloping rooflines and bold design features make this home attractive for any neighborhood.
- Inside, a vaulted entry takes visitors into an impressive vaulted Great Room with a wood stove and window-wall facing the house-spanning rear deck.
- Clerestory windows flanking the stove area and large windows front and rear flood the Great Room with natural light.
- The magnificent kitchen includes a stylish island and opens to the informal dining area which in turn flows into the Great Room.
- Two bedrooms on the main floor share a full bath, and bedroom #2 boasts easy access to the rear deck which spans the width of the house.
- The upstairs comprises an "adult retreat," with a roomy master suite, luxurious bath with double sinks, and a large walk-in closet.
- A daylight basement version adds another 1,410 sq. ft. of space for entertaining and recreation, plus a fourth bedroom and a large shop/storage area.

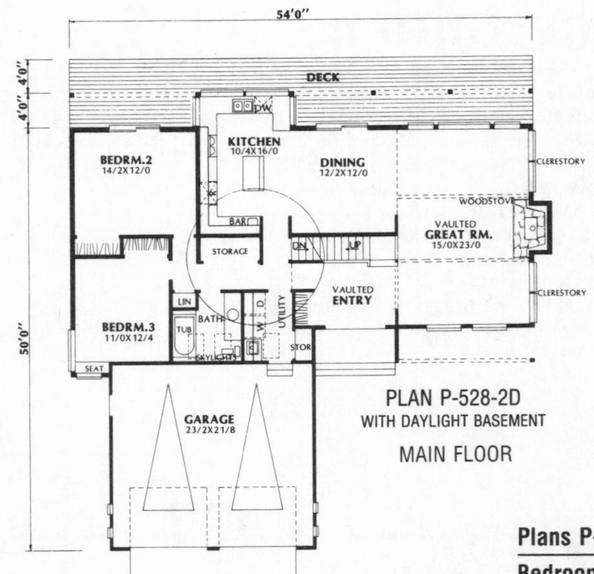

PLAN P-528-2D
WITH DAYLIGHT BASEMENT
MAIN FLOOR

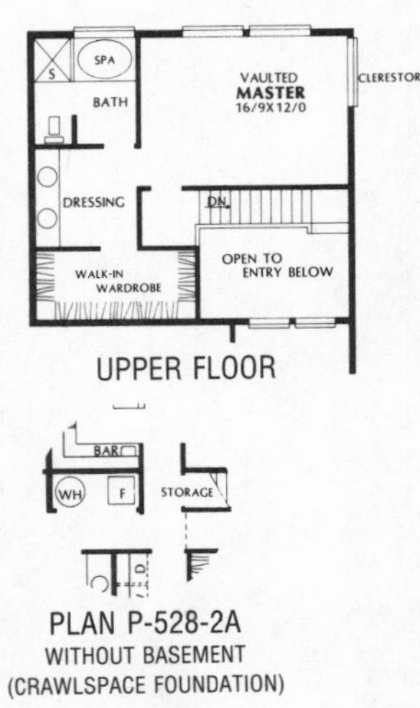

UPPER FLOOR

PLAN P-528-2A
WITHOUT BASEMENT
(CRAWLSPACE FOUNDATION)

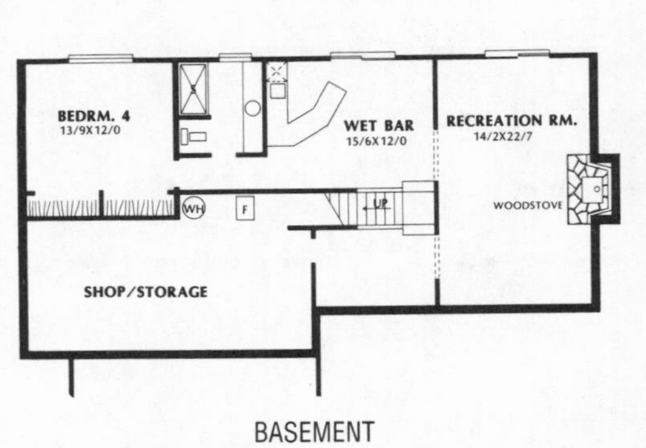

BASEMENT

Plans P-528-2A & -2D

Bedrooms: 3-4 | **Baths:** 2-3

Space:

Upper floor:	498 sq. ft.
Main floor:	1,456 sq. ft.
Total living area:	1,954 sq. ft.
Basement:	1,410 sq. ft.
Garage:	502 sq. ft.
Exterior Wall Framing:	2x6

Foundation options:
Daylight basement (Plan P-528-2D).
Crawlspace (Plan P-528-2A).
(Foundation & framing conversion diagram available — see order form.)

Blueprint Price Code:

Without basement:	B
With basement:	E

Plenty of Presence

- A stucco facade complemented by fieldstone, handsome keystones accenting the interesting window treatments and an imposing roofline give this home lots of presence.
- Inside, a two-story foyer an open stairway with a balcony overlook above provides an impressive welcome. Straight ahead, the huge family room is expanded by a vaulted ceiling, plus a tall window and a French door that frame the fireplace.
- The adjoining dining room flows into the kitchen and breakfast room, which feature an angled serving bar, lots of sunny windows and a French door that opens to a covered patio.
- The main-floor master suite is the pride of the floor plan, offering a tray ceiling, a vaulted spa bath and a spacious walk-in closet brightened by a window.
- The upper floor has two bedrooms, each with a walk-in closet, and a full bath. Abundant attic storage space is easily accessible.

Plan FB-1681

Bedrooms: 3	**Baths:** 2½
Living Area:	
Upper floor	449 sq. ft.
Main floor	1,232 sq. ft.
Total Living Area:	**1,681 sq. ft.**
Daylight basement	1,232 sq. ft.
Garage	420 sq. ft.
Storage	15 sq. ft.
Exterior Wall Framing:	2x4

Foundation Options:
Daylight basement
Slab
(Typical foundation & framing conversion diagram available—see order form.)

BLUEPRINT PRICE CODE: **B**

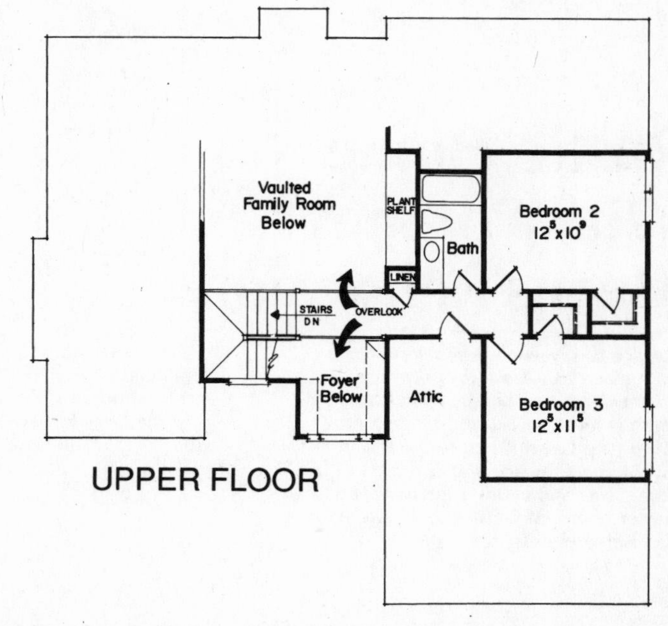

UPPER FLOOR

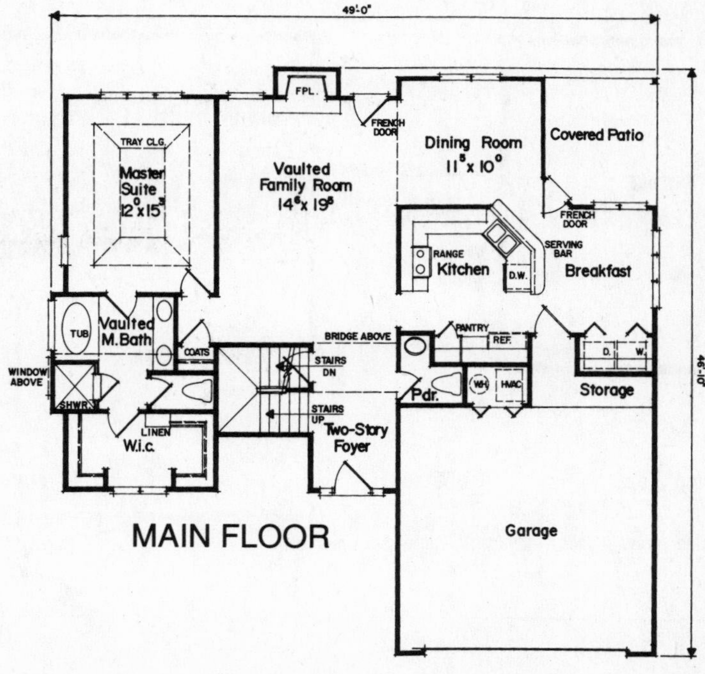

MAIN FLOOR

Rustic Home With Porches Means Relaxation

A spacious screened porch serves as a great place to eat out during warm summer days and nights, while the front porch is ideal for relaxed rocking or a swing. The Great Room to the left of the entry has a fireplace and connects to the dining area and country kitchen. The large master bedroom features a private bath and ample closets.

For entertaining large groups, the combined dining area, living room and screened porch provide lots of space. Also note the large kitchen/utility and pantry area.

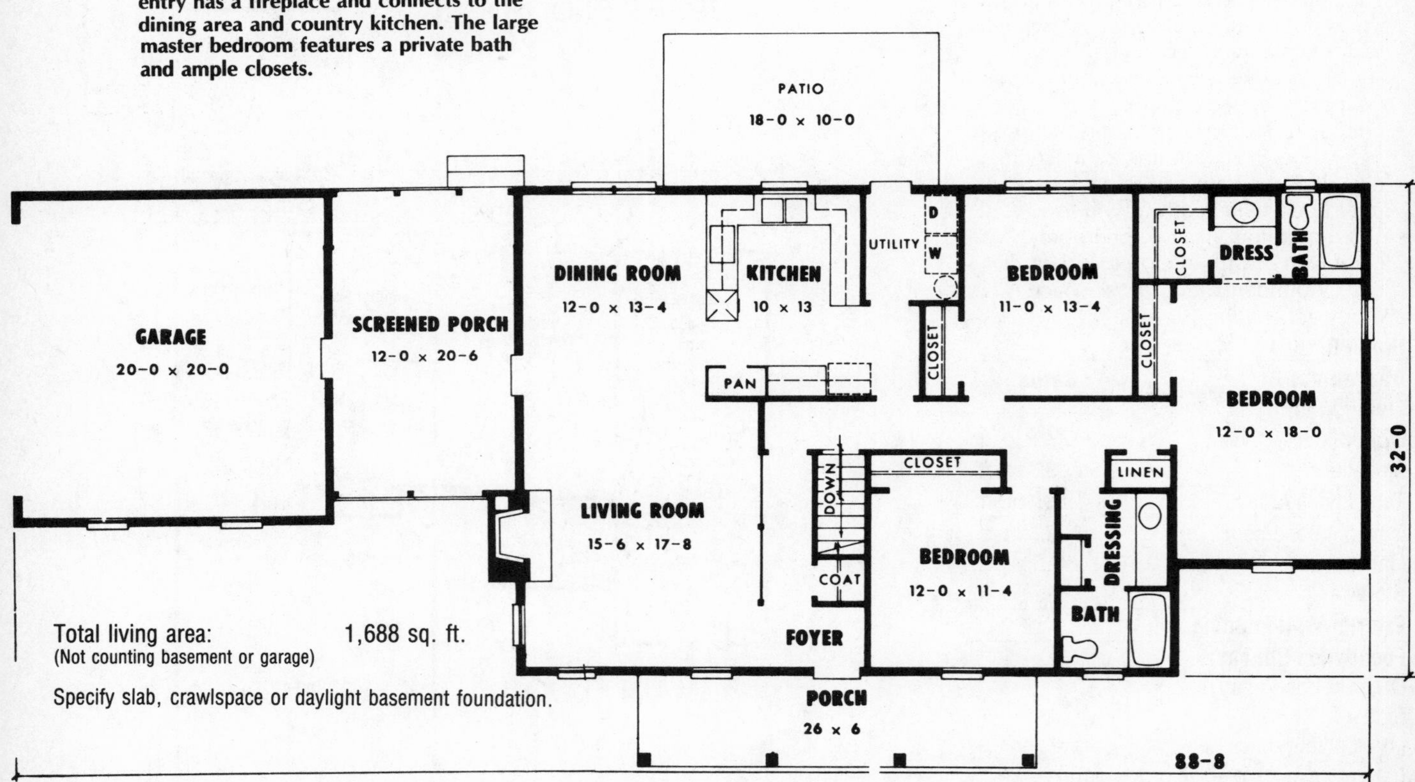

Total living area: 1,688 sq. ft.
(Not counting basement or garage)

Specify slab, crawlspace or daylight basement foundation.

Blueprint Price Code B

Plan C-7557

PRICES AND DETAILS ON PAGES 12-15

Instant Impact

- Bold rooflines, interesting angles and unusual window treatments give this stylish home lots of impact.
- Inside, high ceilings and an open floor plan maximize the home's square footage. At only 28 ft. wide, the home also is ideal for a narrow lot.
- A covered deck leads to the main entry, which features a sidelighted door, angled glass walls and a view of the striking open staircase.
- The Great Room is stunning, with its vaulted ceiling, energy-efficient woodstove and access to a large deck.
- A flat ceiling distinguishes the dining area, which shares an angled snack bar/cooktop with the step-saving kitchen. A laundry/mudroom is nearby.
- Upstairs, the master suite offers a sloped ceiling and a clerestory window. A walk-through closet leads to the private bath, which is enhanced by a skylighted, sloped ceiling.
- Linen and storage closets line the hallway leading to the smaller bedrooms, one of which has a sloped ceiling and double closets.

Plans H-1427-3A & -3B	
Bedrooms: 3	**Baths:** 2½
Living Area:	
Upper floor	880 sq. ft.
Main floor	810 sq. ft.
Total Living Area:	**1,690 sq. ft.**
Daylight basement	810 sq. ft.
Garage	409 sq. ft.
Exterior Wall Framing:	2x4
Foundation Options:	**Plan #**
Daylight basement	H-1427-3B
Crawlspace	H-1427-3A

(All plans can be built with your choice of foundation and framing. A generic conversion diagram is available. See order form.)

BLUEPRINT PRICE CODE:	**B**

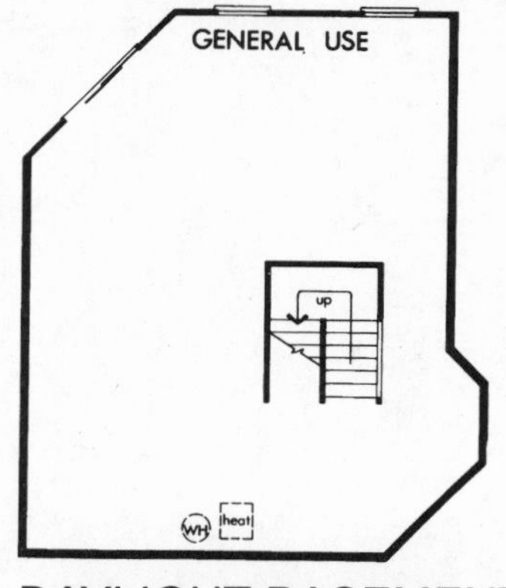

DAYLIGHT BASEMENT

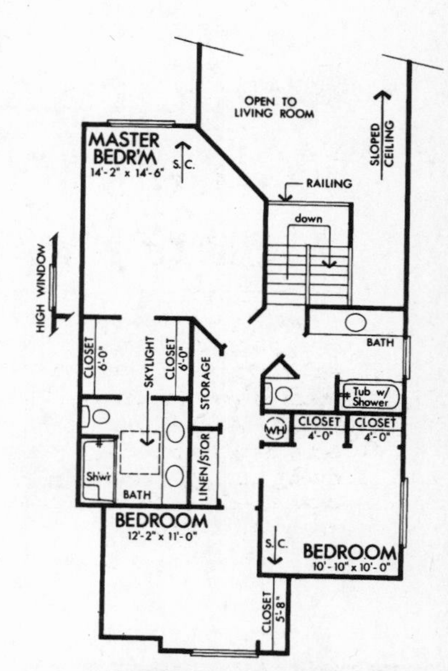

UPPER FLOOR

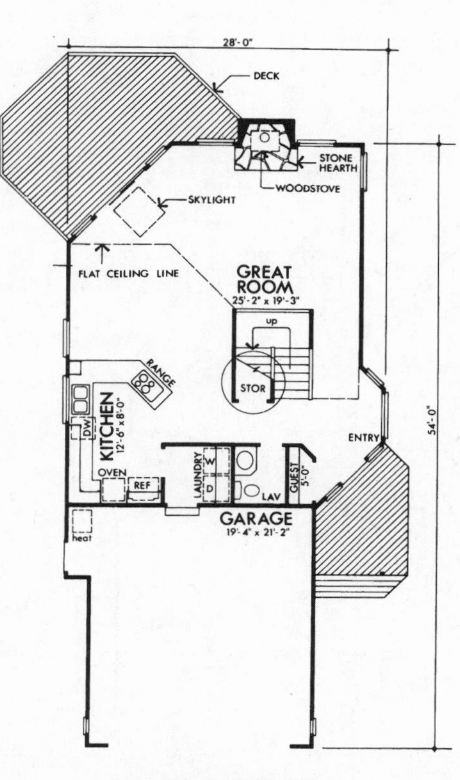

MAIN FLOOR

STAIRWAY AREA IN CRAWLSPACE VERSION

Exciting Interior Angles

- A relatively modest-looking exterior encloses an exciting interior design that's loaded with surprises.
- The Y-shaped entry directs traffic to the more formal living/dining area or to the family room or bedroom wing.
- The family room features an unusual shape, a vaulted ceiling and a fireplace.
- The living room is brightened by a bay window, and also includes a fireplace.
- The dining area, the sun room, the family room and the outdoor patios are grouped around the large kitchen.
- The roomy master suite includes a deluxe bath and a large closet.
- The daylight-basement version adds 1,275 square feet of space.

Plans P-7661-3A & -3D

Bedrooms: 2-3	**Baths:** 2
Space:	
Main floor	1,693 sq. ft.
Total Living Area	**1,693 sq. ft.**
Basement	1,275 sq. ft.
Garage	462 sq. ft.
Exterior Wall Framing	2x4
Foundation options:	**Plan #**
Daylight Basement	P-7661-3D
Crawlspace	P-7661-3A

(Foundation & framing conversion diagram available—see order form.)

Blueprint Price Code	**B**

55'-0"
54'-0"
PATIO
WALK IN WARDROBE
MASTER 13/0x15/6
VAULTED FAMILY RM. 17/0x13/6
KITCHEN 11/0x10/0
PATIO
WOODSTOVE
VAULTED SUN RM.
LINEN
LIN
PANTRY
ENTRY
DINING AREA
BEDRM. 2 10/0x10/0
DEN/ BEDRM. 3 10/0x11/6
LIVING RM. 18/4x18/4
GARAGE 21/4x21/8

MAIN FLOOR
PLAN P-7661-3A
WITH CRAWLSPACE

BAR
MASTER
DN

PLAN P-7661-3D
WITH DAYLIGHT BASEMENT

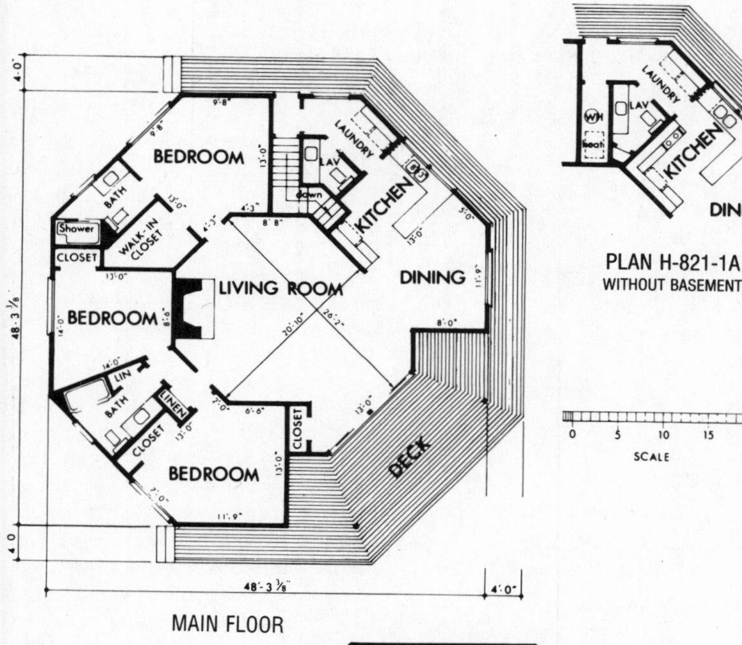

MAIN FLOOR

WH
LAV
LAUNDRY
KITCHEN
DINING

PLAN H-821-1A
WITHOUT BASEMENT

0 5 10 15 20
SCALE

Versatile Octagon

- Popular octagonal design features a secondary raised roof to allow light into the 500 sq. ft. living room.
- Unique framing design allows you to divide the living space any way you choose: left open, with 3 or more bedrooms, a den, library or other options.
- Large, winding deck can accommodate outdoor parties and guests.
- Optional basement expands recreational opportunities.

Plans H-821-1 & -1A

Bedrooms: 3	**Baths:** 2½
Space:	
Main floor:	1,699 sq. ft.
Total living area:	1,699 sq. ft.
Basement:	approx. 1,699 sq. ft.
Exterior Wall Framing:	2x4

Foundation options:
Daylight basement (Plan H-821-1).
Crawlspace (Plan H-821-1A).
(Foundation & framing conversion diagram available — see order form.)

Blueprint Price Code:	
Without basement	B
With basement	E

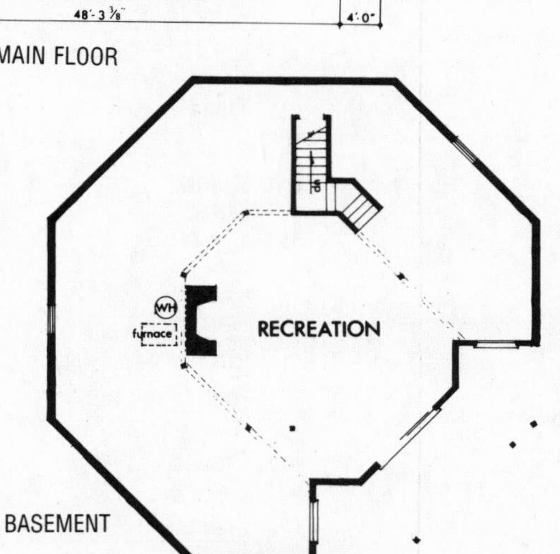

BASEMENT

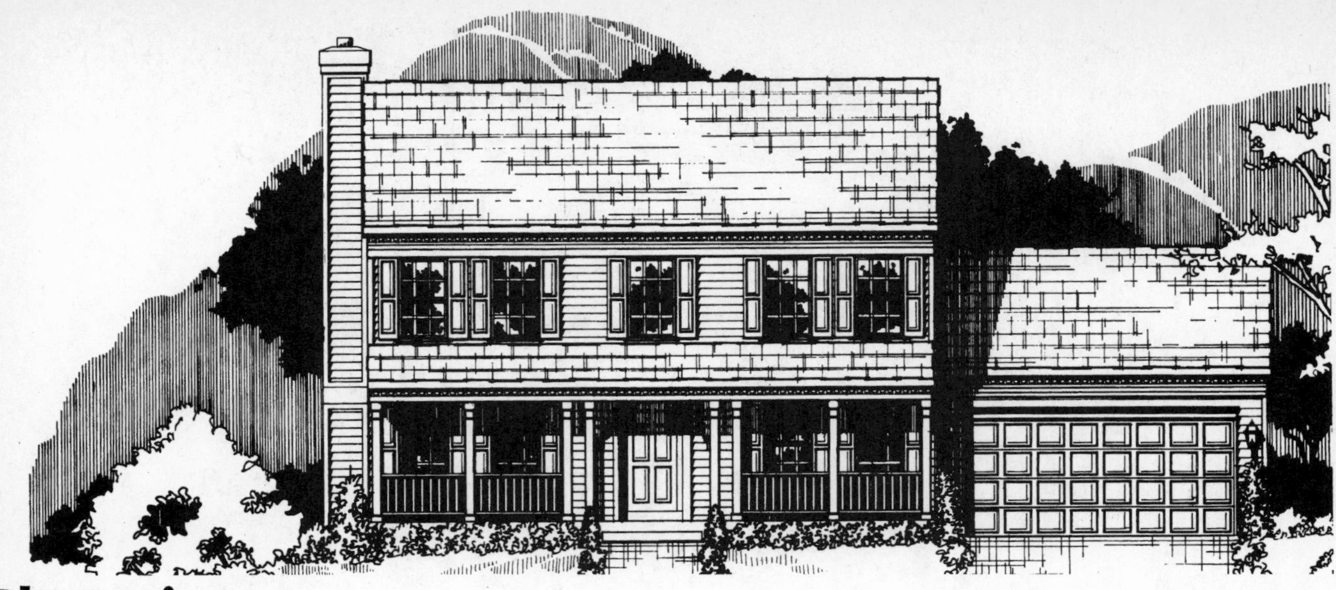

Charming Choices

- This charming farmhouse design has a simple and economical structure that can be finished with siding or brick. With four bedrooms, the home is ideal for a large or growing family.
- Comfortably sized formal spaces, open informal areas and lots of windows make the floor plan light and bright. An optional bay window in the living room and fireplace in the family room can add further ambience.
- The breakfast nook's delightful boxed bay provides a sunny site for casual dining. The adjoining kitchen has a windowed sink and easy access to the garage and to the formal dining room.
- All four bedrooms are housed on the upper floor. The master bedroom has a private bath, while the secondary bedrooms share another.

Plan CH-110-B

Bedrooms: 4	**Baths:** 2½
Living Area:	
Upper floor	860 sq. ft.
Main floor	846 sq. ft.
Total Living Area:	**1,706 sq. ft.**
Basement	834 sq. ft.
Garage	380 sq. ft.
Exterior Wall Framing:	2x4

Foundation Options:

Daylight basement
Standard basement
Crawlspace

(All plans can be built with your choice of foundation and framing. A generic conversion diagram is available. See order form.)

BLUEPRINT PRICE CODE: B

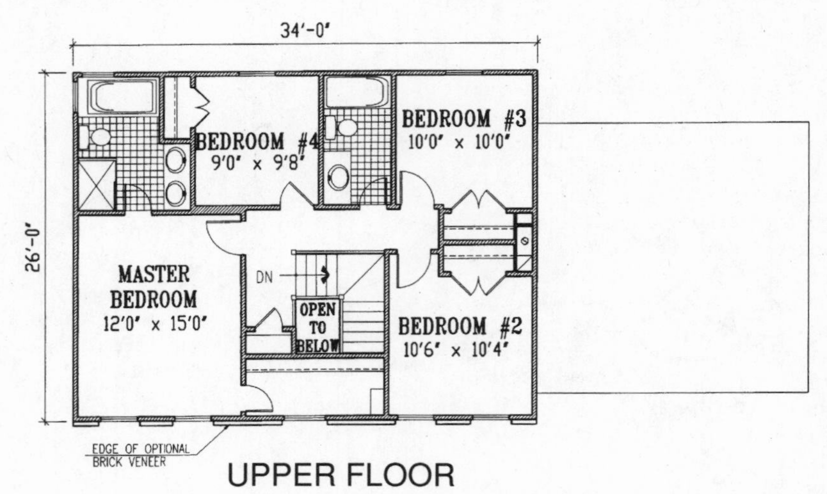

UPPER FLOOR

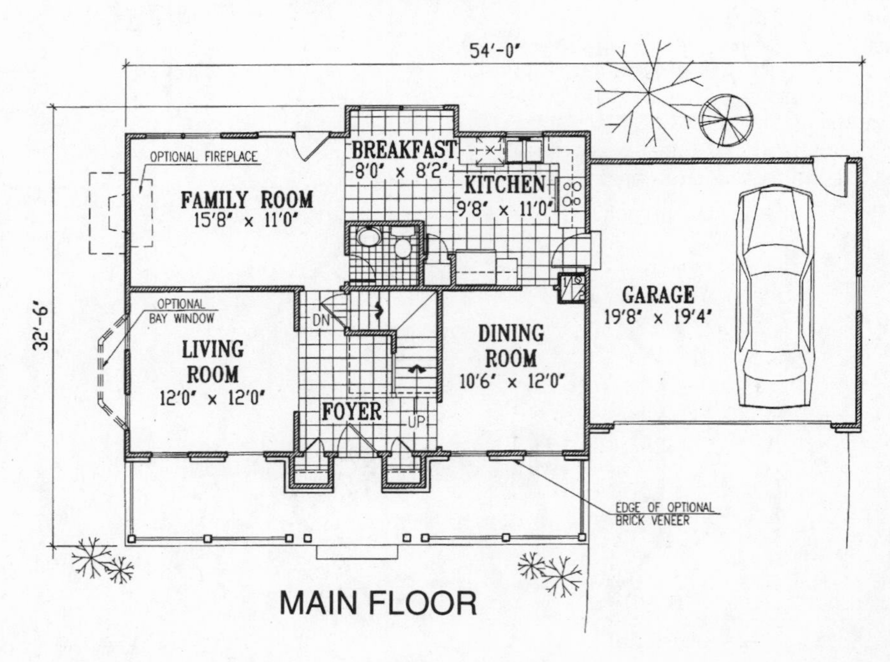

MAIN FLOOR

 TO ORDER THIS BLUEPRINT, CALL TOLL-FREE 1-800-547-5570

Plan CH-110-B

PRICES AND DETAILS ON PAGES 12-15

Very Versatile!

- You won't find a more versatile design than this one! The attractive traditional facade gives way to a dramatic rear deck, making the home suitable for a lakeside lot. With its modest width and daylight basement, the home also adapts to a narrow or sloping site.
- A nice railed porch welcomes guests into the main entry and into the Great Room straight ahead. The Great Room is enhanced by a 21-ft. vaulted ceiling, a metal fireplace and sliding glass doors to the expansive deck.
- The U-shaped kitchen offers a pantry and a serving bar.
- A convenient hall bath serves the quiet main-floor bedroom.
- Upstairs, a spacious loft allows views of the Great Room over a wood rail.
- Double doors introduce the posh master suite, which boasts a walk-in closet, a whirlpool bath and attic access.
- The loft and the master bedroom are visually expanded by 12-ft. ceilings.

Plan PI-92-373	
Bedrooms: 2	**Baths:** 2
Living Area:	
Upper floor	546 sq. ft.
Main floor	1,212 sq. ft.
Total Living Area:	**1,758 sq. ft.**
Daylight basement	1,212 sq. ft.
Garage	475 sq. ft.
Exterior Wall Framing:	2x6
Foundation Options:	
Daylight basement	
(All plans can be built with your choice of foundation and framing. A generic conversion diagram is available. See order form.)	
BLUEPRINT PRICE CODE:	**B**

REAR VIEW

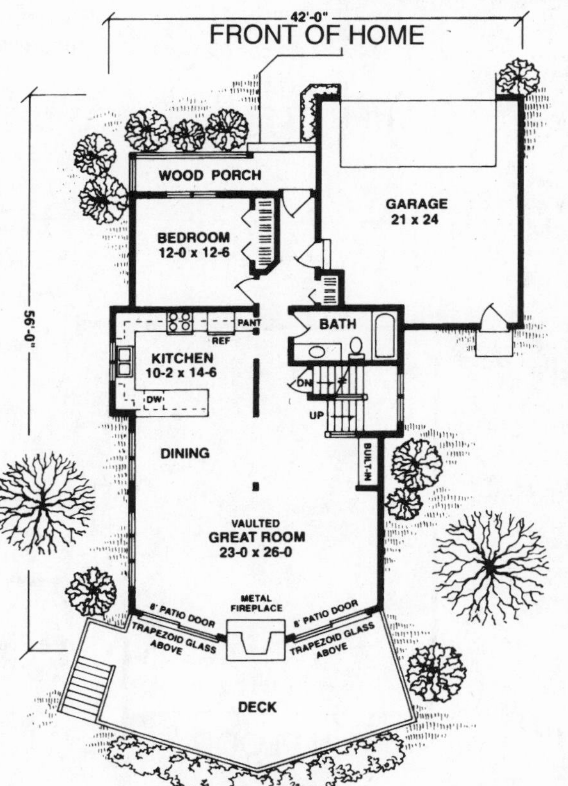

MAIN FLOOR

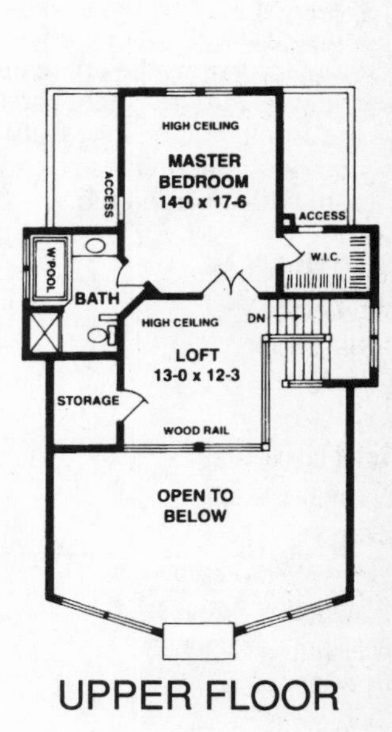

UPPER FLOOR

Class with Comfort

- Twin gables, great window treatments and the rich look of brick lend a sophisticated air to this design.
- Inside, the floor plan is comfortable and unpretentious. The foyer is open to the formal spaces, which flow freely into the casual living areas.
- The kitchen, breakfast nook and family room combine to create a highly livable area with no wasted space.
- The kitchen's angled serving bar accommodates those in the family room and in the nook. The bay-windowed nook has a convenient, space-saving laundry closet. The family room's fireplace warms the entire area.
- The upper floor is highlighted by an irresistible master suite featuring his-and-hers walk-in closets and a vaulted bath with a garden tub.

Plan FB-1744-L

Bedrooms: 4	**Baths:** 2½
Living Area:	
Upper floor	860 sq. ft.
Main floor	884 sq. ft.
Total Living Area:	**1,744 sq. ft.**
Daylight basement	884 sq. ft.
Garage	456 sq. ft.
Exterior Wall Framing:	2x4
Foundation Options:	
Daylight basement	
Crawlspace	
Slab	
(Typical foundation & framing conversion diagram available—see order form.)	
BLUEPRINT PRICE CODE:	**B**

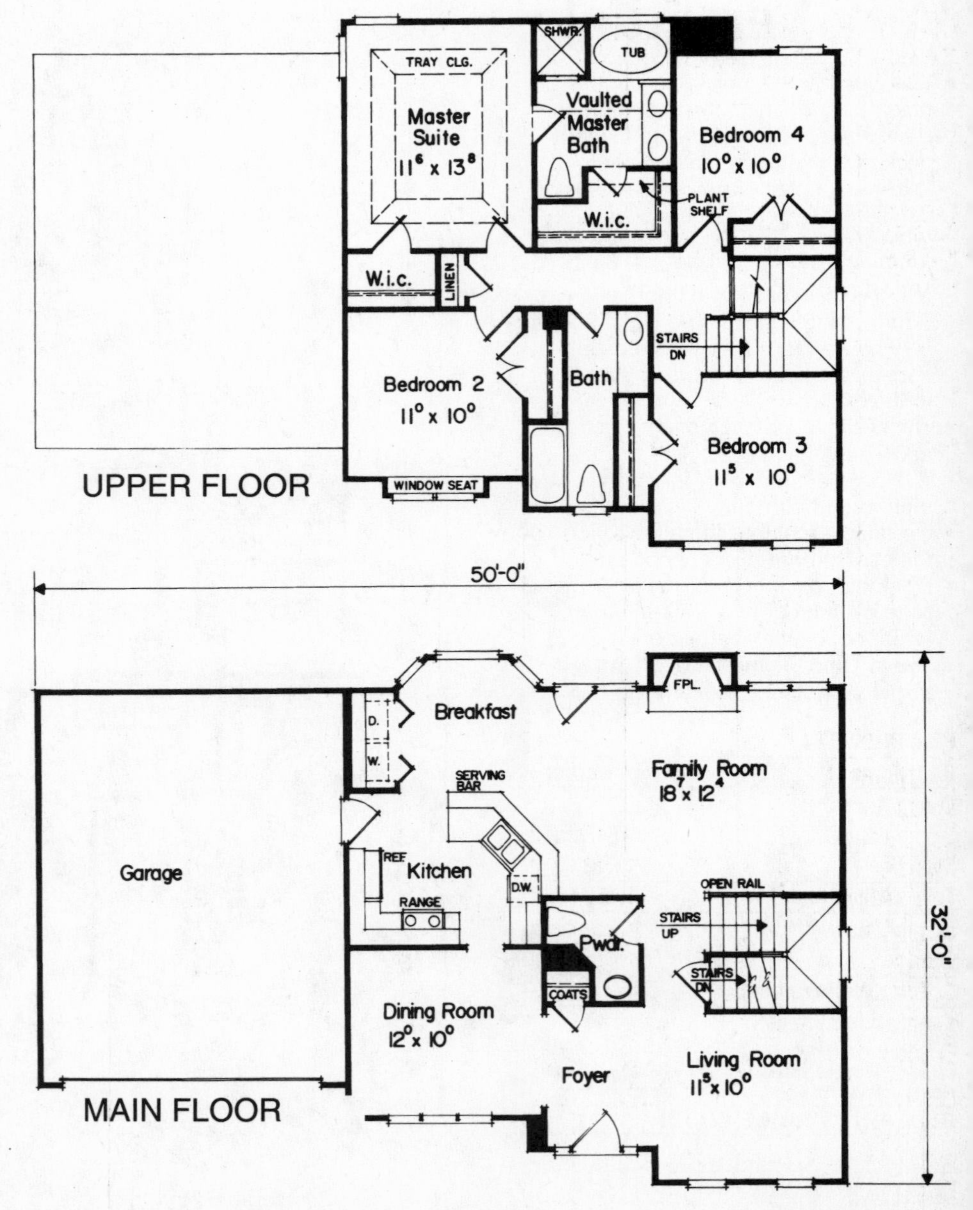

Rustic Home Offers Comfort, Economy

- Rustic and compact, this home offers economy of construction and good looks.
- The homey front porch, multi-paned windows, shutters and horizontal siding combine to create a rustic exterior.
- An L-shaped kitchen is open to the dining room and also to the living room to create a Great Room feel to the floor plan.
- The living room includes a raised-hearth fireplace.
- The main-floor master suite features a large walk-in closet and a double vanity in the master bath.
- An open two-story-high foyer leads to the second floor, which includes two bedrooms with walk-in closets and a full bath with two linen closets.

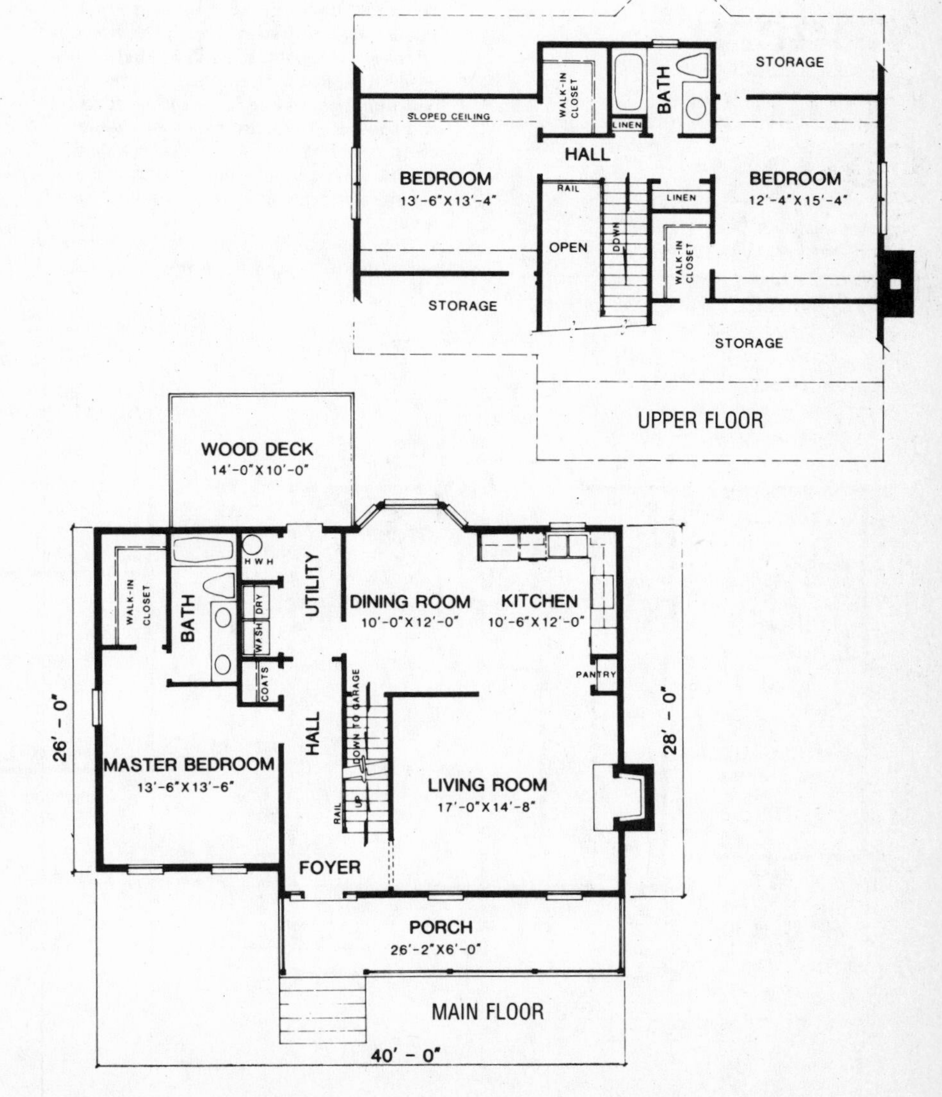

Plan C-8339	
Bedrooms: 3	**Baths:** 2
Space:	
Upper floor	660 sq. ft.
Main floor	1,100 sq. ft.
Total Living Area	**1,760 sq. ft.**
Basement	approx. 1,100 sq. ft.
Garage	Included in basement
Exterior Wall Framing	2x4
Foundation options:	
Daylight Basement	
(Foundation & framing conversion diagram available—see order form.)	
Blueprint Price Code	B

TO ORDER THIS BLUEPRINT, CALL TOLL-FREE 1-800-547-5570

Plan C-8339

PRICES AND DETAILS ON PAGES 12-15

Modern Country Cottage for Small Lot

This drive-under garage design is great for smaller lots. But even though the home is relatively compact, it's still loaded with modern features. The deluxe master bedroom has a large bath with garden tub and shower. The country kitchen/dining room combination has access to a deck out back. The large living room with fireplace is accessible from the two story foyer.

The upper floor has two large bedrooms and a full bath, and the large basement has room for two cars and expandable living areas.

This plan is available with daylight basement foundation only.

Main floor:	1,100 sq. ft.
Second floor:	664 sq. ft.
Total living area: (Not counting basement or garage)	1,764 sq. ft.
Basement:	1,100 sq. ft.

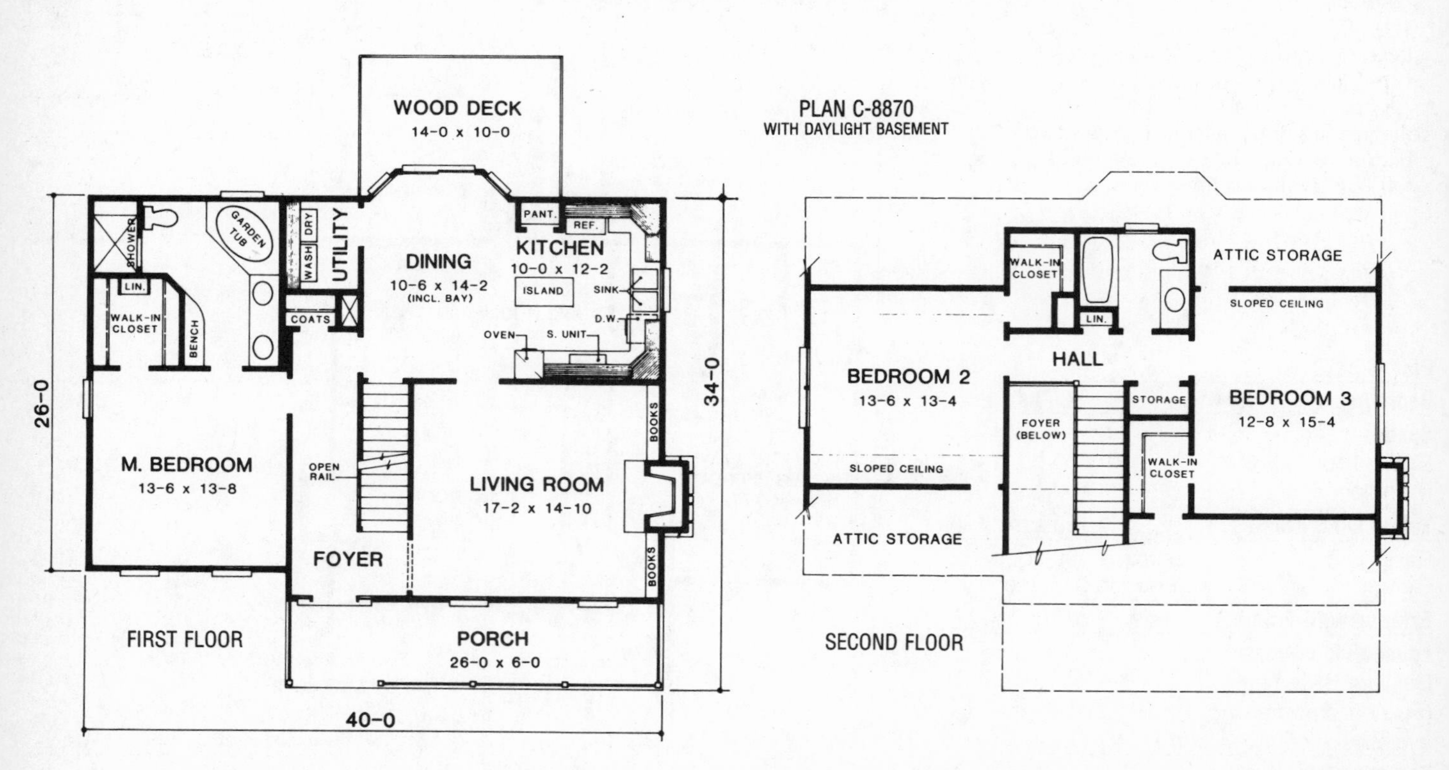

Blueprint Price Code B

Plan C-8870

Multi-Level Ideal for Difficult Lot

- This compact design is well suited for a lot that slopes steeply up to the rear.
- Massive open spaces and windows create a light and airy feeling inside.
- A mid-level landing at the entry takes you to the vaulted living room, which offers a pass-through to the kitchen; completing the main level are a dining room, two bedrooms and a bath.
- The master bedroom is an upper level loft arrangement. The attached master bath is entered through double doors and features dual vanities, large tub and separate toilet.
- The basement/lower level houses the garage, utility room and fourth bedroom.

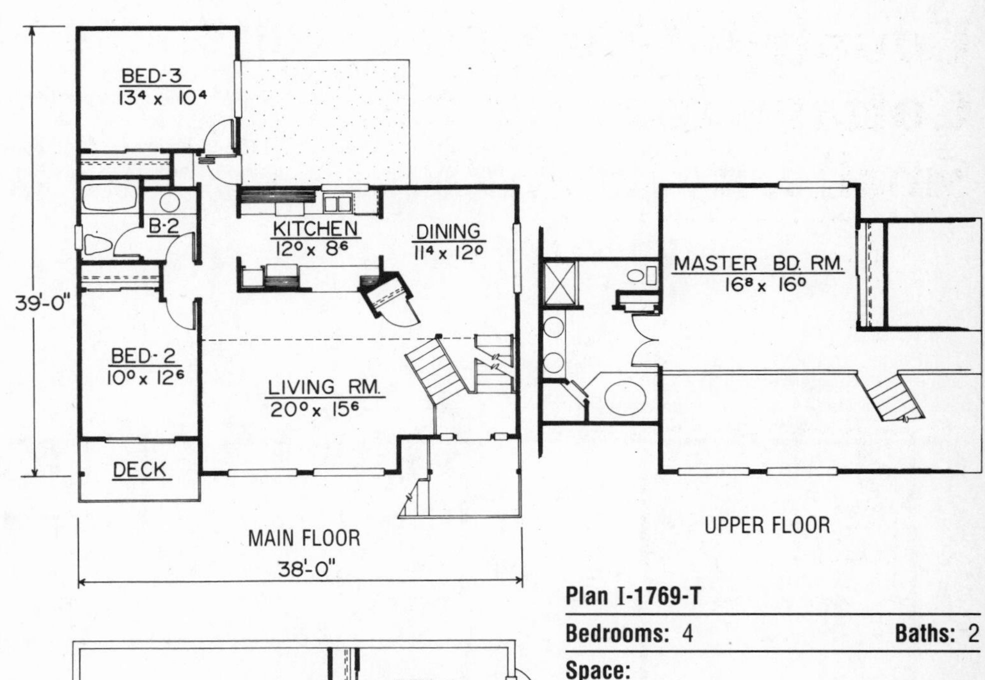

Plan I-1769-T

Bedroooms: 4	**Baths:** 2
Space:	
Upper floor:	418 sq. ft.
Main floor:	1,021 sq. ft.
Lower floor:	330 sq. ft.
Total living area:	1,769 sq. ft.
Garage:	441 sq. ft.
Exterior Wall Framing:	2x6

Foundation options:
Daylight basement.
(Foundation & framing conversion diagram available — see order form.)

Blueprint Price Code:	B

Rustic Home for Relaxed Living

A screened-in breezeway provides a cool place to dine out on warm summer days and nights, and the rustic front porch is ideal for relaxed rocking or a swing. A Great Room to the left of the entry has a fireplace and connects the dining area to the country kitchen.

The large master suite contains separate shower, garden tub, vanities and walk-in closets.

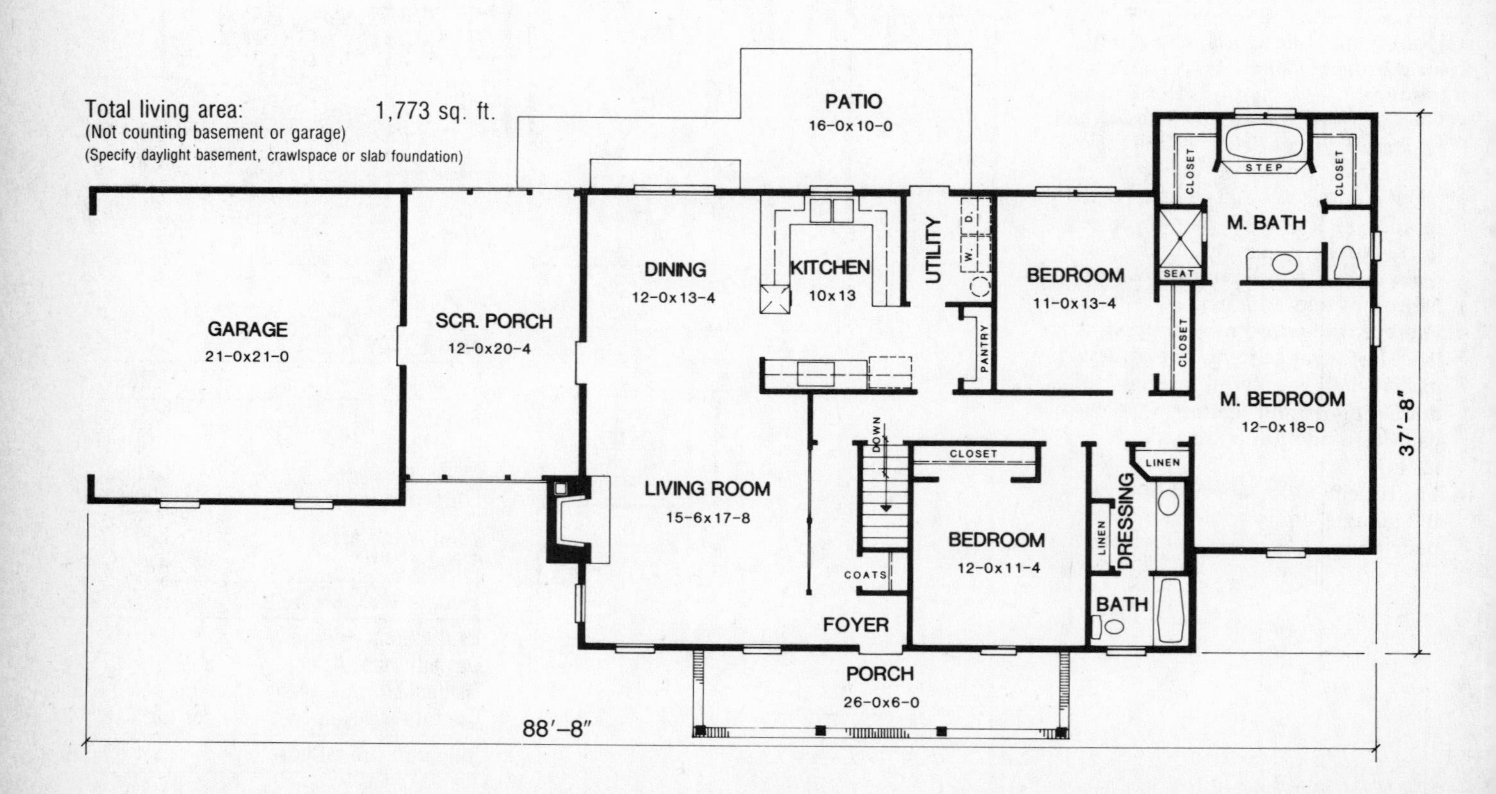

Total living area: 1,773 sq. ft.
(Not counting basement or garage)
(Specify daylight basement, crawlspace or slab foundation)

Blueprint Price Code B

Plan C-8650

TO ORDER THIS BLUEPRINT, CALL TOLL-FREE 1-800-547-5570

PRICES AND DETAILS ON PAGES 12-15

Dramatic Visual Impact

Rich brick accents this unique hillside home. The family room is sequestered on the lower level for informal, relaxed living and is overlooked not only by the nook and entry but the stairway landing above as well. The added height creates a dramatic visual impact and opens up the core of the house.

The landing itself presents an unusual decorating opportunity. It is light and spacious enough for plants, handsome book shelves, or perhaps your own art collection!

Upstairs, double doors lead into a spacious master suite getaway featuring a large walk-in closet.

This design features 2x6 exterior walls for energy efficiency.

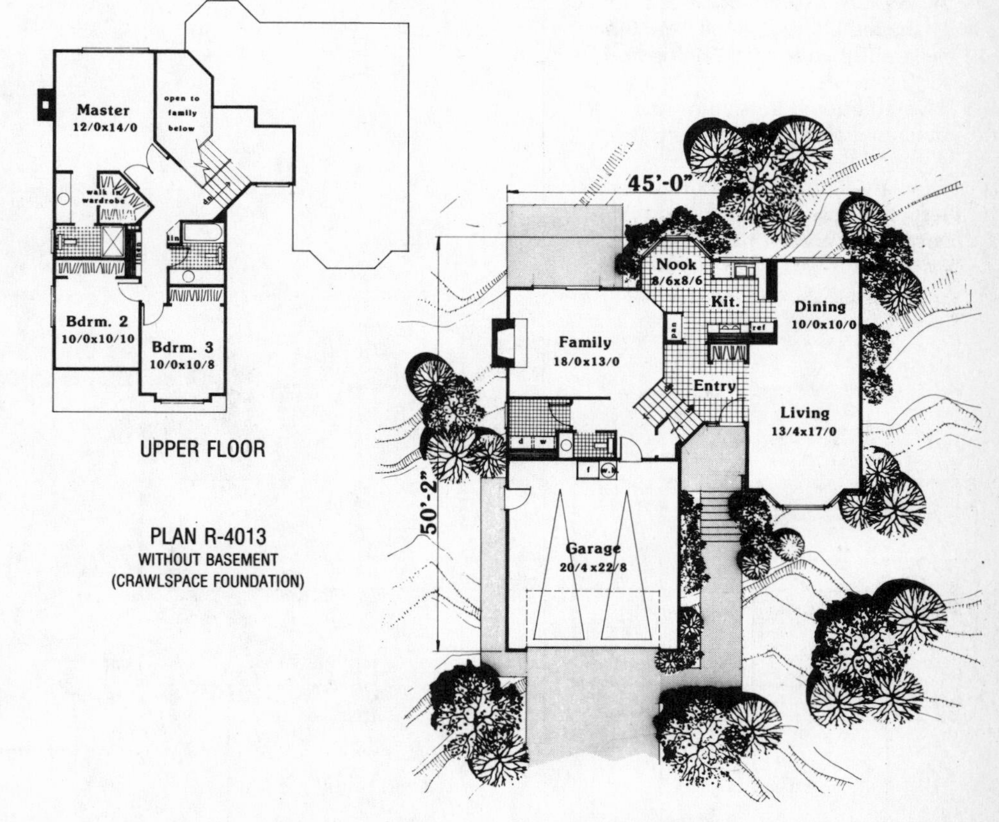

UPPER FLOOR

PLAN R-4013
WITHOUT BASEMENT
(CRAWLSPACE FOUNDATION)

MAIN FLOOR

Main floor:	1,048 sq. ft.
Upper floor:	726 sq. ft.
Total living area: (Not counting garage)	1,774 sq. ft.

Blueprint Price Code B

Plan R-4013

Popular Plan for Any Setting

- City, country, or casual living is possible in this versatile two-story design.
- A spa room and sunning area lie between the master suite and Great Room, all encased in an extended eating and viewing deck.
- U-shaped kitchen, nook, and dining area fulfill your entertaining and dining needs.
- Two additional bedrooms and a balcony hall are located on the second level.
- Daylight basement option provides a fourth bedroom, shop, and recreation area.

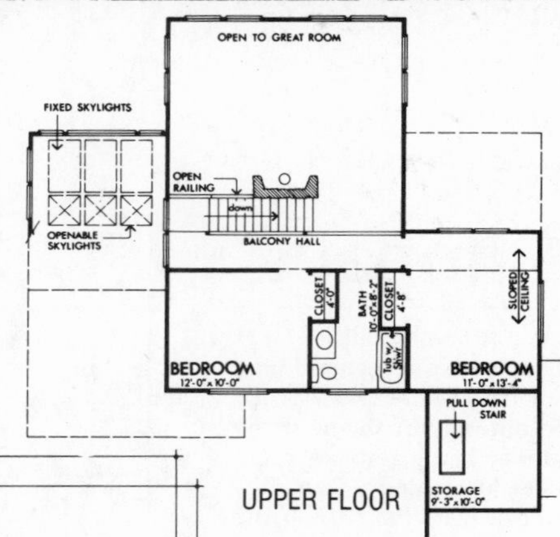

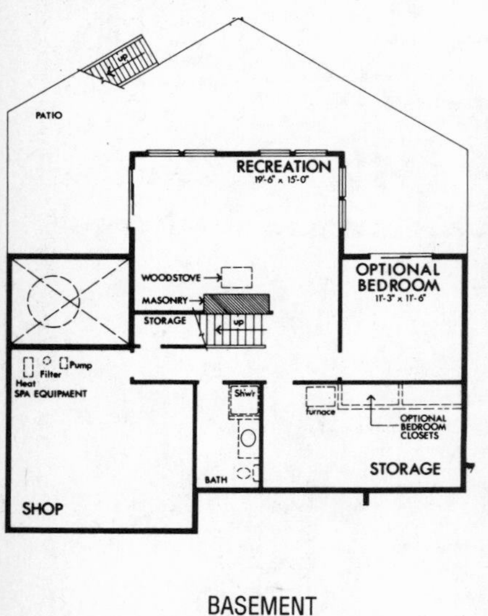

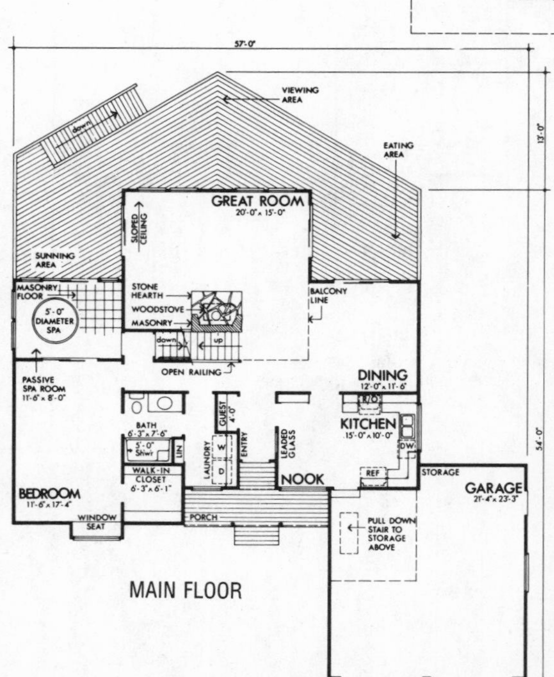

Plans H-952-1A &-1B

Bedrooms: 3-4	**Baths:** 2-3
Space:	
Upper floor:	470 sq. ft.
Main floor:	1,207 sq. ft.
Passive spa room:	102 sq. ft.
Total living area:	1,779 sq. ft.
Basement:	1,105 sq. ft.
Garage:	496 sq. ft.
Exterior Wall Framing:	2x6

Foundation options:
Daylight Basement (Plan H-952-1B).
Crawlspace (Plan H-952-1A).
(Foundation & framing conversion diagram available — see order form.)

Blueprint Price Code:

H-952-1A:	B
H-952-1B:	D

Raised Interest

- The raised living and deck areas of this design take full advantage of surrounding views. A sloping lot can be accommodated with the shown lower level retaining wall.
- The lower level foyer feels high and is bright with a two-and-a-half-story opening lighting the stairwell.
- A two-car tuck-under garage and two bedroom suites complete the lower level.
- At the top of the stairs, guests are wowed with a view into the Grand Room, with high vaulted ceiling, fireplace and atrium doors and windows overlooking the main deck.
- The kitchen incorporates a sunny good morning room.
- The master suite dazzles with a vaulted ceiling, plant shelves, a private deck and a splashy master bath.

MAIN FLOOR

Plan EOF-44	
Bedrooms: 4	**Baths:** 2
Living Area:	
Main floor	1,256 sq. ft.
Daylight basement	541 sq. ft.
Total Living Area:	**1,797 sq. ft.**
Garage	460 sq. ft.
Exterior Wall Framing:	2x4
Foundation Options:	
Daylight basement	
(Typical foundation & framing conversion diagram available—see order form.)	
BLUEPRINT PRICE CODE:	**B**

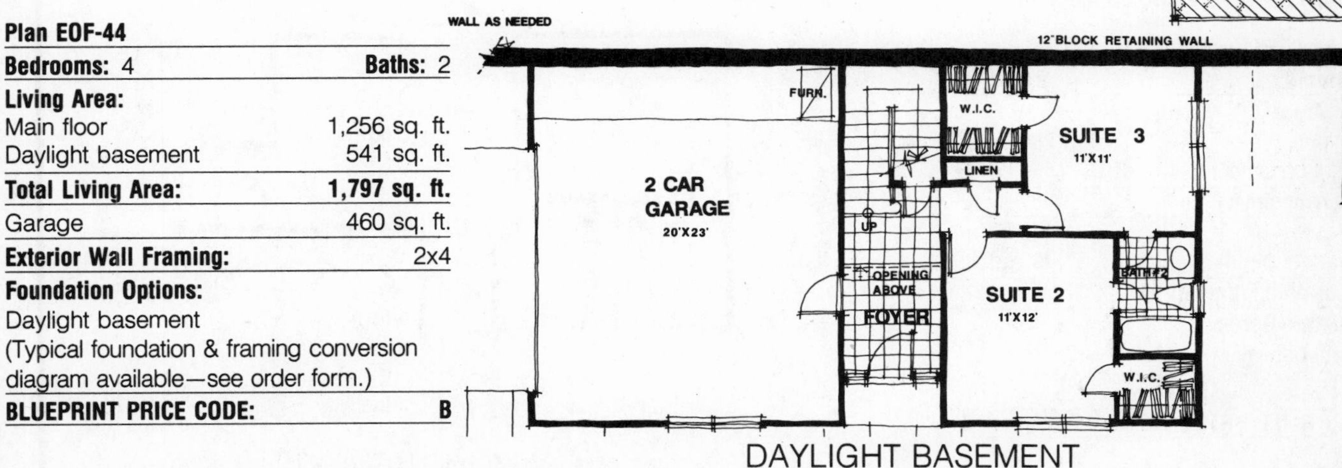

DAYLIGHT BASEMENT

Practical Perfection

- This practical split-foyer home is perfect for a growing family, offering a huge lower area for a future recreation room.
- The vaulted foyer is brightened by transom and sidelight windows.
- A few steps up from the foyer, the living room boasts a cathedral ceiling and a fireplace flanked by angled window walls, one viewing to a large rear patio and the other to a wraparound deck.
- Sliding glass doors in the adjoining dining room open to the deck. The nearby eat-in kitchen also accesses the deck and has views of the front yard.
- The large master bedroom boasts a walk-in closet and a private bathroom with glass-block walls framing the designer shower. Two more main-floor bedrooms share a full bath.
- Downstairs, the future recreation room has space set aside for a wet bar and another fireplace. Laundry facilities and garage access are also convenient.

Plan AX-97511	
Bedrooms: 3	**Baths:** 2
Living Area:	
Main floor	1,286 sq. ft.
Daylight basement (finished)	565 sq. ft.
Total Living Area:	**1,851 sq. ft.**
Utility room	140 sq. ft.
Tuck-under garage	400 sq. ft.
Exterior Wall Framing:	2x4
Foundation Options:	
Daylight basement	
(All plans can be built with your choice of foundation and framing. A generic conversion diagram is available. See order form.)	
BLUEPRINT PRICE CODE:	**B**

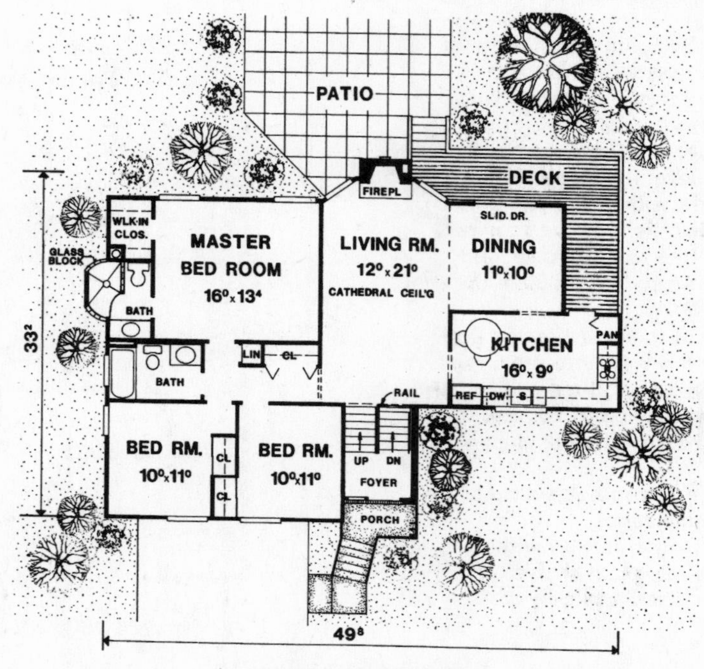

MAIN FLOOR

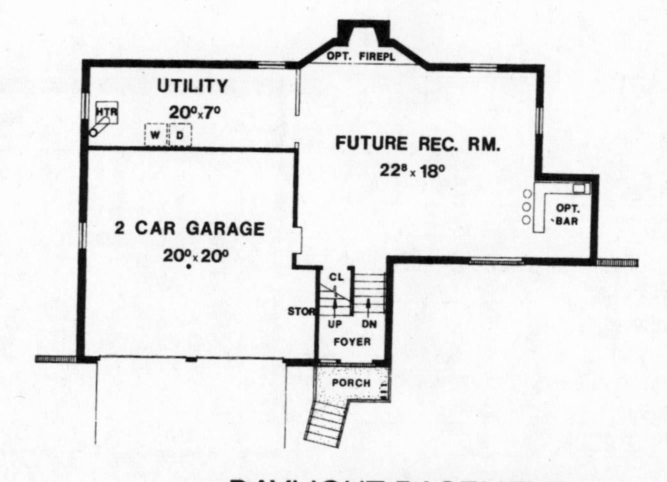

DAYLIGHT BASEMENT

Graceful Wings

- Past the inviting entrance to this graceful contemporary home, the skylighted foyer welcomes guests into the dramatic interior.
- Off the foyer, the tray-ceilinged dining room is graced by a wall of windows. The spacious country kitchen has a bright skylight and sliding glass doors to an enormous wraparound deck.
- The spectacular vaulted Great Room's 17-ft. ceiling soars to greet a row of large clerestory windows. Flanked by sliding glass doors, the exciting corner fireplace warms the area.
- The main-floor sleeping wing contains three bedrooms. The master bedroom has a tray ceiling, a private bath and two closets.
- The optional daylight basement includes a den, two more bedrooms, a family room and more!

Plan AX-97837

Bedrooms: 3+	**Baths:** 2½-3½
Living Area:	
Main floor	1,816 sq. ft.
Daylight basement (finished)	1,435 sq. ft.
Total Living Area:	**1,816/3,251 sq. ft.**
Utility and storage	381 sq. ft.
Garage	400 sq. ft.
Exterior Wall Framing:	2x4

Foundation Options:

Daylight basement
Crawlspace
Slab

(All plans can be built with your choice of foundation and framing. A generic conversion diagram is available. See order form.)

BLUEPRINT PRICE CODE: B/E

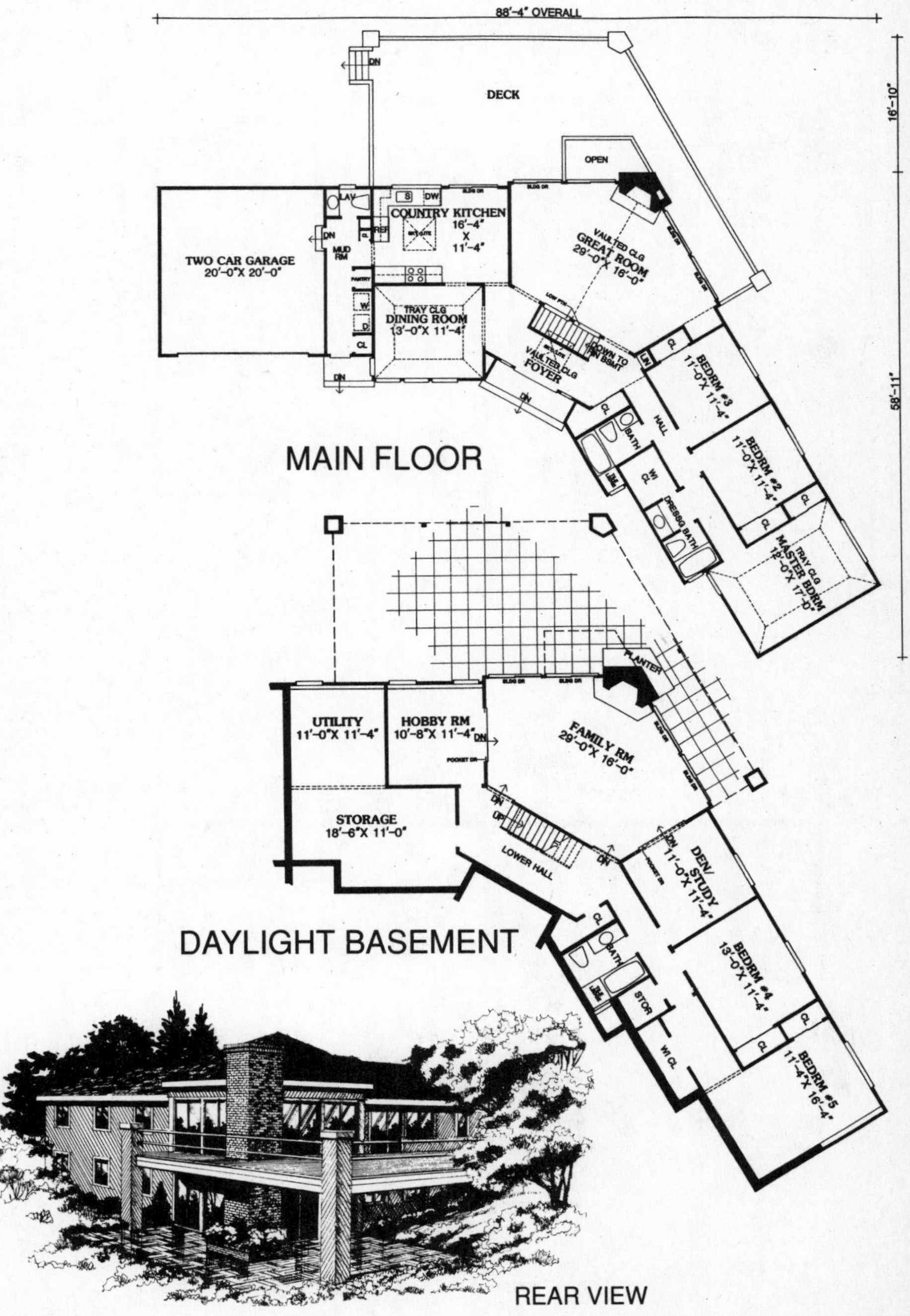

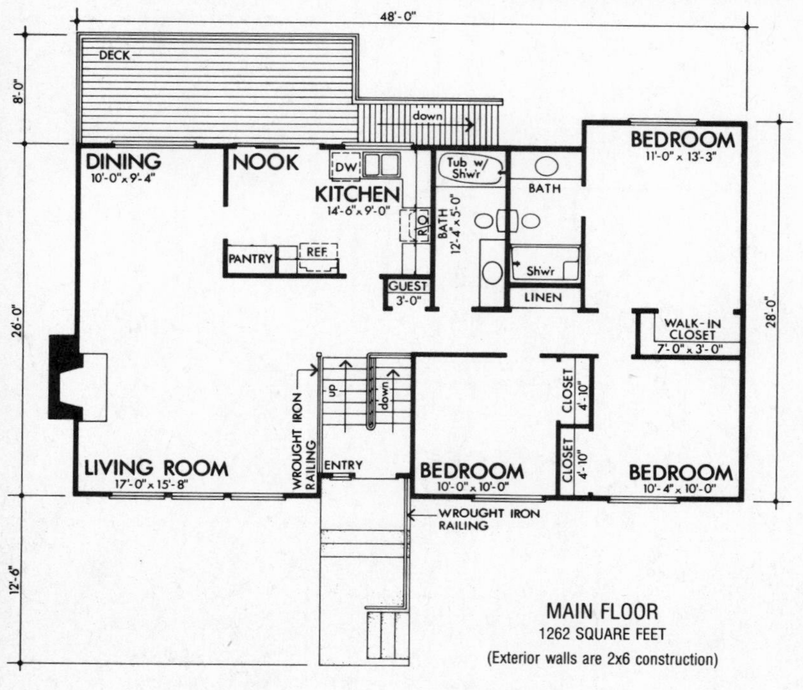

MAIN FLOOR
1262 SQUARE FEET
(Exterior walls are 2x6 construction)

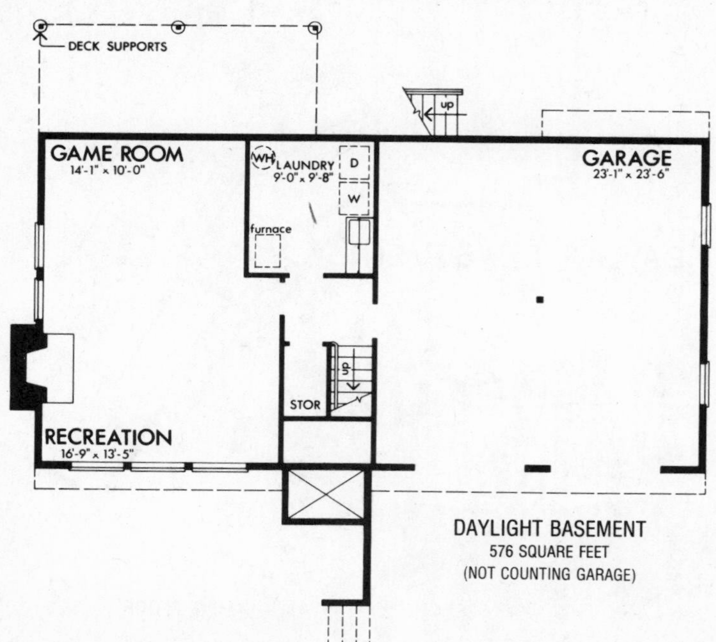

DAYLIGHT BASEMENT
576 SQUARE FEET
(NOT COUNTING GARAGE)

Economical Hillside Design

The solid, expansive, well-to-do appearance of this home plan belies the fact that it contains only 1,262 sq. ft. on the main floor and 1,152 sq. ft. on the lower level, including garage space.

This plan has a simple framing pattern, rectangular shape and straight roof line, and it lacks complicated embellishments. Even the excavation, only half as deep as usual, helps make this an affordable and relatively quick and easy house to build.

A split-level entry opens onto a landing between floors, providing access up to the main living room or down to the recreation and work areas.

The living space is large and open. The dining and living rooms combine with the stairwell to form a large visual space. A large 8'x20' deck, visible through the picture window in the dining room, adds visual expansiveness to this multi-purpose space.

The L-shaped kitchen and adjoining nook are perfect for daily food preparation and family meals, and the deck is also accessible from this area through sliding glass doors. The kitchen features a 48 cubic foot pantry closet.

The master bedroom has a complete private bathroom and oversized closet. The remaining bedrooms each have a large closet and access to a full-size bathroom.

A huge rec and game room is easily accessible from the entry, making it ideal for a home office or business.

Main floor:	1,262 sq. ft.
Lower level:	576 sq. ft.
Total living area: (Not counting garage)	1,838 sq. ft.

Blueprint Price Code B

Plan H-1332-5

PRICES AND DETAILS ON PAGES 12-15

Three Bedrooms in Daylight Basement

- Front porch offers warm welcome to vaulted entry area.
- Main floor offers plenty of space for family living and entertaining.
- Lower level provides three bedrooms, with the master suite including a private bath and walk-in closet.

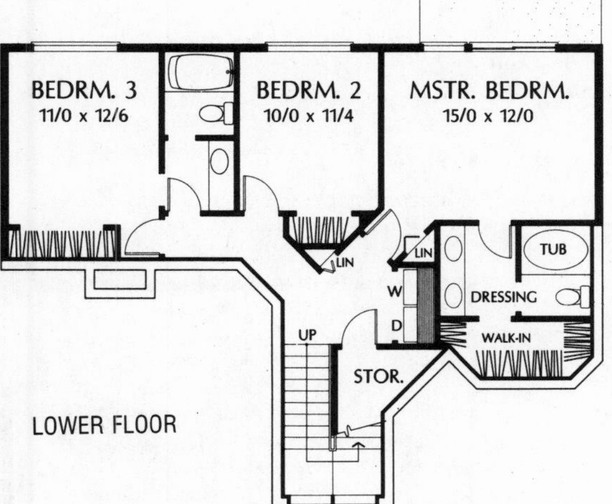

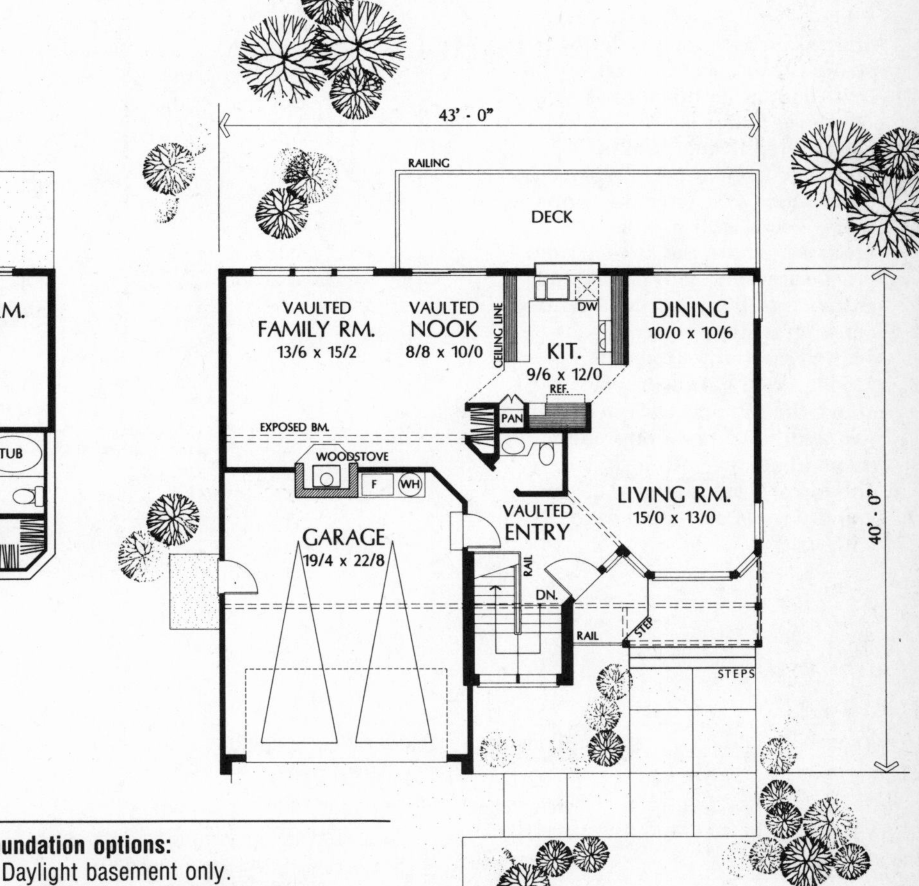

Plan P-7725-2D

Bedrooms: 3	**Baths:** 2½
Space:	
Main floor:	921 sq. ft.
Lower floor:	921 sq. ft.
Total living area:	1,842 sq. ft.
Garage:	438 sq. ft.
Exterior Wall Framing:	2x6

Foundation options:
Daylight basement only.
(Foundation & framing conversion diagram available — see order form.)

Blueprint Price Code: B

TO ORDER THIS BLUEPRINT, CALL TOLL-FREE 1-800-547-5570

Plan P-7725-2D

PRICES AND DETAILS ON PAGES 12-15

Spirited Split

- A lovely front porch, expressed timber and ascending exterior stairs create an anticipation that is well rewarded inside this three-bedroom split-level.
- The vaulted living room off the foyer has a handsome fireplace and front window; it joins the formal dining room with wet bar.
- Also vaulted are the kitchen and breakfast room, with pantry and entrance to the wrapping rear deck.
- Up several steps is the elegant vaulted master bedroom and private skylit bath with plant shelf above the tub and walk-in closet; two additional bedrooms and a second bath are also included.
- The lower level offers a half bath, laundry room and a bonus area with bar.

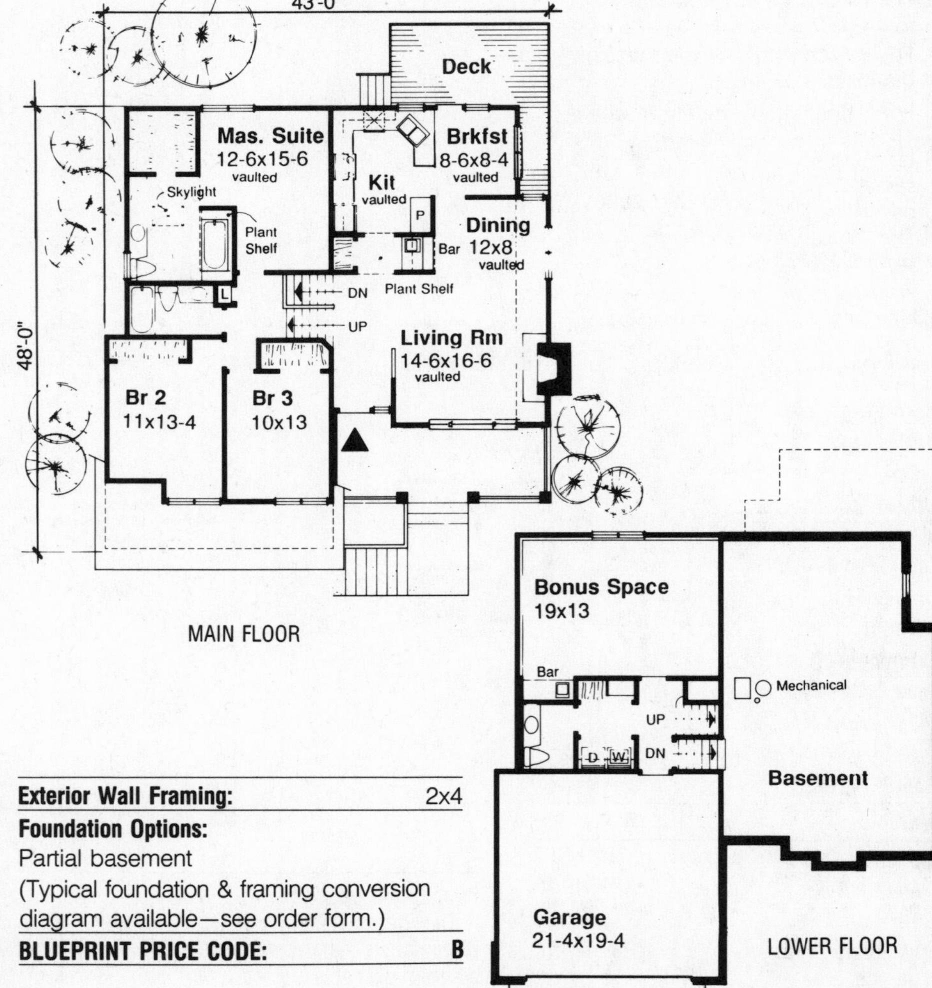

Plan B-89032

Bedrooms: 3	**Baths:** 2½
Living Area:	
Main floor	1,424 sq. ft.
Lower floor	150 sq. ft.
Bonus space	273 sq. ft.
Total Living Area:	**1,847 sq. ft.**
Partial basement	575 sq. ft.
Garage	412 sq. ft.

Exterior Wall Framing:	2x4
Foundation Options:	
Partial basement	
(Typical foundation & framing conversion diagram available—see order form.)	
BLUEPRINT PRICE CODE:	**B**

PRICES AND DETAILS ON PAGES 12-15

Two-Story Great Room

- An expansive two-story-high Great Room with an oversized hearth and high transom windows highlights this updated traditional design.
- The cozy front porch and bright, open foyer welcome visitors.
- The nice-sized dining room opens to the backyard and is nestled between the Great Room and the efficient island kitchen. This trio of rooms creates a large, open expanse for a dramatic setting. The spacious kitchen boasts a pantry and windows above the sink.
- The main-floor master suite is in a separate wing for privacy and features a whirlpool tub and a separate shower.
- Upstairs, a balcony joins two bedrooms and a hall bath. The balcony overlooks the Great Room and the foyer.

Plan PI-92-510

Bedrooms: 3	**Baths:** 2½
Living Area:	
Upper floor	574 sq. ft.
Main floor	1,298 sq. ft.
Total Living Area:	**1,872 sq. ft.**
Daylight basement	1,298 sq. ft.
Garage	660 sq. ft.
Exterior Wall Framing:	2x6
Foundation Options:	
Daylight basement	
(Typical foundation & framing conversion diagram available—see order form.)	
BLUEPRINT PRICE CODE:	**B**

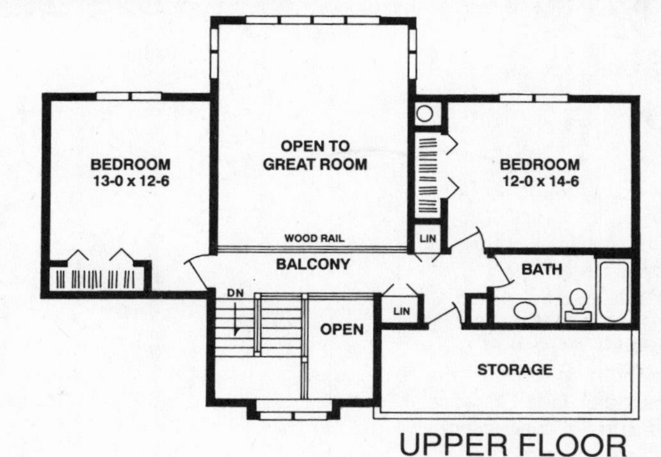

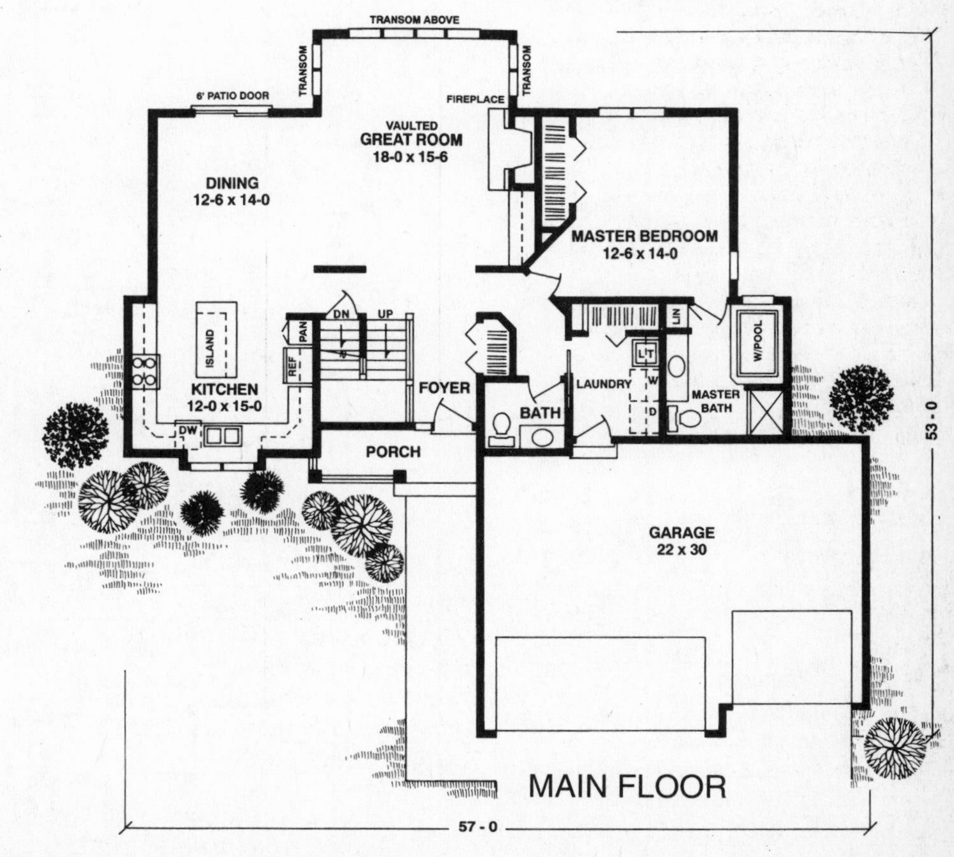

Customize Your Floor Plan!

- An optional bonus room and a choice between a loft or a bedroom allow you to customize the floor plan of this striking two-story traditional.
- The vaulted foyer leads guests past a handy powder room and directly into the vaulted family room straight ahead or into the formal dining room on the right. A beautiful open-railed staircase pleasantly breaks up the spaces while giving more privacy to the kitchen and the breakfast room.
- The sunny breakfast room is open to the island kitchen. A pantry closet, loads of counter space and direct access to the laundry room and the garage add to the kitchen's efficiency.
- The main-floor master suite is a treasure, with its tray ceiling and vaulted, amenity-filled master bath.
- Upstairs, two bedrooms, a full bath and an optional loft as well as a bonus room provide plenty of opportunity for expansion and customization.

Plan FB-1874	
Bedrooms: 3+	**Baths:** 2½
Living Area:	
Upper floor	554 sq. ft.
Main floor	1,320 sq. ft.
Bonus room	155 sq. ft.
Total Living Area:	**2,029 sq. ft.**
Daylight basement	1,320 sq. ft.
Garage	240 sq. ft.
Storage	38 sq. ft.
Exterior Wall Framing:	2x4
Foundation Options:	
Daylight basement	
(Typical foundation & framing conversion diagram available—see order form.)	
BLUEPRINT PRICE CODE:	C

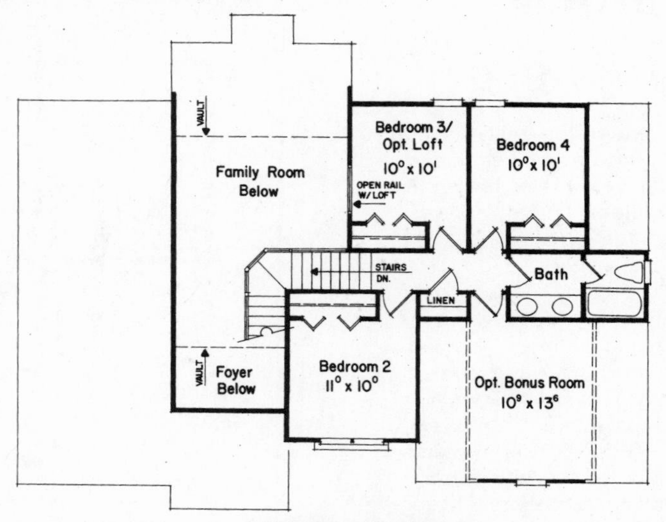

UPPER FLOOR

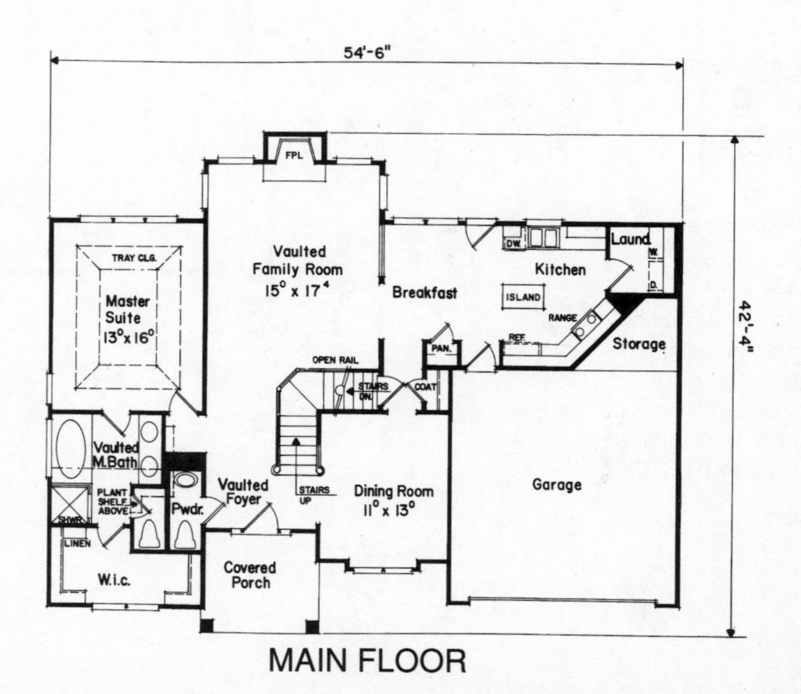

MAIN FLOOR

Split-Level for Side-to-Side Slope

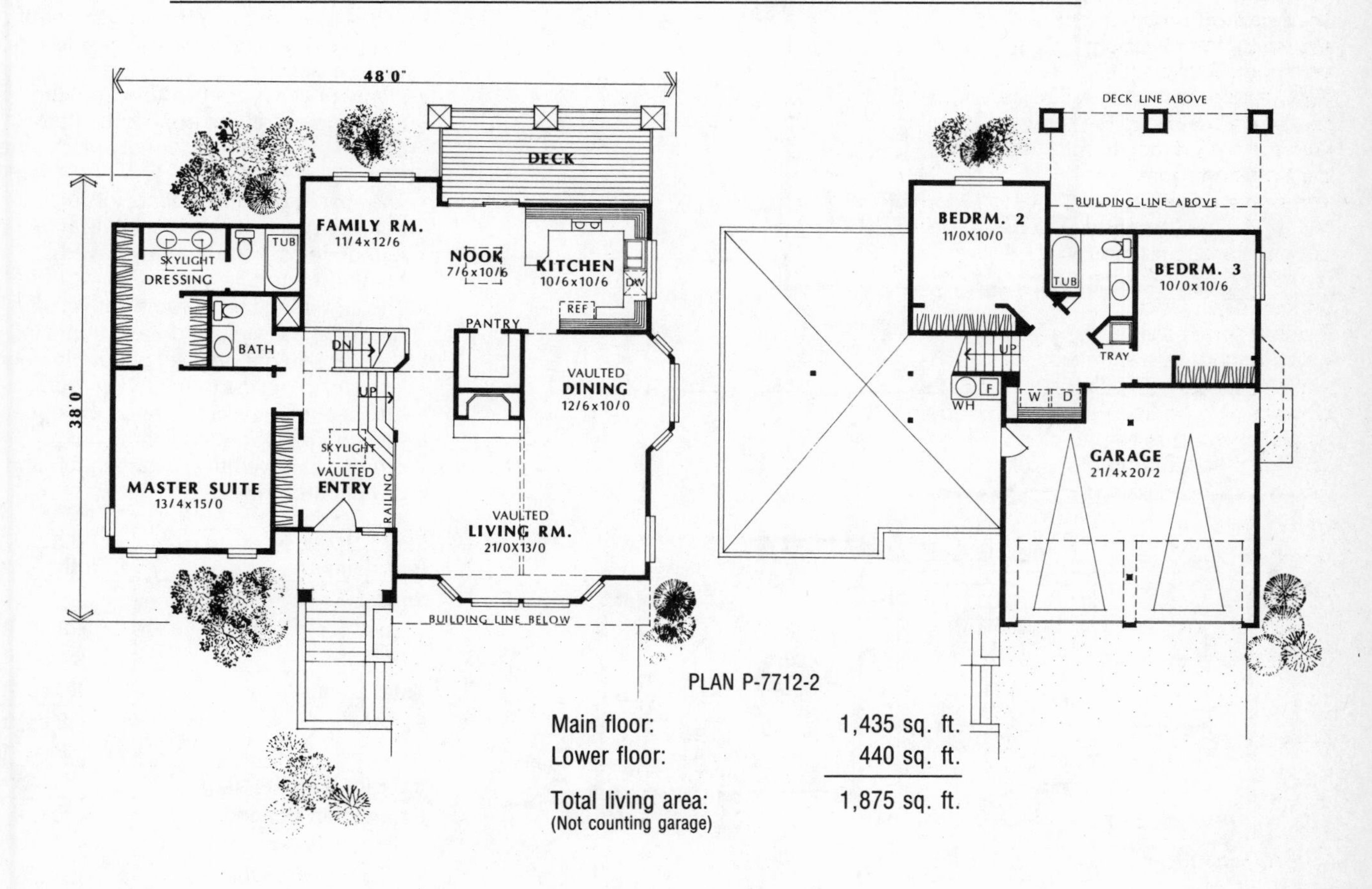

PLAN P-7712-2

Main floor:	1,435 sq. ft.
Lower floor:	440 sq. ft.
Total living area: (Not counting garage)	1,875 sq. ft.

Blueprint Price Code B

Plan P-7712-2

Exemplary Colonial

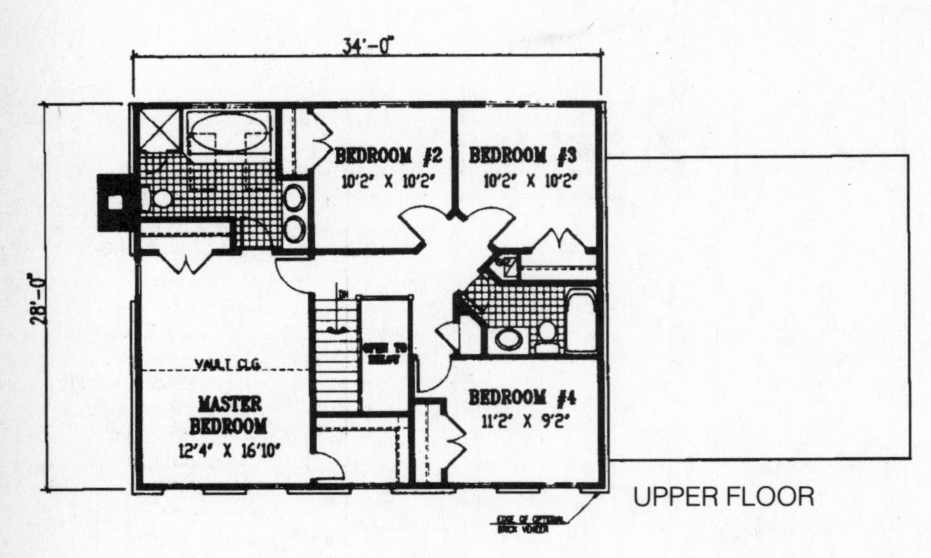

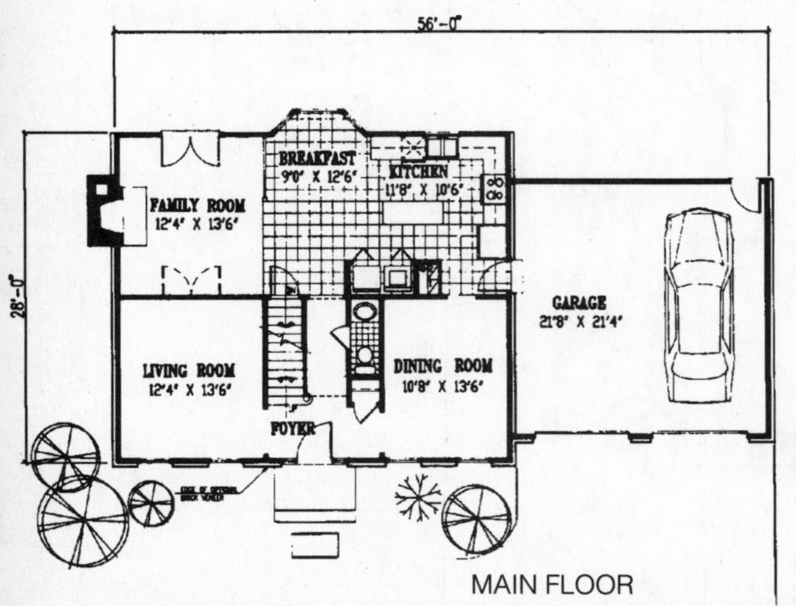

- Inside this traditionally designed home is an exciting floor plan for today's lifestyles.
- The classic center-hall arrangement of this Colonial allows easy access to all living areas.
- Plenty of views are possible from the formal rooms at the front of the home, as well as from the informal areas at the rear.
- The spacious kitchen offers lots of counter space, a handy work island, a laundry closet and a sunny bayed breakfast nook.
- The adjoining family room shows off a fireplace and elegant double doors to the rear. An optional set of double doors offers easy access to the living room.
- The beautiful master suite on the upper level boasts a vaulted ceiling, two closets, twin vanities, a garden tub and a separate shower.

Plan CH-100-A

Bedrooms: 4	**Baths:** 2 ½
Space:	
Upper floor	923 sq. ft.
Main floor	965 sq. ft.
Total Living Area	**1,888 sq. ft.**
Basement	952 sq. ft.
Garage	462 sq. ft.
Exterior Wall Framing	2x4

Foundation options:
Standard Basement
Daylight Basement
Crawlspace
(Foundation & framing conversion diagram available—see order form.)

Blueprint Price Code	B

P-524-5D Exterior

P-524-2D Exterior

Spacious Great Room

- This same floor plan is available with two different exterior treatments, as illustrated.
- In either case, a spacious Great Room is the highlight, with its vaulted ceiling, wide windows and sliding glass doors which open to a deck, and to the view beyond.
- The dining room and kitchen also feature vaulted ceilings.
- A loft room adds another sleeping area, and the daylight basement offers even more usable space.

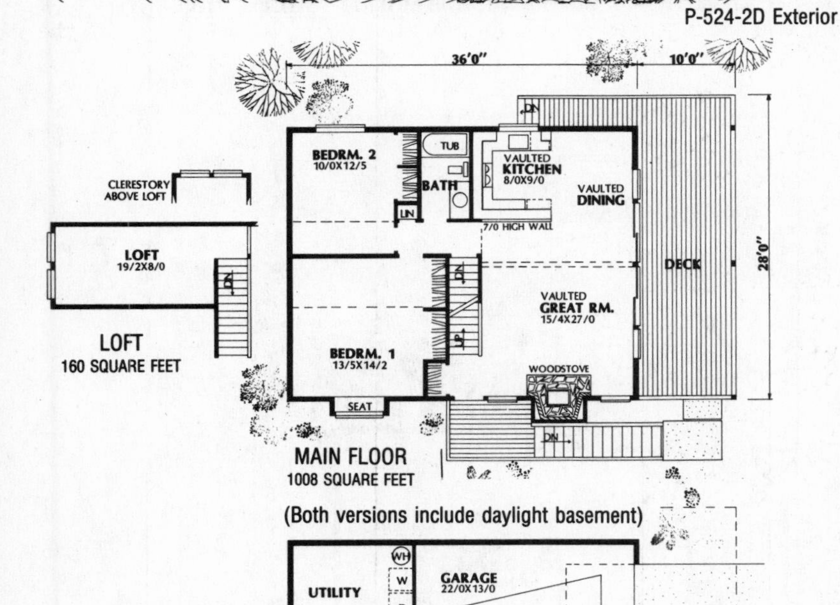

LOFT
160 SQUARE FEET

MAIN FLOOR
1008 SQUARE FEET

(Both versions include daylight basement)

BASEMENT
FLOOR AREA 722 SQUARE FEET
(Not counting garage)

Plans P-524-2D & -5D

Bedrooms: 2+	**Baths:** 1
Space:	
Loft:	160 sq. ft.
Main floor:	1,008 sq. ft.
Lower level:	722 sq. ft.
Total living area:	1,890 sq. ft.
Garage:	286 sq. ft.
Exterior Wall Framing:	2x6

Foundation options:
Daylight basement.
(Foundation & framing conversion diagram available — see order form.)

Blueprint Price Code:	B

Playful Floor Plan

- High, hip roofs and a recessed entry give this home a smart-looking exterior. A dynamic floor plan—punctuated with angled walls, high ceilings and playful window treatments—gives the home an exciting interior.
- The sunken Great Room, the circular dining room and the angled island kitchen are the heartbeat of the home. The Great Room offers a 14-ft. vaulted ceiling, a fireplace, a built-in corner entertainment center and tall arched windows overlooking the backyard.
- An angled railing separates the Great Room from the open kitchen and dining room. An atrium door next to the glassed-in dining area leads to the backyard. The kitchen includes an island snack bar and a garden window.
- The master bedroom is nestled into one corner for quiet and privacy. This deluxe suite features two walk-in closets and a luxurious whirlpool bath.
- An extra-large laundry area, complete with a clothes-folding counter and a coat closet, is accessible from the three-car garage.
- The home is expanded by 9-ft. ceilings throughout, with the exception of the vaulted Great Room.

Plan PI-90-435

Bedrooms: 3	**Baths:** 2
Living Area:	
Main floor	1,896 sq. ft.
Total Living Area:	**1,896 sq. ft.**
Basement	1,889 sq. ft.
Garage	667 sq. ft.
Exterior Wall Framing:	2x6

Foundation Options:

Daylight basement

Standard basement

(All plans can be built with your choice of foundation and framing. A generic conversion diagram is available. See order form.)

BLUEPRINT PRICE CODE: B

68'

Atrium Dr.

Vaulted Ceiling

Sunken Great Room 16'-6" x 18'

F.P.

Dining Room 14' x 11'

Master Bedroom 13' x 17'

Snack Bar

DW

Whirlpool

Lin.

Pantry

Kitchen 13' x 14'

Foyer

D

W

Lin.

Bedroom 11' x 11'

Bedroom 10'-6" x 15'

3 Car Garage 29' x 23'

44'

MAIN FLOOR

TO ORDER THIS BLUEPRINT, CALL TOLL-FREE 1-800-547-5570

Plan PI-90-435

PRICES AND DETAILS ON PAGES 12-15

CH-210-B

Alternate Exteriors

- Timeless exterior detailing and a functional, cost-effective interior are found in this traditional home.
- The kitchen, bayed breakfast room and vaulted family room with skylights and fireplace flow together to form the heart of the home.
- Lots of light filters into the front-facing formal living room.
- Upstairs, the master suite boasts a vaulted ceiling, large walk-in closet and private luxury bath.
- For the flavor of a full, covered front porch, Plan CH-210-B should be your choice.

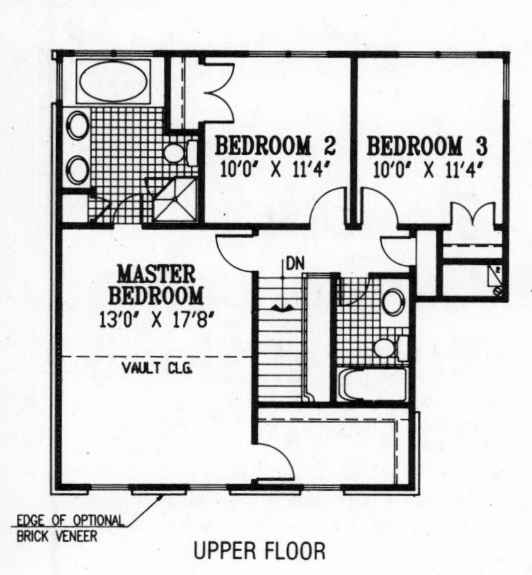

UPPER FLOOR

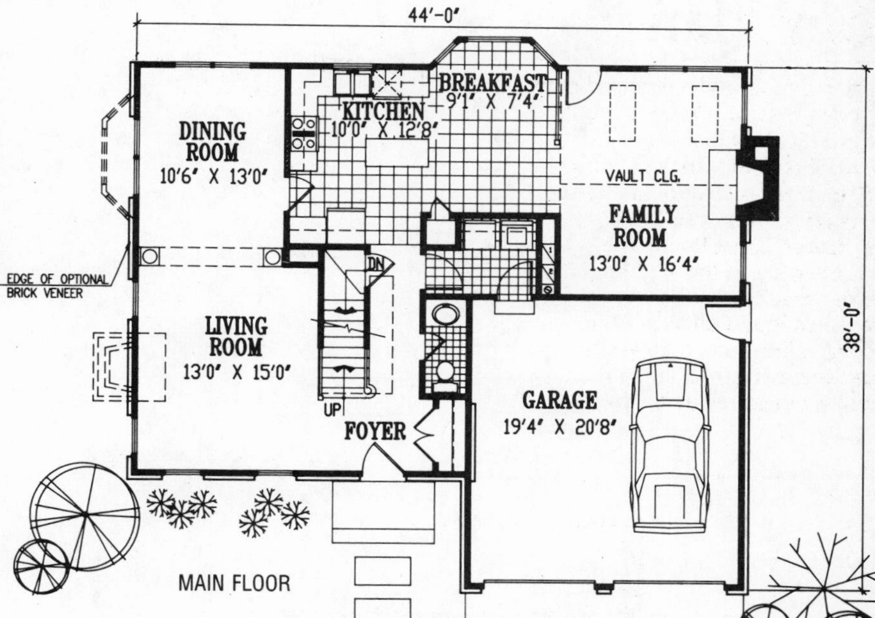

MAIN FLOOR

Plan CH-210-A & -B	
Bedroms: 3	**Baths:** 2½
Space:	
Upper floor	823 sq. ft.
Main floor	1,079 sq. ft.
Total Living Area	**1,902 sq. ft.**
Basement	978 sq. ft.
Garage	400 sq. ft.
Exterior Wall Framing	2x4
Foundation options:	
Standard Basement	
Daylight Basement	
Crawlspace	
(Foundation & framing conversion diagram available—see order form.)	
Blueprint Price Code	B

CH-210-A

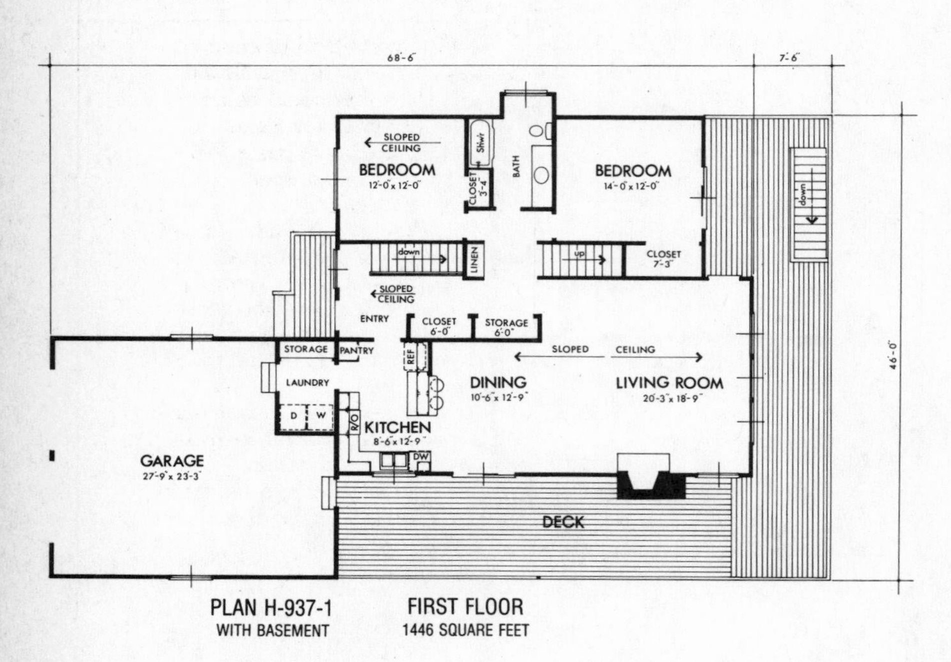

PLAN H-937-1
WITH BASEMENT

FIRST FLOOR
1446 SQUARE FEET

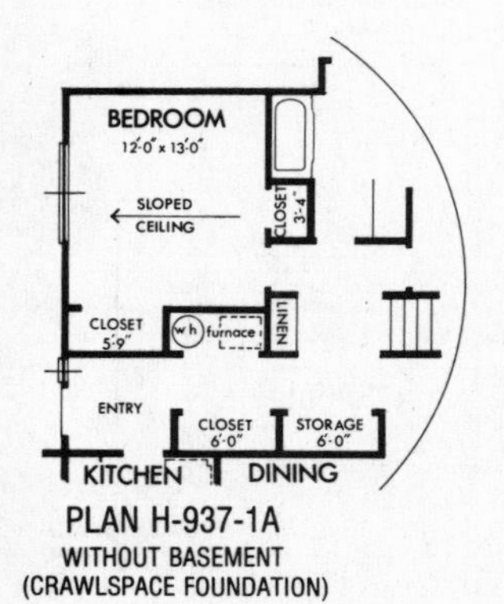

PLAN H-937-1A
WITHOUT BASEMENT
(CRAWLSPACE FOUNDATION)

UPPER LEVEL
462 SQUARE FEET

Smooth Comfort on Rugged Slope or Level Site

This home is designed for a rugged sloping hillside, but is also adaptable to a level lot. It provides for a comfortable interior arrangement. The entry hall allows privacy to the sleeping area and access to the living area. One bath efficiently serves both first-floor bedrooms. Closet space is plentiful.

Abundant windows enhance the living-dining area. The snack bar for easy and fast meals is especially useful. Ample kitchen cabinets, outside view and access to laundry-storage room and two-car garage make the working space especially attractive.

An open bedroom is located on the upper level. A walk-in closet, complete bathroom and vanity area enhance this arrangement.

Delightful decks surround two sides of this home, perfect for those who enjoy the outdoors.

First floor:	1,446 sq. ft.
Upper level:	462 sq. ft.
Total living area:	1,908 sq. ft.

(Not counting basement or garage)
(Exterior walls are 2x6 construction)

Blueprint Price Code B

Plans H-937-1 & H-937-1A

 TO ORDER THIS BLUEPRINT, CALL TOLL-FREE 1-800-547-5570

PRICES AND DETAILS ON PAGES 12-15

A Blend of Extras

- A sophisticated blend of country and contemporary design flows through this exceptional home.
- Specially designed for a side sloping lot, the home has a tuck-under garage and an open, economical interior.
- Attractive features include vaulted ceilings, a front wrapping deck, a rear deck off the family room, skylights, interior plant shelves in the kitchen and master bath, and an optional fourth bedroom, guest room or study.
- The vaulted family room is uniquely set below the main level, separated from the nook by a handrail.
- Three bedrooms and two full baths are found on the upper floor.

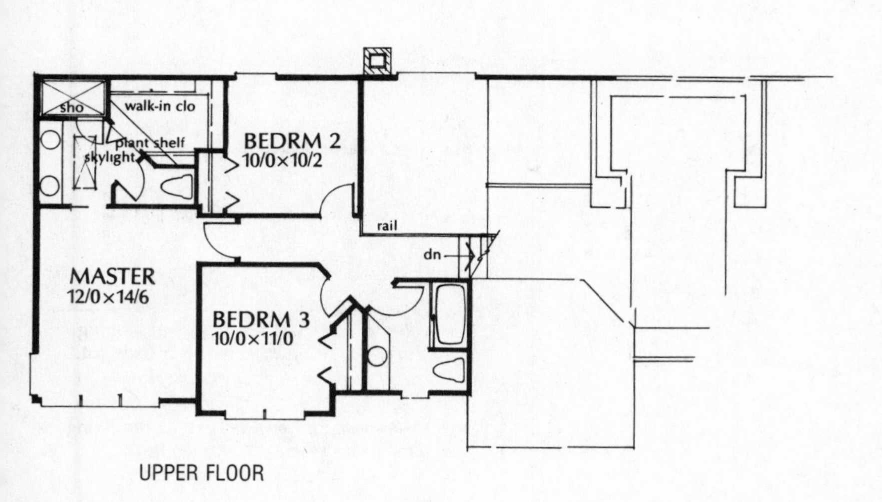

UPPER FLOOR

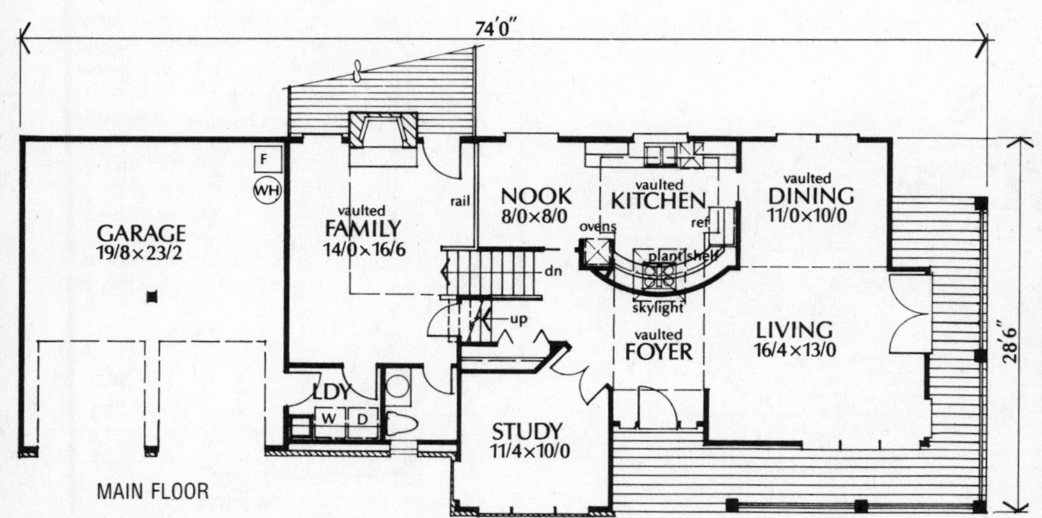

MAIN FLOOR

Plan CDG-4005	
Bedrooms: 3-4	**Baths:** 2½
Space:	
Upper floor:	732 sq. ft.
Main floor:	1,178 sq. ft.
Total living area:	1,910 sq. ft.
Garage:	456 sq. ft.
Exterior Wall Framing:	2x4
Foundation options:	
Crawlspace.	
(Foundation & framing conversion diagram available — see order form.)	
Blueprint Price Code:	B

Octagonal Home with Lofty View

- There's no better way to avoid the ordinary than by building an octagonal home and escaping from square corners and rigid rooms.
- The roomy main floor offers plenty of space for full-time family living or for a comfortable second-home retreat.
- The vaulted entry hall leads to the bedrooms on the right or down the hall to the Great Room.
- Warmed by a woodstove, the Great Room offers a panoramic view of the surrounding scenery.
- The center core of the main floor houses two baths, one of which contains a spa tub and is private to the master bedroom.
- This plan also includes a roomy kitchen and handy utility area.
- A large loft is planned as a recreation room, also with a woodstove.
- The daylight basement version adds another bedroom, a bath, a garage and a large storage area.

Plans P-532-3A & -3D	
Bedrooms: 3-4	**Baths:** 2-3
Living Area:	
Upper floor	355 sq. ft.
Main floor	1,567 sq. ft.
Daylight basement	430 sq. ft.
Total Living Area:	**1,922/2,352 sq. ft.**
Garage and storage	1,137 sq. ft.
Exterior Wall Framing:	2x6
Foundation Options:	**Plan #**
Daylight basement	P-532-3D
Crawlspace	P-532-3A
(Typical foundation & framing conversion diagram available—see order form.)	
BLUEPRINT PRICE CODE:	**B/C**

FRONT VIEW

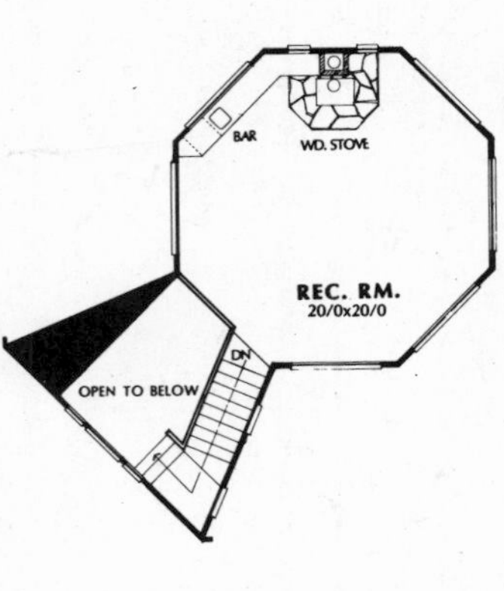

UPPER FLOOR

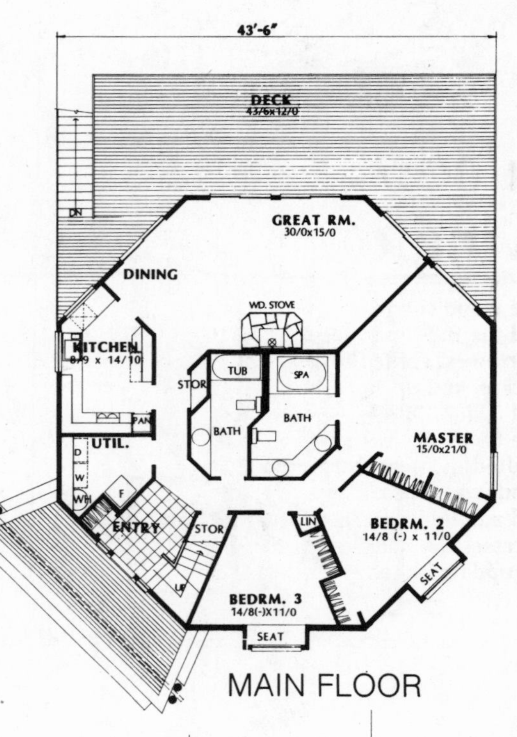

MAIN FLOOR

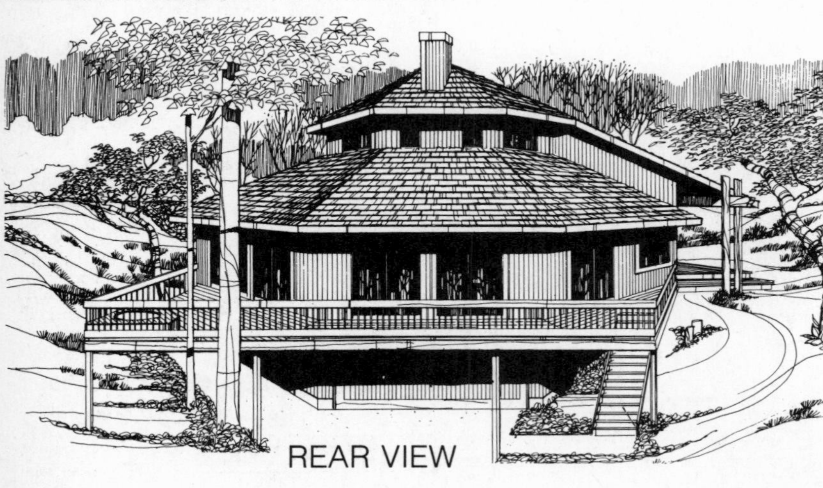

REAR VIEW

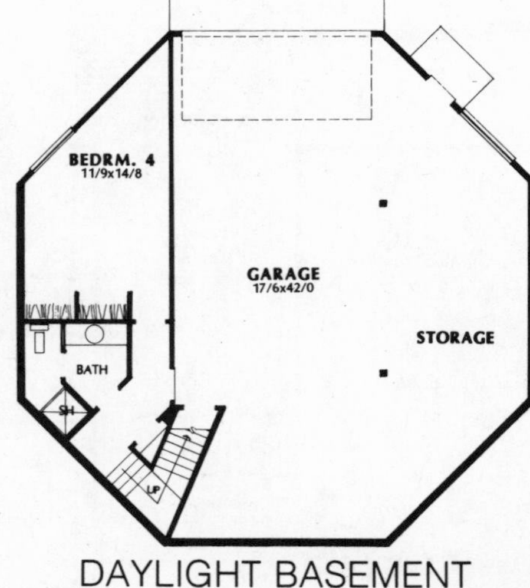

DAYLIGHT BASEMENT

Indoor/Outdoor Living on A Sloping Lot

- The wood siding, the front deck, and the multi-paned exterior of this Northwest contemporary will beckon you up to the entry stairs and inside.
- The two-story entry opens up to a vaulted living room with tall windows, exposed beam ceiling and adjoining dining area which accesses the hand-railed deck.
- An updated kitchen offers a walk-in pantry, eating bar and breakfast nook with sliders to a rear deck.
- A fireplace and rear patio highlight the attached family room.
- A washer/dryer in the upper level bath is convenient to all three bedrooms, making laundry a breeze.

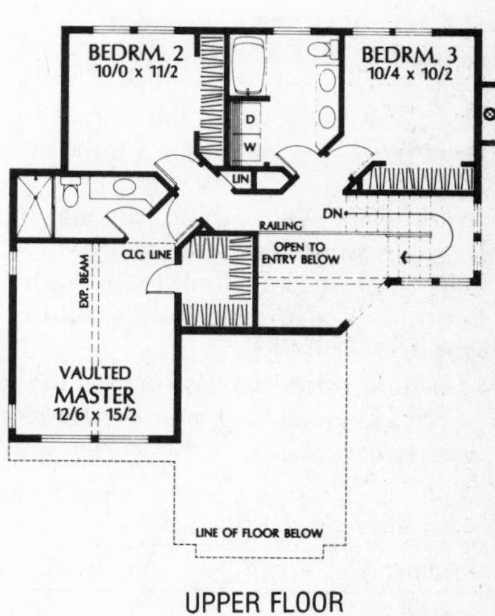

UPPER FLOOR

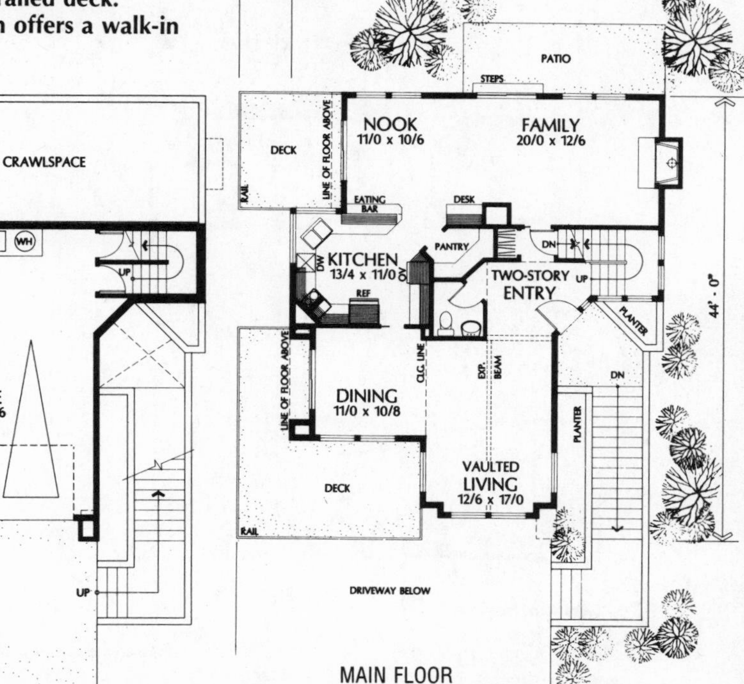

BASEMENT

MAIN FLOOR

Plan P-7737-4D

Bedrooms: 3	**Baths:** 2½
Space:	
Upper floor:	802 sq. ft.
Main floor:	1,158 sq. ft.
Total living area:	1,960 sq. ft.
Garage/basement:	736 sq. ft.
Exterior Wall Framing:	2x6

Foundation options:
Crawlspace.
(Foundation & framing conversion diagram available — see order form.)

Blueprint Price Code: B

Spacious Vaulted Great Room

- Behind an unpretentious facade lies an exciting and highly livable floor plan.
- A vaulted entry leads visitors to an impressive vaulted Great Room with exposed-beam ceiling.
- The roomy kitchen also boasts a vaulted ceiling, and skylights as well.
- The sunny nook looks out onto a large patio, and includes a built-in desk.
- A first-class master suite includes a large dressing area, enormous walk-in closet and sumptuous bath.
- Bedroom 2 also contains a walk-in closet.
- Also note other details such as the pantry, linen storage and convenient washer/dryer area in the garage entry.

Plans P-6577-3A & -3D

Bedrooms: 3 **Baths:** 2

Space:

Main floor (crawlspace version):	1,978 sq. ft.
Main floor (basement version):	2,047 sq. ft.
Basement:	1,982 sq. ft.
Garage:	438 sq. ft.

Exterior Wall Framing: 2x4

Foundation options:
Daylight basement (Plan P-6577-3D).
Crawlspace (Plan P-6577-3A).
(Foundation & framing conversion diagram available — see order form.)

Blueprint Price Code:

Without basement:	B
With basement:	C

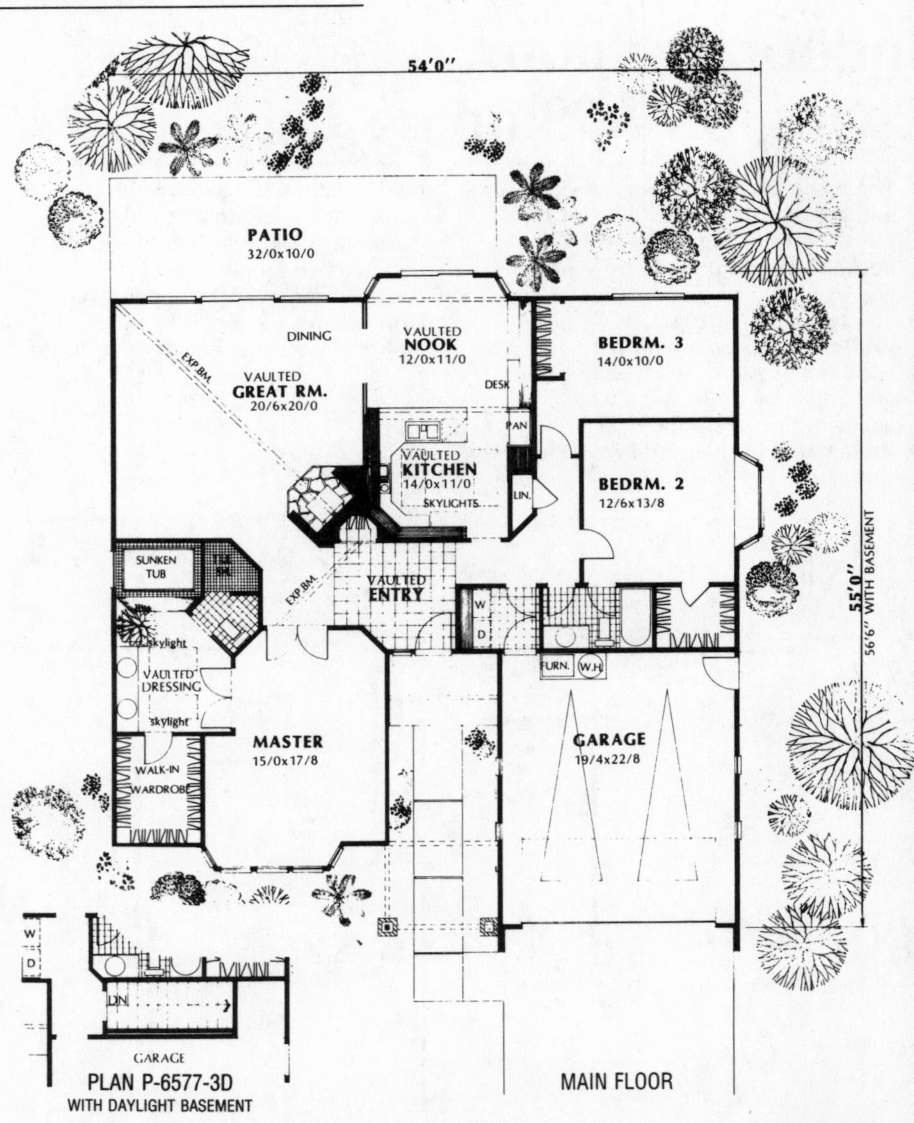

Rustic Country Design

- A welcoming front porch, window shutters and a bay window on the exterior of this rustic design are complemented by a comfortable, informal interior.
- A spacious country kitchen includes a bay-windowed breakfast area, center work island and abundant counter and cabinet space.
- Note the large utility room in the garage entry area.
- The large Great Room includes an impressive fireplace and another informal eating area with double doors opening to a deck, patio or screened porch. Also note the half-bath.
- The main floor master suite features a walk-in closet and compartmentalized private bath.
- Upstairs, you will find two more bedrooms, another full bath and a large storage area.

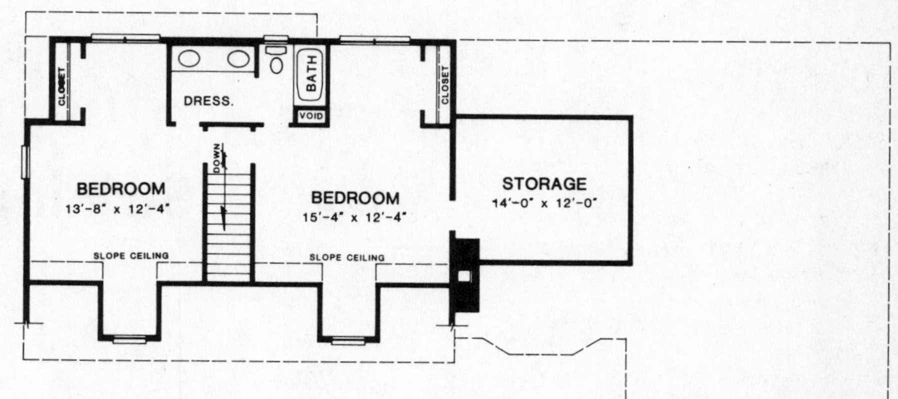

UPPER FLOOR

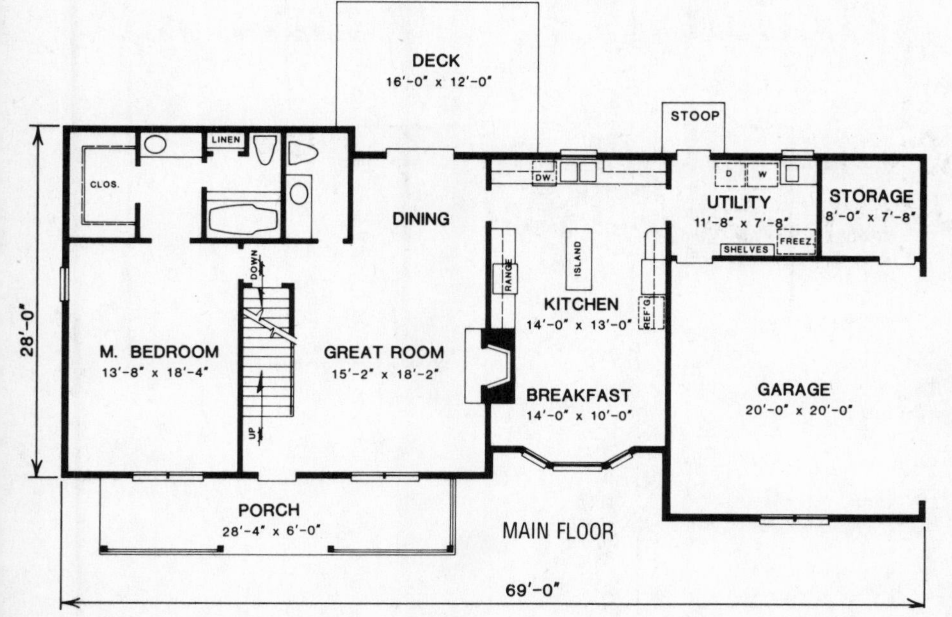

MAIN FLOOR

Plan C-8476

Bedrooms: 3	**Baths:** 2½
Space:	
Upper floor:	720 sq. ft.
Main floor:	1,277 sq. ft.
Total living area:	1,997 sq. ft.
Basement:	approx. 1,200 sq. ft.
Garage:	400 sq. ft.
Storage:	(in garage) 61 sq. ft.
Exterior Wall Framing:	2x4

Foundation options:
Daylight basement.
Standard basement.
Crawlspace.
Slab.
(Foundation & framing conversion diagram available — see order form.)

Blueprint Price Code: B

Striking Hillside Design

Main floor:	1,899 sq. ft.
Lower floor:	127 sq. ft.
Total living area: (Not counting garage)	2,026 sq. ft.

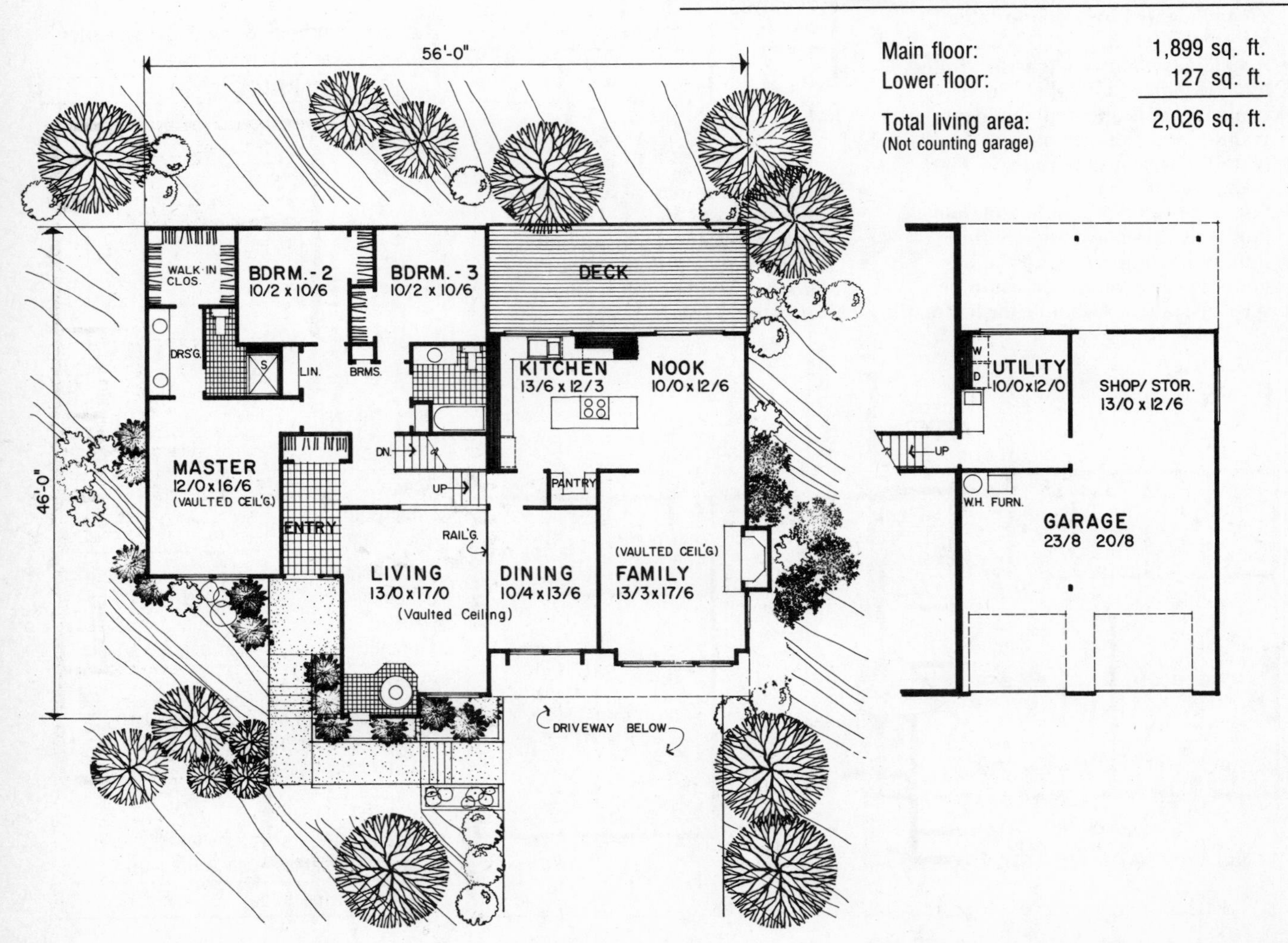

Blueprint Price Code C

Plan P-7597-2

PRICES AND DETAILS ON PAGES 12-15

REAR VIEW

Victorian Vacation Home

- Victorian design accents, horizontal wood siding and decorative windows create an exciting exterior for this versatile home.
- A stairway to the back porch presents accesses to the living room, dining room and master suite.
- The spacious master suite offers a large sleeping area, built-in bookshelves, a walk-in closet, a dressing area and a corner tub. The toilet and a second vanity are set off to serve as a half-bath for rest of the main floor.
- The tiled kitchen offers a U-shaped counter, ample storage space and nearby laundry facilities.
- Three secondary bedrooms share the upper floor with two baths.
- Plenty of storage space is available in the attic.
- The open space underneath the house makes an excellent carport or storage area for boats or other equipment.

Plan E-2006

Bedrooms: 4	**Baths:** 3
Living Area:	
Upper floor	838 sq. ft.
Main floor	1,182 sq. ft.
Total Living Area:	**2,020 sq. ft.**
Carport/storage	1,450 sq. ft.
Exterior Wall Framing:	2x6

Foundation Options:

Pole

(Typical foundation & framing conversion diagram available—see order form.)

BLUEPRINT PRICE CODE: **C**

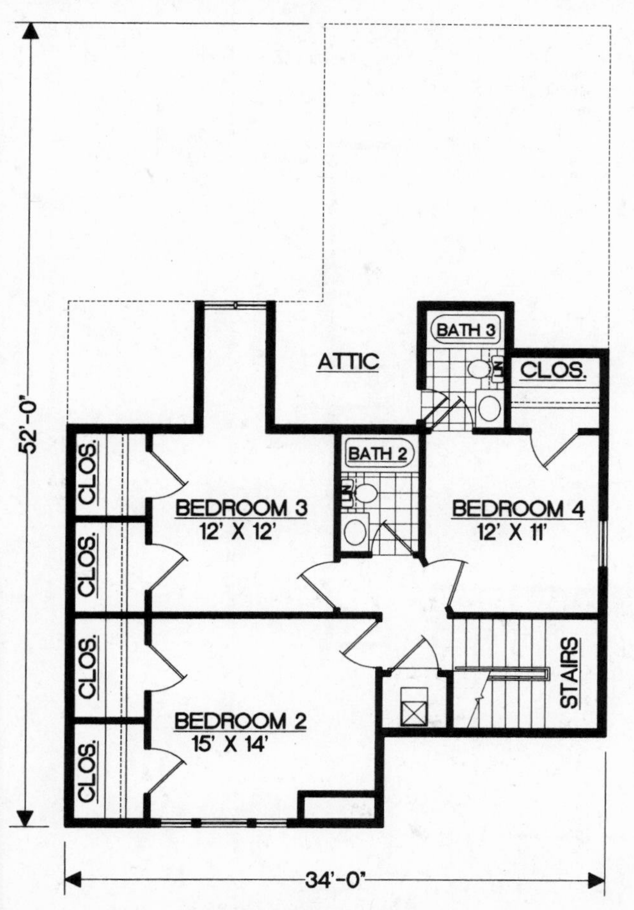

UPPER FLOOR

52'-0"
CLOSET
VANITY
LINEN
DRESS 1
MASTER SUITE
12' X 16'
BATH
PORCH 2
BOOKS
LINEN
DRY
WASH
KITCHEN
10' x 12'
REF
DW
DINING
12' x 12'
SINK
RANGE
STAIRS
LIVING
20' x 14'
PORCH 1
11' x 4'
34'-0"

MAIN FLOOR

Stylish Design for Sloping Lot

- With its walk-up entry and tuck-under garage, this stylish design conforms well to a sloping lot.
- The entry is accented with a brick column and flanking bay windows.
- Inside, an 11-ft. vaulted ceiling presides over a split entry that accesses the living areas and the garage below. Straight ahead, four graceful columns set off a central reception area.
- A sunken living room, outlined from the entry by two columns, features a 12-ft. vaulted ceiling and a large bay window. A decorative railing allows a view into the formal dining room above.
- The island kitchen and the breakfast nook create an intimate setting that overlooks a covered and skylighted backyard patio.
- The adjacent family room also views the patio through a spectacular window wall. A 9-ft. vaulted ceiling and a dramatic fireplace are also featured.
- The sleeping wing includes two baths and two bedrooms, with a den serving as an optional third bedroom. The master suite boasts a 9-ft. vaulted ceiling, a bayed sitting area and a skylighted bath with a garden spa tub.

Plan CDG-4001

Bedrooms: 2+	**Baths:** 2
Living Area:	
Main floor	2,022 sq. ft.
Total Living Area:	**2,022 sq. ft.**
Tuck-under garage/lower floor	546 sq. ft.
Exterior Wall Framing:	2x6
Foundation Options:	
Crawlspace	

(All plans can be built with your choice of foundation and framing. A generic conversion diagram is available. See order form.)

BLUEPRINT PRICE CODE: C

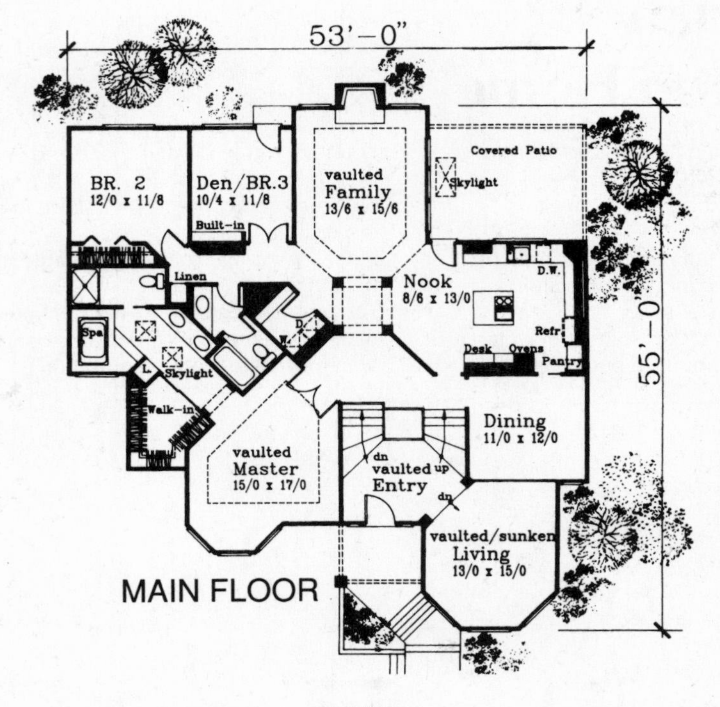

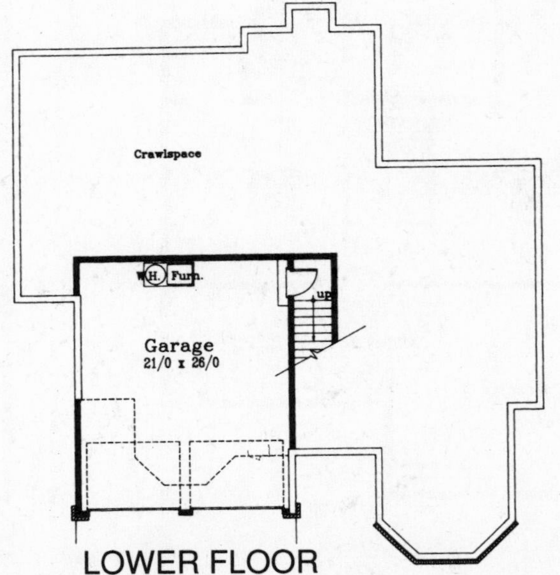

Expandable One-Story

- The hipped roof and covered entry give this well-appointed home a distinguished look.
- Inside, the foyer leads directly into the expansive Great Room, which boasts a vaulted ceiling, a fireplace with a built-in entertainment center, tall windows and access to the full-width deck with a hot tub.
- A half-wall separates the Great Room from the nook, which is open to the U-shaped kitchen. The impressive kitchen includes a snack bar, a walk-in pantry and a greenhouse window.
- The isolated main-floor master suite offers a vaulted ceiling, private access to the deck and the nearby hot tub, and a walk-in closet. The sumptuous master bath has a spa tub backlighted by a glass-block wall.
- Two more bedrooms on the lower level share another full bath. The optional expansion areas provide an additional 730 sq. ft. of space.

Plan S-41792	
Bedrooms: 3	**Baths:** 3
Living Area:	
Main floor	1,450 sq. ft.
Partial daylight basement	590 sq. ft.
Total Living Area:	**2,040 sq. ft.**
Garage	429 sq. ft.
Unfinished expansion areas	730 sq. ft.
Exterior Wall Framing:	2x6
Foundation Options:	
Partial daylight basement	
(Typical foundation & framing conversion diagram available—see order form.)	
BLUEPRINT PRICE CODE:	**C**

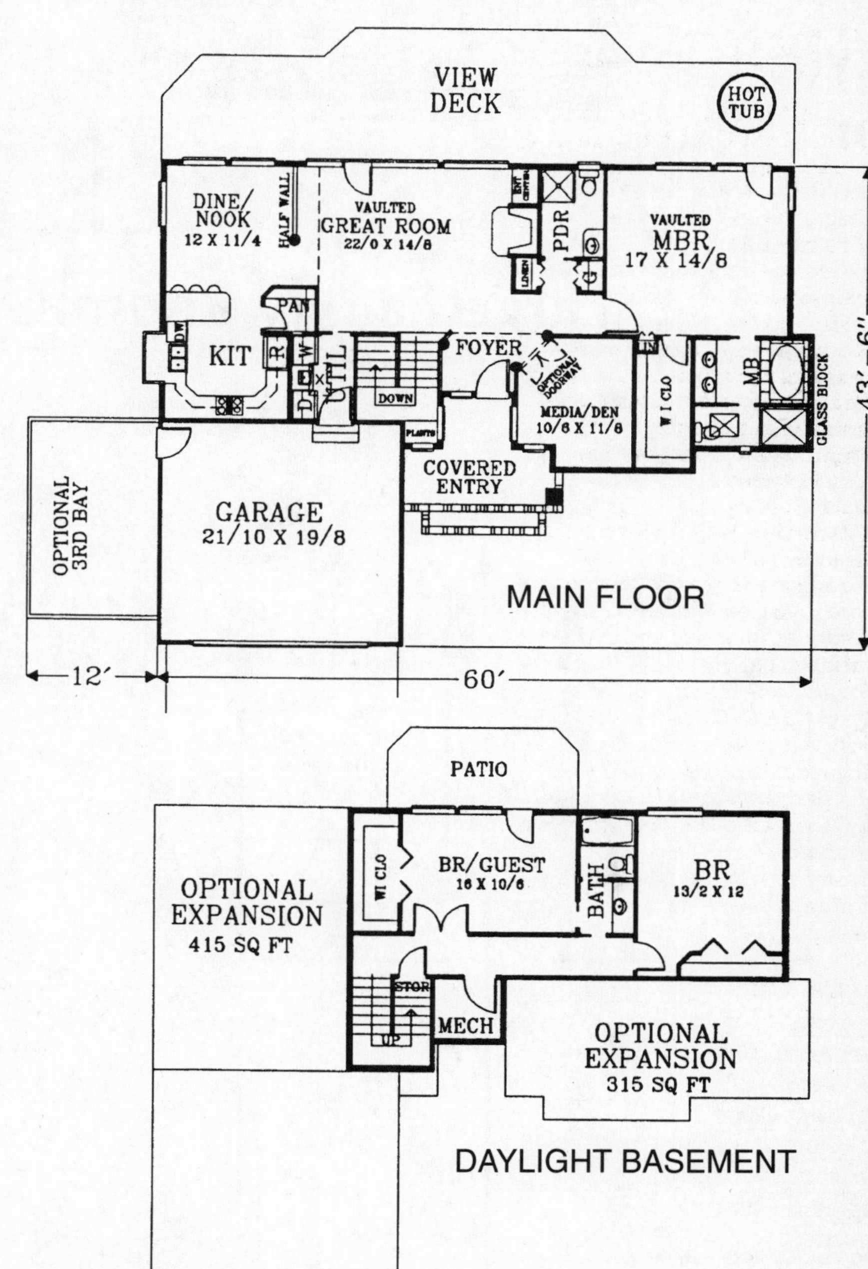

Large Family Room Upstairs

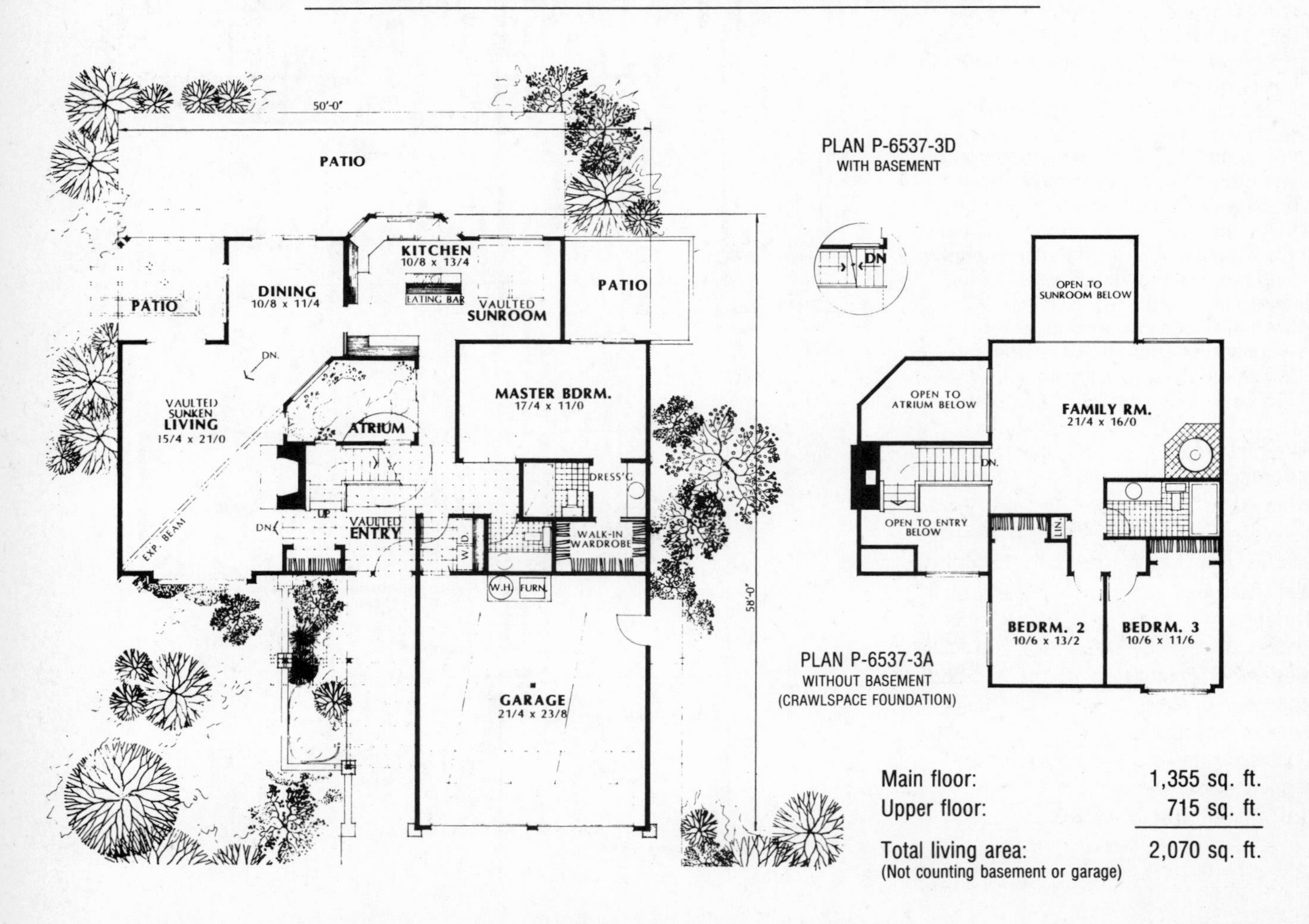

Main floor:	1,355 sq. ft.
Upper floor:	715 sq. ft.
Total living area:	2,070 sq. ft.

(Not counting basement or garage)

Blueprint Price Code C

Plans P-6537-3A & -3D

Spacious Contemporary

- Perfect for a sloping site overlooking splendid scenery, this home features a large deck, a patio, plenty of glass and a walk-out basement.
- Guests are welcomed by a roomy front porch with a decorative planter.
- The vaulted entry leads to a spectacular Great Room with vaulted ceiling, fireplace and rear window wall. The dining area is adjacent to the kitchen, which boasts an angled serving counter. French doors expand the entertaining area to include the spacious deck.
- The main-floor master suite offers a window seat, a walk-in closet and a skylighted dressing area.
- Two bedrooms and a full bath share the basement with a roomy family room, which boasts a second fireplace and sliders to a rear patio.

Plan P-6606-2D

Bedrooms: 3	**Baths:** 2½
Living Area:	
Main floor	1,140 sq. ft.
Daylight basement	935 sq. ft.
Total Living Area:	**2,075 sq. ft.**
Garage	451 sq. ft.
Exterior Wall Framing:	2x6
Foundation Options:	
Daylight basement	
(Typical foundation & framing conversion diagram available—see order form.)	
BLUEPRINT PRICE CODE:	**C**

Simple, Spacious, Easy to Build

For a simple, spacious, easy-to-construct home away from home, you should definitely consider this plan.

Entrance to the home is by way of the lower level or the side door to the living room, or both, where grade levels permit. This has the advantage of elevating the second floor to take advantage of a view that otherwise may be blocked out by surrounding buildings.

The living area, consisting of the living room, dining room and kitchen, occupies 565 sq. ft. of the main floor. The open room arrangement allows the cook to remain part of the family even when occupied with necessary chores.

The design's basically simple rectangular shape allows for easy construction, and the home could be built by any moderately experienced do-it-yourselfer. All you have to do is order the plan that fits your setting.

Plan H-833-5 has the garage entry to the street side. H-833-6 puts the garage under the view-side deck.

Upper floor:	1,200 sq. ft.
Lower level:	876 sq. ft.
Total living area: (Not counting garage)	2,076 sq. ft.

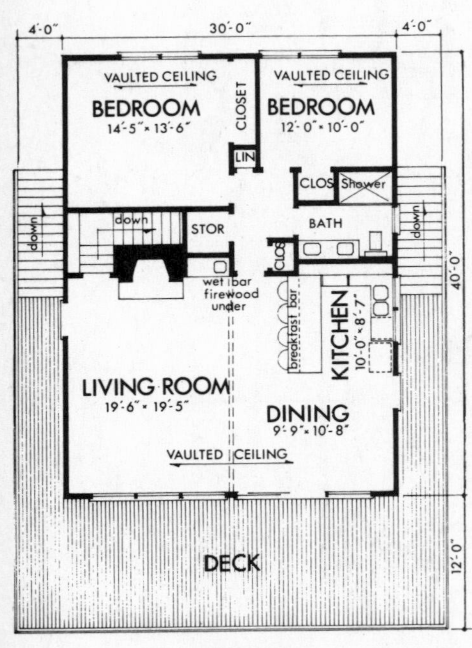

UPPER FLOOR
1200 SQUARE FEET

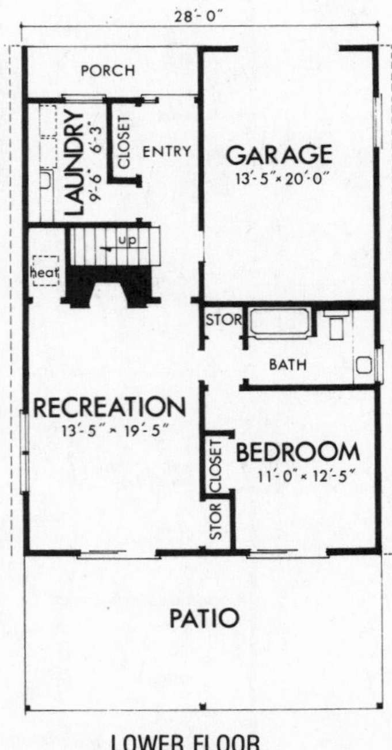

LOWER FLOOR
876 SQUARE FEET
PLAN H-833-5

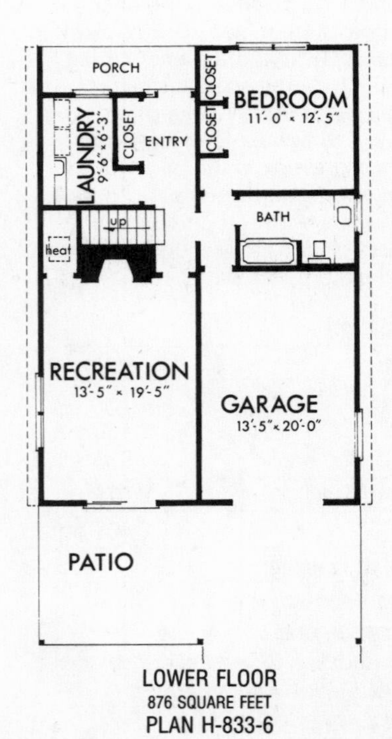

LOWER FLOOR
876 SQUARE FEET
PLAN H-833-6

Blueprint Price Code C

Plans H-833-5 & -6

PRICES AND DETAILS ON PAGES 12-15

Volume with Charm

- This charming two-story has an interesting variety of exterior elements and an open, airy interior.
- The two-story foyer has direct access to the main living areas. The formal spaces are oriented to the front of the home and include a dining room that overlooks a covered porch.
- A long view into the family room reveals a dramatic fireplace flanked by windows. The vaulted family room can also be viewed from the balcony above.
- A large kitchen and a vaulted breakfast room adjoin the family room. The breakfast room features a built-in work desk and a bayed sitting area. The kitchen offers a pantry closet and two convenient serving bars.
- A spectacular vaulted master suite is the perfect adult retreat. The bedroom opens to a private vaulted bath with a corner tub, a separate shower, dual sinks and a walk-in closet.

Plan FB-2081	
Bedrooms: 4	**Baths:** 2½
Living Area:	
Upper floor	492 sq. ft.
Main floor	1,589 sq. ft.
Bonus room	226 sq. ft.
Total Living Area:	**2,307 sq. ft.**
Daylight basement	1,589 sq. ft.
Garage	400 sq. ft.
Storage	24 sq. ft.
Exterior Wall Framing:	2x4

Foundation Options:
Daylight basement
(Typical foundation & framing conversion diagram available—see order form.)

BLUEPRINT PRICE CODE: C

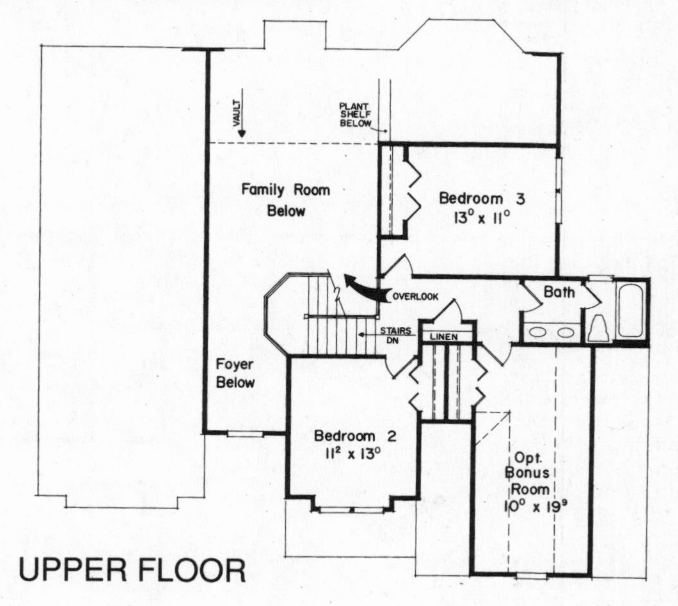

UPPER FLOOR

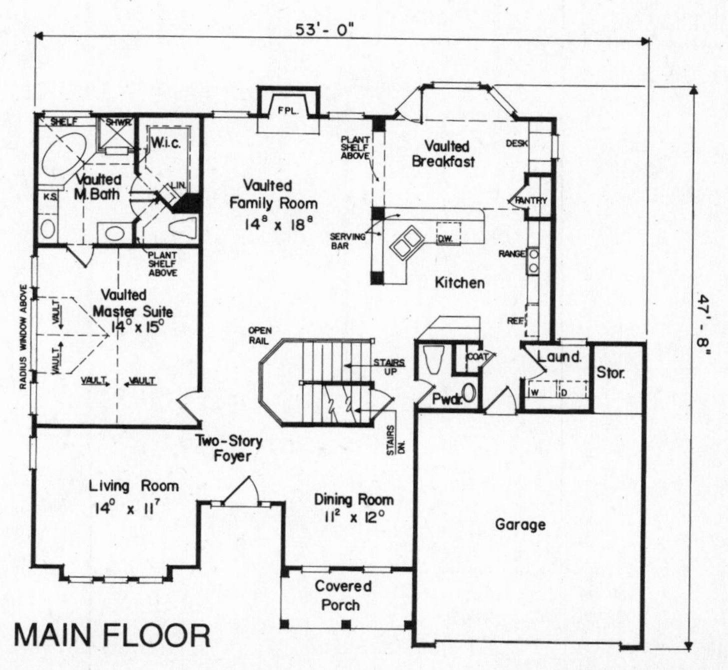

MAIN FLOOR

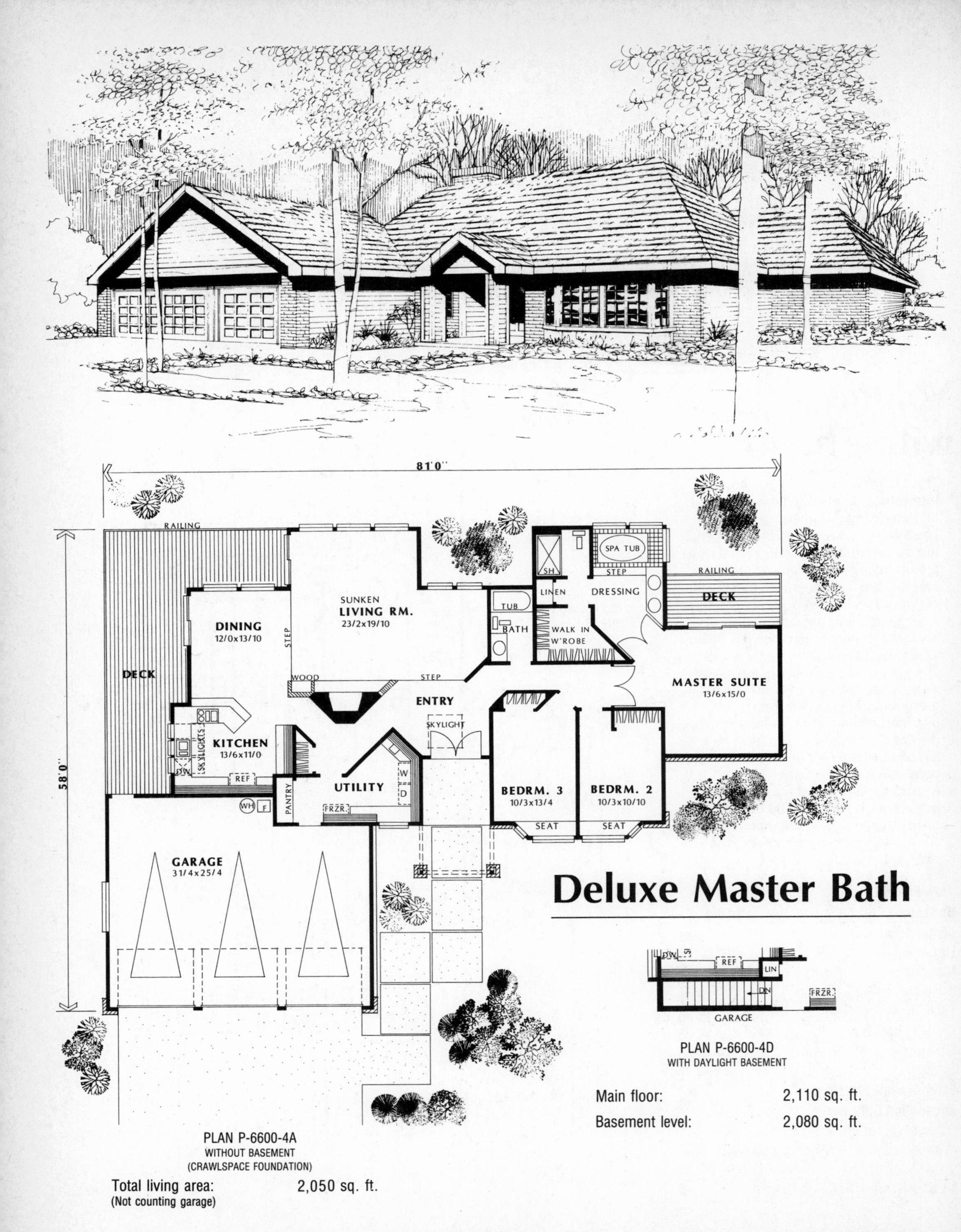

Blueprint Price Code C

Plans P-6600-4A & -4D

TO ORDER THIS BLUEPRINT, CALL TOLL-FREE 1-800-547-5570

PRICES AND DETAILS ON PAGES 12-15

Wonderful Windows

- This one-story's striking stucco and stone facade is enhanced with wonderful windows and great gables.
- A beautiful bay augments the living room/den, which can be closed off.
- A wall of windows lets sunbeams brighten the exquisite formal dining room, which is open but defined by decorative columns.
- The oversized family room offers a nice fireplace and a handy serving bar.
- The walk-through kitchen boasts a large pantry and a corner sink.
- A lovely window seat is found in one of the two secondary bedrooms.
- The magnificent master suite features a symmetrical tray ceiling that sets off a round-top window.
- Large walk-in closets flank the entry to the master bath, which offers a garden tub and two vanities. One of the vanities has knee space for a sit-down makeup area.

Plan FB-5009-CHAD	
Bedrooms: 3	**Baths:** 2
Living Area:	
Main floor	2,115 sq. ft.
Total Living Area:	**2,115 sq. ft.**
Daylight basement	2,115 sq. ft.
Garage	517 sq. ft.
Storage	18 sq. ft.
Exterior Wall Framing:	2x4
Foundation Options:	
Daylight basement	
Slab	
(Typical foundation & framing conversion diagram available—see order form.)	
BLUEPRINT PRICE CODE:	**C**

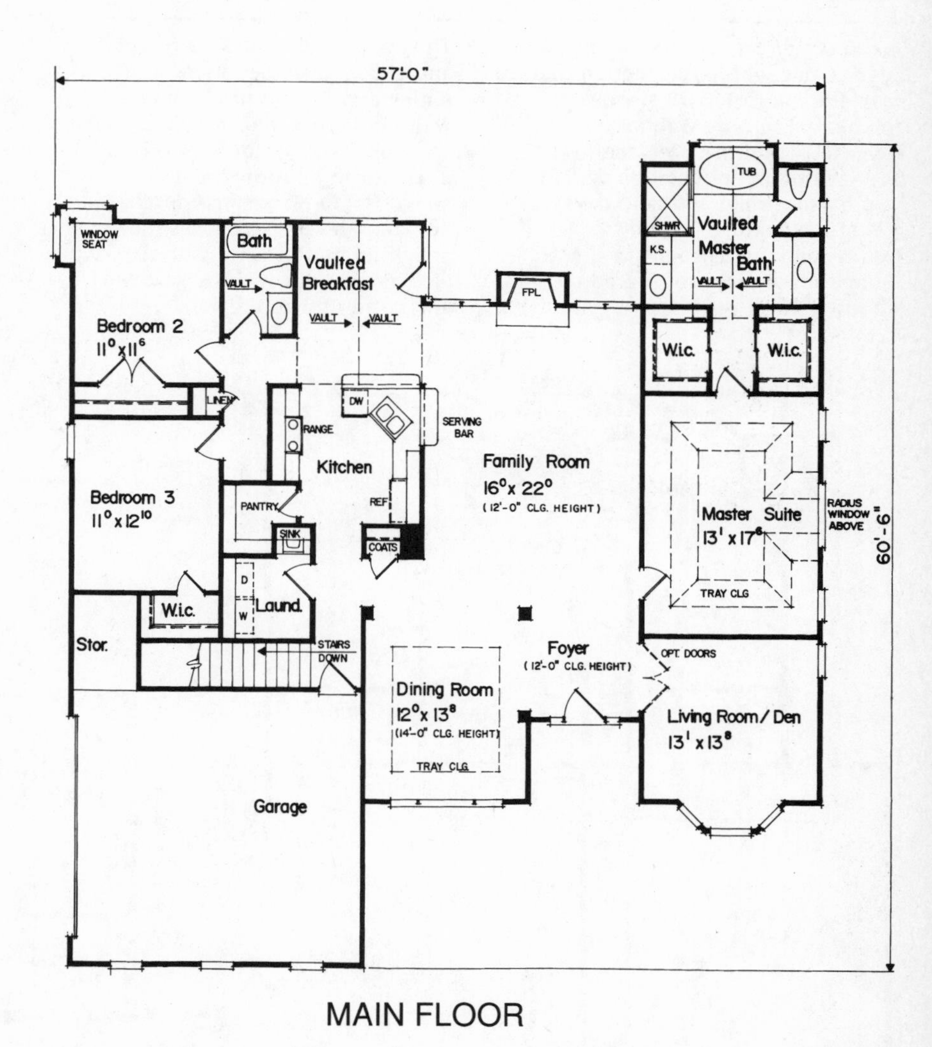

MAIN FLOOR

Built for All Seasons

- Spectacular rear viewing is yours in this exciting, yet homey design that provides comfort in all seasons.
- The heat-absorbing wall in the lower level and the fireplace-to-furnace "tie-in" circulation system help balance mild and cold days during the heating season.
- Two secondary bedrooms and extra storage space are also offered on the lower level.
- The main level features a bright and cheery L-shaped living and dining area with a brick column wall that absorbs heat from the sun.
- The upper side patio deck off the kitchen can be roofed and converted to a screened porch.
- The main level also houses the delightful master suite with dressing alcove and bath with step-up tub and corner mirrored wall.

Plan CPS-1045-SE

Bedrooms: 3	**Baths:** 2½
Space:	
Lower floor:	1,095 sq. ft.
Main floor:	1,040 sq. ft.
Total living area:	2,135 sq. ft.
Garage:	624 sq. ft.
Exterior Wall Framing:	2x6
Foundation options:	
Daylight basement.	
(Foundation & framing conversion diagram available — see order form.)	
Blueprint Price Code:	C

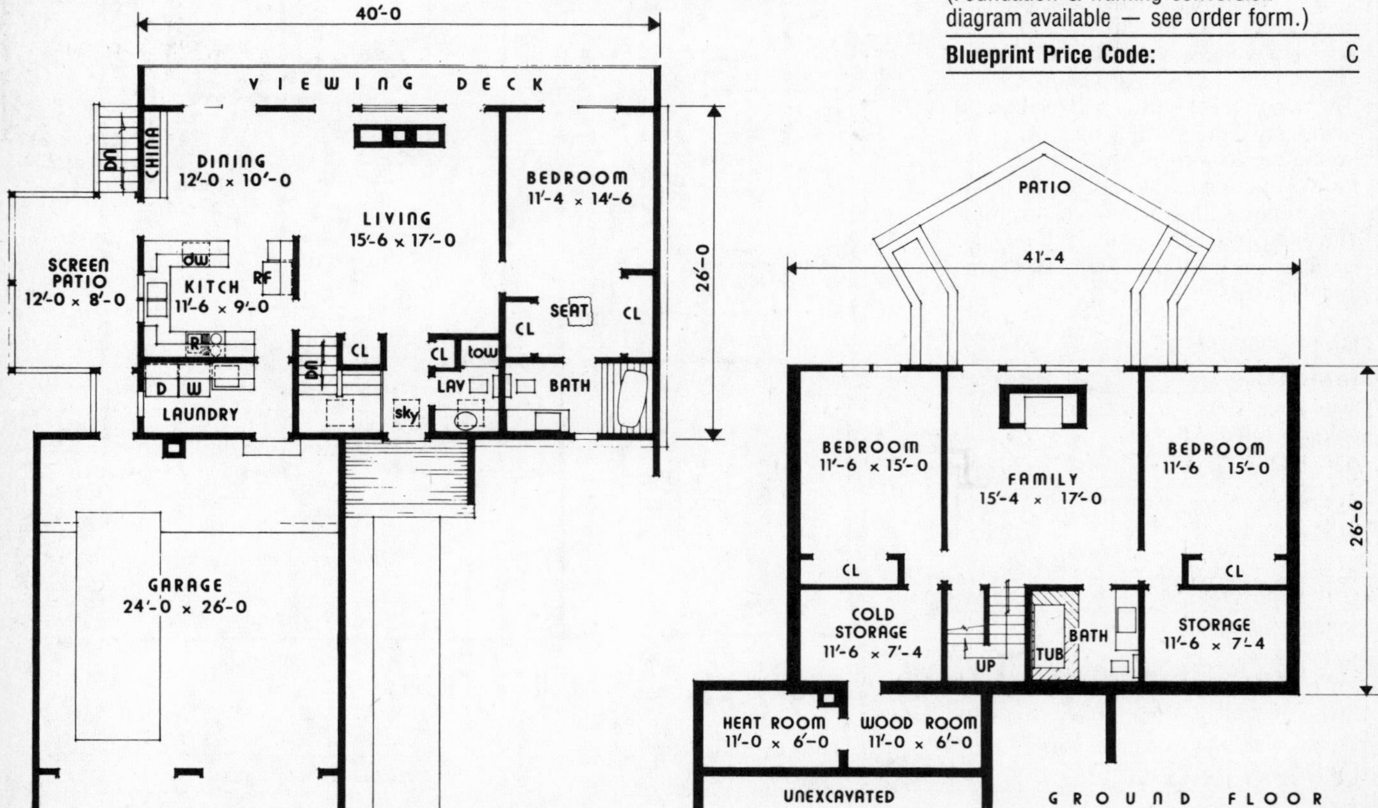

Plan CPS-1045-SE

PRICES AND DETAILS ON PAGES 12-15

Upstairs Suite Creates Adult Retreat

- This multi-level design is ideal for a gently sloping site with a view to the rear.
- Upstairs master suite is a sumptuous "adult retreat" complete with magnificent bath, vaulted ceiling, walk-in closet, private deck and balcony loft.
- Living room includes wood stove area and large windows to the rear. Wood bin can be loaded from outside.
- Main floor also features roomy kitchen and large utility area.

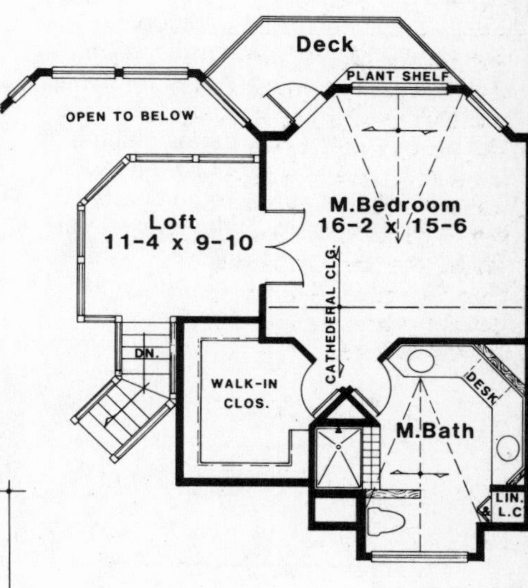

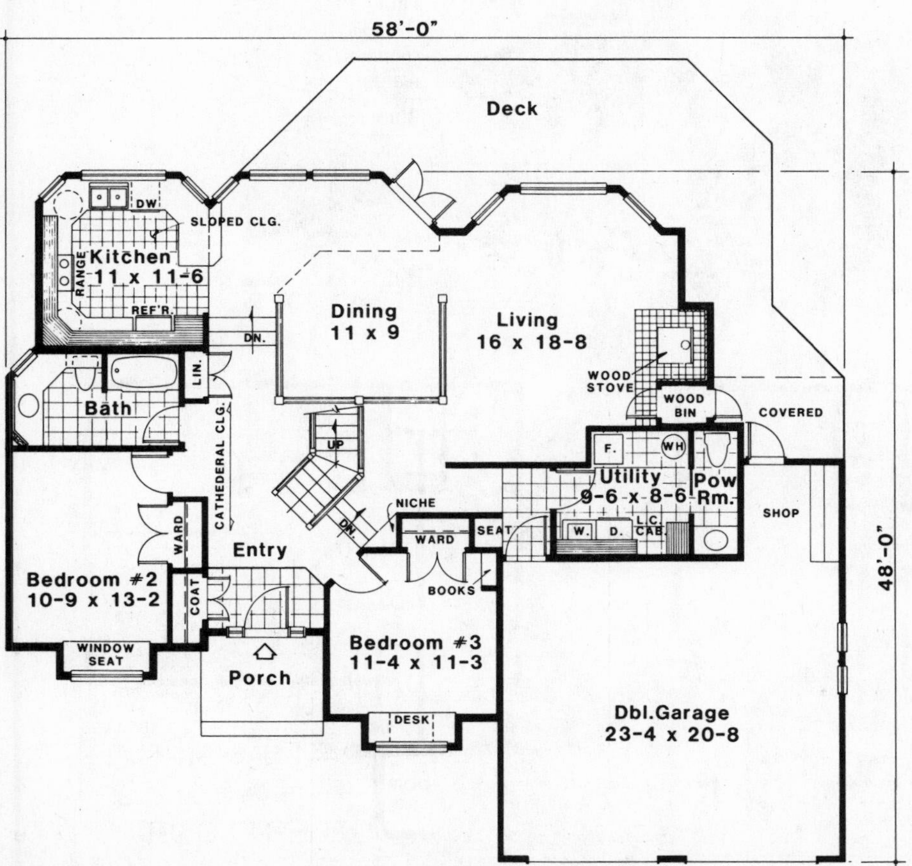

Plan NW-544-S

Bedrooms: 3	**Baths:** 2½
Space:	
Upper floor:	638 sq. ft.
Main floor:	1,500 sq. ft.
Total living area:	2,138 sq. ft.
Garage:	545 sq. ft.
Exterior Wall Framing:	2x6
Foundation options:	
Crawlspace only. (Foundation & framing conversion diagram available — see order form.)	
Blueprint Price Code:	C

ELEVATION A

Spectacular Family Room

- Available with either a traditional or a contemporary exterior, this handsome home's floor plan is designed for living.
- The inviting skylighted entry flows into the comfortable living room, which is brightened by a boxed-out window.
- The spectacular family room boasts a 14-ft. vaulted ceiling, bright boxed-out windows and a warm fireplace flanked by French doors to a backyard deck.
- The modern U-shaped kitchen services the family room via a handy pass-through. The adjoining nook is ideal for informal meals. A laundry room and a half-bath are nearby.
- Three nice-sized bedrooms are upstairs. The master bedroom has a private, compartmentalized master bath that features a designer shower and a dual-sink vanity.
- A tuck-under garage and a big multi-purpose area make up the daylight basement.
- When ordering blueprints, please specify Elevation A or Elevation B.

Plan LMB-9611-E

Bedrooms: 3	**Baths:** 2½
Living Area:	
Upper floor	826 sq. ft.
Main floor	1,332 sq. ft.
Total Living Area:	**2,158 sq. ft.**
Daylight basement	669 sq. ft.
Tuck-under garage	484 sq. ft.
Exterior Wall Framing:	2x6
Foundation Options:	
Daylight basement	

(All plans can be built with your choice of foundation and framing. A generic conversion diagram is available. See order form.)

BLUEPRINT PRICE CODE: C

ELEVATION B

WOOD DECK 24'-0" x 12'-0"
FAMILY ROOM 13'-6" x 23'-0"
KITCHEN 9'-0" x 9'-6"
UTILITY 6'-0" x 9'-0"
BATH
DINING ROOM 12'-0 x 13'-9"
NOOK 9'-2" x 9'-4"
LIVING ROOM 14'-0" x 17'-0"
ENTRY
COVERED PORCH
33'
49'

MAIN FLOOR

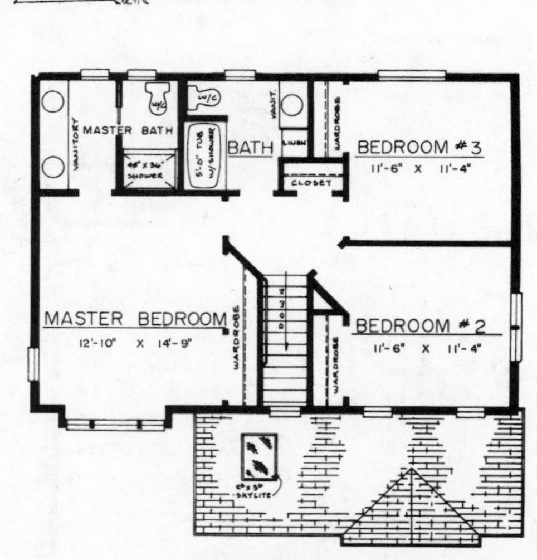

UPPER FLOOR

Chalet Style for Town or Country

- The exterior features exposed beams, board siding and viewing decks with cut-out railings to give this home the look of a mountain chalet.
- Inside, the design lends itself equally well to year-round family living or part-time recreational enjoyment.
- An expansive Great Room features an impressive fireplace and includes a dining area next to the well-planned kitchen.
- The upstairs offers the possibility of an adult retreat, with a fine master bedroom with private bath and large closets, plus a loft area available for many uses.
- Two secondary bedrooms are on the main floor, and share another bath.
- The daylight basement level includes a garage and a large recreation room with a fireplace and a half-bath.

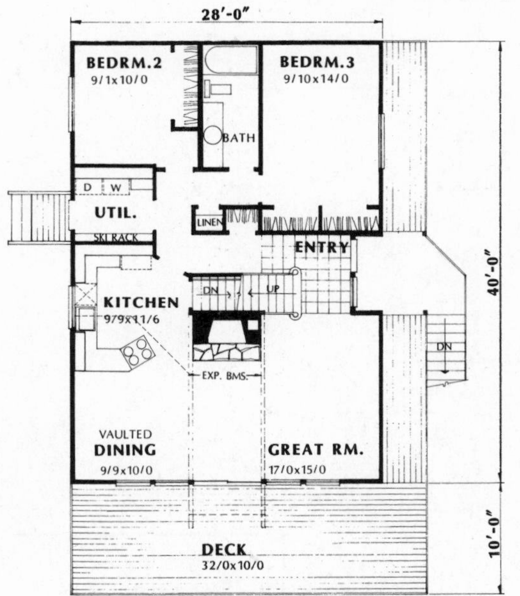

MAIN FLOOR

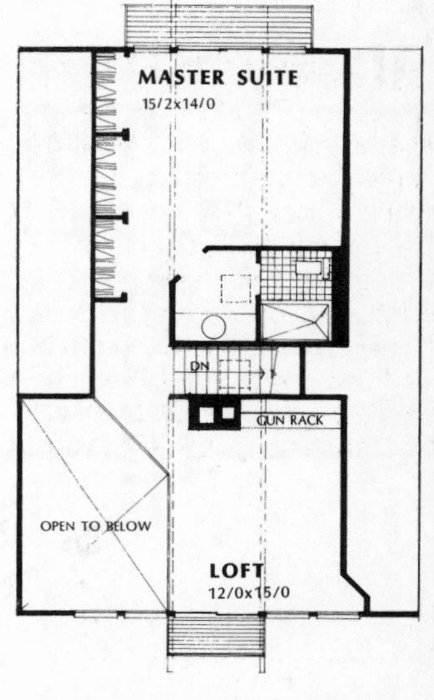

UPPER FLOOR

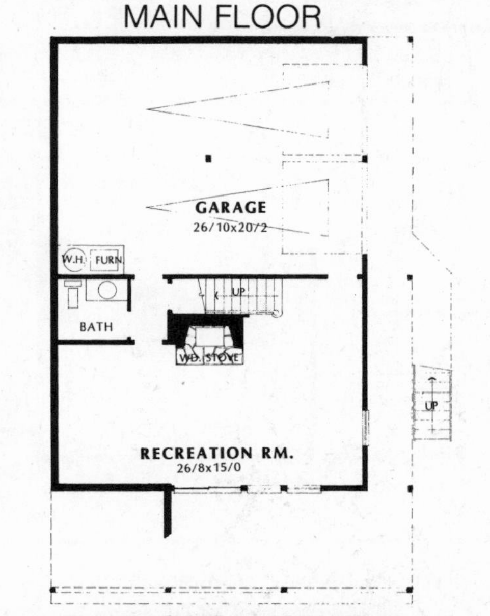

DAYLIGHT BASEMENT

Plan P-531-2D	
Bedrooms: 3	**Baths:** 2½
Living Area:	
Upper floor	573 sq. ft.
Main floor	1,120 sq. ft.
Daylight basement	532 sq. ft.
Total Living Area:	**2,225 sq. ft.**
Garage	541 sq. ft.
Exterior Wall Framing:	2x6
Foundation Options:	
Daylight basement	
(Typical foundation & framing conversion diagram available—see order form.)	
BLUEPRINT PRICE CODE:	**C**

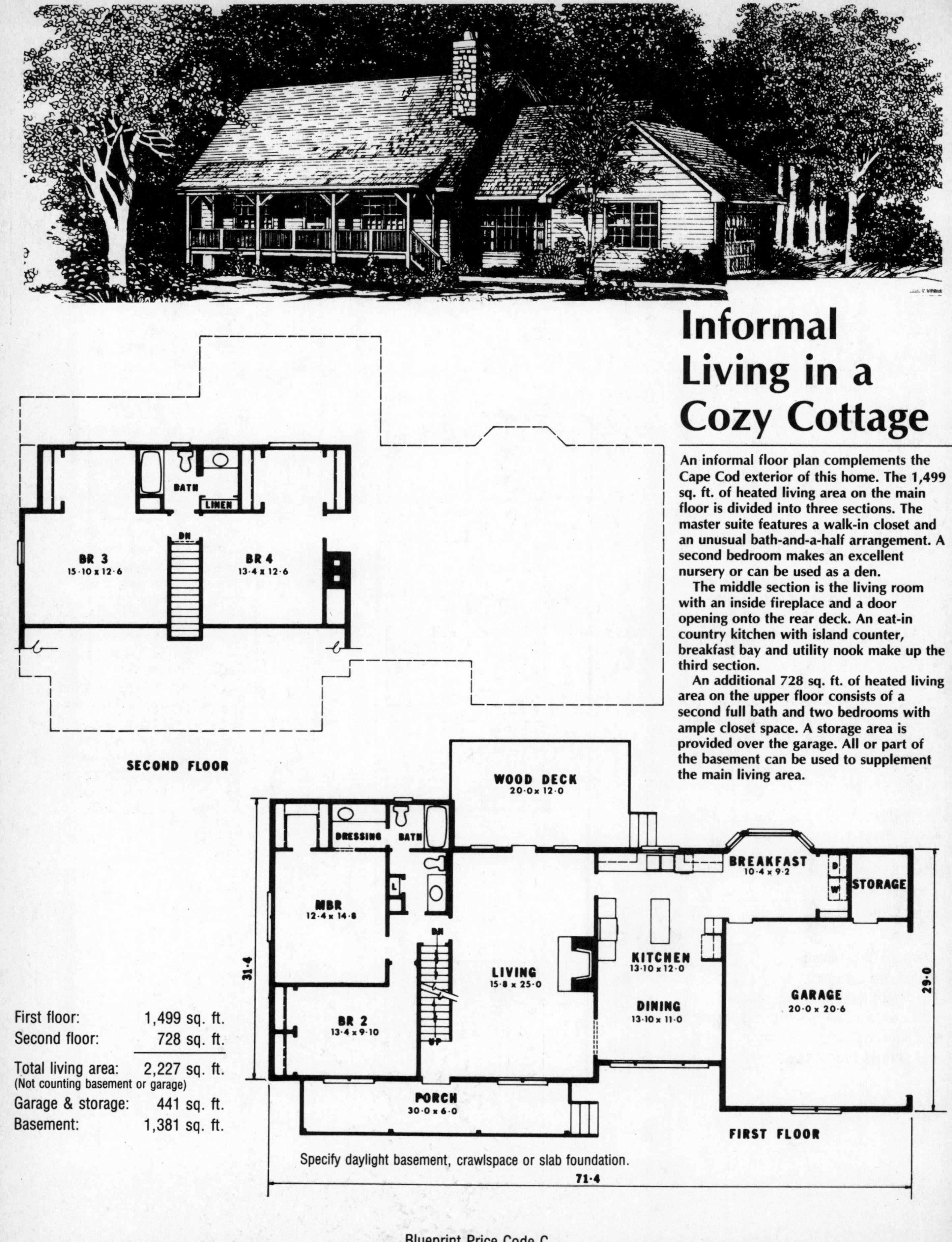

Informal Living in a Cozy Cottage

An informal floor plan complements the Cape Cod exterior of this home. The 1,499 sq. ft. of heated living area on the main floor is divided into three sections. The master suite features a walk-in closet and an unusual bath-and-a-half arrangement. A second bedroom makes an excellent nursery or can be used as a den.

The middle section is the living room with an inside fireplace and a door opening onto the rear deck. An eat-in country kitchen with island counter, breakfast bay and utility nook make up the third section.

An additional 728 sq. ft. of heated living area on the upper floor consists of a second full bath and two bedrooms with ample closet space. A storage area is provided over the garage. All or part of the basement can be used to supplement the main living area.

First floor:	1,499 sq. ft.
Second floor:	728 sq. ft.
Total living area:	2,227 sq. ft.
(Not counting basement or garage)	
Garage & storage:	441 sq. ft.
Basement:	1,381 sq. ft.

Specify daylight basement, crawlspace or slab foundation.

Blueprint Price Code C

Plan C-8030

PRICES AND DETAILS ON PAGES 12-15

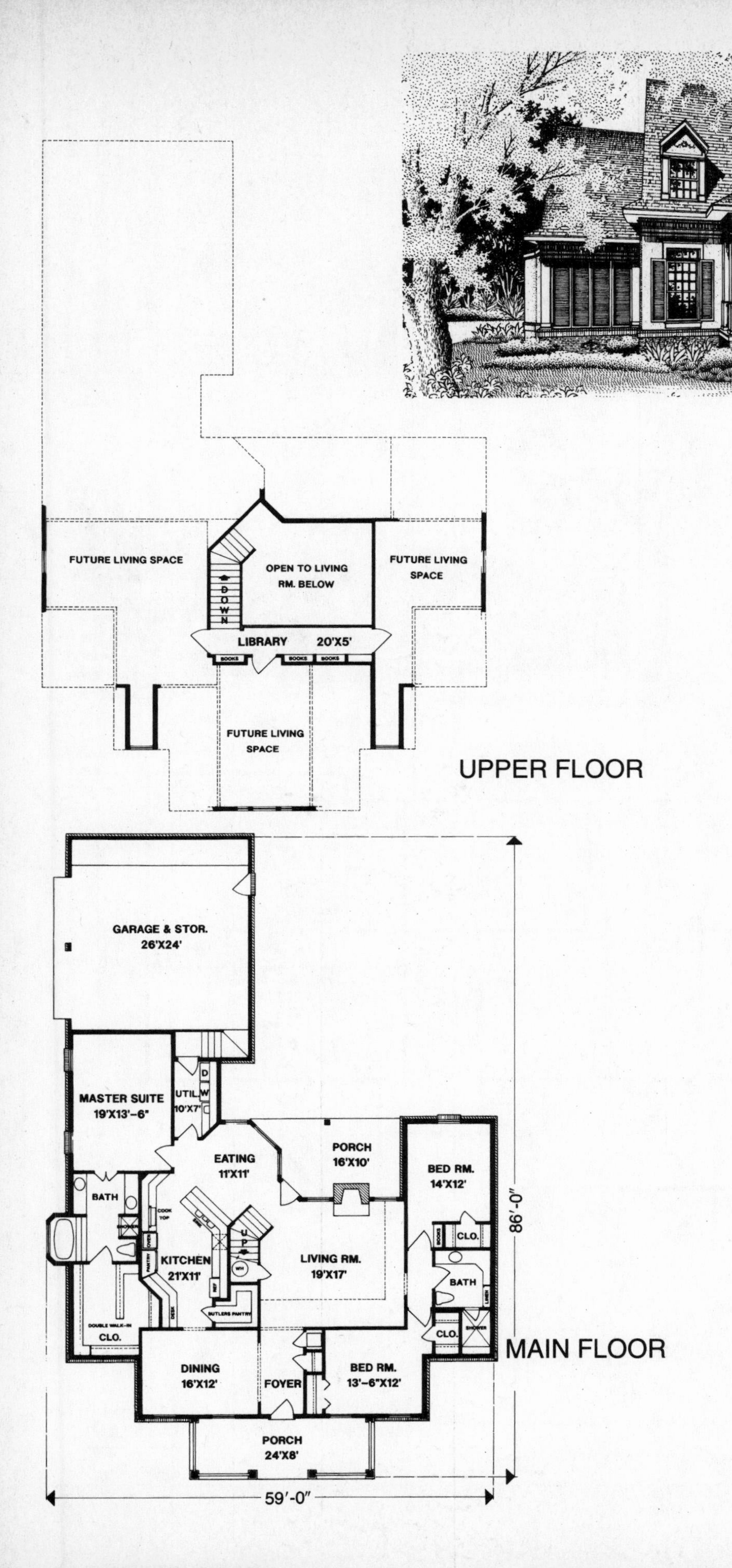

Rural and Refined

- This refined and graceful two-story is at home in the country or in the city.
- Visitors are given a warm welcome by the railed, covered front porch.
- A quiet balcony library overlooks the dramatic two-story living room, with its fireplace and access to a rear porch.
- Nine-foot ceilings give a spacious feeling to the rest of the home.
- An angled counter separates the gourmet kitchen from the sunny, angled eating area. The formal dining room is also easily serviced from the kitchen, which boasts a butler's pantry, a second pantry and a built-in desk.
- An enormous walk-in closet is found in the isolated master suite. The master bath has an enticing garden tub, a separate shower and dual vanities.
- A hall bath with an oversized shower is shared by two additional bedrooms.
- The upstairs attic areas could easily accommodate future expansion.

Plan THD-220-0	
Bedrooms: 3	**Baths:** 2
Living Area:	
Upper floor	96 sq. ft.
Main floor	2,159 sq. ft.
Total Living Area:	**2,255 sq. ft.**
Daylight basement	2,159 sq. ft.
Garage and storage	664 sq. ft.
Future expansion area	878 sq. ft.
Exterior Wall Framing:	2x6
Foundation Options:	
Daylight basement	
Crawlspace	
Slab	
(Typical foundation & framing conversion diagram available—see order form.)	
BLUEPRINT PRICE CODE:	**C**

PLAN H-2107-1B

Solarium for Sloping Lots

This plan is available in two versions. Plan H-2107-1B, shown above, is most suitable for a lot sloping upward from front to rear, providing a daylight front for the lower floor. The other version, Plan H-2107-1 (at right), is more suitable for a lot that slopes from side to side.

Either way, this moderately sized home has a number of interesting and imaginative features. Of these, the passive sun room will provoke the most comment. Spanning two floors between recreation and living rooms, this glass-enclosed space serves the practical purpose of collecting, storing and redistributing the sun's natural heat, while acting as a conservatory for exotic plants, an exercise room, or any number of other uses. A link between the formal atmosphere of the living room and the carefree activities of the recreation area is created by this two-story solarium by way of an open balcony railing. Living, dining, and entry blend together in one huge space made to seem even larger by the vaulted ceiling spanning the entire complex of rooms.

PLAN H-2107-1

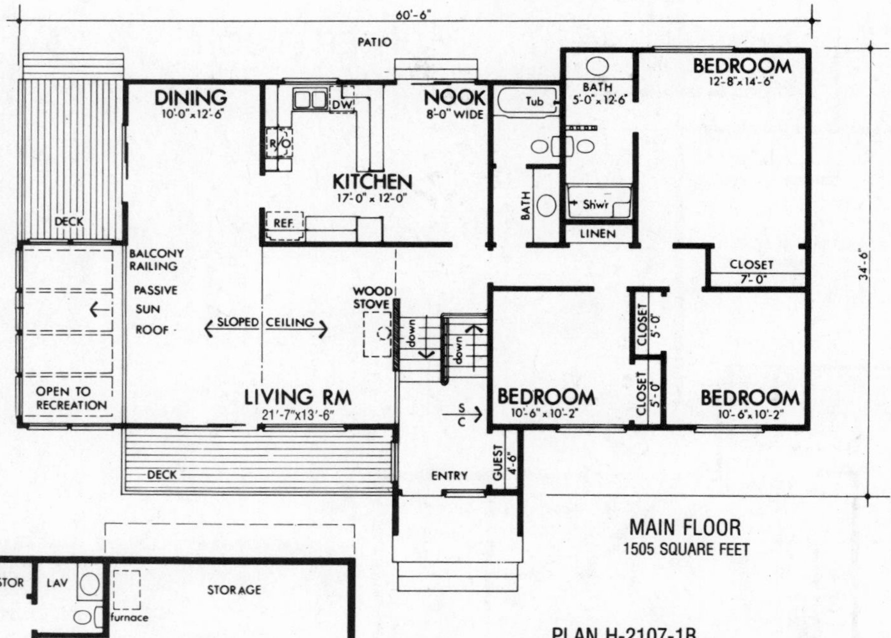

MAIN FLOOR
1505 SQUARE FEET

PLAN H-2107-1B
DAYLIGHT BASEMENT

PLAN H-2107-1
WITH STANDARD BASEMENT
(BOTH VERSIONS INCLUDE
2X6 EXTERIOR WALL CONSTRUCTION)

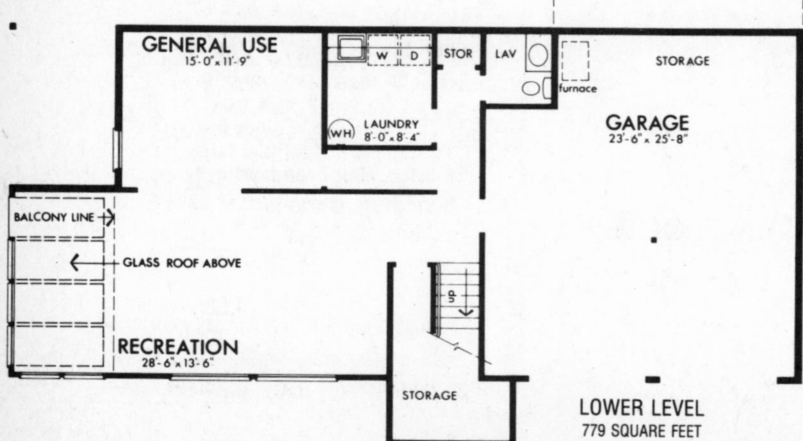

LOWER LEVEL
779 SQUARE FEET

Main floor:	1,505 sq. ft.
Lower level:	779 sq. ft.
Total living area: (Not counting garage)	2,284 sq. ft.

Blueprint Price Code C

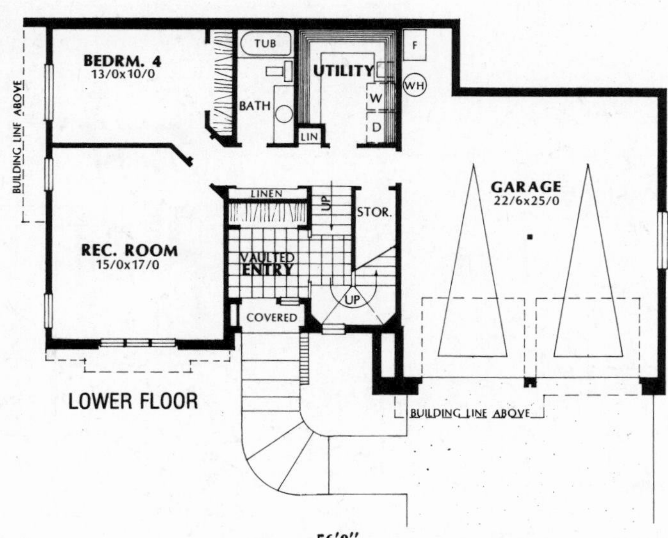

LOWER FLOOR

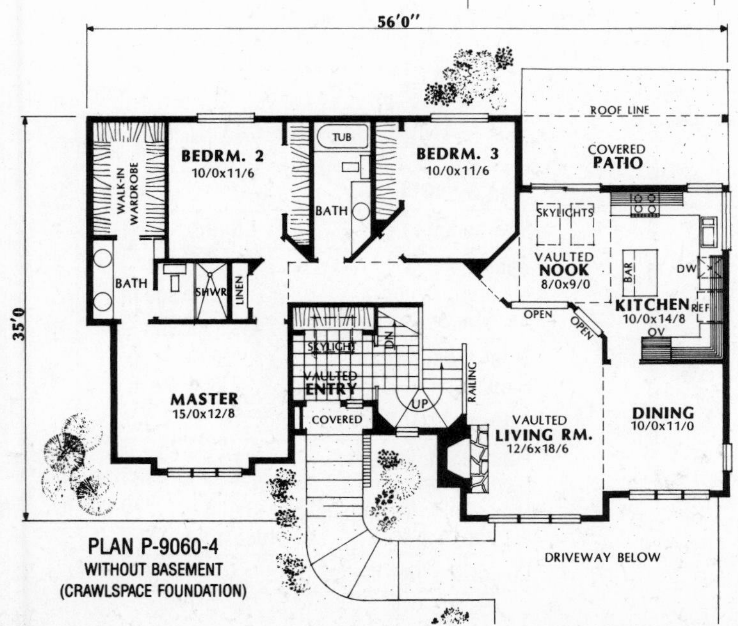

PLAN P-9060-4
WITHOUT BASEMENT
(CRAWLSPACE FOUNDATION)

Tudor Charm in a Modern Split-Level

The board-and-stucco charm of English Tudor styling is accented by the brick facade and tall chimney of this split-level, four-bedroom house, designed to fit comfortably on a sloping lot. The front door, sheltered by a brick archway, opens into a vaulted and skylighted entry hall.

An open stairway takes you from the entry to the 1,585-sq. ft. main floor, and directly into the vaulted living room and adjacent dining area. This formal space, with tall and wide windows, also is perfect for firelit family activities in front of the stone-hearth fireplace. The U-shaped island kitchen, skylighted nook and partially covered patio round out the living/dining wing of the house.

The master bedroom, with walk-in wardrobe and full bath, and two more bedrooms, separated by a full bath, occupy the other side of the main floor.

Down a short flight of steps from the entry, the 700-sq. ft. lower floor includes a fourth bedroom and full bath, a large family/recreation room and a utility/storage room. A door leads to the two-car garage, which has space for storage or a workbench.

Main floor:	1,585 sq. ft.
Lower floor:	700 sq. ft.
Total living area: (Not counting garage)	2,285 sq. ft.

Blueprint Price Code C

Plan P-9060-4

Three-Bedroom Split-Entry

- This lovely split-entry combines contemporary and traditional styling in an affordable floor arrangement.
- The main/upper level houses the sleeping rooms, two baths, convenient laundry facilities, and the main living areas.
- A formal dining room is divided from the foyer by an open handrail; the room can also overlook the front yard through a large, boxed window wall.
- The adjacent living room boasts a handsome fireplace and sliders to the rear patio.
- A large, versatile bonus space and a garage are found on the lower level.

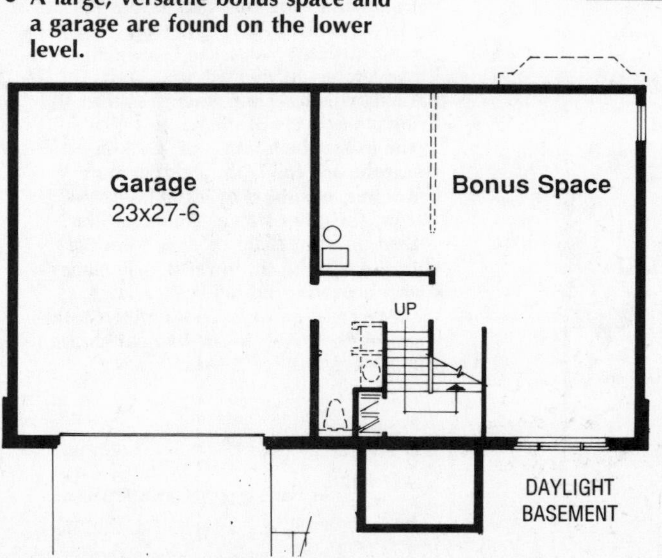

Plan B-90014

Bedrooms: 3	**Baths:** 2-2½
Space:	
Main/upper floor:	1,549 sq. ft.
Basement:	750 sq. ft.
Total living area:	2,299 sq. ft.
Garage:	633 sq. ft.
Exterior Wall Framing:	2x4

Foundation options:
Daylight basement.
(Foundation & framing conversion diagram available — see order form.)

Blueprint Price Code:	C

Plan B-90014

PRICES AND DETAILS ON PAGES 12-15

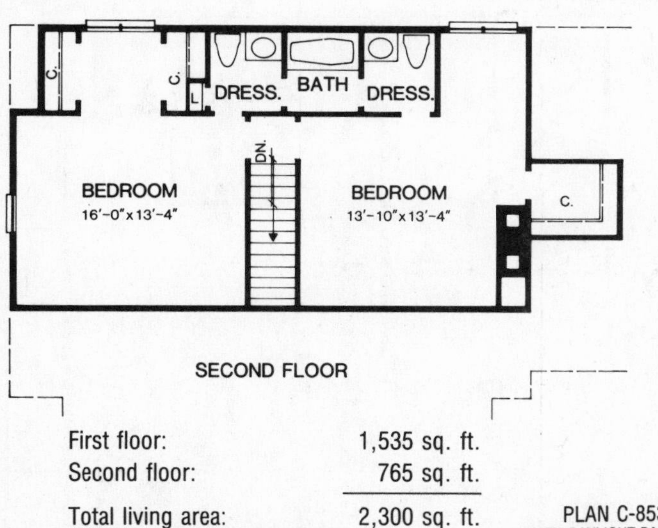

First floor:	1,535 sq. ft.
Second floor:	765 sq. ft.
Total living area: (Not counting basement or garage)	2,300 sq. ft.

PLAN C-8535
WITH DAYLIGHT BASEMENT

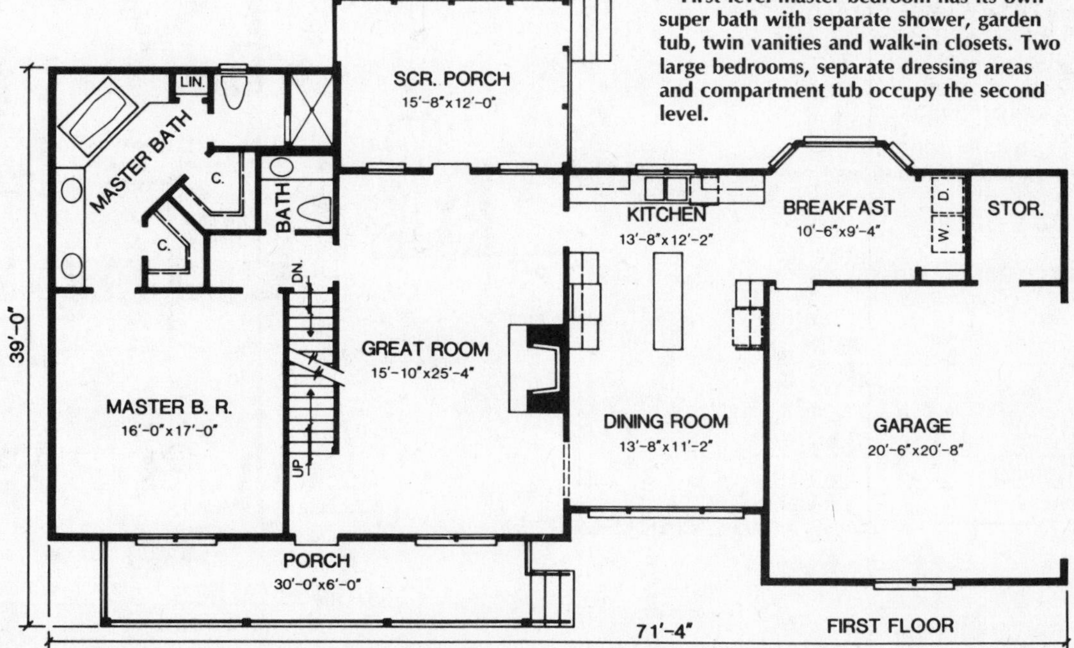

Traditional Touches Dress Up a Country Cottage

Multipaned windows, shutters and a covered porch embellish the traditional exterior of this country cottage. The floor plan incorporates a central Great Room. A raised-hearth stone fireplace forms part of a wall separating the Great Room from the kitchen.

The large country kitchen features an island and abundant counter space. The breakfast room includes a bay window. A large dining room faces the front.

First-level master bedroom has its own super bath with separate shower, garden tub, twin vanities and walk-in closets. Two large bedrooms, separate dressing areas and compartment tub occupy the second level.

Blueprint Price Code C

Plan C-8535

Distinctive Design

- Distinctive rooflines and elegant windows give this home an eye-catching, contemporary look.
- Inside, the two-story entry flows to the formal living spaces on the right, which host 9½-ft. raised ceilings. A pocket door closes off the dining room from the octagonal-shaped kitchen.
- An eating bar in the island kitchen serves the sunny breakfast nook, where sliding glass doors open to a covered patio. The adjoining family room features a 16-ft. vaulted ceiling, a fireplace framed by built-in shelves and access to a second patio.
- Entered through elegant double doors, the main-floor master suite offers a private bath with a step-up spa tub, a separate shower and a walk-in closet.
- A nice-sized laundry room and a half-bath are just off the garage entrance.
- Upstairs are two more bedrooms, a full bath and a study or loft with a fireplace.

Plans P-7750-3A & -3D

Bedrooms: 3+	**Baths:** 2½
Living Area:	
Upper floor	616 sq. ft.
Main floor	1,685 sq. ft.
Total Living Area:	**2,301 sq. ft.**
Daylight basement	1,685 sq. ft.
Garage	699 sq. ft.
Exterior Wall Framing:	2x6
Foundation Options:	**Plan #**
Daylight basement	P-7750-3D
Crawlspace	P-7750-3A

(All plans can be built with your choice of foundation and framing. A generic conversion diagram is available. See order form.)

BLUEPRINT PRICE CODE: C

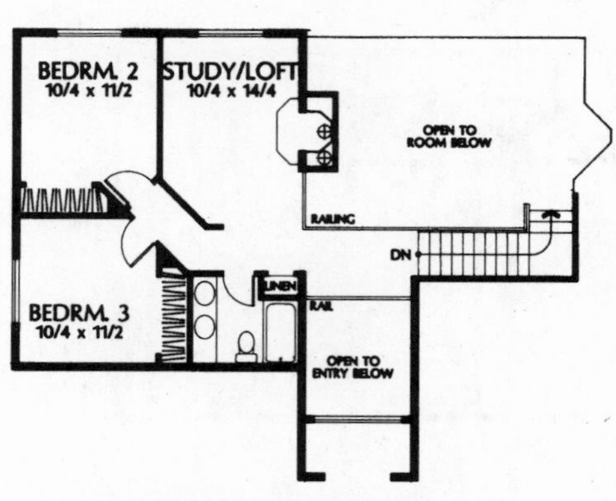

UPPER FLOOR

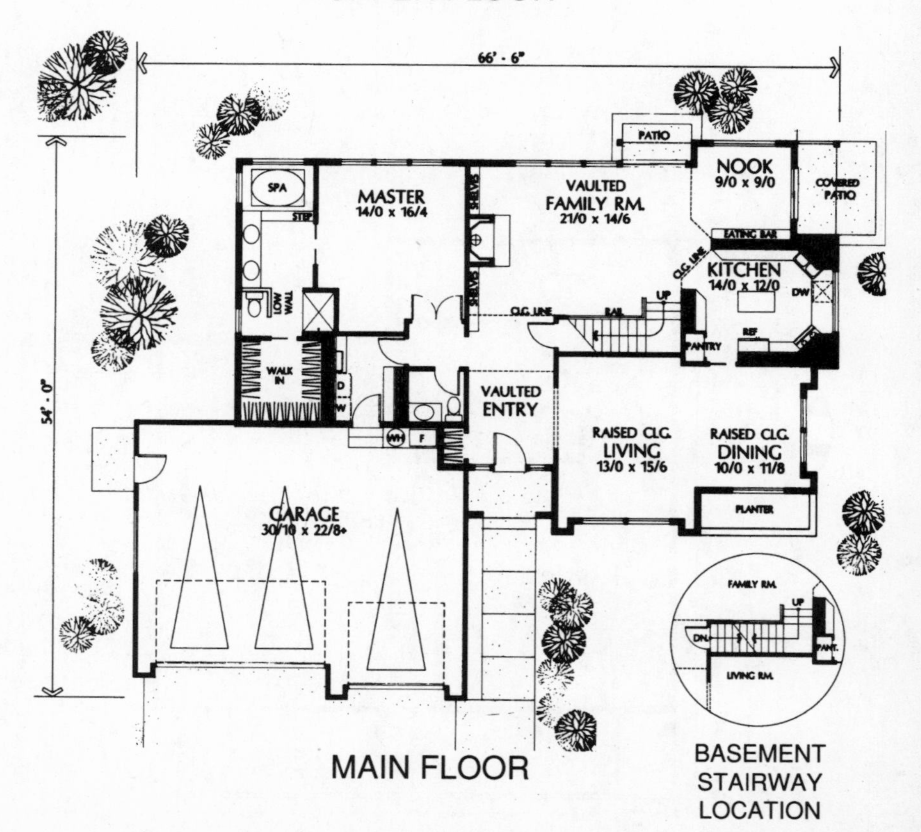

MAIN FLOOR

BASEMENT STAIRWAY LOCATION

Plans P-7750-3A & -3D

PRICES AND DETAILS ON PAGES 12-15

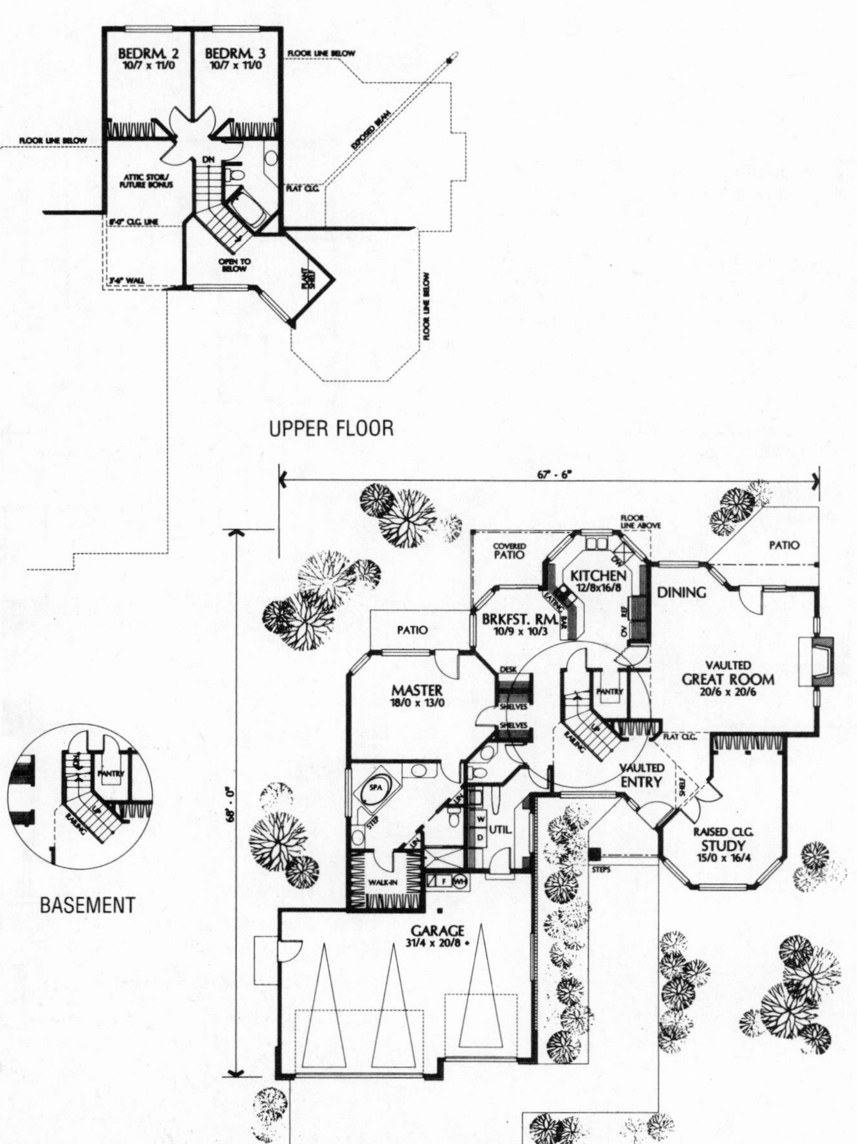

Unique Octagonal Styling

- Volume ceilings and multiple angled windows add style and luxury to this two-level, brick-accented home.
- The vaulted entry reveals double doors that access the study with raised ceiling and a large bay window.
- A vaulted Great Room and dining area share a fireplace and a patio view.
- A second patio joins the bayed kitchen and breakfast room, which share an eating bar. A large pantry is secluded near the stairway.
- The spacious main-level master bedroom offers a private patio and generous bath with walk-in closet, spa tub and separate vanities.

Plans P-6613-3A & -3D	
Bedrooms: 3	**Baths:** 2 ½
Space:	
Upper floor	410 sq. ft.
Main floor	1,925 sq. ft.
Total Living Area	**2,335 sq. ft.**
Basement	1,925 sq. ft.
Garage	648 sq. ft.
Exterior Wall Framing	2x6
Foundation options:	**Plan #**
Daylight Basement	P-6613-3D
Crawlspace	P-6613-3A
(Foundation & framing conversion diagram available—see order form.)	
Blueprint Price Code	C

Design for Steep Terrain

- A railing separates the sunken living room from the vaulted dining room for a great visual flow of space.
- The kitchen is highlighted by a corner window sink, an island and a walk-in pantry.
- The master suite includes a luxury bath illuminated by a skylight and a spacious walk-in closet.
- The partial basement could be omitted for building on flat lots.

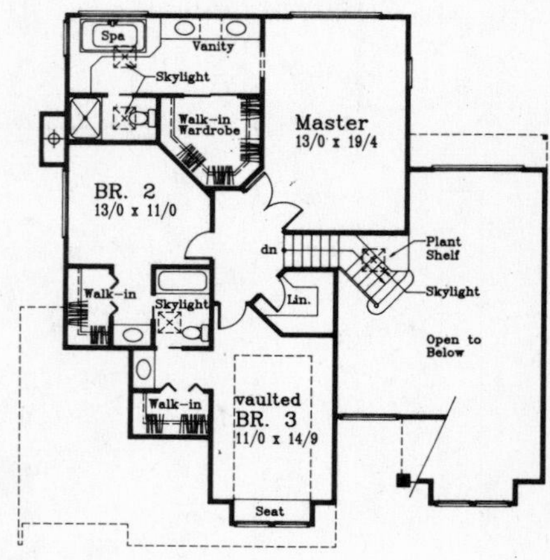

UPPER FLOOR

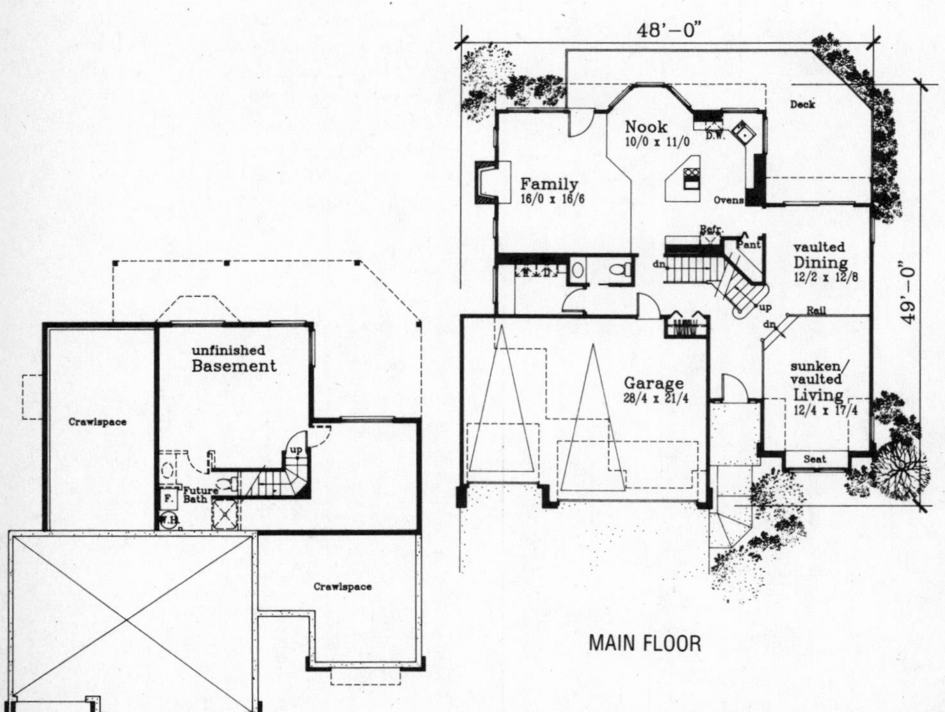

BASEMENT

MAIN FLOOR

Plan CDG-2009	
Bedrooms: 3	**Baths:** 2½
Living Area:	
Upper floor	1,113 sq. ft.
Main floor	1,230 sq. ft.
Total Living Area:	**2,343 sq. ft.**
Partial daylight basement	606 sq. ft.
Garage	604 sq. ft.
Exterior Wall Framing:	2x6
Foundation Options:	
Partial daylight basement	
(Typical foundation & framing conversion diagram available—see order form.)	
BLUEPRINT PRICE CODE:	**C**

PRICES AND DETAILS
ON PAGES 12-15

Roomy Four-Bedroom Home

57'0"
48'0"
RAILING
DECK
SHWR
LINEN
MASTER 12/4x15/4
STOR.
UP
RAILING
VAULTED FAMILY RM. 13/4x14/6
CEILING LINE
BAR
NOOK 12/8x8/0
REF
DW
KITCHEN 13/6x13/4
PANTRY
DRESSING
WALK IN WARDROBE
FREEZER
UTILITY
W
D
F
WH
VAULTED ENTRY
VAULTED DINING 12/0x11/8
VAULTED LIVING RM. 13/4x18/8
GARAGE 21/4x21/8

MAIN FLOOR

PLAN P-7592-2A
WITHOUT BASEMENT

Main floor:	1,685 sq. ft.
Upper floor:	665 sq. ft.
Total living area:	2,350 sq. ft.

(Not counting basement or garage)

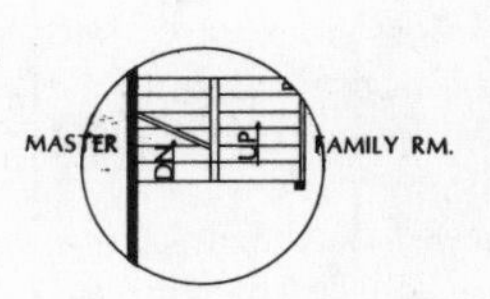

PLAN P-7592-2D
WITH DAYLIGHT BASEMENT

Basement level:	1,634 sq. ft.
Storage:	484 sq. ft.

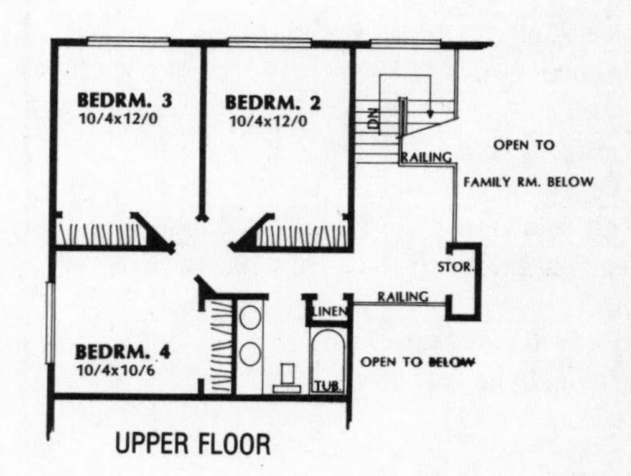

Blueprint Price Code C

TO ORDER THIS BLUEPRINT, CALL TOLL-FREE 1-800-547-5570

Plans P-7592-2A & -2D

PRICES AND DETAILS ON PAGES 12-15

Arched Accents

- Elegant exterior arches add drama to the covered porch of this lovely home.
- Once inside, interior arches flank the two-story-high foyer, offering eye-catching entrances to the formal dining room and the intimate living room.
- A dramatic window-framed fireplace and a 17-ft. ceiling enhance the spacious family room. A columned archway leads into the island kitchen, which offers a convenient serving bar.
- The adjoining breakfast area features a pantry closet, open shelves and a French door to the backyard. A half-bath and a laundry room are close by.
- The ceilings in all main-floor rooms are 9 ft. high unless otherwise specified.
- Upstairs, a balcony overlooks the family room and the foyer below. The master bedroom flaunts a 10-ft. tray ceiling, a beautiful window showpiece and a private bath with 13-ft. vaulted ceiling and a garden tub. The bedroom may be extended to include a sitting area.
- Boasting its own dressing vanity, the rear-facing bedroom offers private access to a compartmentalized bath that also serves the two remaining bedrooms.

Plan FB-2368	
Bedrooms: 4	**Baths:** 2½
Living Area:	
Upper floor	1,168 sq. ft.
Main floor	1,200 sq. ft.
Total Living Area:	**2,368 sq. ft.**
Daylight basement	1,200 sq. ft.
Garage	504 sq. ft.
Exterior Wall Framing:	2x4
Foundation Options:	
Daylight basement	
Slab	
(All plans can be built with your choice of foundation and framing. A generic conversion diagram is available. See order form.)	
BLUEPRINT PRICE CODE:	**C**

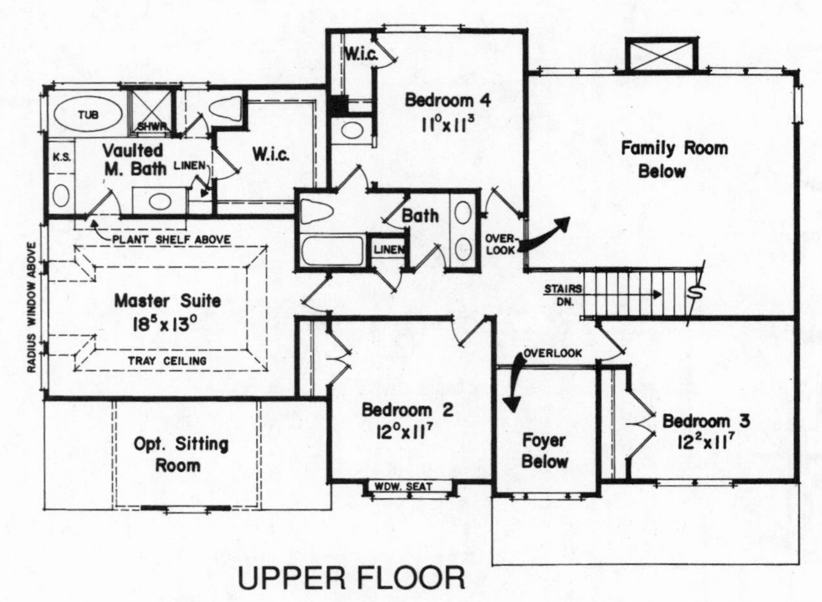

UPPER FLOOR

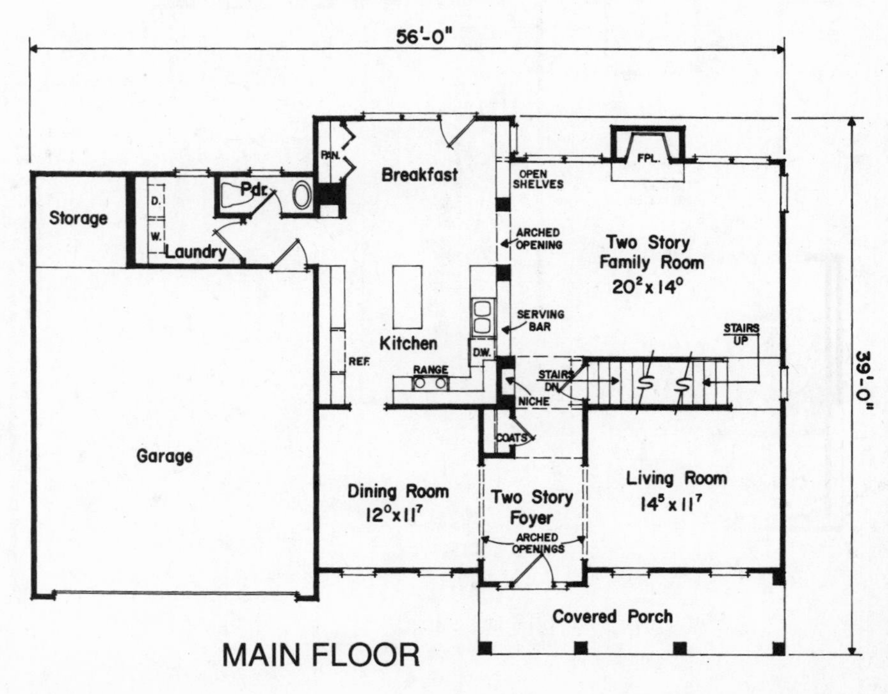

MAIN FLOOR

UPPER FLOOR

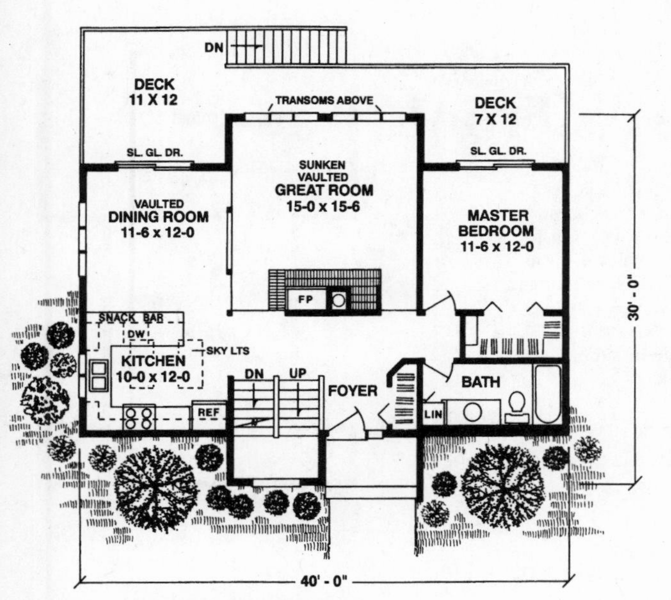

MAIN FLOOR

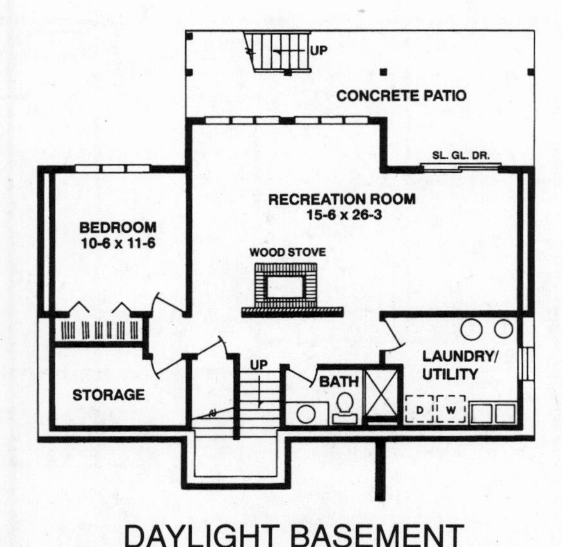

DAYLIGHT BASEMENT

Three Levels of Privacy

- With a bedroom on each of its three floors, this home offers private quarters for everyone in the family.
- The home takes full advantage of the sun's rays, with transoms, skylights and four sets of sliding glass doors.
- The two-story foyer with plant shelves above ushers guests into the sunken Great Room, which features a vaulted ceiling, a two-sided fireplace and a window wall with transoms on top.
- The vaulted dining room has sliders leading to an expansive deck.
- The U-shaped, vaulted kitchen boasts skylights and a peninsula snack bar.
- The master bedroom offers a walk-in closet and sliding glass doors to the rear deck. A full bath is just steps away.
- The upper-floor balcony and loft overlook the Great Room and foyer. A secluded bedroom has a private deck.
- The highlight of the daylight basement is the huge recreation room with abundant windows, a warm woodstove and sliders to a large patio.

Plan PI-100	
Bedrooms: 3	**Baths:** 2
Living Area:	
Upper floor	456 sq. ft.
Main floor	976 sq. ft.
Daylight basement	976 sq. ft.
Total Living Area:	**2,408 sq. ft.**
Exterior Wall Framing:	2x6
Foundation Options:	
Daylight basement	
(Typical foundation & framing conversion diagram available—see order form.)	
BLUEPRINT PRICE CODE:	**C**

Rear of Home As Attractive As Front

The rear of this rustic/contemporary home features a massive stone fireplace and a full-length deck which make it ideal for mountain, golf course, lake or other locations where both the front and rear offer scenic views.

Sliding glass doors in the family room and breakfast nook open onto the deck. The modified A-Frame design combines a 20′6″ cathedral ceiling over the sunken family room with a large studio over the two front bedrooms. An isolated master suite features a walk-in closet and compartmentalized bath with double vanity and linen closet. The front bedrooms include ample closet space and share a unique bath-and-a-half arrangement.

On one side of the U-shaped kitchen and breakfast nook is the formal dining room which opens onto the foyer. On the other side is a utility room which can be entered from either the kitchen or garage.

The exterior features a massive stone fireplace, large glass areas and a combination of vertical wood siding and stone.

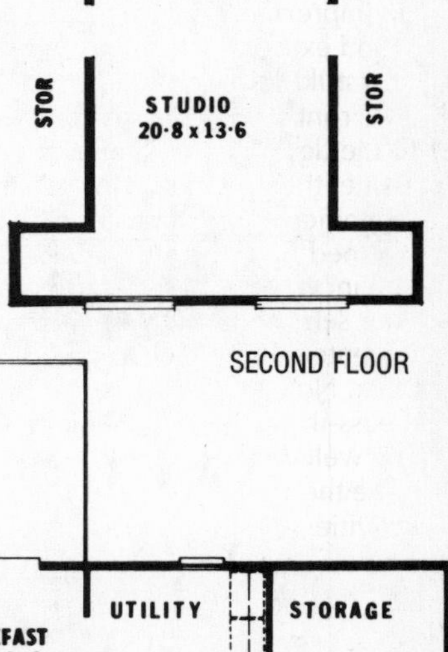

SECOND FLOOR

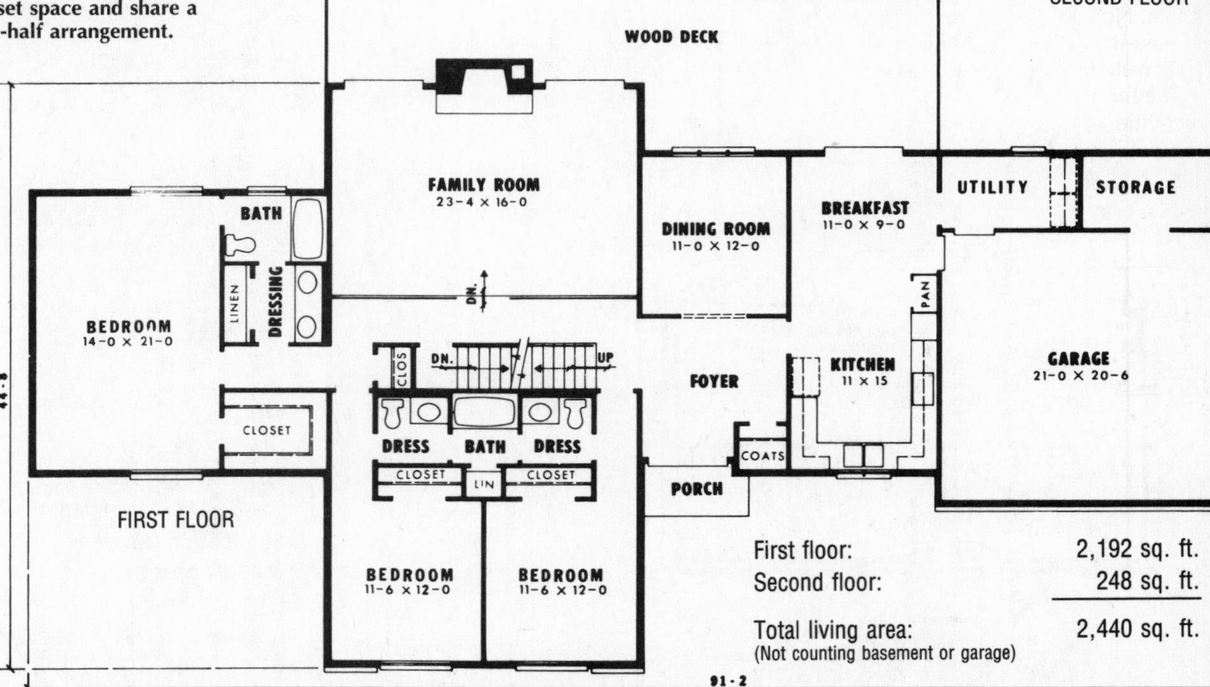

FIRST FLOOR

First floor:	2,192 sq. ft.
Second floor:	248 sq. ft.
Total living area: (Not counting basement or garage)	2,440 sq. ft.

Specify daylight basement, crawlspace or slab foundation when ordering.

Blueprint Price Code C

Plan C-7710

PRICES AND DETAILS ON PAGES 12-15

Rustic Year-Round Home

- This rustic home allows the year-round enjoyment of a scenic site. Visitors will be impressed by the home's attractive wood exterior, enormous railed deck and striking chimney.
- The front stairs lead past a storage closet to the deck and the main entrance.
- Inside, the open foyer introduces the magnificent Great Room, which is warmed by a cozy fireplace and enhanced by a 15½-ft. cathedral ceiling. Four sets of sliding glass doors extend the entertaining area to the wraparound deck. Note the handy serving shelf with a pass-through from the kitchen.
- The welcoming country kitchen is sure to be the center of casual family activities. Features here include a handy pantry closet, a large snack bar and a second fireplace.
- The spacious master bedroom offers private access to the main-floor bath, which shows off a relaxing whirlpool tub and a linen closet.
- Convenient laundry and coat closets complete the main floor.
- A railed, skylighted stairway leads to two bedrooms, a second bath and another linen closet on the upper floor. The railed hallway provides views to the Great Room below.
- Perfect for a sloping lot, this home's daylight basement includes a fabulous recreation room with a third fireplace and sliding glass doors to a nice patio. A third bath and an unfinished area are other extras.
- Also on the lower level is a unique tuck-under garage, which may be entered from two ways and is suitable for boat storage.

Plan AX-7944-A

Bedrooms: 3	**Baths:** 3
Living Area:	
Upper floor	457 sq. ft.
Main floor	1,191 sq. ft.
Daylight basement (finished)	545 sq. ft.
Total Living Area:	**2,193 sq. ft.**
Daylight basement (unfinished)	246 sq. ft.
Tuck-under garage	382 sq. ft.
Exterior Wall Framing:	2x4
Foundation Options:	
Daylight basement	

(All plans can be built with your choice of foundation and framing. A generic conversion diagram is available. See order form.)

BLUEPRINT PRICE CODE: C

MAIN FLOOR

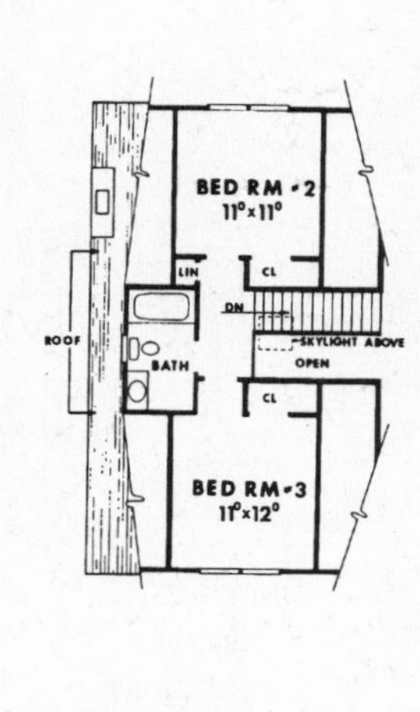

UPPER FLOOR

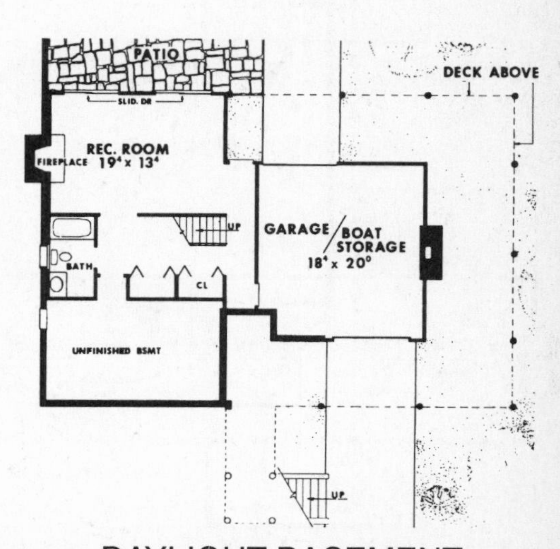

DAYLIGHT BASEMENT

PRICES AND DETAILS ON PAGES 12-15

Designed for Rear-Sloping Lot

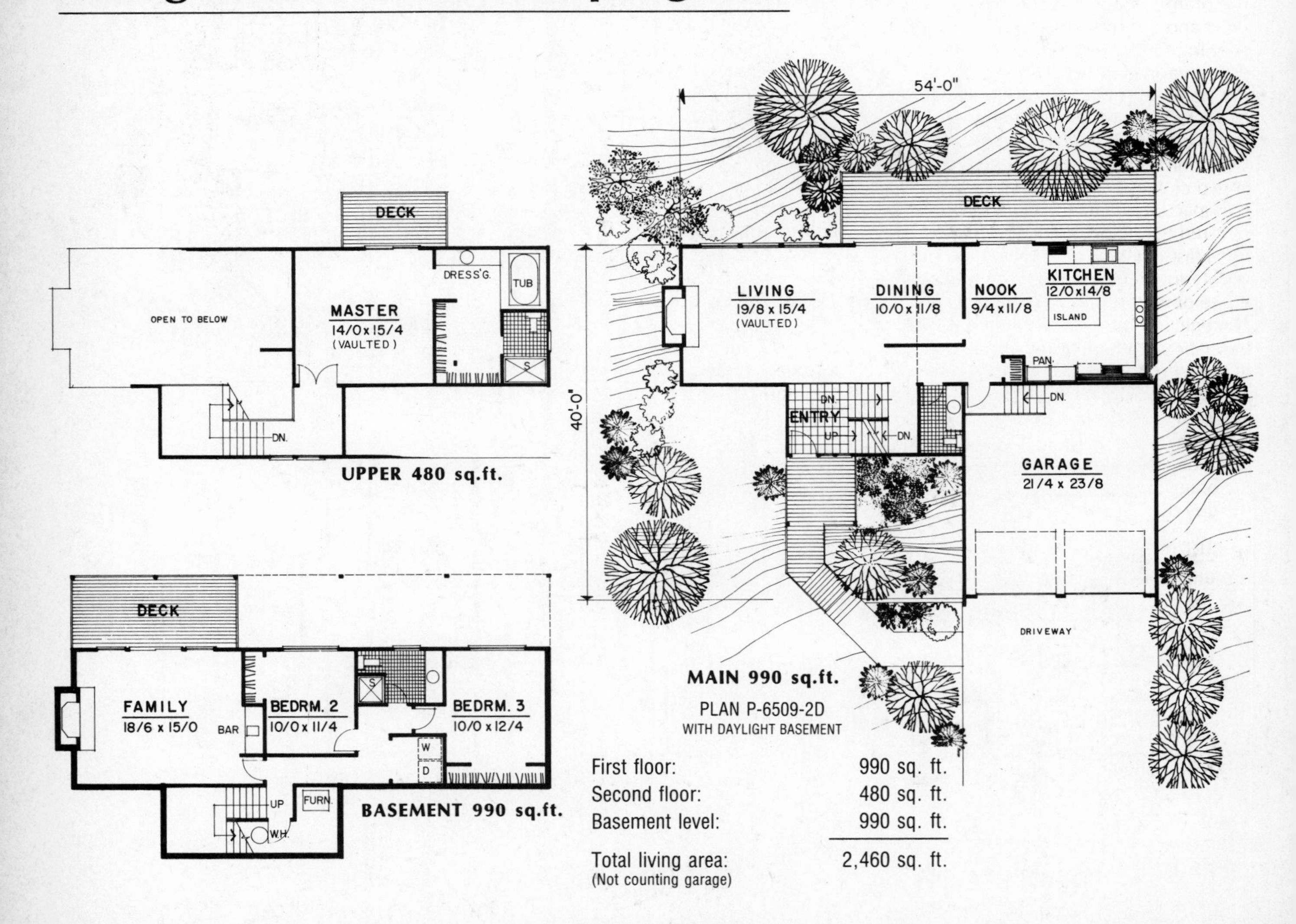

First floor:	990 sq. ft.
Second floor:	480 sq. ft.
Basement level:	990 sq. ft.
Total living area: (Not counting garage)	2,460 sq. ft.

Blueprint Price Code C

Plan P-6509-2D

PRICES AND DETAILS ON PAGES 12-15

Suited For a Downhill Slope

- Ideally suited for a lot that slopes downhill, this contemporary home suggests a carefree, relaxed spirit. Open railings are used throughout the interior to designate living areas without restricting the flow of space.
- The dramatic vaulted entry accesses the main and lower levels, while directly opening to a large, sunken living room with a vaulted ceiling. The living room can be viewed through an open railing in the formal dining room above.
- At the center of the floor plan is a reception area with a unique octagonal coved ceiling.
- The spacious island kitchen overlooks a covered patio and adjoins an angled breakfast nook.
- Family room activities can be extended to the patio through a French door. Strategically placed skylights brighten the patio and the interior of the house as well.
- A vaulted master bedroom with a bayed sitting alcove and a private, skylighted bath shares the sleeping wing with two secondary bedrooms and another bath.
- A storage area and a three-car garage occupy the lower level.

Plan CDG-4014	
Bedrooms: 3+	**Baths:** 2
Living Area:	
Main floor	2,462 sq. ft.
Total Living Area:	**2,462 sq. ft.**
Garage	806 sq. ft.
Storage	80 sq. ft.
Exterior Wall Framing:	2x6
Foundation Options:	
Crawlspace	
(Typical foundation & framing conversion diagram available—see order form.)	
BLUEPRINT PRICE CODE:	**C**

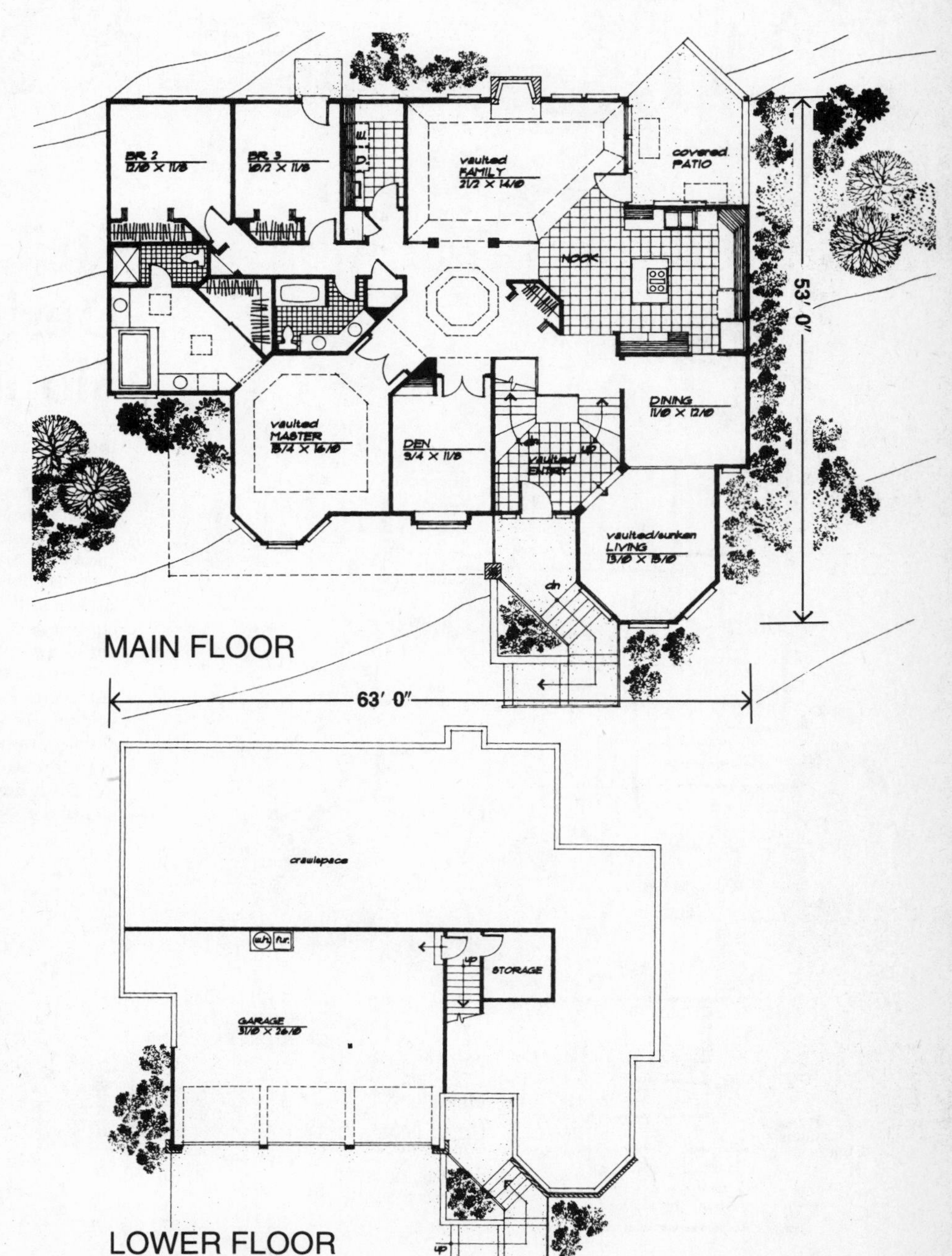

Striking Design for Sloping Lot

The brick accents, beautiful windows and stairway up to the entry are striking, and there are many extra features in this 2,467 sq. ft. home. The upstairs has two bedrooms plus a bath, and the hallway is lined with book shelves.

For the homemaker, there is a large kitchen with an island, a separate pantry, a built-in desk, and even a nook which looks out to a nice patio.

Then, for the "piece de resistance", see the master bedroom suite. The bedroom is vaulted and the bath includes a spa, double vanity and a long walk-in wardrobe.

To top off all these wonderful features, there is a three-car garage, which also includes a storage area.

50'-0"
47'-6"
Patio
Nook
Kitchen 10/0x15/6
Family 17/0x13/6
Mstr.Bath
spa
desk
pantry
Dining 10/6/10/0
Foyer
vaulted Master 17/8x17/4
Den/Br.4 11/0x12/4
vaulted Living 13/0x16/0
DRIVEWAY below
MAIN FLOOR

Exterior walls are 2x6 construction.

furn.
wh
up
Garage 26/0x28/8
Storage

PLAN R-4036
WITHOUT BASEMENT
(CRAWLSPACE FOUNDATION)

Main floor:	2,002 sq. ft.
Upper floor:	465 sq. ft.
Total living area: (Not counting garage)	2,467 sq. ft.
Storage:	60 sq. ft.

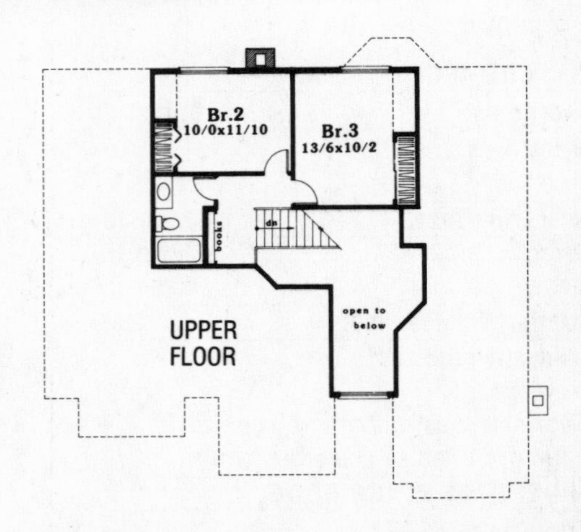

Blueprint Price Code C

Plan R-4036

TO ORDER THIS BLUEPRINT, CALL TOLL-FREE 1-800-547-5570

PRICES AND DETAILS ON PAGES 12-15

Soaring, Vaulted Spaces

- A dignified exterior and a gracious, spacious interior combine to make this an outstanding plan.
- The living, dining, family rooms and breakfast nook all feature soaring vaulted ceilings.
- An interior atrium provides an extra touch of elegance, with its sunny space for growing plants and sunbathing.
- The master suite is first class all the way, with a spacious sleeping area, opulent bath, large skylight and enormous walk-in closet.
- A gorgeous kitchen includes a large work/cooktop island, corner sink with large corner windows and plenty of counter space.

Plans P-7697-4A & -4D

Bedrooms: 3	**Baths:** 2
Space:	
Main floor (crawlspace version):	2,003 sq. ft.
Main floor (basement version):	2,030 sq. ft.
Basement:	2,015 sq. ft.
Garage:	647 sq. ft.
Exterior Wall Framing:	2x6

Foundation options:
Daylight basement (Plan P-7697-4D).
Crawlspace (Plan P-7697-4A).
(Foundation & framing conversion diagram available — see order form.)

Blueprint Price Code: C

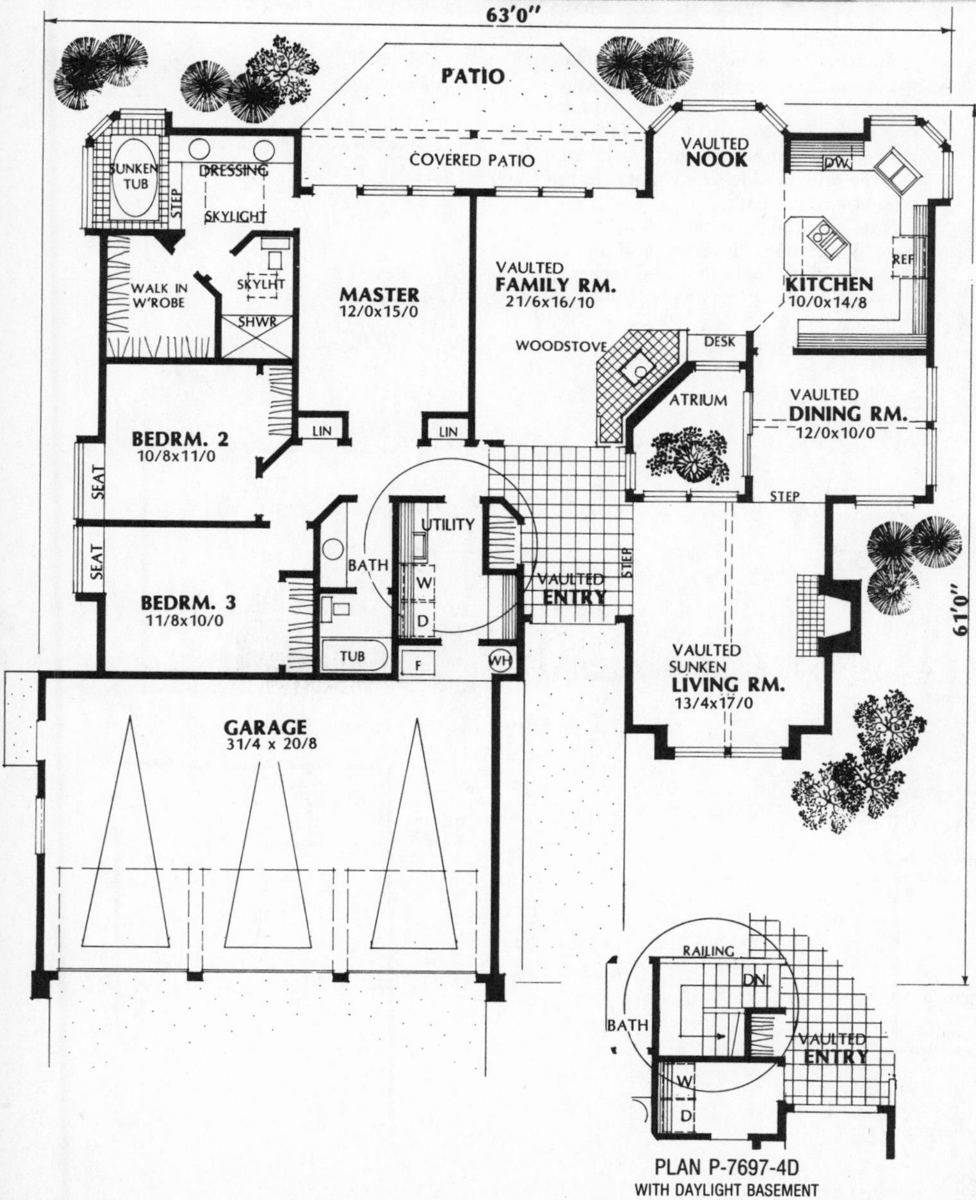

PLAN P-7697-4D
WITH DAYLIGHT BASEMENT

A Glorious Blend of New and Old

This three-bedroom, two and one-half-bath home is a glorious blend of contemporary and traditional lines. Inside, its 2,035 sq. ft. are wisely distributed among amply proportioned, practically appointed rooms. A vaulted entry gives way to a second reception area bordering on a broad, vaulted living room nearly 20′ long.

With its walls of windows overlooking the back yard, this grand room's centerpiece is a massive woodstove, whose central location contributes extra energy efficiency to the home — upstairs as well as down. The dining room offers quiet separation from the living room, while still enjoying the warmth from its woodstove. Its sliding door accesses a large wraparound covered patio to create a cool, shady refuge.

For sun-seeking, another wraparound patio at the front is fenced but uncovered, and elegantly accessed by double doors from a well-lighted, vaulted nook.

Placed conveniently between the two dining areas is a kitchen with all the trimmings: pantry, large sink window, and an expansive breakfast bar.

A stylish upstairs landing overlooks the living room on one side and the entry on the other, and leads to a master suite that rambles over fully half of the second floor.

Adjacent to the huge bedroom area is a spacious dressing area bordered by an abundance of closet space and a double-sink bath area. Unusual extras include walk-in wardrobe in the third bedroom and the long double-sink counter in the second upstairs bath.

Note also the exceptional abundance of closet space on both floors, and the separate utility room that also serves as a clean-up room connecting with the garage.

Upper floor:	1,085 sq. ft.
Main floor:	950 sq. ft.
Total living area:	2,035 sq. ft.

(Not counting basement or garage)

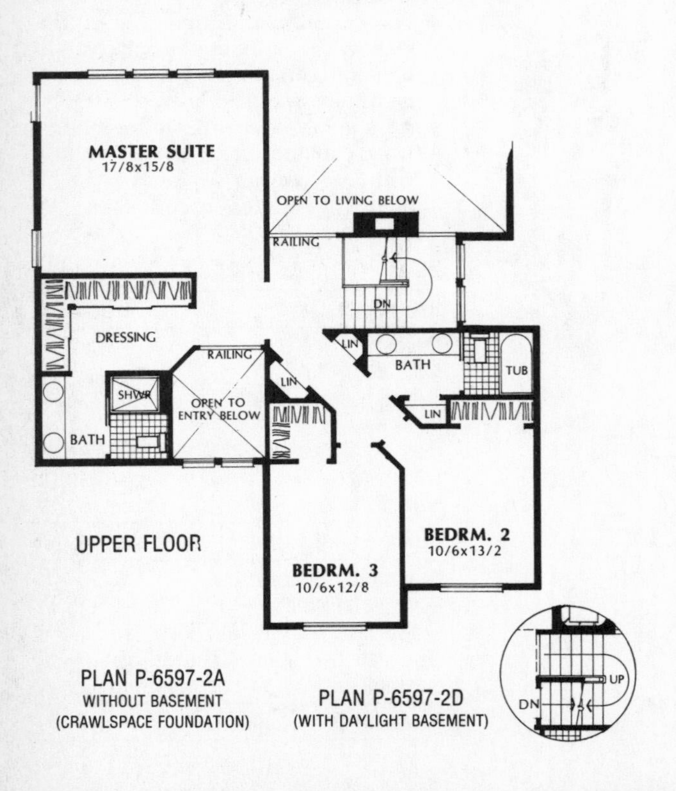

PLAN P-6597-2A
WITHOUT BASEMENT
(CRAWLSPACE FOUNDATION)

PLAN P-6597-2D
(WITH DAYLIGHT BASEMENT)

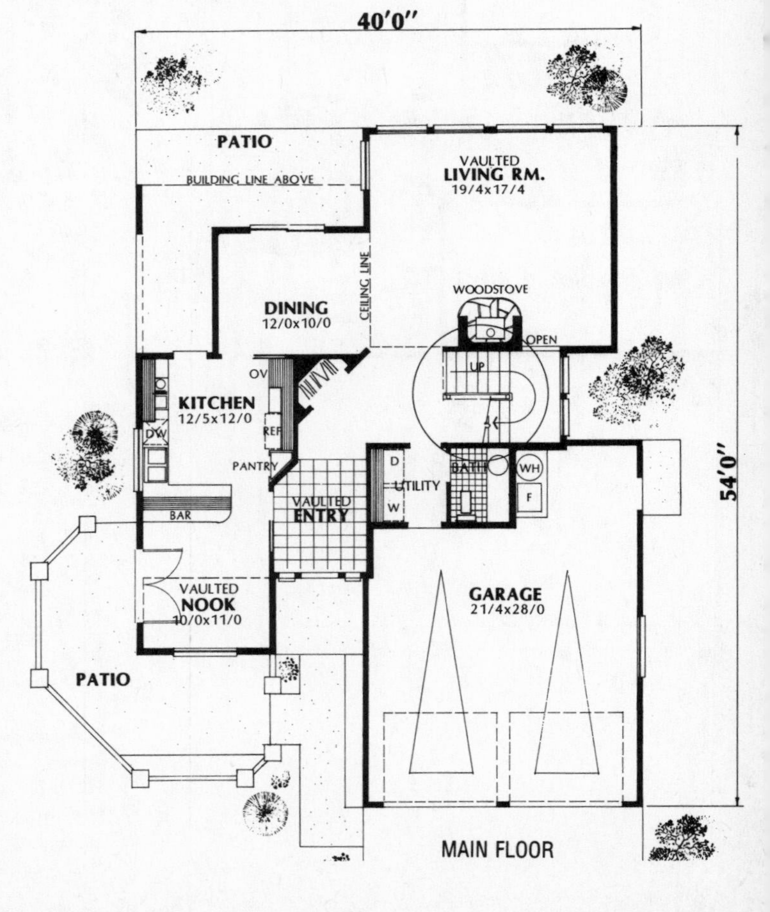

Blueprint Price Code C

Plans P-6597-2A & -2D

Bold Contemporary Style

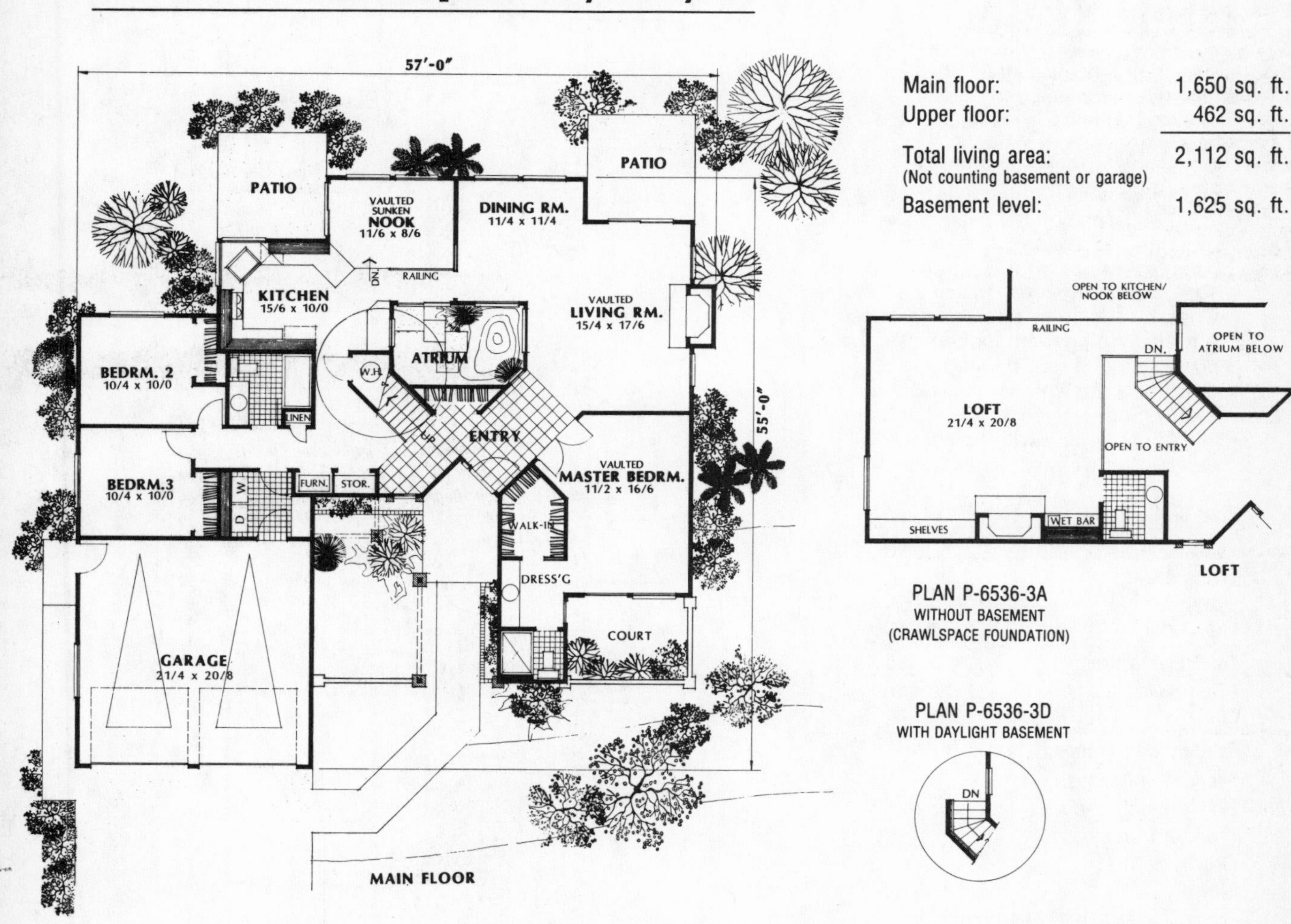

Main floor:	1,650 sq. ft.
Upper floor:	462 sq. ft.
Total living area: (Not counting basement or garage)	2,112 sq. ft.
Basement level:	1,625 sq. ft.

PLAN P-6536-3A
WITHOUT BASEMENT
(CRAWLSPACE FOUNDATION)

PLAN P-6536-3D
WITH DAYLIGHT BASEMENT

Blueprint Price Code C

Plans P-6536-3A & -3D

TO ORDER THIS BLUEPRINT, CALL TOLL-FREE 1-800-547-5570

PRICES AND DETAILS ON PAGES 12-15

Home with High Style

- Sweeping rooflines attract attention to this stylish contemporary home.
- The vaulted entry is enhanced by a clerestory window above.
- Sunlight invades the main floor by way of a window wall in the living room and a sunspace off the patio or deck.
- A main-floor den could serve as a handy guest bedroom.
- The open family room shares a woodstove with the kitchen and nook.
- A formal dining room looks out on the home's natural surroundings.
- Upstairs, a large master bedroom features a private deck, a walk-in closet and a master bath with corner tub, separate shower and dual vanities.

Plan S-2001	
Bedrooms: 3-4	**Baths:** 2½
Living Area:	
Upper floor	890 sq. ft.
Main floor	1,249 sq. ft.
Total Living Area:	**2,139 sq. ft.**
Basement	1,249 sq. ft.
Garage	399 sq. ft.
Exterior Wall Framing:	2x6
Foundation Options:	
Daylight basement	
Standard basement	
Crawlspace	
Slab	
(Typical foundation & framing conversion diagram available—see order form.)	
BLUEPRINT PRICE CODE:	**C**

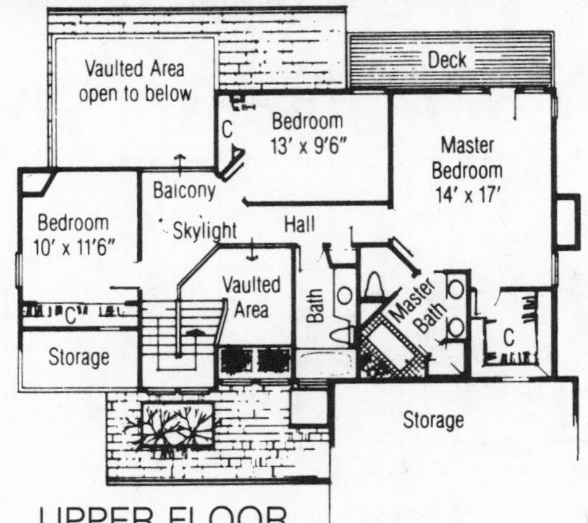

UPPER FLOOR

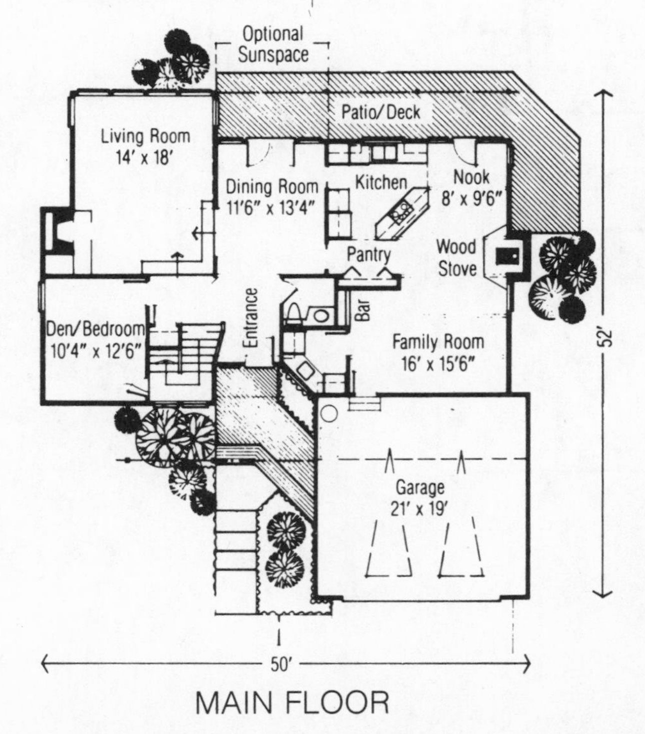

MAIN FLOOR

Today's Tradition

- The traditional two-story design is brought up to today's standards with this exciting new design.
- The front half of the main floor is devoted to formal entertaining. The living and dining rooms offer symmetrical bay windows overlooking the wrap-around front porch.
- The informal living zone faces the rear deck and yard. It includes a family room with fireplace and beamed ceiling as well as a modern kitchen with cooktop island and snack bar.
- There are four large bedrooms and two full baths on the upper sleeping level.

Plan AGH-2143

Bedrooms: 4	**Baths:** 2½
Space:	
Upper floor:	1,047 sq. ft.
Main floor:	1,096 sq. ft.
Total living area:	2,143 sq. ft.
Daylight basement:	1,096 sq. ft.
Garage:	852 sq. ft.
Exterior Wall Framing:	2x6

Foundation options:
Daylight basement.
(Foundation & framing conversion diagram available — see order form.)

Blueprint Price Code: C

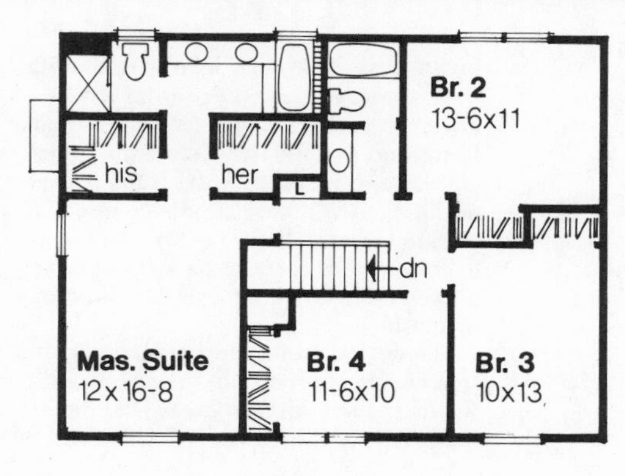

UPPER FLOOR

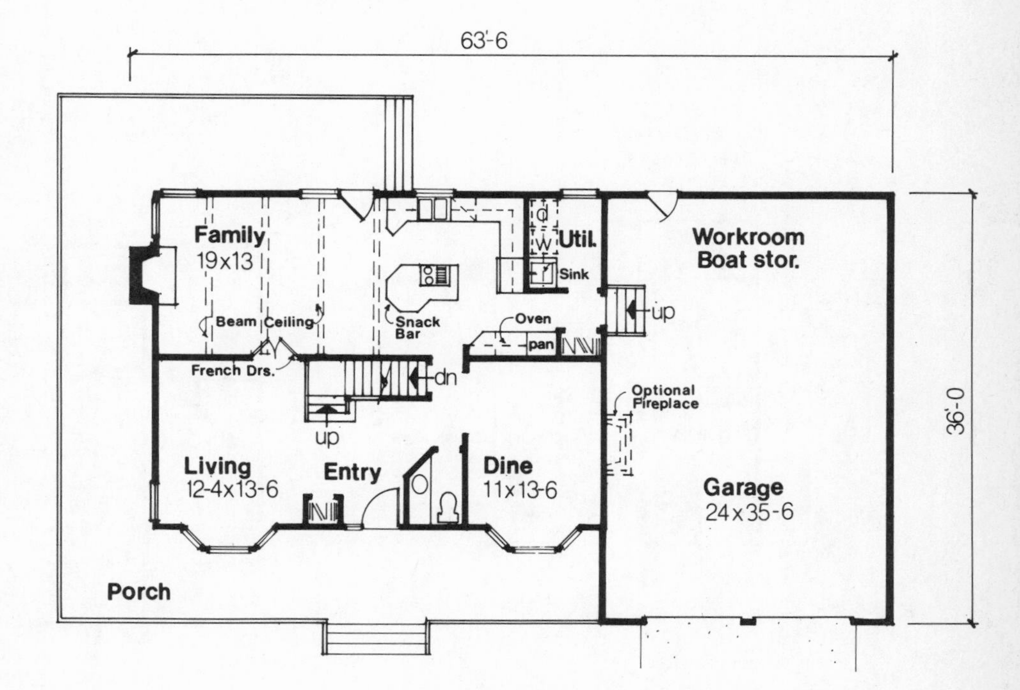

MAIN FLOOR

A Striking Contemporary

A multiplicity of decks and outcroppings along with unusual window arrangements combine to establish this striking contemporary as a classic type of architecture. To adapt to the sloping terrain, the structure has three levels of living space on the downhill side. As one moves around the house from the entry to the various rooms and living areas, both the appearance and function of the different spaces change, as do the angular forms and cutouts that define the floor plan arrangement. Almost all the rooms are flooded with an abundance of daylight, yet are shielded by projections of wing walls and roof surfaces to assure privacy as well as to block undesirable direct rays of sunshine.

The design projects open planning of a spacious living room that connects with the dining and kitchen area. The home features four large bedrooms, two of which have walk-in closets and private baths. The remaining two bedrooms also have an abundance of wardrobe space, and the rooms are of generous proportions.

For energy efficiency, exterior walls are framed with 2x6 studs.

First floor:	1,216 sq. ft.
Second floor:	958 sq. ft.
Total living area: (Not counting basement or garage)	2,174 sq. ft.
Basement:	1,019 sq. ft.

FIRST FLOOR
1216 SQUARE FEET

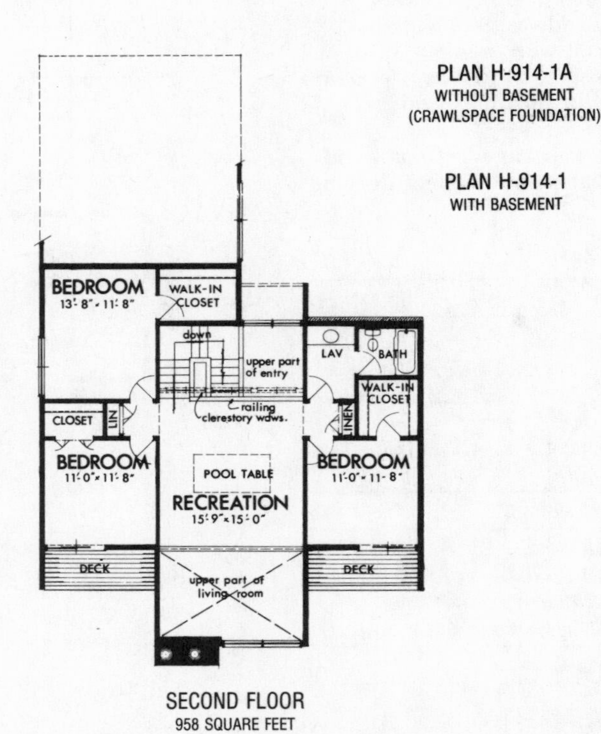

SECOND FLOOR
958 SQUARE FEET

PLAN H-914-1A
WITHOUT BASEMENT
(CRAWLSPACE FOUNDATION)

PLAN H-914-1
WITH BASEMENT

Blueprint Price Code C

Plans H-914-1 & -1A

TO ORDER THIS BLUEPRINT, CALL TOLL-FREE 1-800-547-5570

PRICES AND DETAILS ON PAGES 12-15

Country Kitchen and Deluxe Master Bath

- Front porch, dormers and shutters give this home a decidedly country look on the outside, which is complemented by an informal modern interior.
- The roomy country kitchen connects with a sunny breakfast nook and utility area on one hand and a formal dining room on the other.
- The central portion of the home consists of a large family room with a fireplace and easy access to a rear deck.
- The downstairs master suite is particularly impressive for a home of this size, a features a majestic master bath with two walk-in closets and double vanities.
- Upstairs, you will find two more ample-sized bedrooms, a double bath and a large storage area.

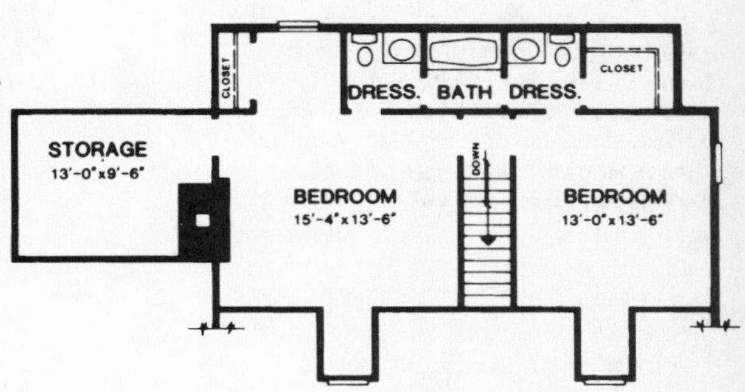

UPPER FLOOR

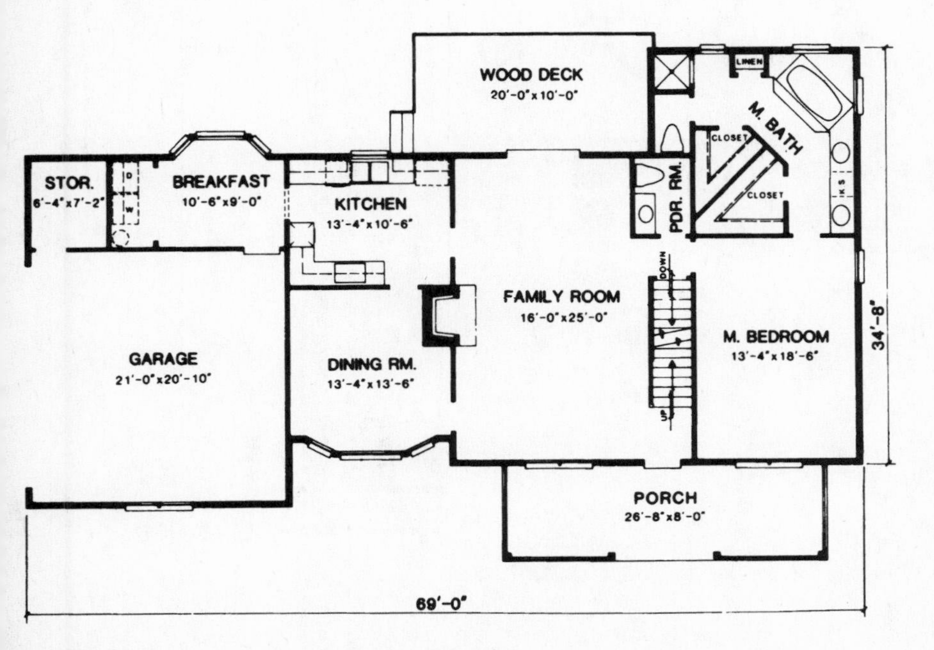

MAIN FLOOR

Plan C-8645	
Bedrooms: 3	**Baths:** 2½
Living Area:	
Upper floor	704 sq. ft.
Main floor	1,477 sq. ft.
Total Living Area:	**2,181 sq. ft.**
Daylight basement	Approx. 1,400 sq. ft.
Garage	438 sq. ft.
Storage	123 sq. ft.
Exterior Wall Framing:	2x4
Foundation Options:	
Daylight basement	
Crawlspace	
Slab	
(Typical foundation & framing conversion diagram available—see order form.)	
BLUEPRINT PRICE CODE:	**C**

Photo by Mark Englund/HomeStyles

Stunning One-Story Design

- This home gets off to a great start with a vaulted, skylighted foyer.
- The sunken living room simply sparkles, with its tray ceiling, fireplace and turret-like bay with high arched windows.
- The adjoining dining room also features a tray ceiling and a bay window.
- The unusual kitchen includes a built-in desk, a garden sink and an island cooktop with an eating bar.
- The adjacent nook and family room boast vaulted ceilings, an abundance of windows facing the rear patio and a woodstove tucked into one corner.
- A plant shelf provides an elegant introduction to the bedroom hall, where double doors open to a den.
- Also entered through double doors, the master bedroom is highlighted by a tray ceiling, a rear window wall and access to the patio. The magnificent master bath includes a raised, skylighted ceiling and a step-up garden spa tub.

Plans P-7754-3A & -3D	
Bedrooms: 2+	**Baths:** 2
Living Area:	
Main floor (crawlspace version)	2,200 sq. ft.
Main floor (basement version)	2,288 sq. ft.
Total Living Area:	**2,200/2,288 sq. ft.**
Daylight basement	2,244 sq. ft.
Garage	722 sq. ft.
Exterior Wall Framing:	2x4
Foundation Options:	**Plan #**
Daylight basement	P-7754-3D
Crawlspace	P-7754-3A

(All plans can be built with your choice of foundation and framing. A generic conversion diagram is available. See order form.)

BLUEPRINT PRICE CODE: C

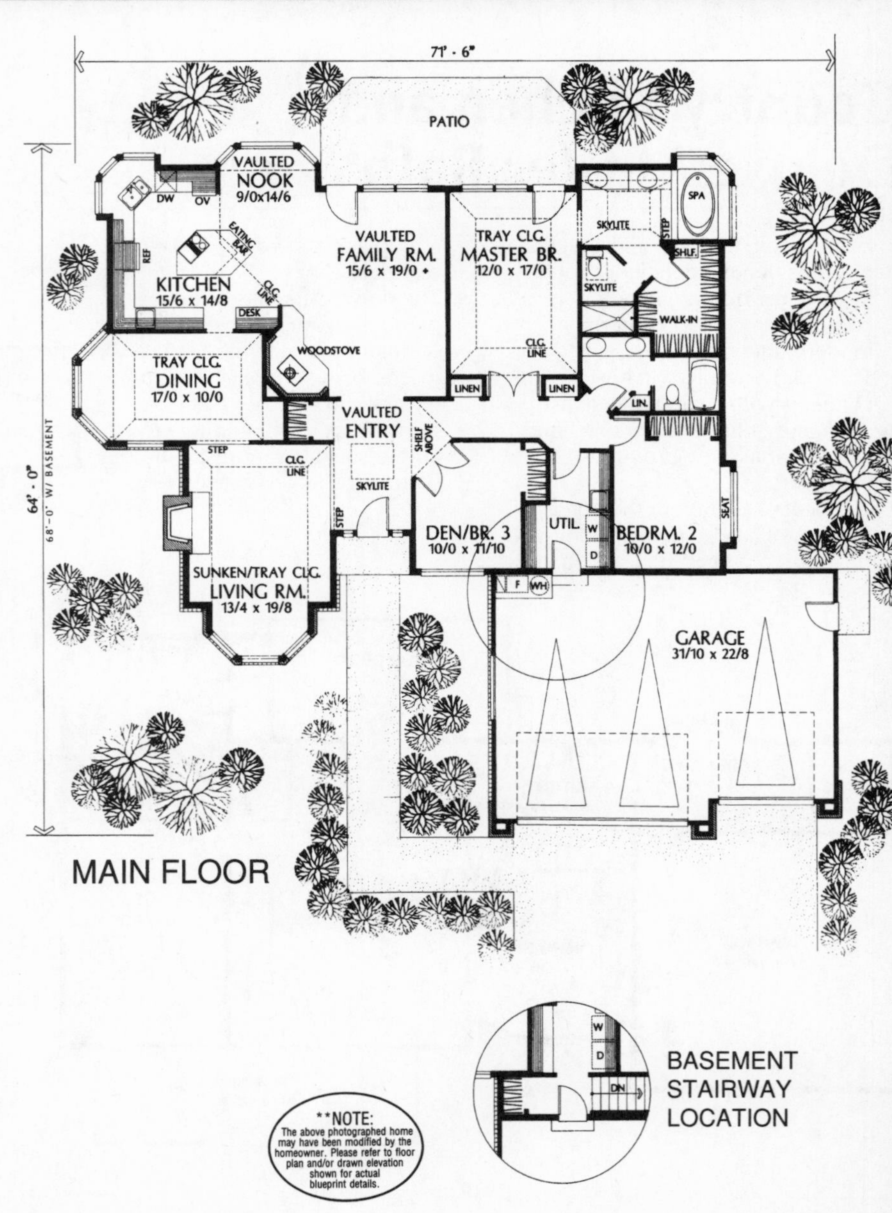

Distinctive Uphill Design

- This distinctive home is perfect for an uphill slope, with double-door access to a soaring two-story-high entry that leads up to the main living areas.
- From the central stairway, an open railing reveals the the living room, with its striking fireplace and access to a covered front deck. Sliding glass doors in the adjoining dining room open to the backyard.
- A pocket door leads from the dining room to the U-shaped kitchen, which offers a snack counter facing the sunny breakfast nook.
- A full bath serves the two smaller bedrooms on this floor, while the larger bedroom features its own bath.
- Downstairs, another full bath is centrally located for easy access from the garage, the bedroom and the two recreation areas. One area includes a fireplace, while the other provides room for expansion or a home office.
- Also on this floor are a large laundry room and access to the tuck-under, two-car garage.

Plan H-2093-1

Bedrooms: 4	**Baths:** 3
Living Area:	
Main floor	1,325 sq. ft.
Daylight basement	932 sq. ft.
Total Living Area:	**2,257 sq. ft.**
Tuck-under garage	452 sq. ft.
Exterior Wall Framing:	2x6

Foundation Options:

Daylight basement

(All plans can be built with your choice of foundation and framing. A generic conversion diagram is available. See order form.)

BLUEPRINT PRICE CODE: C

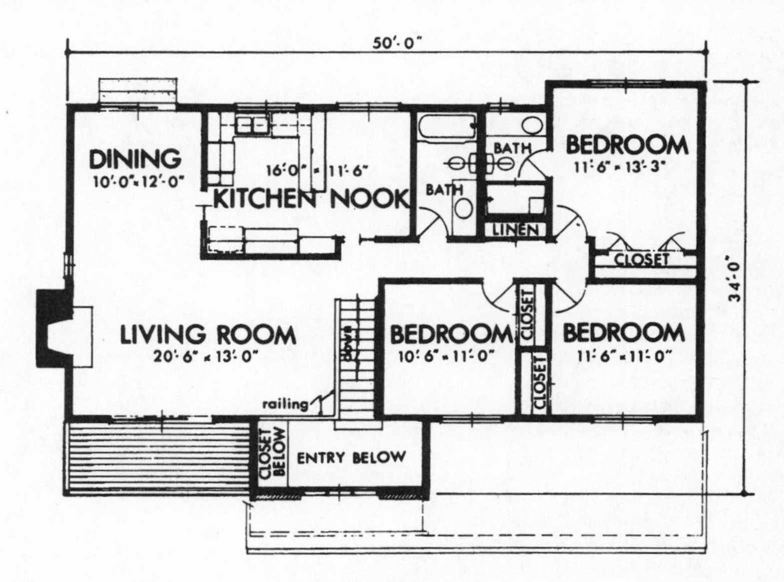

MAIN FLOOR

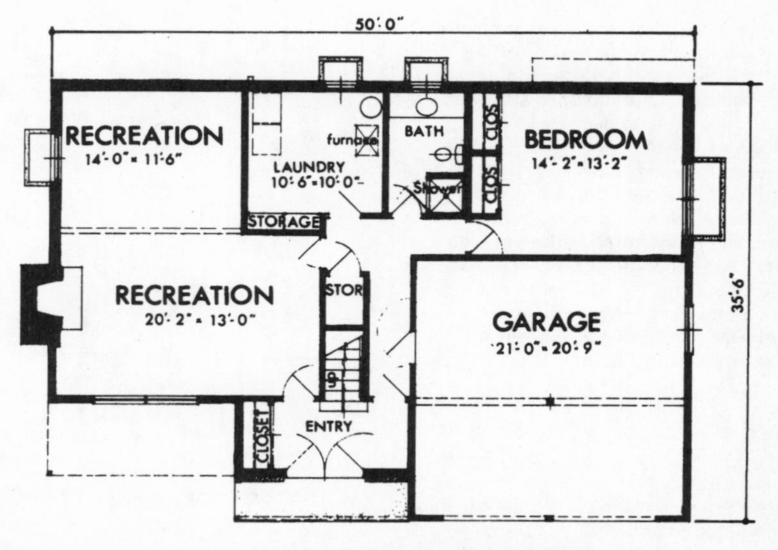

DAYLIGHT BASEMENT

Photo by Mark Englund/HomeStyles

Four-Bedroom Contemporary Style

Steeply pitched, multi-level gable rooflines accented by diagonal board siding and tall windows add imposing height to this contemporary, 2,289 sq. ft. home. With most of the 1,389 sq. ft. main floor devoted to the living, dining and family rooms, and a long patio or wood deck accessible off the nook, the home lends itself ideally to family activities and gracious entertaining.

Directly off the spacious foyer is the vaulted-ceiling living room and dining area, brightened with high windows and warmed by a log-sized fireplace. The wide U-shaped kitchen, nook and family room, with wood stove, join and extend across the back half of the main floor. With doors off the nook and utility room leading to a large patio, this area combines for large, informal activities. Also off the front entry hall is a full bathroom, a den or fourth bedroom, and the open stairway, brightened by a skylight, leading to the upper floor.

The master bedroom suite, occupying about half of the upper floor, has a wide picture window, walk-in dressing room/ wardrobe, and a skylighted bathroom with sunken tub and separate shower. The other two bedrooms share the hall bathroom. A daylight basement version of the plan further expands the family living and recreation areas of this home.

Main floor:	1,389 sq. ft.
Upper floor:	900 sq. ft.
Total living area: (Not counting basement or garage)	2,289 sq. ft.
Basement level:	1,389 sq. ft.

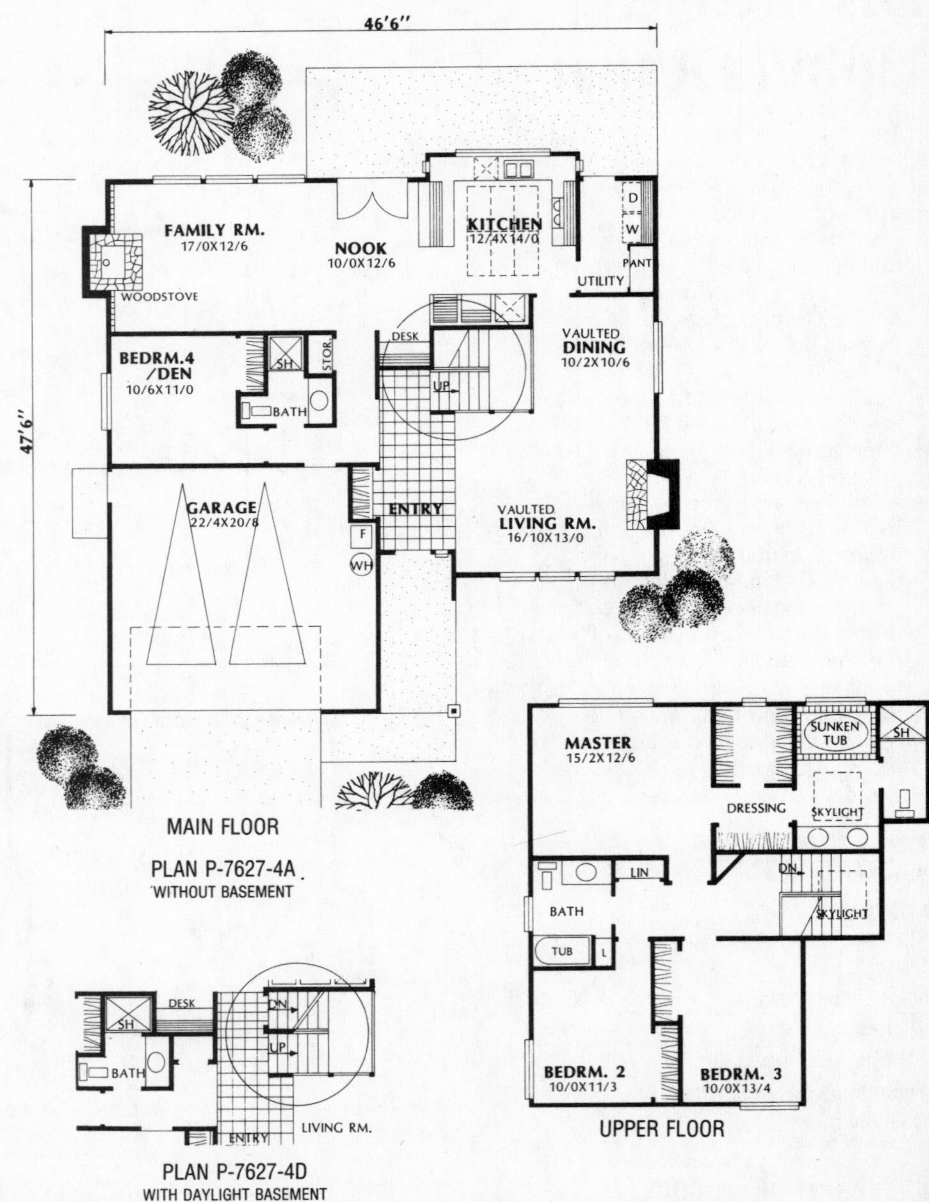

Blueprint Price Code C

 TO ORDER THIS BLUEPRINT, CALL TOLL-FREE 1-800-547-5570

Plans P-7627-4A & -4D

PRICES AND DETAILS ON PAGES 12-15

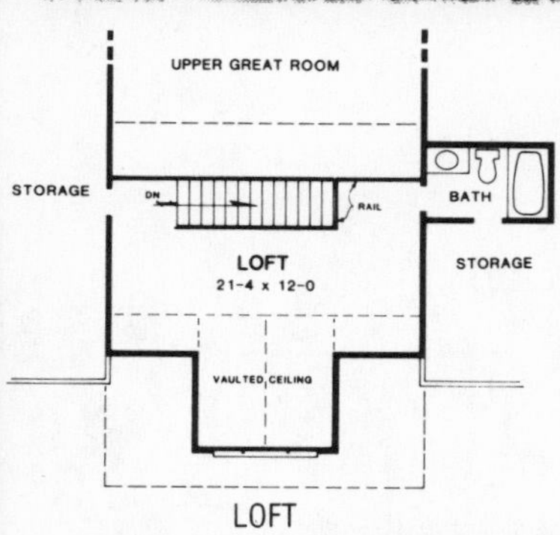

LOFT

Gracious Traditional

- This traditional-style ranch is perfect for a corner building lot. Long windows and dormers add distinctive elegance.
- The floor plan has a popular "split-bedroom" design. The master bedroom is secluded away from the other bedrooms.
- The large Great Room has a vaulted ceiling and stairs leading up to a loft.
- The upstairs loft is perfect for a recreation area, and has a full bath.
- The master bedroom bath has a large corner tub and his and hers vanities. A large walk-in closet provides plenty of storage space.
- The two other bedrooms have large walk-in closets, desks, and a shared bath.
- The kitchen and private breakfast nook are located conveniently near the utility/garage area.

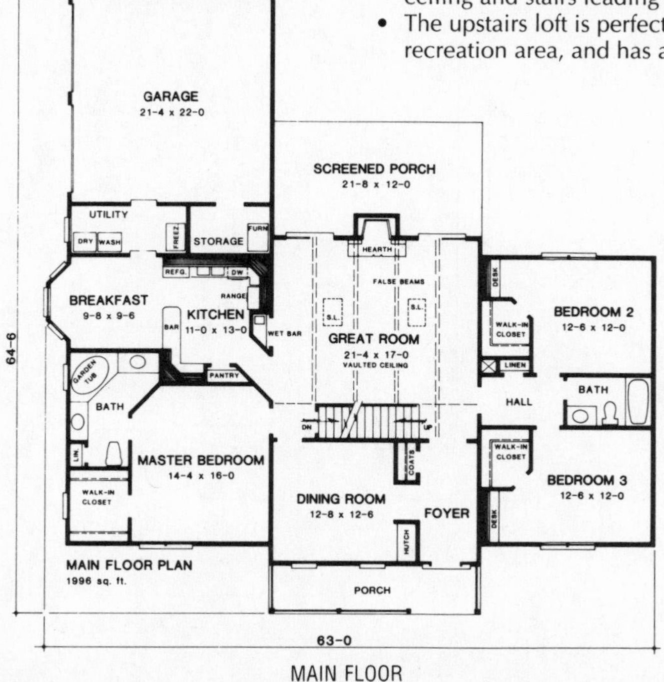

MAIN FLOOR

Plan C-8920

Bedrooms: 3	**Baths:** 3
Living Area:	
Upper floor	305 sq. ft.
Main floor	1,996 sq. ft.
Total Living Area:	**2,301 sq. ft.**
Daylight basement	1,996 sq. ft.
Garage	469 sq. ft.
Exterior Wall Framing:	2x4
Foundation Options:	
Daylight basement	
Crawlspace	
(Typical foundation & framing conversion diagram available—see order form.)	
BLUEPRINT PRICE CODE:	**C**

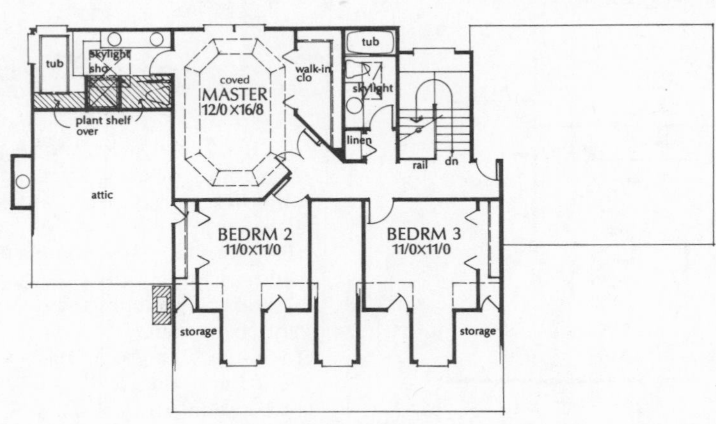

UPPER FLOOR

**NOTE:
The above photographed home may have been modified by the homeowner. Please refer to floor plan and/or drawn elevation shown for actual blueprint details.

Space:

Upper floor:	920 sq. ft.
Main floor:	1,385 sq. ft.
Total living area:	2,305 sq. ft.
Garage:	501 sq. ft.

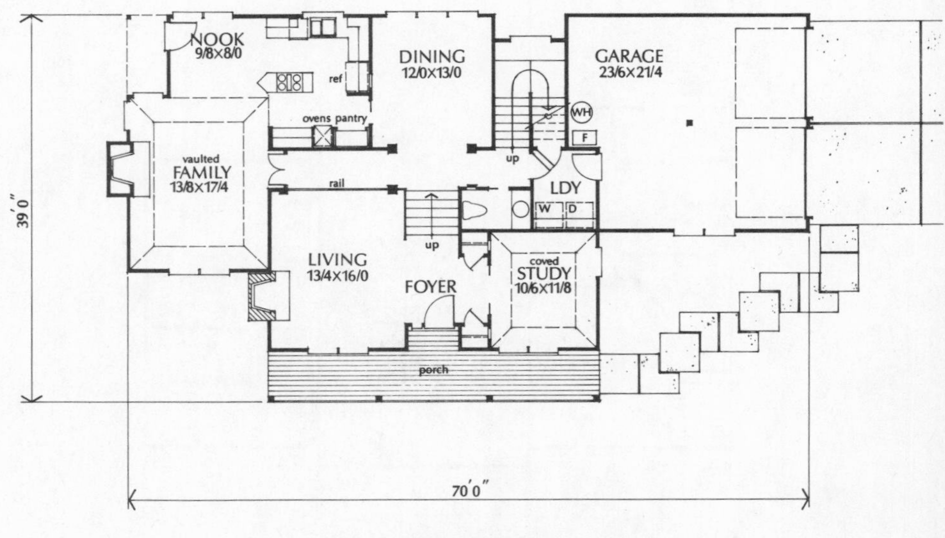

MAIN FLOOR

Plan CDG-4002

PRICES AND DETAILS ON PAGES 12-15

Photo by Mark Englund

Charming Design for Hillside Site

- Split-level design puts living room on entry level, other rooms up or down a half-flight of steps.
- Kitchen includes work/eating island and combines with dining/family room for informal living.
- Vaulted master suite includes private bath and large closet.
- Daylight basement includes two bedrooms, bath, utility area and a rec room.

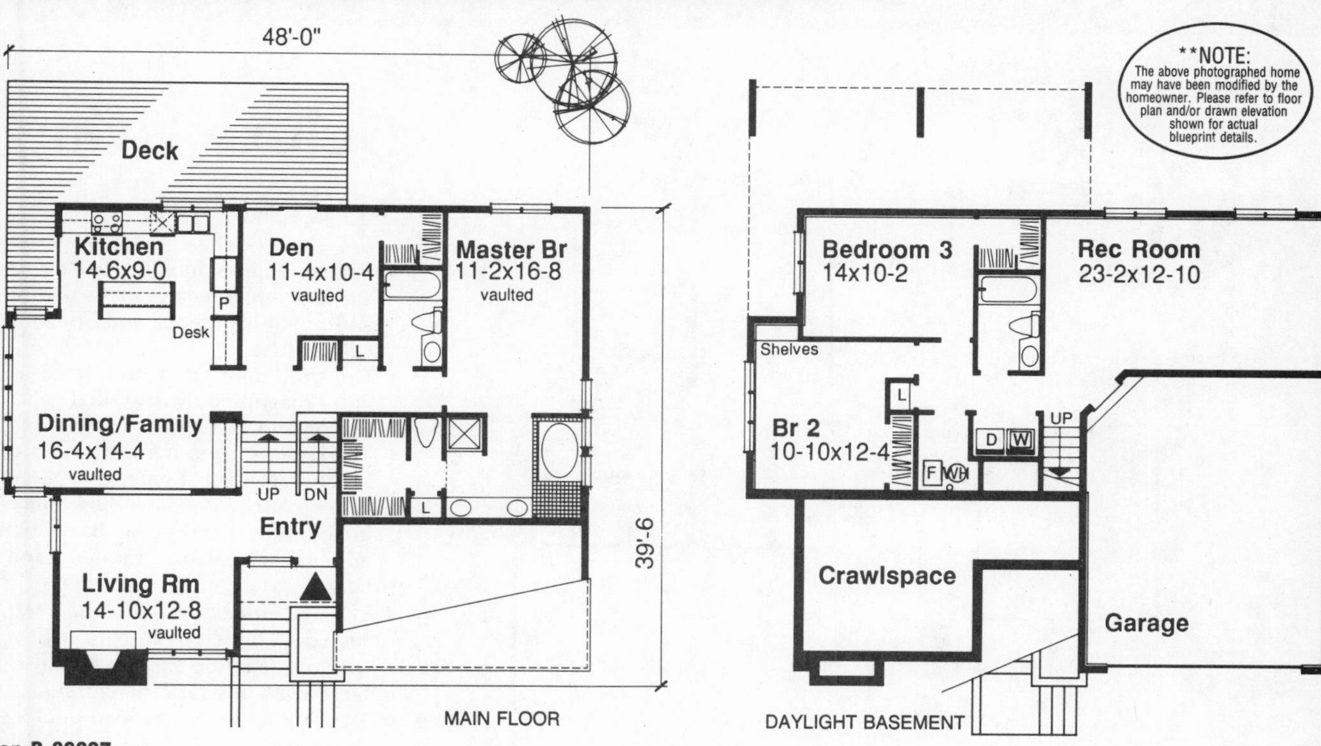

Plan B-89037

Bedrooms: 3+	**Baths:** 3
Living Area:	
Main floor	1,422 sq. ft.
Partial daylight basement	913 sq. ft.
Total Living Area:	**2,335 sq. ft.**
Garage	480 sq. ft.
Exterior Wall Framing:	2x6

Foundation Options:
Partial daylight basement
(Typical foundation & framing conversion diagram available—see order form.)

BLUEPRINT PRICE CODE: **C**

Photo courtesy of Piercy & Barclay Designers, Inc.

Deluxe Living Spaces

- Visitors approaching the front entry are welcomed by a courtyard with a wrought-iron fence and brick columns.
- The front door opens to a large entry magnified by a vaulted ceiling and skylight.
- The large, sunken living/dining area is great for formal entertaining.
- A huge kitchen/nook combination includes an island eating bar which adjoins the spacious, vaulted family room.
- The magnificent master suite includes an incredible bath with spa tub, separate shower and a large walk-in wardrobe closet.
- Daylight basement version doubles the space.

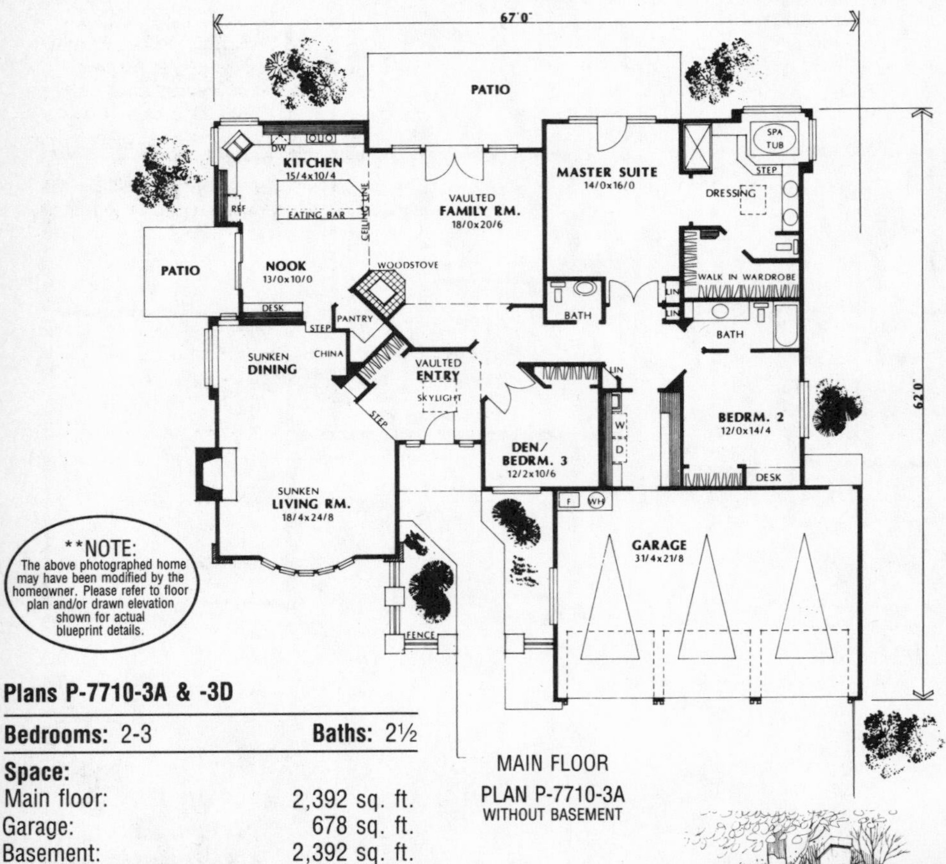

**NOTE: The above photographed home may have been modified by the homeowner. Please refer to floor plan and/or drawn elevation shown for actual blueprint details.

MAIN FLOOR
PLAN P-7710-3A
WITHOUT BASEMENT

Plans P-7710-3A & -3D

Bedrooms: 2-3	**Baths:** 2½
Space:	
Main floor:	2,392 sq. ft.
Garage:	678 sq. ft.
Basement:	2,392 sq. ft.
Exterior Wall Framing:	2x6

Foundation options:
Daylight basement, Plan P-7710-3D.
Crawlspace, Plan P-7710-3A.
(Foundation & framing conversion diagram available — see order form.)

Blueprint Price Code: C

PLAN P-7710-3D
WITH DAYLIGHT BASEMENT

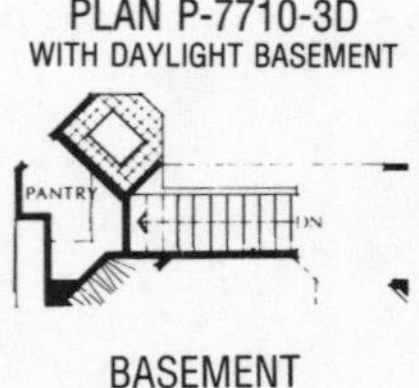
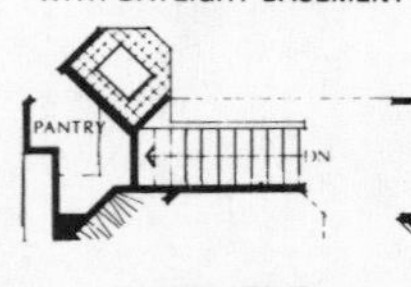

BASEMENT

Plans P-7710-3A &-3D

PRICES AND DETAILS ON PAGES 12-15

Gracious Living on a Grand Scale

Well suited to either a gently sloping or flat building site, this home is also geared to a conservative building budget. First, it saves money through the partial enclosure of the lower level with foundation walls. A portion of the lower level that is surrounded by concrete walls is devoted to a 15'-10" x 13'-0" bedroom or optional den with wardrobe closet, a spacious recreation room with fireplace, and a third complete bathroom along with an abundance of storage space.

The balance of the area at this level is devoted to a two-car garage. Access from this portion of the home to the floor directly above is via a central staircase.

In Plan H-2082-2, a formal dining room and large kitchen provide two places for family eating.

Plan H-2082-1 includes a combination family room and U-shaped kitchen in one open area. Spatial continuity is further extended into the cantilevered deck that projects over the garage driveway below and is accessible through sliding glass doors off the family room.

This system of multi-level planning offers economy in building where grading would otherwise be required.

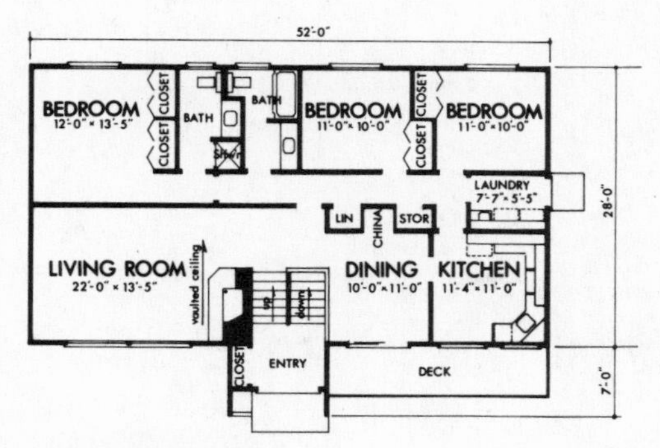

PLAN H-2082-2
MAIN FLOOR
1500 SQUARE FEET

PLAN H-2082-1
MAIN FLOOR
1500 SQUARE FEET

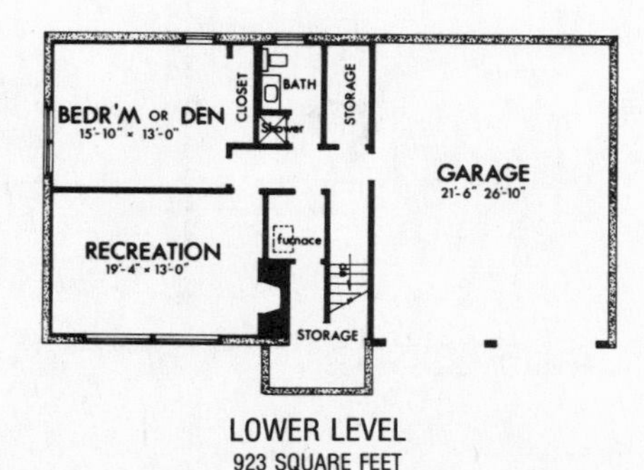

LOWER LEVEL
923 SQUARE FEET

Main floor:	1,500 sq. ft.
Lower level:	923 sq. ft.
Total living area: (Not counting garage)	2,423 sq. ft.

Blueprint Price Code C

Plans H-2082-1 & -2

PRICES AND DETAILS ON PAGES 12-15

Photo by Mark Englund/HomeStyles

Old-Fashioned Charm

- A trio of dormers add old-fashioned charm to this modern design.
- Both the living room and the dining room offer vaulted celings, and the two rooms flow together to create a sense of even more spaciousness.
- The open kitchen, nook and family room combination features a sunny alcove, a walk-in pantry and an inviting wood stove.
- A first-floor den and a walk-through utility room are other big bonuses.
- Upstairs, the master suite includes a walk-in closet and a deluxe bath with a spa tub and a separate shower and water closet.
- Two more bedrooms, each with a window seat, and a bonus room complete this stylish design.

Plan CDG-2004	
Bedrooms: 4	**Baths:** 2½
Living Area:	
Upper floor	928 sq. ft.
Main floor	1,317 sq. ft.
Bonus room	192 sq. ft.
Total Living Area:	**2,437 sq. ft.**
Partial daylight basement	780 sq. ft.
Garage	537 sq. ft.
Exterior Wall Framing:	2x6
Foundation Options:	
Partial daylight basement	
Crawlspace	
(Typical foundation & framing conversion diagram available—see order form.)	
BLUEPRINT PRICE CODE:	C

NOTE: The above photographed home may have been modified by the homeowner. Please refer to floor plan and/or drawn elevation shown for actual blueprint details.

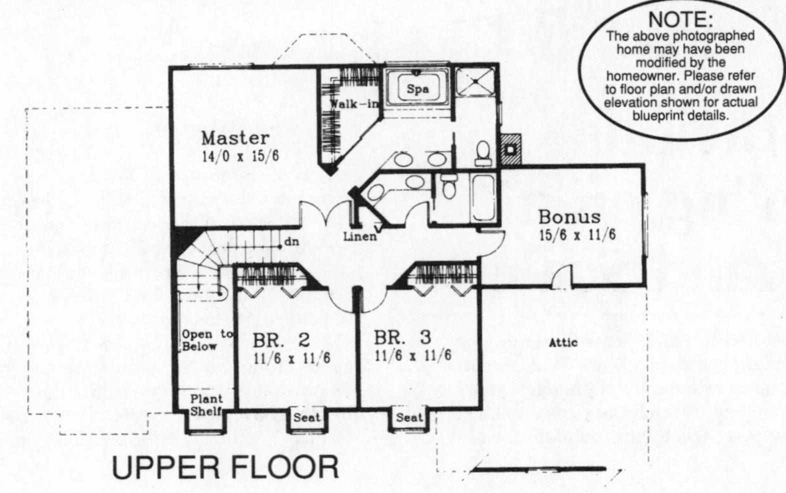

UPPER FLOOR

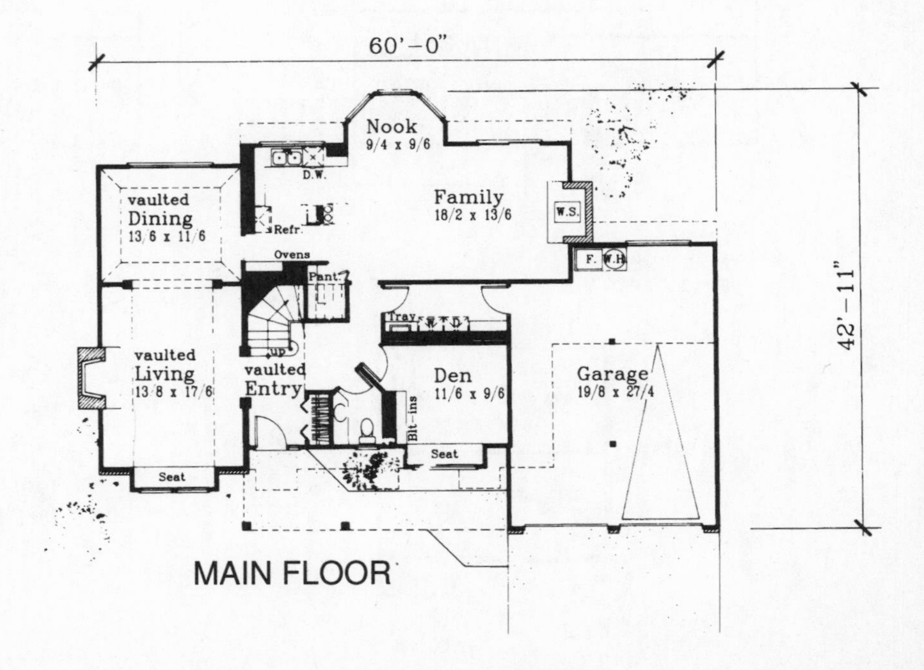

MAIN FLOOR

Large-Scale Living

- Eye-catching windows and an appealing wraparound porch highlight the exterior of this outstanding home.
- High ceilings and large-scale living spaces prevail inside, beginning with the two-story-high foyer.
- The spacious living room flows into the formal dining room, which accesses the front porch as well as the rear deck.
- The island kitchen combines with a bright breakfast room, also with deck access. The fabulous family room offers a warm corner fireplace, a soaring 18-ft. vaulted ceiling, a wall of windows and a view of the balcony hall above.
- The upper floor hosts four large bedrooms, including a luxurious master suite. The vaulted sleeping area is brightened by an arched window and has two walk-in closets. The skylighted master bath features a spa tub, a separate shower and a dual-sink vanity.
- The three remaining bedrooms are reached via a balcony hall, which offers stunning views of the family room.

Plan AX-93309

Bedrooms: 4	**Baths:** 2½
Living Area:	
Upper floor	1,180 sq. ft.
Main floor	1,290 sq. ft.
Total Living Area:	**2,470 sq. ft.**
Basement	1,290 sq. ft.
Garage	421 sq. ft.
Exterior Wall Framing:	2x4

Foundation Options:
Daylight basement
Standard basement
Slab
(All plans can be built with your choice of foundation and framing. A generic conversion diagram is available. See order form.)

BLUEPRINT PRICE CODE: C

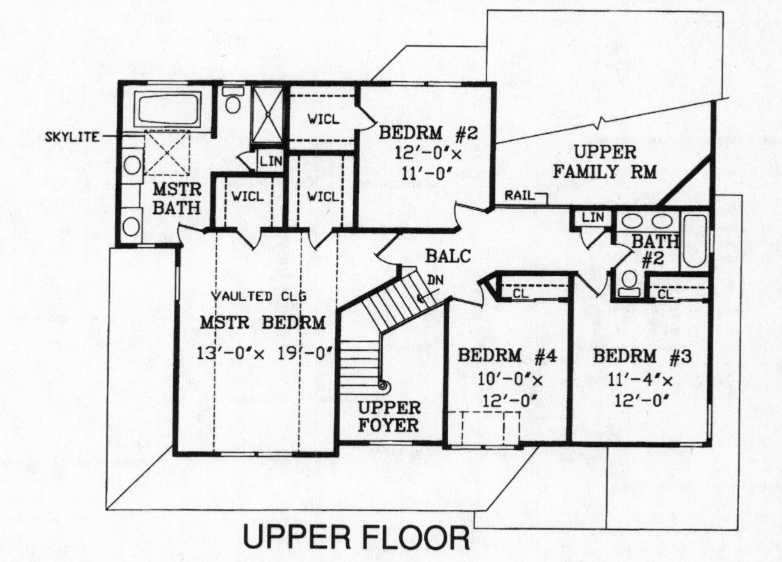

UPPER FLOOR

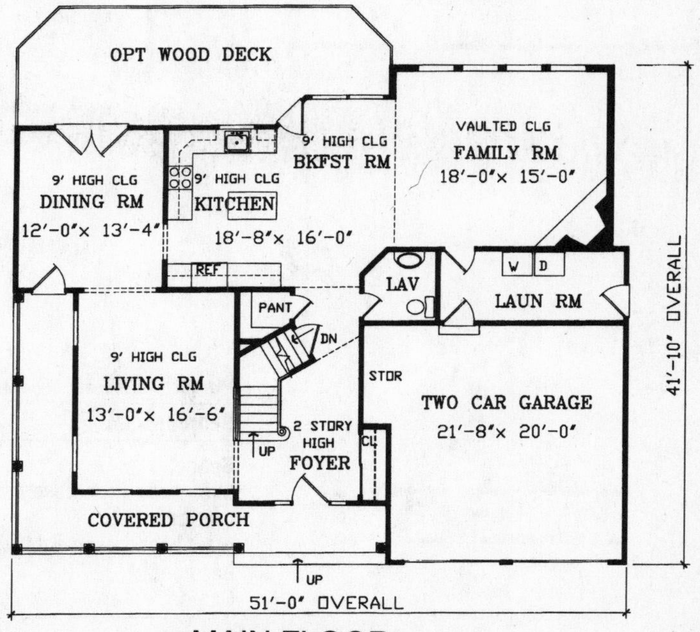

MAIN FLOOR

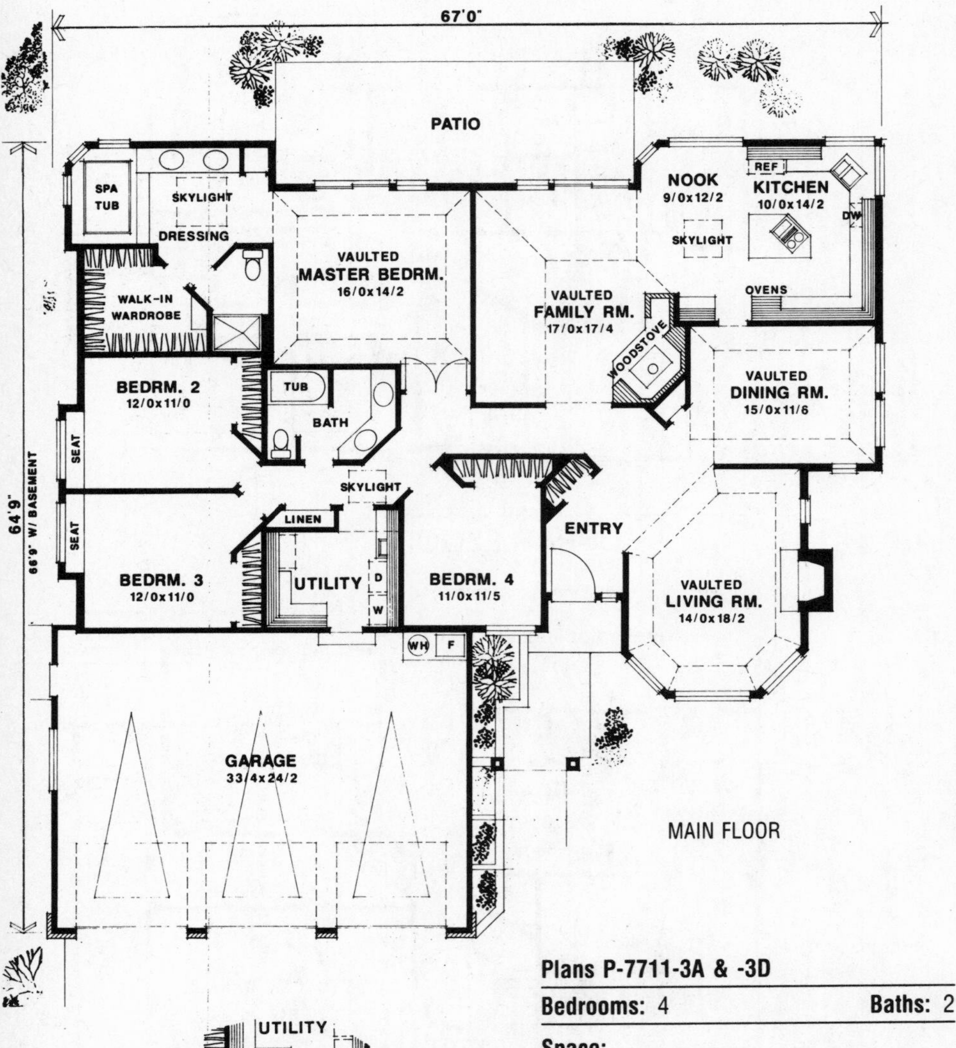

GARAGE

PLAN P-7711-3D

WITH DAYLIGHT BASEMENT

Full of Surprises

- While dignified and reserved on the outside, this plan presents delightful surprises throughout the interior.
- Interesting angles, vaulted ceilings, surprising spaces and bright windows abound everywhere you look in this home.
- The elegant, vaulted living room is off the expansive foyer, and includes an imposing fireplace and large windows areas.
- The delightful kitchen includes a handy island and large corner windows in front of the sink.
- The nook is brightened not only by large windows, but also by a skylight.
- The vaulted family room includes a corner wood stove area plus easy access to the outdoors.
- A superb master suite includes an exquisite bath with a skylighted dressing area and large walk-in closet.
- Three secondary bedrooms share another full bath, and the large laundry room is conveniently positioned near the bedrooms.

Plans P-7711-3A & -3D

Bedrooms: 4 **Baths:** 2

Space:

Main floor (non-basement version):	2,510 sq. ft.
Main floor (basement version):	2,580 sq. ft.
Basement:	2,635 sq. ft.
Garage:	806 sq. ft.

Exterior Wall Framing: 2x6

Foundation options:
Daylight basement (Plan P-7711-3D).
Crawlspace (Plan P-7711-3A).
(Foundation & framing conversion diagram available — see order form.)

Blueprint Price Code: D

TO ORDER THIS BLUEPRINT, CALL TOLL-FREE 1-800-547-5570

Plans P-7711-3A & -3D

PRICES AND DETAILS ON PAGES 12-15

Fine Details

- Elegant window treatments, eye-catching gables and a finely detailed stucco facade give this home a distinctive look.
- The spacious interior begins with an 18-ft.-high foyer and a dramatic two-way stairway with open railings.
- Decorative columns introduce the formal living room. Straight ahead, the spacious family room features a focal-point fireplace framed by windows.
- A French door between the family room and the breakfast room provides easy access to the backyard. The gourmet kitchen is highlighted by an angled serving bar/snack counter.
- Upstairs, the luxurious master bedroom features a 10-ft. tray ceiling and an intimate sitting room with a two-sided fireplace. Double doors open to the opulent master bath, which includes a huge walk-in closet and a 13½-ft.-high bathing area with an oval tub.
- Three more bedrooms share a compartmentalized bath. A balcony overlook with a beautiful plant shelf is open to the foyer below.

Plan FB-2600	
Bedrooms: 4	**Baths:** 2½
Living Area:	
Upper floor	1,348 sq. ft.
Main floor	1,252 sq. ft.
Total Living Area:	**2,600 sq. ft.**
Daylight basement	1,252 sq. ft.
Garage	448 sq. ft.
Storage	36 sq. ft.
Exterior Wall Framing:	2x4

Foundation Options:

Daylight basement

Crawlspace

(All plans can be built with your choice of foundation and framing. A generic conversion diagram is available. See order form.)

BLUEPRINT PRICE CODE: D

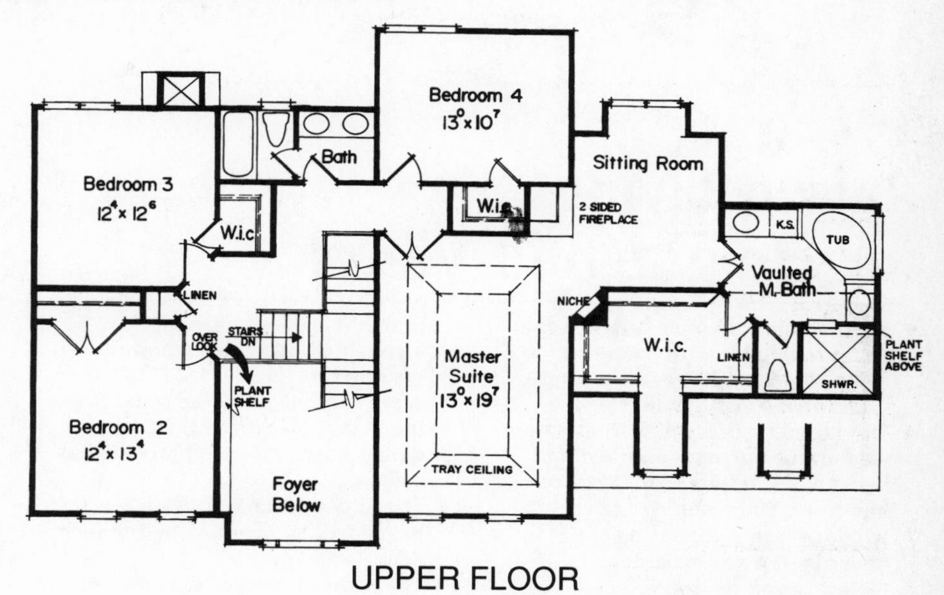

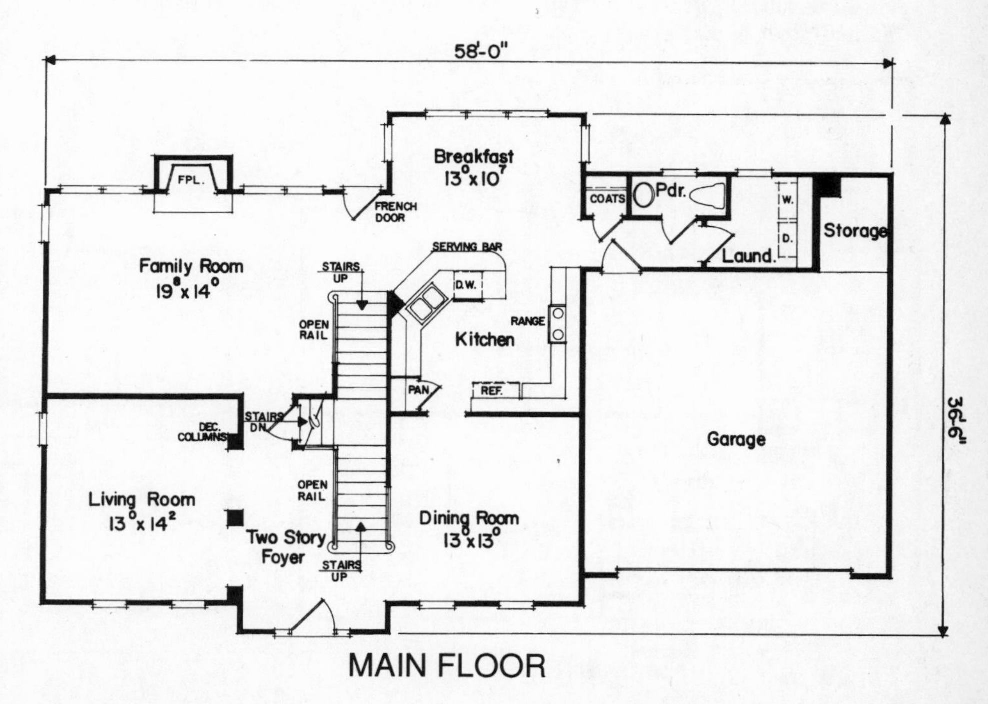

Raised Living for Heightened Views

- Picture your new home nestled into an upsloping lot with an entire living room window wall looking back to your panoramic view.
- The raised main level gives a better view of the surroundings, without being blocked by a road, cars, or low trees. The resulting larger windows and walk-out on the lower level avoid a basement feeling in the rec room.
- The sunken living room, at the top of a half-flight of stairs, has a dramatic cathedral ceiling highlighted by angled transom windows.
- A see-through fireplace separates the living room from the formal dining room, also with a cathedral ceiling.
- The kitchen incorporates a spacious breakfast bay overlooking the rear deck.
- The main floor also houses three bedrooms and two full baths.

Plan AX-8486-A

Bedrooms: 3	**Baths:** 2
Space:	
Main floor:	1,630 sq. ft.
Basement & rec room:	978 sq. ft.
Total living area:	2,608 sq. ft.
Garage:	400 sq. ft.
Storage area:	110 sq. ft.
Exterior Wall Framing:	2x4

Foundation options:
Daylight basement.
(Foundation & framing conversion diagram available — see order form.)

Blueprint Price Code: D

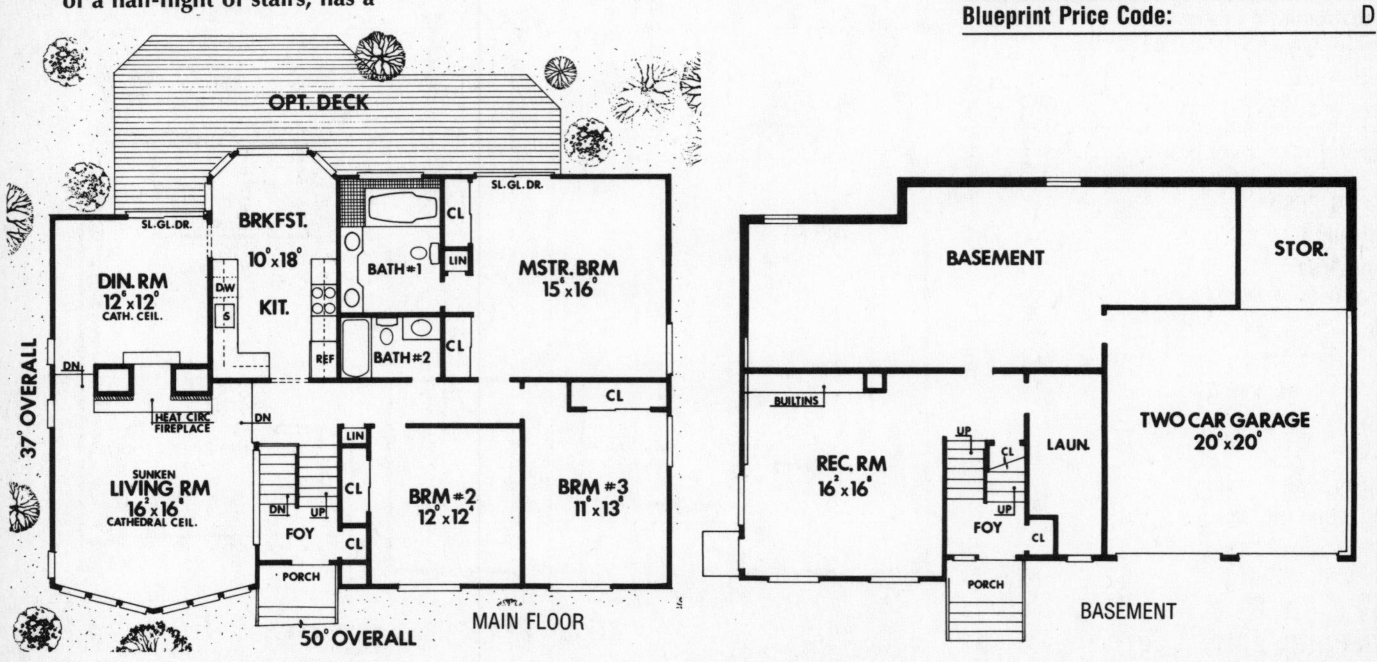

Plan AX-8486-A

PRICES AND DETAILS ON PAGES 12-15

Large Deck Wraps Home

- A full deck and an abundance of windows surround this exciting two-level contemporary.
- Skywalls brighten the island kitchen and the dining room.
- The brilliant living room boasts a huge fireplace and a cathedral ceiling, plus a stunning prow-shaped window wall.
- The master bedroom offers private access to the deck. The master bath includes a dual-sink vanity, a large tub and a separate shower.
- A generous-sized family room, another bath and two extra bedrooms share the lower level with a two-car garage and a shop area.

Plan NW-579

Bedrooms: 4	**Baths:** 3
Living Area:	
Main floor	1,707 sq. ft.
Daylight basement	901 sq. ft.
Total Living Area:	**2,608 sq. ft.**
Tuck-under garage	588 sq. ft.
Shop	162 sq. ft.
Exterior Wall Framing:	2x6
Foundation Options:	
Daylight basement	

(All plans can be built with your choice of foundation and framing. A generic conversion diagram is available. See order form.)

BLUEPRINT PRICE CODE: D

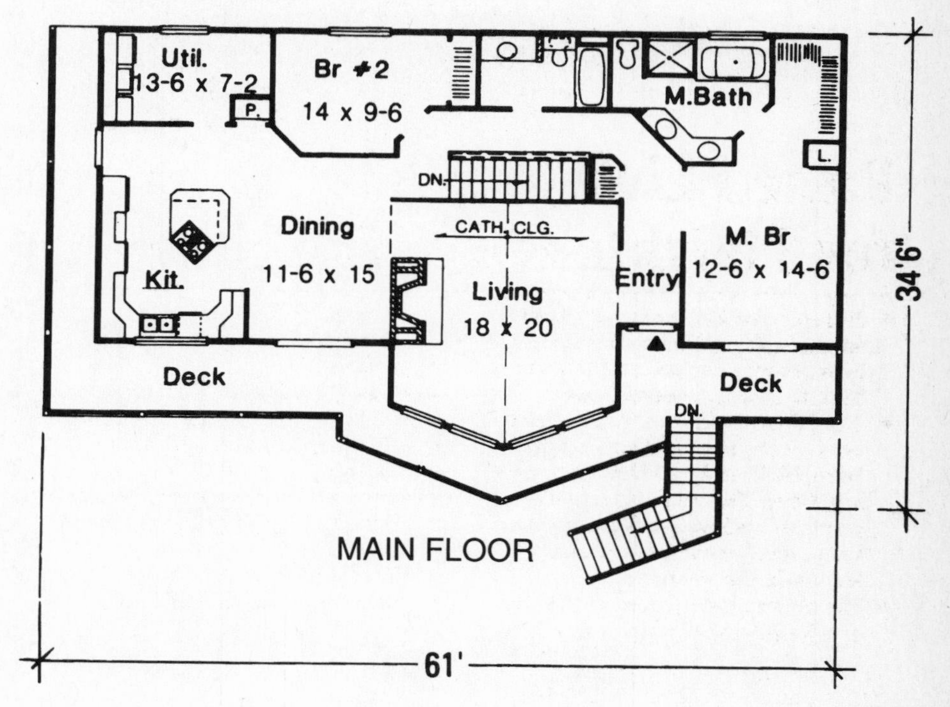

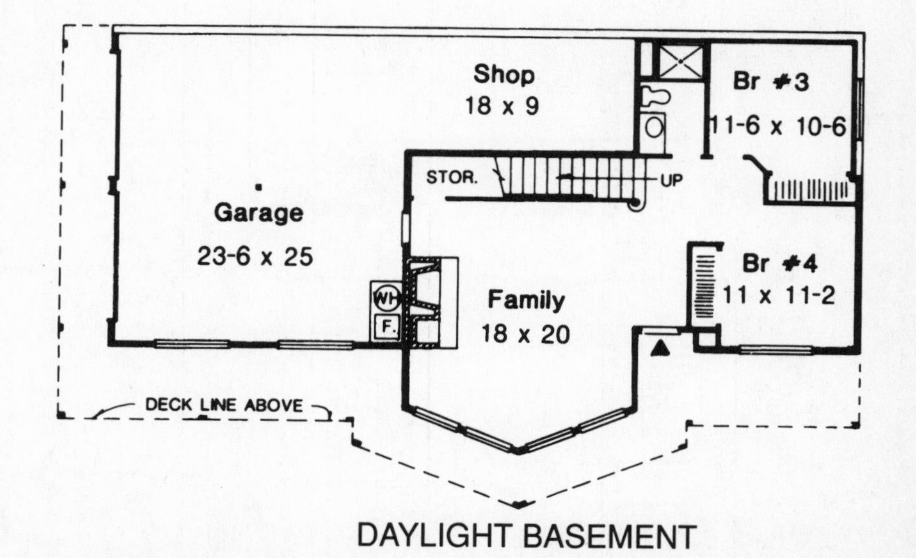

Roomy Four- or Five-Bedroom Plan

First floor:	1,523 sq. ft.
Second floor:	1,101 sq. ft.
Total living area: (Not counting basement or garage)	2,624 sq. ft.

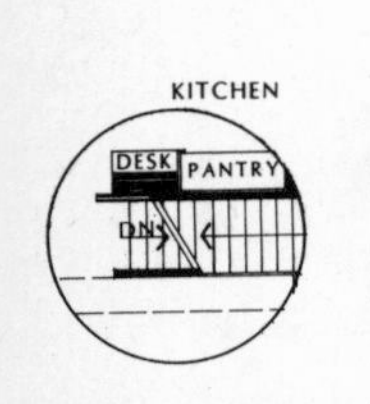

PLAN P-7644-2D
WITH DAYLIGHT BASEMENT
BASEMENT LEVEL: 1,286 sq. ft.

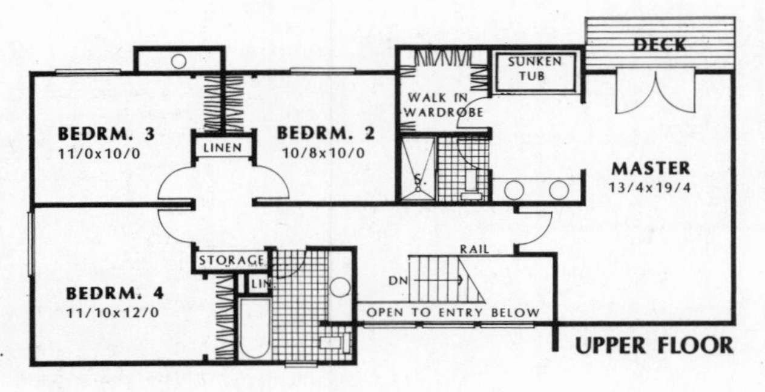

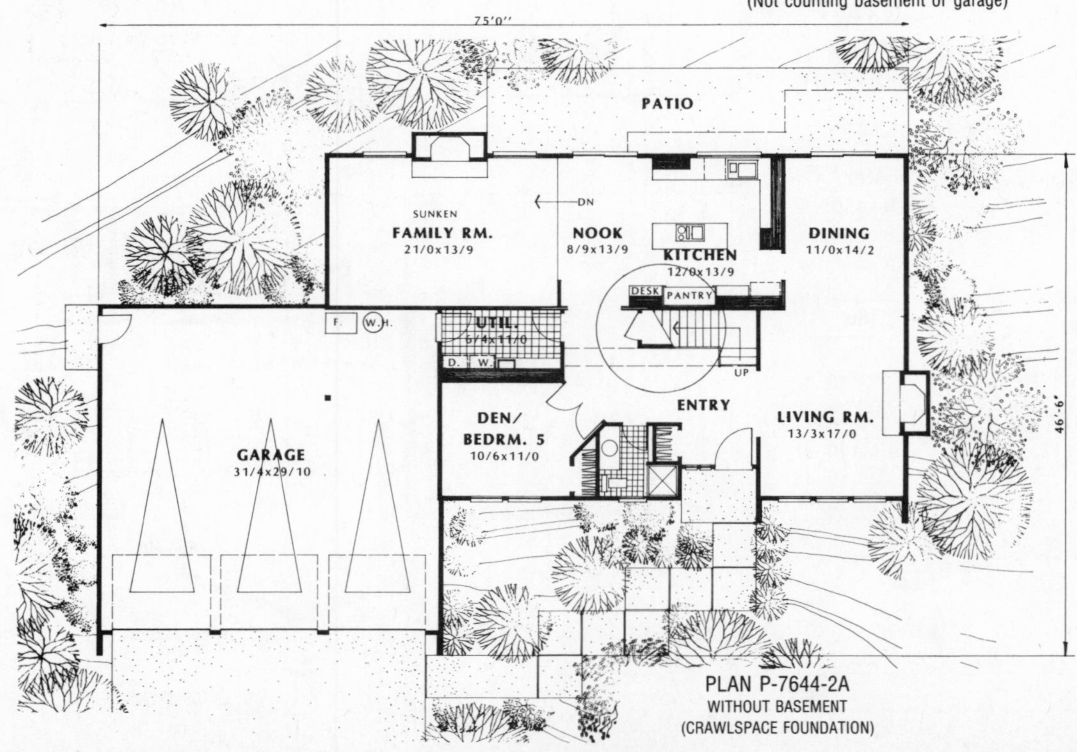

PLAN P-7644-2A
WITHOUT BASEMENT
(CRAWLSPACE FOUNDATION)

Blueprint Price Code D

Plans P-7644-2A & -2D

PRICES AND DETAILS ON PAGES 12-15

Well-Planned Walkout

- A dramatic double-back stair atrium descending from the Great Room to the bonus family room below ties the main floor design to the walkout lower level.
- A traditional exterior leads into a dramatic, open-feeling interior.
- The vaulted Great Room and dining room are separated by stylish columns.
- A see-thru fireplace is shared by the Great Room and the exciting kitchen with octagonal breakfast bay.
- A double-doored den/guest room opens off the Great Room.
- The spacious main floor master suite includes a huge walk-in closet and lavish master bath.

Plan AG-9105

Bedrooms: 3-4	**Baths:** 2½
Space:	
Main floor:	1,838 sq. ft.
Daylight basement:	800 sq. ft.
Total living area:	2,638 sq. ft.
Unfinished basement area:	1,038 sq. ft.
Garage:	462 sq. ft.
Exterior Wall Framing:	2x6

Foundation options:
Daylight basement.
(Foundation & framing conversion diagram available — see order form.)

Blueprint Price Code: D

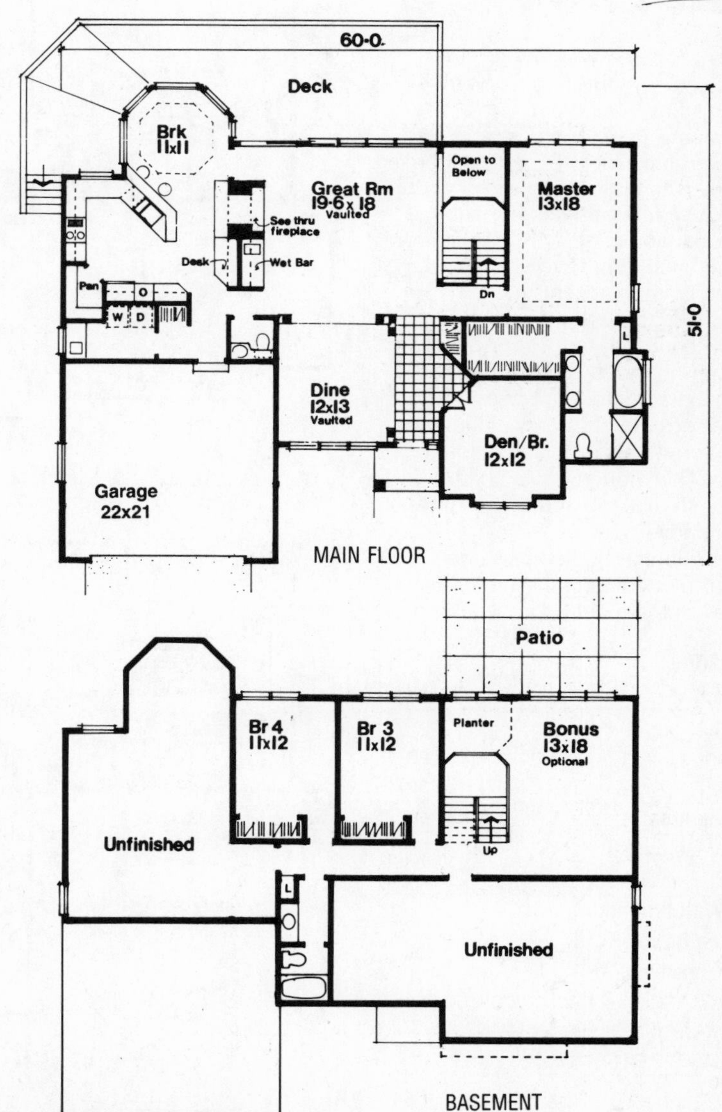

Fantastic Front Entry

- A fantastic arched window presides over the entry of this two-story, giving guests a sunny welcome.
- The spacious living room is separated from the dining room by a pair of boxed columns with built-in shelves.
- The kitchen offers a walk-in pantry, a serving bar and a sunny breakfast room with a French door to the backyard.
- A boxed column accents the entry to the vaulted family room, which boasts a window bank and an inviting fireplace.
- The main-floor den is easily converted into an extra bedroom or guest room.
- The master suite has a tray ceiling, a walk-in closet and decorative plant shelves. The vaulted private bath features an oval tub and two vanities, one with knee space.
- Three additional bedrooms share another full bath near the second stairway to the main floor.

Plan FB-2680	
Bedrooms: 4+	**Baths:** 3
Living Area:	
Upper floor	1,256 sq. ft.
Main floor	1,424 sq. ft.
Total Living Area:	**2,680 sq. ft.**
Daylight basement	1,424 sq. ft.
Garage	496 sq. ft.
Exterior Wall Framing:	2x4
Foundation Options:	
Daylight basement	
(Typical foundation & framing conversion diagram available–see order form.)	
BLUEPRINT PRICE CODE:	**D**

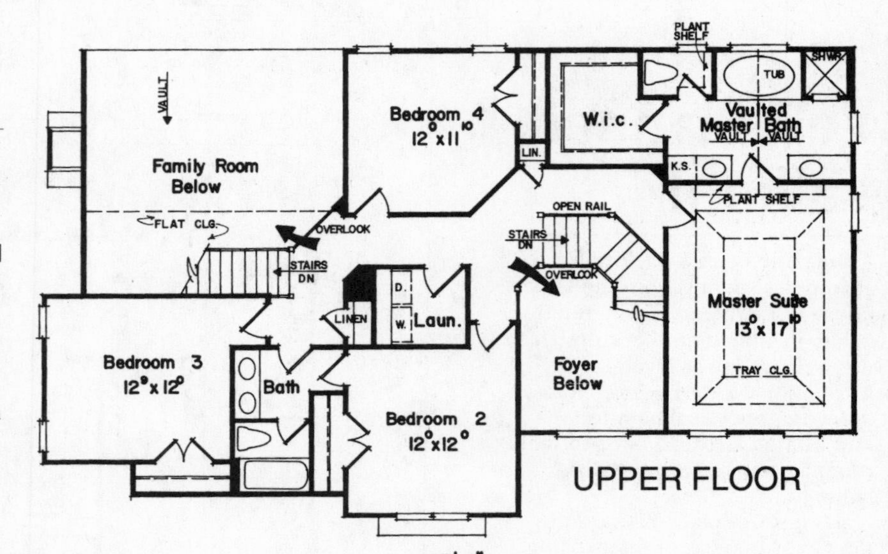

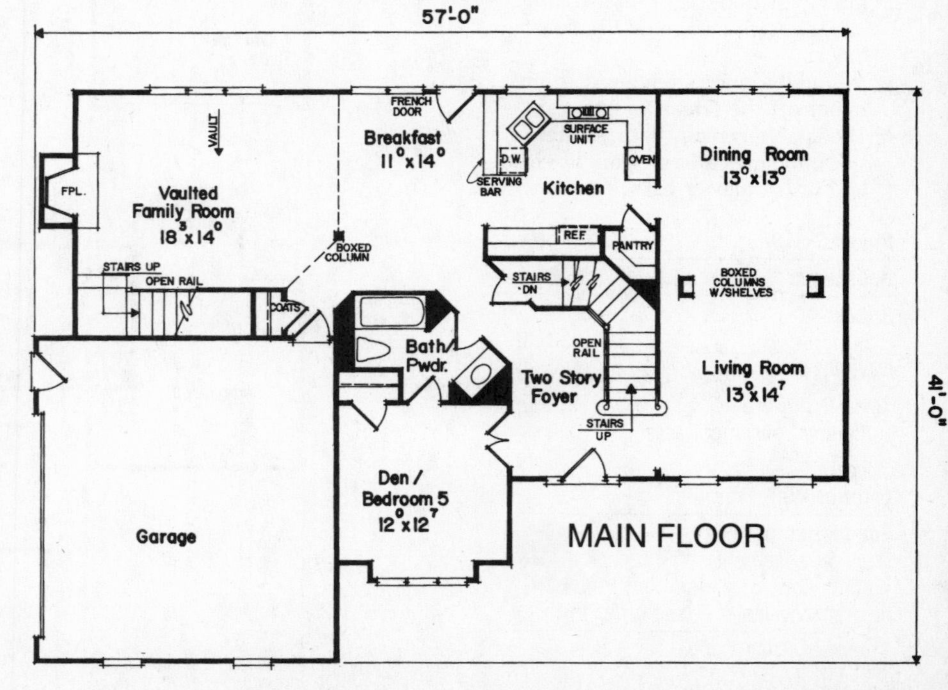

PRICES AND DETAILS ON PAGES 12-15

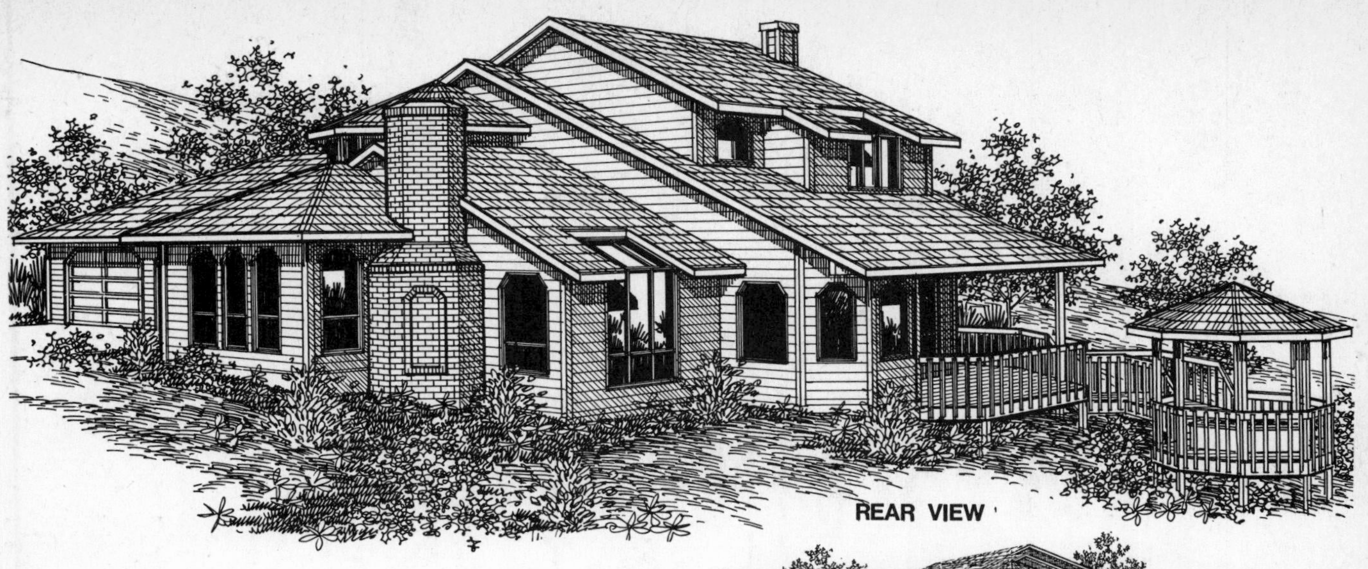

Luxurious Living Areas

- This striking exterior design also provides plenty of excitement inside as well, with its angles, curves and bay windows.
- Especially note the eye-popping entry, with its curving stairway soaring through the two-story high foyer.
- The large family room is surrounded by a spacious deck, and a sunny nook adjoins the efficient kitchen.
- The upper floor is devoted mostly to a luxurious master suite with a spa bath and large closet. An adjoining space can serve as a nursery, library or den.

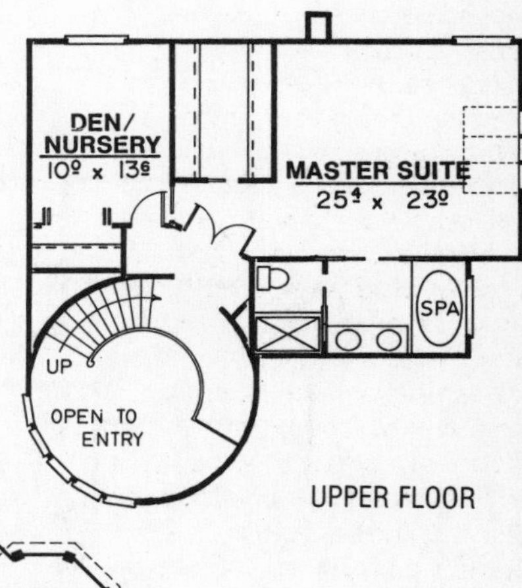

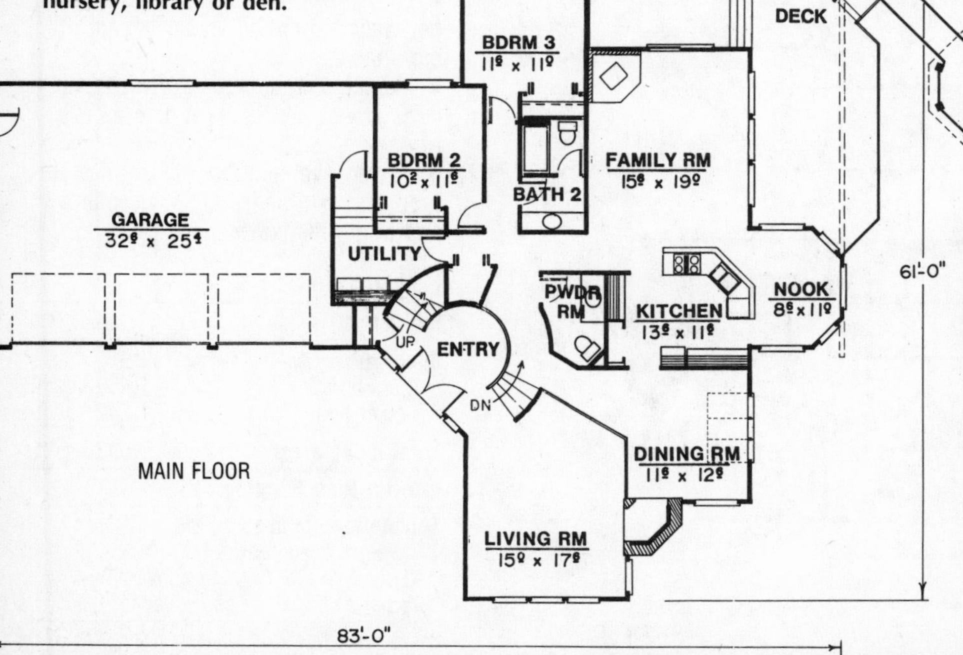

Plan I-2686

Bedrooms: 3	**Baths:** 2½
Space:	
Upper floor:	785 sq. ft.
Main floor:	1,901 sq. ft.
Total living area:	2,686 sq. ft.
Basement: approx.	1,900 sq. ft.
Garage:	823 sq. ft.
Exterior Wall Framing:	2x6

Foundation options:
Standard basement.
Crawlspace.
Slab.
(Foundation & framing conversion diagram available — see order form.)

Blueprint Price Code: D

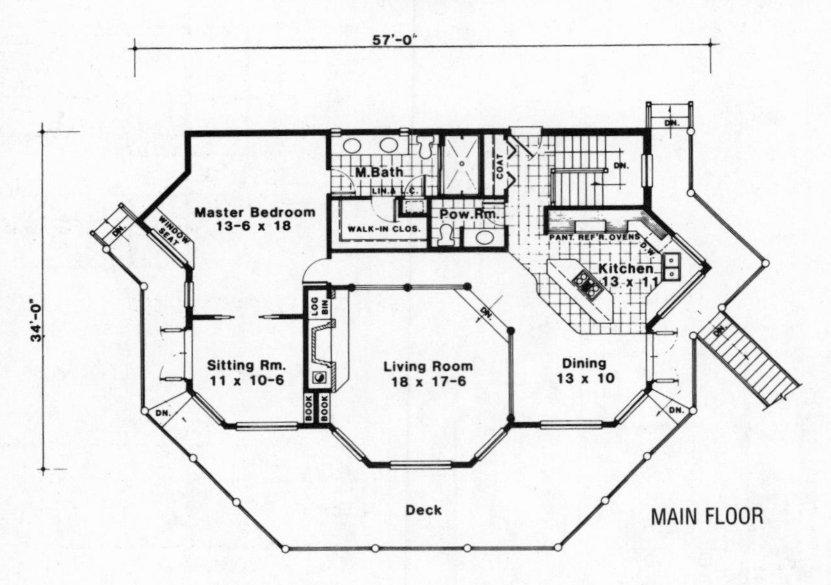

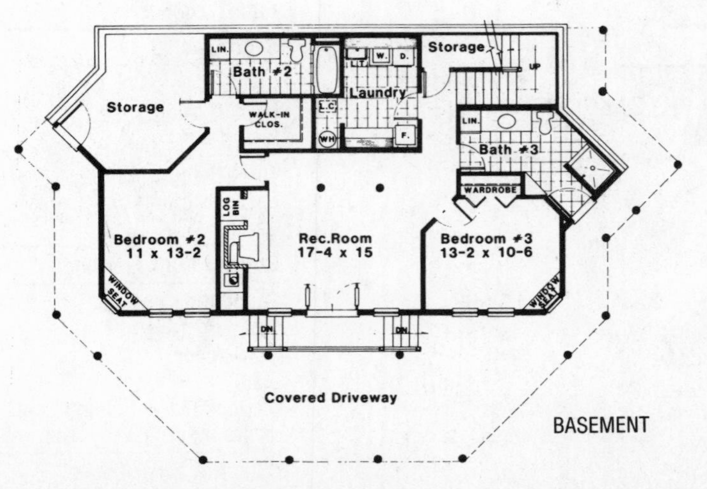

Panoramic View for Scenic Site

- Large deck offers a panoramic view and plenty of space for outdoor living.
- Sunken living room features big windows and impressive fireplace.
- Living room is set off by railings, not walls, to create visual impact of big space.
- Master suite includes private bath, large closet, sitting area and access to deck.
- Lower level includes rec room with fireplace, two bedrooms, two baths and large utility area.

Plan NW-779

Bedrooms: 3 **Baths:** 3½

Space:
Main floor: 1,450 sq. ft.
Lower floor: 1,242 sq. ft.

Total living area: 2,692 sq. ft.

Exterior Wall Framing: 2x6

Foundation options:
Daylight basement only.
(Foundation & framing conversion diagram available — see order form.)

Blueprint Price Code: D

PRICES AND DETAILS ON PAGES 12-15

FRONT VIEW

Luxury on a Compact Foundation

Sky-lighted sloped ceilings, an intriguing stairway and overhead bridge and a carefully planned first floor arrangement combine to delight the senses as one explores this spacious 2737 sq. ft. home. A major element of the design is the luxurious master suite that is reached via the stairway and bridge. An abundance of closet space and an oversized bath are welcome features here.

Two bedrooms, generous bath facilities and a large family room provide lots of growing room for the younger members of the household.

All these features are available within a mere 36′ width which allows the house to be built on a 50′ wide lot — a real bonus these days.

Main floor:	1,044 sq. ft.
Upper level:	649 sq. ft.
Lower level:	1,044 sq. ft.
Total living area: (Not counting garage)	2,737 sq. ft.

(Exterior walls are 2x6 construction)

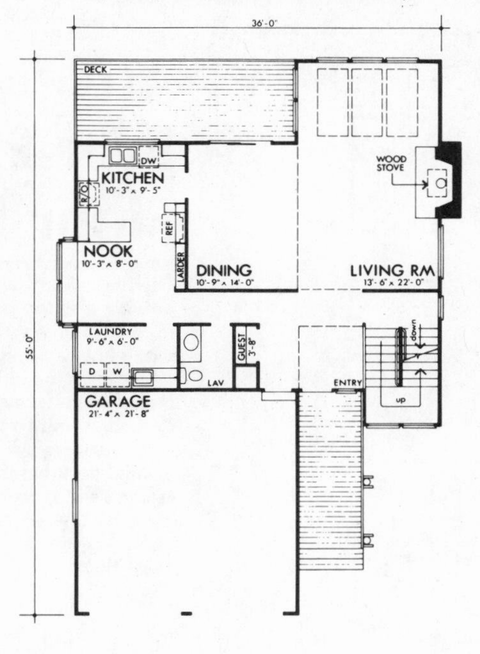

MAIN FLOOR
1044 SQUARE FEET

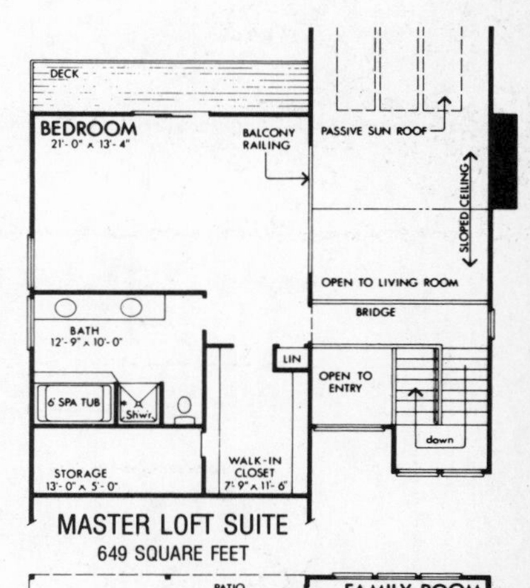

MASTER LOFT SUITE
649 SQUARE FEET

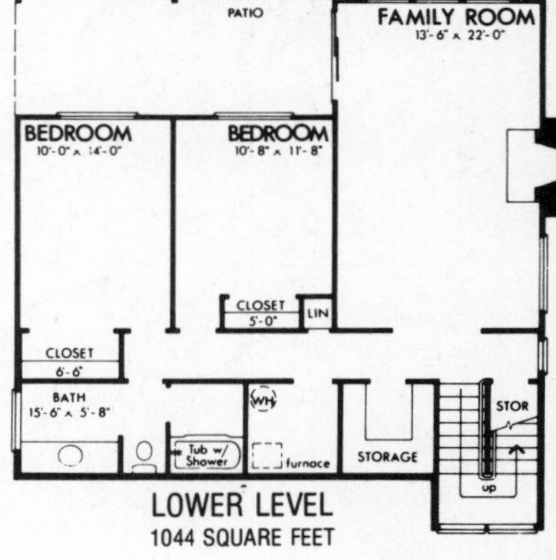

LOWER LEVEL
1044 SQUARE FEET

REAR VIEW

Blueprint Price Code D

Plan H-2110-1B

TO ORDER THIS BLUEPRINT, CALL TOLL-FREE 1-800-547-5570

PRICES AND DETAILS ON PAGES 12-15

An Ever-Popular Floor Plan

The basic concept of this plan is to provide a simple straight-forward design for an uphill site. The plan is available with either a family room or dining room adjacent to the kitchen. Other features include a convenient laundry room, three bedrooms and two full baths. The living room features a fireplace and the wrap-around deck has access through the kitchen and laundry room. Total main floor area is 1,664 sq. ft.

Main floor:	1,664 sq. ft.
Lower level:	1,090 sq. ft.
Total living area:	2,754 sq. ft.
Garage:	573 sq. ft.

(Exterior walls are 2x6 construction)

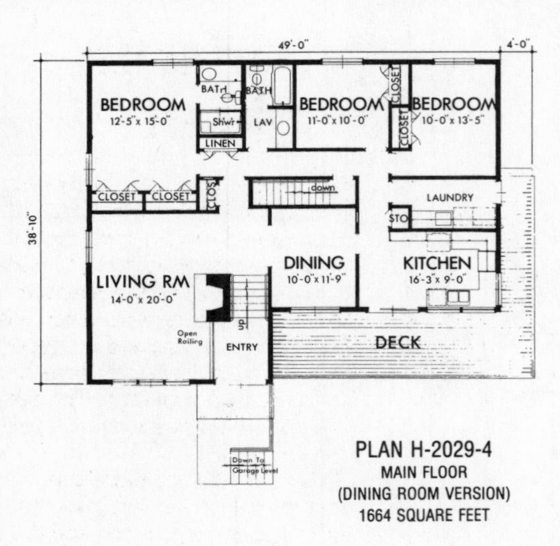

PLAN H-2029-4
MAIN FLOOR
(DINING ROOM VERSION)
1664 SQUARE FEET

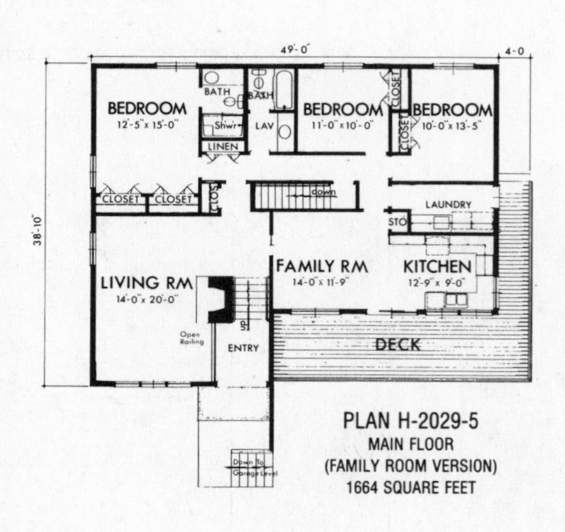

PLAN H-2029-5
MAIN FLOOR
(FAMILY ROOM VERSION)
1664 SQUARE FEET

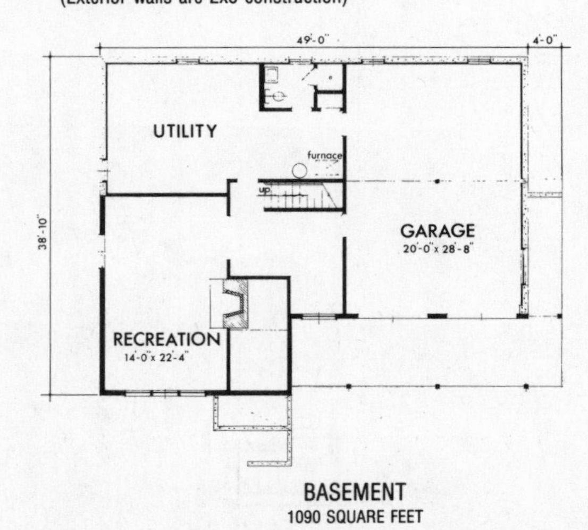

BASEMENT
1090 SQUARE FEET

Blueprint Price Code D

Plans H-2029-4 & -5

PRICES AND DETAILS ON PAGES 12-15

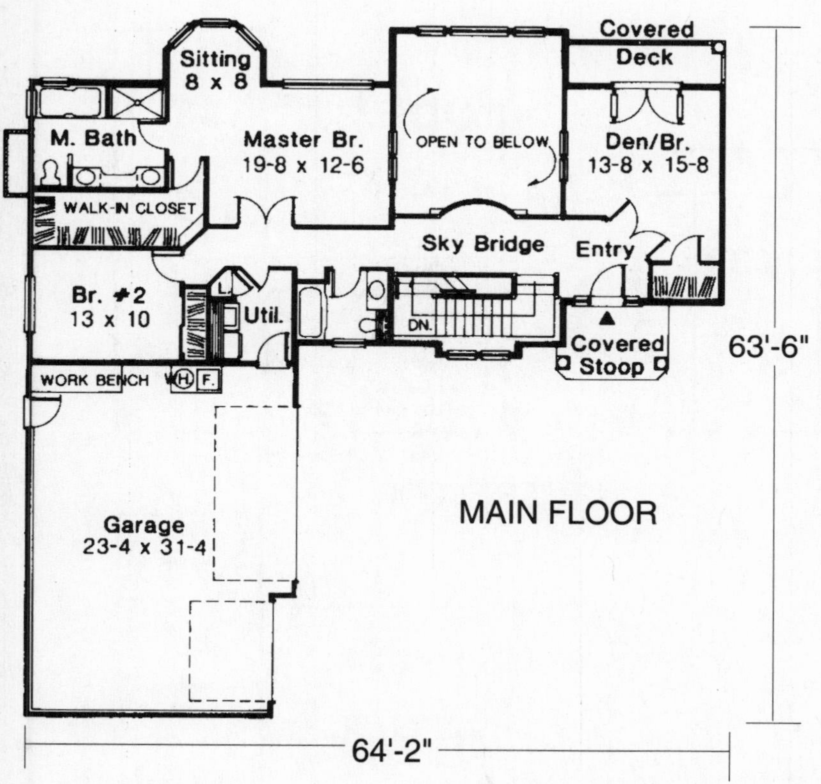

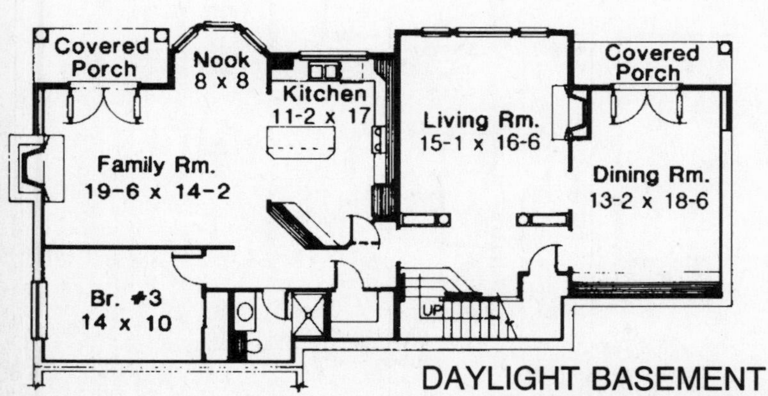

Wonderful Walkout

- Not your ordinary two-story, this wonderful walkout plan creates excitement from the top down.
- The main motorcourt level houses a stunning master suite, a second bedroom and a den/bedroom with French doors to a covered deck. The entry of the main level opens to a dramatic view from a sky bridge to the lower-level living room with two-story window wall.
- The lower level contains the living areas of the house including the formal living and dining rooms and the family room, which is open to the island kitchen and the breakfast bay. There is also a third bedroom and full bath nearby.

Plan NW-915	
Bedrooms: 3-4	**Baths:** 3
Space:	
Main floor	1,522 sq. ft.
Daylight basement	1,267 sq. ft.
Total Living Area	**2,789 sq. ft.**
Garage	731 sq. ft.
Exterior Wall Framing	2x6
Foundation options:	
Daylight Basement	
(Foundation & framing conversion diagram available—see order form.)	
Blueprint Price Code	**D**

Two-Story Great Room

- A spacious vaulted Great Room, with a fireplace and sliding glass doors to a backyard deck, is the highlight of this distinguished brick home.
- The front dining room and study both feature bay windows; the study can be used as an extra bedroom or as a guest room.
- A second stairway off the breakfast room accesses a home office or bonus space; an optional bath could also be built in.
- The main-floor master suite offers his-and-hers walk-in closets, a splashy master bath and private access to the rear deck.
- Three secondary bedrooms are located off the second-floor balcony that overlooks the Great Room and foyer.

Plan C-9010	
Bedrooms: 4+	**Baths:** 2½-3½
Living Area:	
Upper floor	761 sq. ft.
Main floor	1,637 sq. ft.
Bonus room	347 sq. ft.
Optional bath and closet	106 sq. ft.
Total Living Area:	**2,851 sq. ft.**
Daylight basement	1,637 sq. ft.
Garage	572 sq. ft.
Exterior Wall Framing:	2x4
Foundation Options:	
Daylight basement	
Crawlspace	
(Typical foundation & framing conversion diagram available—see order form.)	
BLUEPRINT PRICE CODE:	**D**

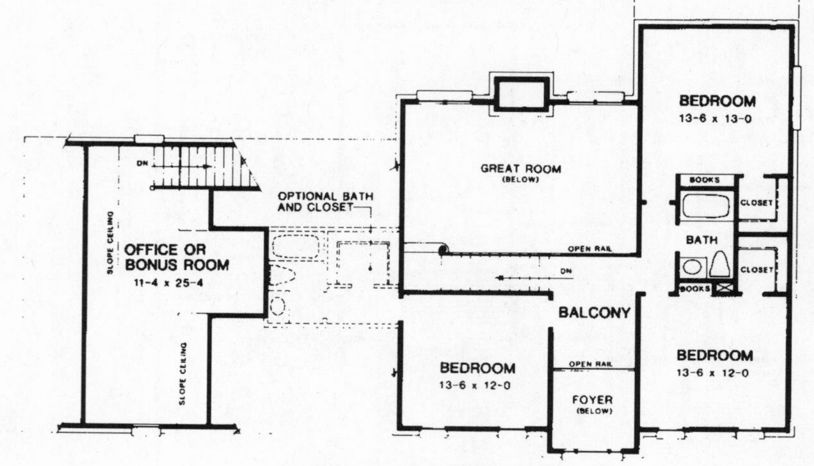

UPPER FLOOR

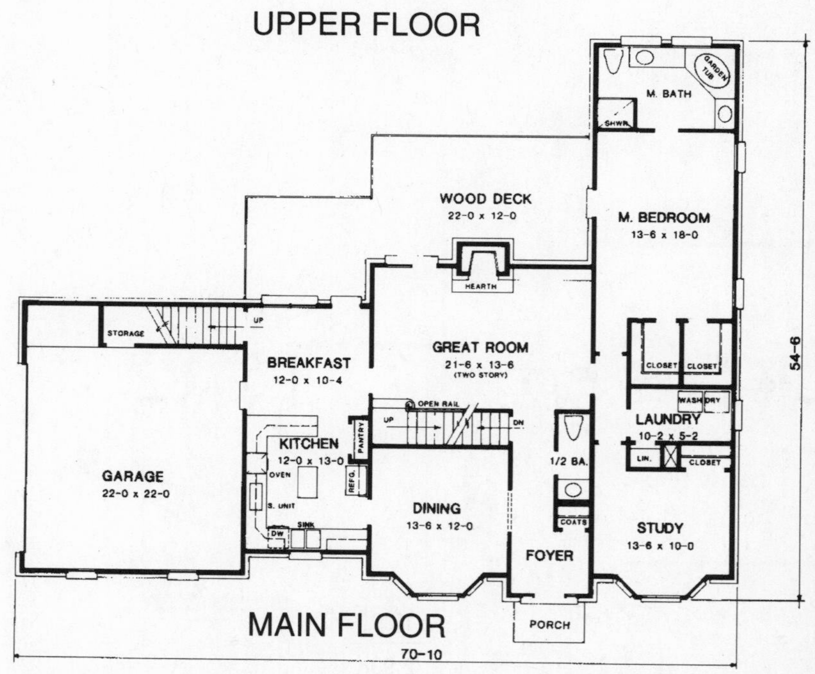

MAIN FLOOR

 TO ORDER THIS BLUEPRINT, CALL TOLL-FREE 1-800-547-5570

Plan C-9010

PRICES AND DETAILS ON PAGES 12-15

Master Suite Features Deluxe Bath

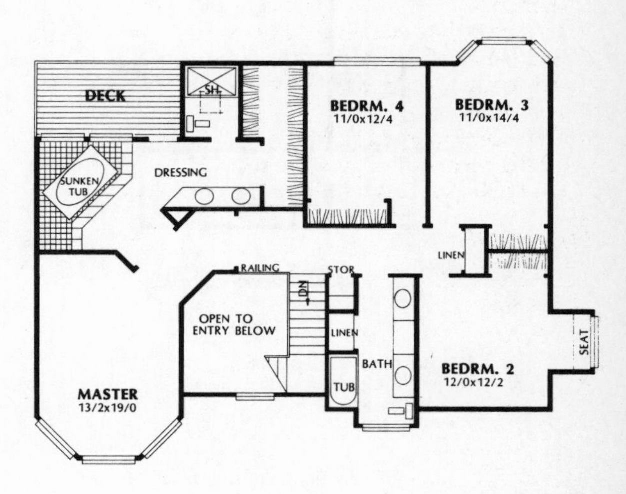

PLAN P-7662-3A
WITHOUT BASEMENT
(CRAWLSPACE FOUNDATION)

First floor:	1,538 sq. ft.
Second floor:	1,392 sq. ft.
Total living area: (Not counting basement or garage)	2,930 sq. ft.

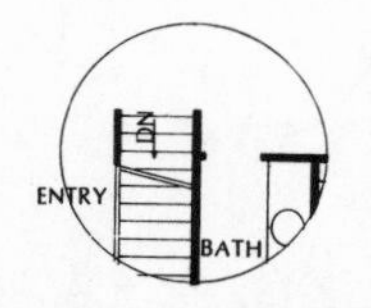

PLAN P-7662-3D
WITH DAYLIGHT BASEMENT
BASEMENT LEVEL: 1,179 sq. ft.

Blueprint Price Code D

Plans P-7662-3A & -3D

For Side-to-Side Slope

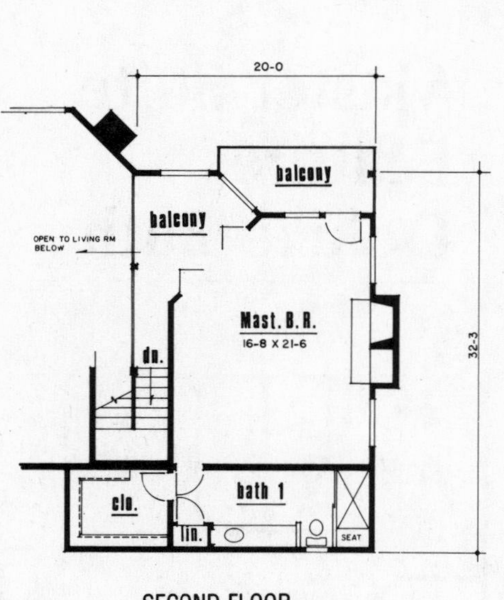

SECOND FLOOR

MAIN FLOOR

48-0
BENCH
deck
44-0
Dining
9-8 X 13-0
VAULTED
Living
18-0 X 21-6
Library
10-6 X 12-0
BALCONY ABV.
Study
opt. b. r.
9-4 X 11-9
Kitchen
14-8 X 8-0
Entry
clo
up.
dn.
bath 2
utility
covered porch
Bed Rm.
11-10 X 13-0
Bed Rm.
10-10 X 11-8

NOTE: This house was designed for a lot sloping down in the direction of the arrow. ◀

PLAN Q-2934-1
WITH BASEMENT
(CRAWLSPACE UNDER NON-BASEMENT PORTION OF HOUSE)

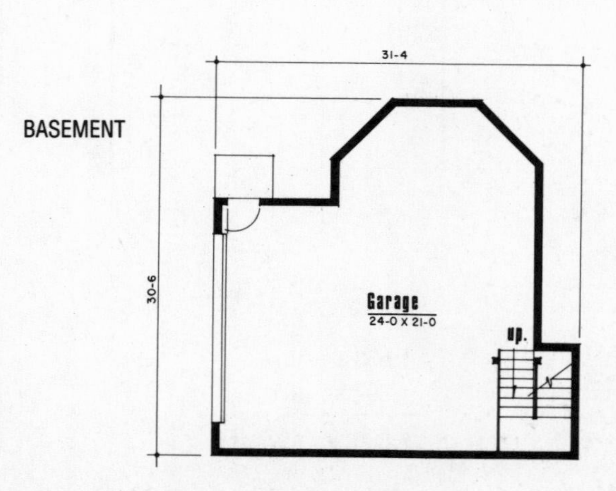

Main level:	1,527 sq. ft.
Second level:	635 sq. ft.
Total living area: (Not counting basement or garage)	2,162 sq. ft.
Basement:	772 sq. ft.

Blueprint Price Code C

Plan Q-2934-1

PRICES AND DETAILS ON PAGES 12-15

Elegant Two-Story

- This elegant two-story home is available with a durable brick or stucco exterior.
- Past the columned entry is an oversized foyer with dual coat closets and a dramatic curved stairway.
- Double doors open to a study or extra bedroom. In the opposite direction are the formal living areas. The living room features a fireplace; the adjoining dining room boasts a lovely bay window.
- The island kitchen and breakfast room form a comfortable and spacious informal setting with the family room. The sunken family room offers a vaulted ceiling and a second fireplace. Rear doors access the outdoor spaces.
- The handy main-floor laundry room is located near the garage entrance.
- The upper floor houses four nice-sized bedrooms and two full baths, each with dual dressing areas. The master bath also includes a garden tub and a separate shower.

Plan CH-280-A

Bedrooms: 4	**Baths:** 2½
Living Area:	
Upper floor	1,262 sq. ft.
Main floor	1,797 sq. ft.
Total Living Area:	**3,059 sq. ft.**
Basement	1,797 sq. ft.
Garage	462 sq. ft.
Exterior Wall Framing:	2x4

Foundation Options:
Daylight basement
Standard basement
Crawlspace
(Typical foundation & framing conversion diagram available—see order form.)

BLUEPRINT PRICE CODE: E

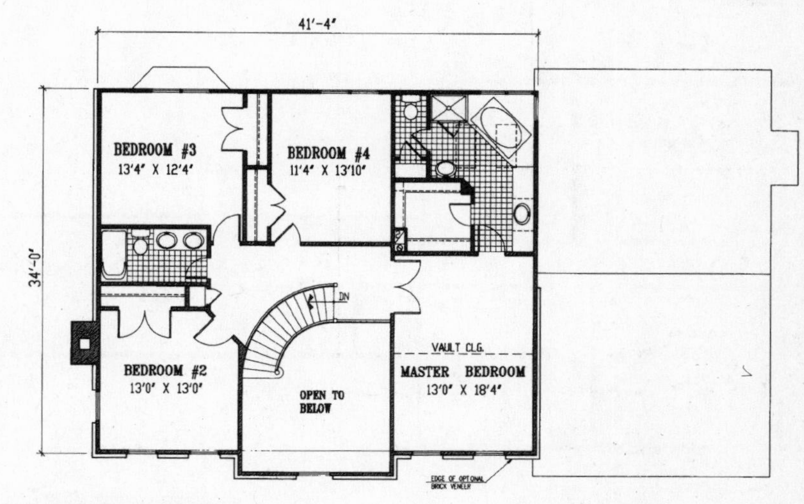

UPPER FLOOR

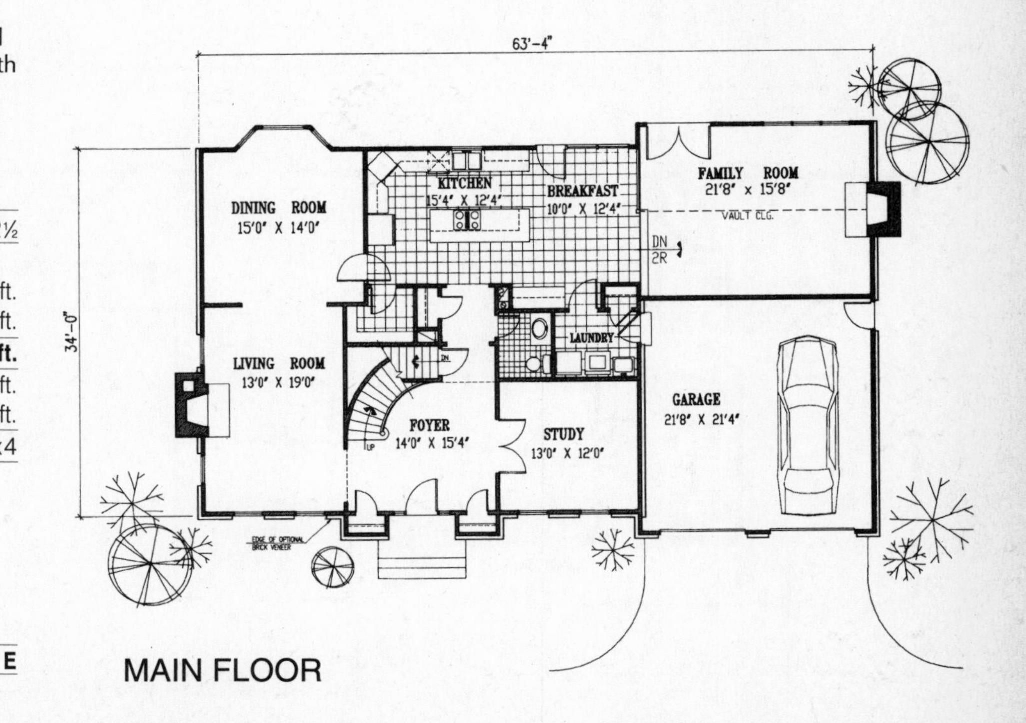

MAIN FLOOR

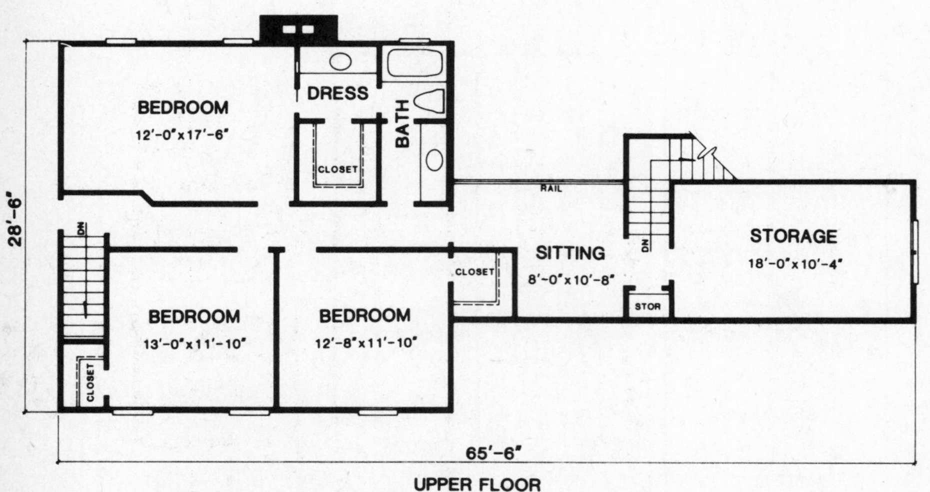

UPPER FLOOR

Bay Windows Enhance a Country Home

A large master bedroom suite includes a deluxe bath with separate shower, garden tub, twin vanities and two large walk-in closets. Kitchen has direct access to both the breakfast nook and the dining room, which features a large bay window. Three bedrooms, a sitting area and storage or bonus room combine to form the second level.

First floor:	2,005 sq. ft.
Second floor:	1,063 sq. ft.
Total living area: (Not counting basement or garage)	3,068 sq. ft.

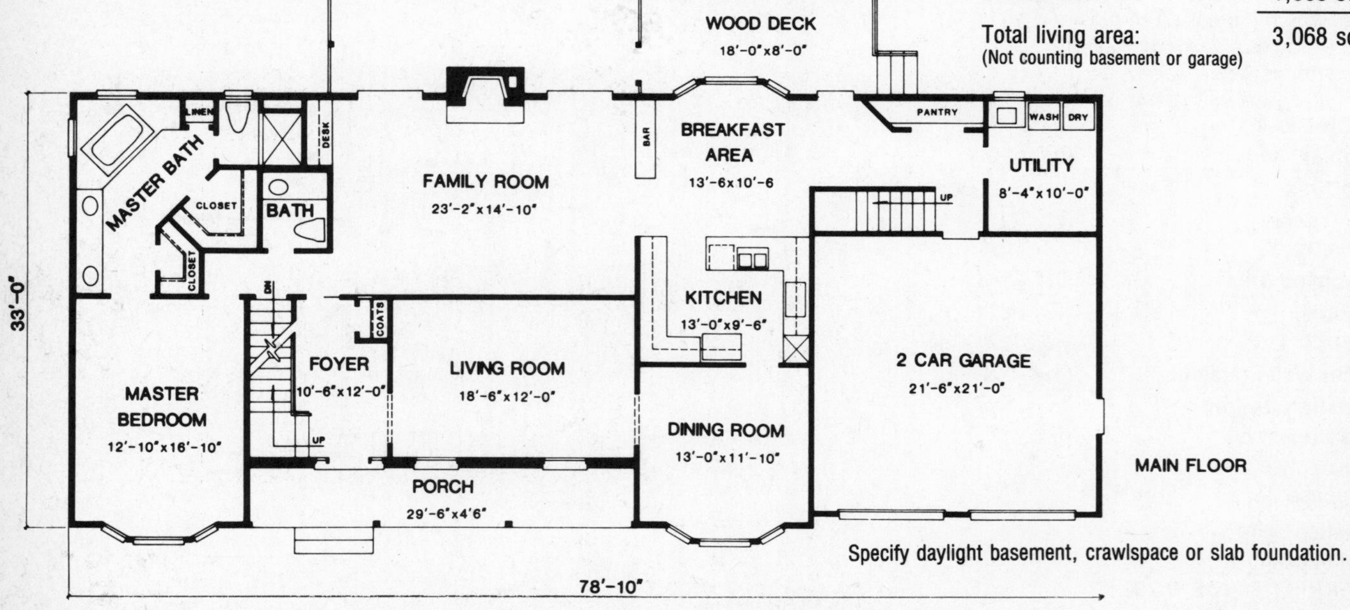

MAIN FLOOR

Specify daylight basement, crawlspace or slab foundation.

Blueprint Price Code E

Plan C-8409

Large and Luxurious

- This two-story home offers large, luxurious living areas with a variety of options to complement any lifestyle.
- The two-story-high foyer shows off an angled stairway and flows to the elegant formal living spaces on the right.
- The gourmet kitchen boasts a sunny sink, a walk-in pantry and an island cooktop with a serving bar. The adjoining breakfast nook has French doors opening to the backyard.
- Highlighting the main floor is a huge sunken family room, which is expanded by a 17-ft. vaulted ceiling and hosts a handy wet bar and a handsome fireplace. An open rail views to the breakfast room and kitchen beyond.
- Completing the main floor is a den or guest bedroom with private access to a full bath, making a great guest suite.
- Upstairs, the master suite boasts a 10-ft. tray ceiling in the sleeping area and a 15-ft. vaulted ceiling in the garden bath.
- Each of the three remaining bedrooms has private access to a bath.

Plan FB-3071

Bedrooms: 4+	**Baths:** 4
Living Area:	
Upper floor	1,419 sq. ft.
Main floor	1,652 sq. ft.
Total Living Area:	**3,071 sq. ft.**
Daylight basement	1,652 sq. ft.
Garage	456 sq. ft.
Exterior Wall Framing:	2x4
Foundation Options:	
Daylight basement	

(All plans can be built with your choice of foundation and framing. A generic conversion diagram is available. See order form.)

BLUEPRINT PRICE CODE: E

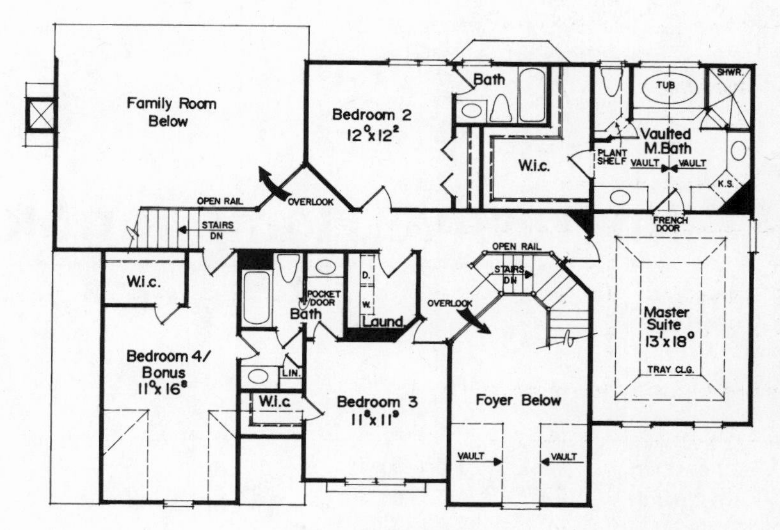

UPPER FLOOR

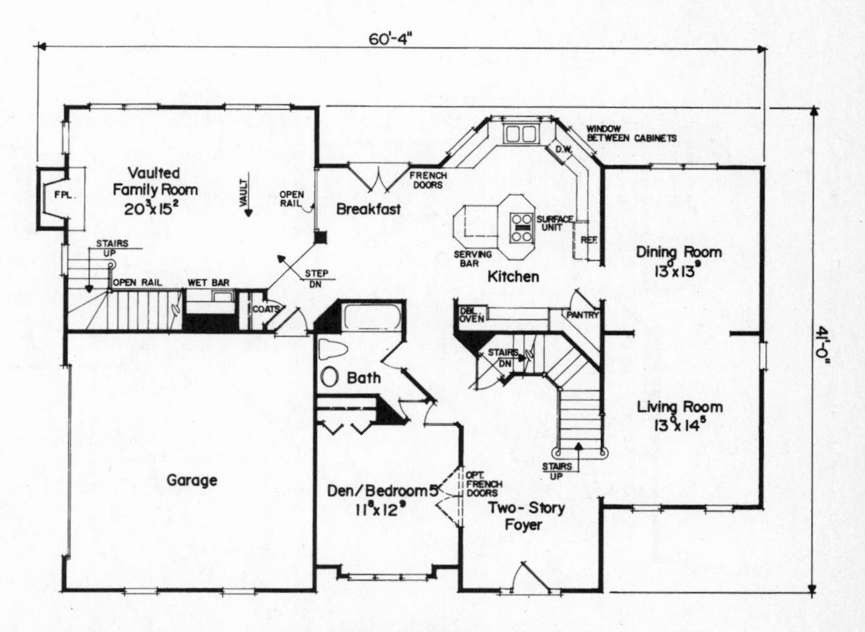

MAIN FLOOR

Impressive Home for Sloping Lot

PLAN Q-3080-1A
WITHOUT BASEMENT
(SLAB-ON-GRADE FOUNDATION)

First floor:	1,505 sq. ft.
Second floor:	1,575 sq. ft.
Total living area: (Not counting garage)	3,080 sq. ft.

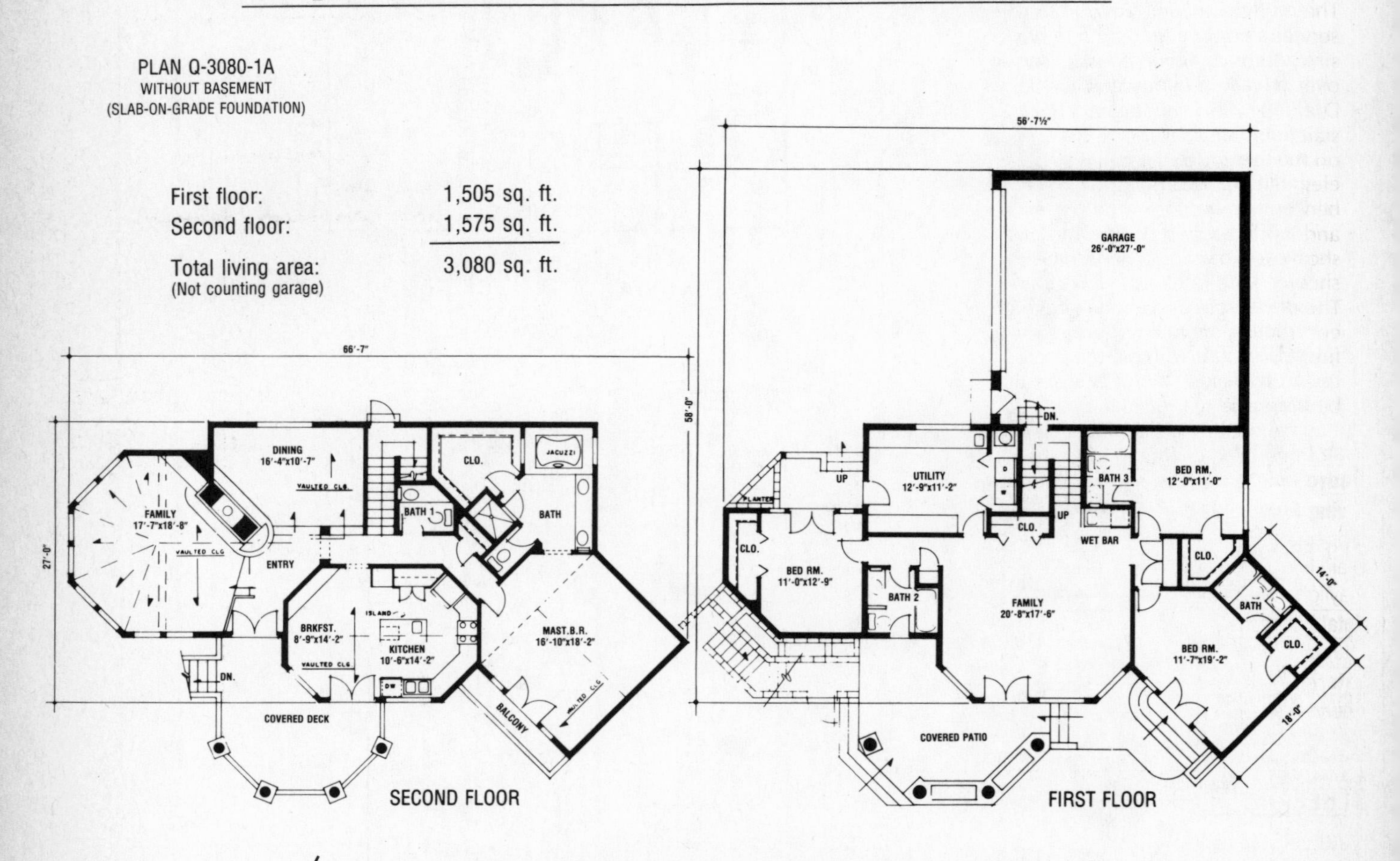

NOTE: This house was designed for a lot sloping down in the direction of the arrow.

Blueprint Price Code E

TO ORDER THIS BLUEPRINT, CALL TOLL-FREE 1-800-547-5570

Plan Q-3080-1A

PRICES AND DETAILS ON PAGES 12-15

Hillside Heaven

- Ideal for a sloping lot, this handsome multi-level home is filled with surprises.
- Past the stately covered entrance, the bright foyer flows into the sunken living room. Boasting a 14-ft.-high vaulted ceiling, the living room features a warm fireplace, a built-in media center and a boxed-out rear window.
- The adjoining sunken dining room opens to the backyard deck and spa.
- The modern kitchen shows off an island service center with a cooktop and bar sink. A convenient half-bath and an oversized laundry room are nearby.
- Dramatic windows brighten the stairway to the luxurious master suite on the upper floor. Entered through elegant double doors, the master bedroom also boasts a coved ceiling and a private deck. The master bath showcases a spa tub, a skylighted shower and a dual-sink vanity.
- The daylight basement offers an enormous family room with a cozy fireplace and deck access. A wine cellar, a full bath and two more bedrooms are also included.

Plan I-3153-A	
Bedrooms: 3	**Baths:** 2½
Living Area:	
Upper floor	579 sq. ft.
Main floor	1,307 sq. ft.
Daylight basement	1,267 sq. ft.
Total Living Area:	**3,153 sq. ft.**
Garage	808 sq. ft.
Exterior Wall Framing:	2x6
Foundation Options:	
Daylight basement	
(All plans can be built with your choice of foundation and framing. A generic conversion diagram is available. See order form.)	
BLUEPRINT PRICE CODE:	E

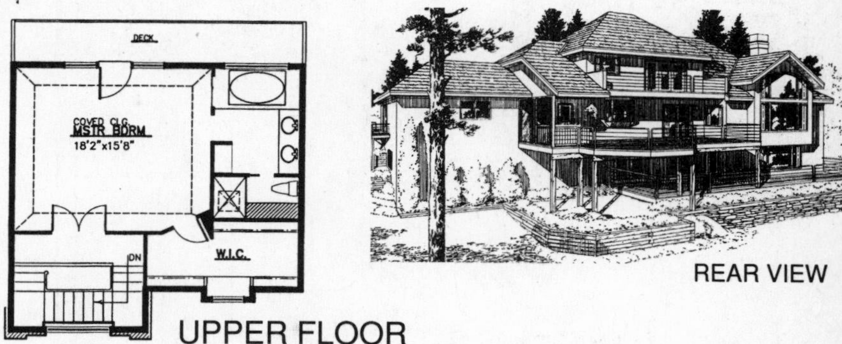

UPPER FLOOR

REAR VIEW

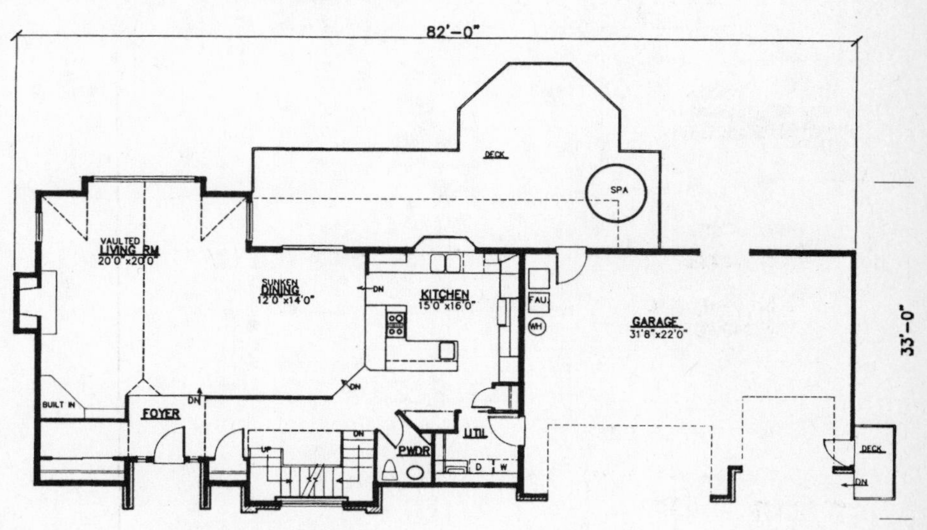

MAIN FLOOR

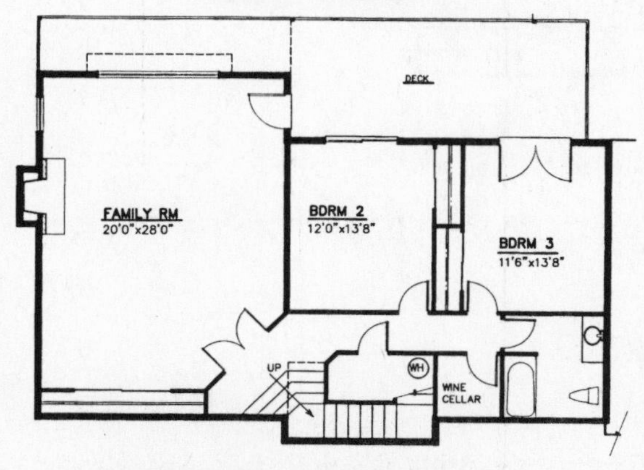

DAYLIGHT BASEMENT

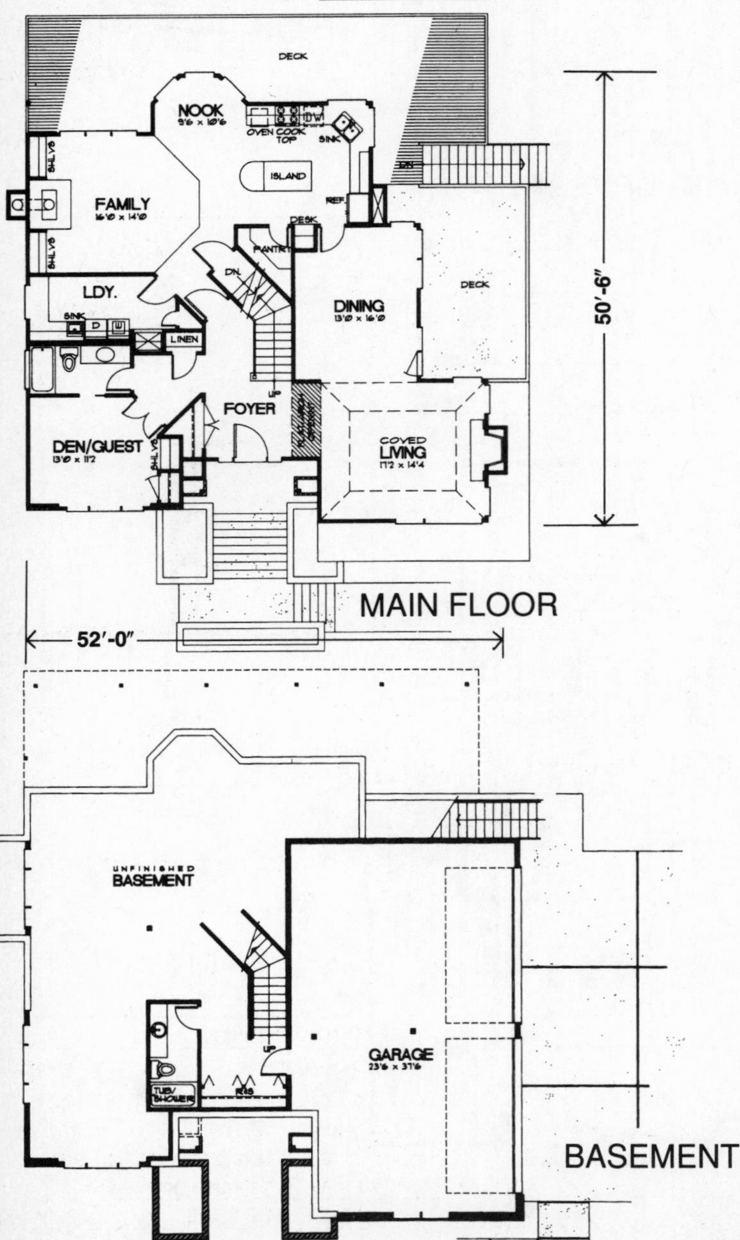

Exciting Home Captures Views

- This extraordinary home uses an abundance of windows and a wraparound deck to capitalize on the surrounding views and enjoy the outdoors.
- The dramatic two-story foyer is brightened by an arched transom window and an illuminating skylight.
- The formal living spaces combine at the right and overlook the deck.
- The rear-oriented informal spaces intersect to form an open activity area. The gourmet kitchen boasts a functional work island and a walk-in pantry. The cozy alcove nook offers a sunny dining experience. A view of the family room's woodstove is possible from both areas.
- The master suite on the upper floor shows off an alcove sitting area and a skylighted private bath, and is entered through elegant double doors.
- Three more bedrooms and a second bath are also included on this floor.

Plan CDG-4016

Bedrooms: 4-5 **Baths:** 4

Living Area:

Upper floor	1,301 sq. ft.
Main floor	1,693 sq. ft.
Standard basement (finished)	180 sq. ft.
Total Living Area:	**3,174 sq. ft.**
Standard basement (unfinished)	991 sq. ft.
Tuck-under garage	903 sq. ft.
Exterior Wall Framing:	2x4

Foundation Options:

Standard basement

(Typical foundation & framing conversion diagram available—see order form.)

BLUEPRINT PRICE CODE: **E**

Creative Spaces

- Here's a home that is not only large, but extremely creative in its use of indoor space.
- A huge area is created by the combination of the vaulted living and dining rooms, which flow together visually but are separated by a railing.
- Another expansive space results from the kitchen/nook/family room arrangement, and their easy access to deck and patio.
- Upstairs, the master suite includes a lavish bath and generous closets.
- Three large secondary bedrooms share another full bath, and each has its own unique design feature.

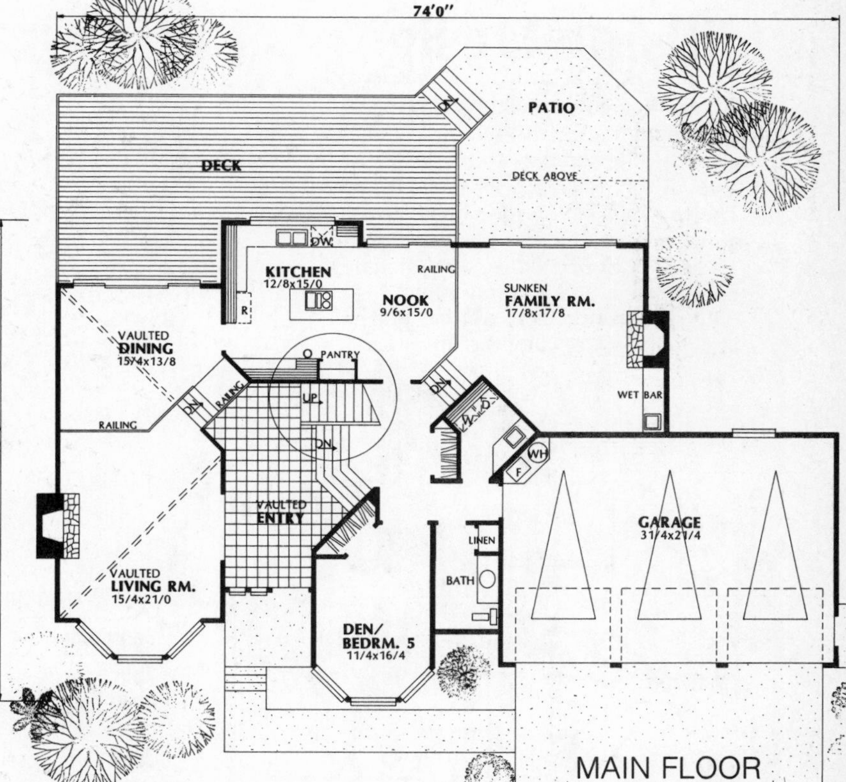

BASEMENT STAIRWAY LOCATION

Plans P-7664-4A & -4D

Bedrooms: 4+	**Baths:** 2½
Living Area:	
Upper floor	1,301 sq. ft.
Main floor	1,853 sq. ft.
Total Living Area:	**3,154 sq. ft.**
Daylight basement	1,486 sq. ft.
Garage	668 sq. ft.

Exterior Wall Framing:	2x4
Foundation Options:	**Plan #**
Daylight basement	P-7664-4D
Crawlspace	P-7664-4A
(Typical foundation & framing conversion diagram available—see order form.)	
BLUEPRINT PRICE CODE:	**E**

Lower Level Opens to Rear in Spacious Hillside Design

- A huge living room with fireplace and dining room with railing overlook the stairway to the lower level of this walk-out, hillside design.
- The spacious country kitchen offers an island cooktop and unique skywall.
- Three to four bedrooms, an optional hobby room, and a family room with second fireplace, wet bar and attached deck occupy the lower level.

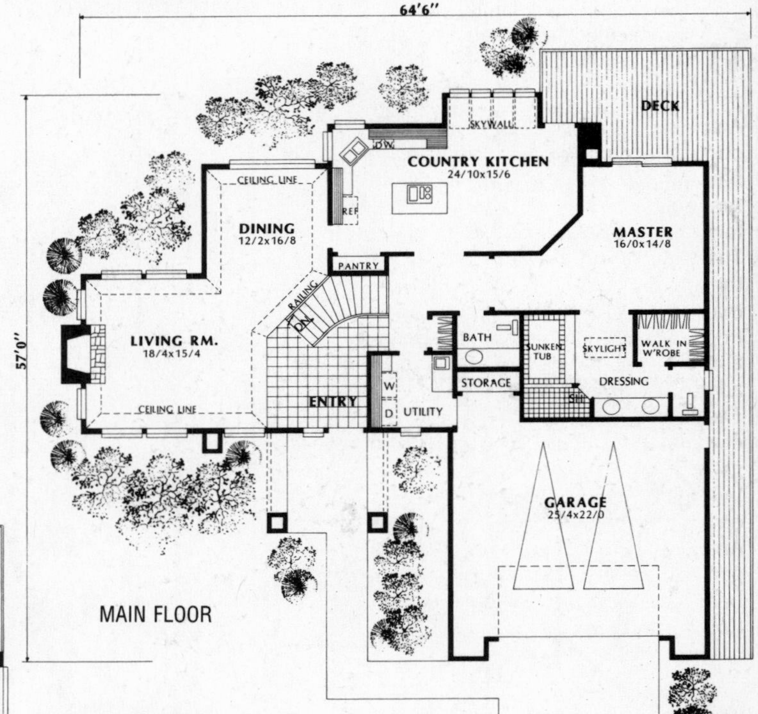

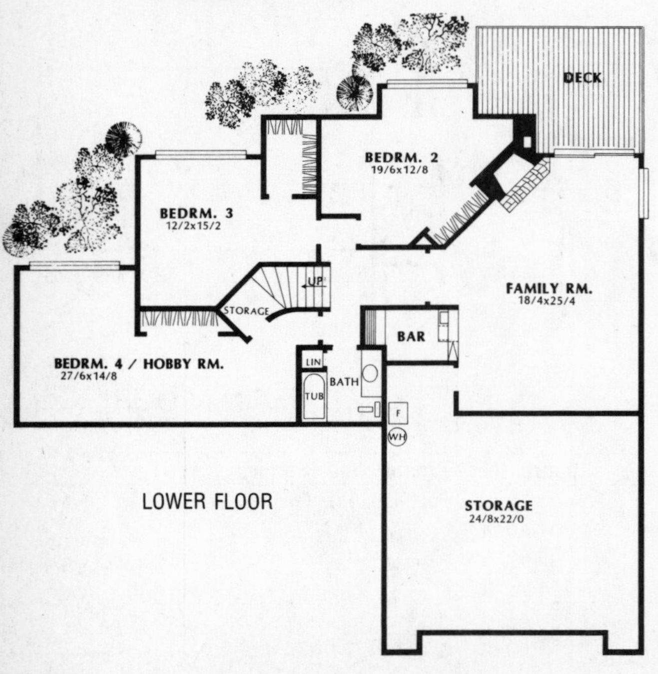

Plan P-7688-3D

Bedrooms: 3-4	**Baths:** 2½
Space:	
Main floor:	1,624 sq. ft.
Lower floor:	1,624 sq. ft.
Total living area:	3,248 sq. ft.
Garage:	557 sq. ft.
Storage:	620 sq. ft.
Exterior Wall Framing:	2x4

Foundation options:
Daylight basement.
(Foundation & framing conversion diagram available — see order form.)

Blueprint Price Code:	E

Anyone for Fun?

- A spectacular sunken game room with a corner window, vaulted ceilings, wet bar and half-wall that separates it from the family room is ideal for the active family or for those who like to entertain.
- The exciting atmosphere continues to the family room, also at a level lower than the rest of the home; here you'll find a fireplace, a rear window wall and a railing that allows a view of the adjoining vaulted nook.
- The spacious kitchen offers an island cooktop, pantry and pass-through to the game room hallway; formal, vaulted living areas are found opposite the entry.
- An upper-level bridge overlooks the game room and joins the two secondary bedrooms with the master suite and luxury, skylit master bath.

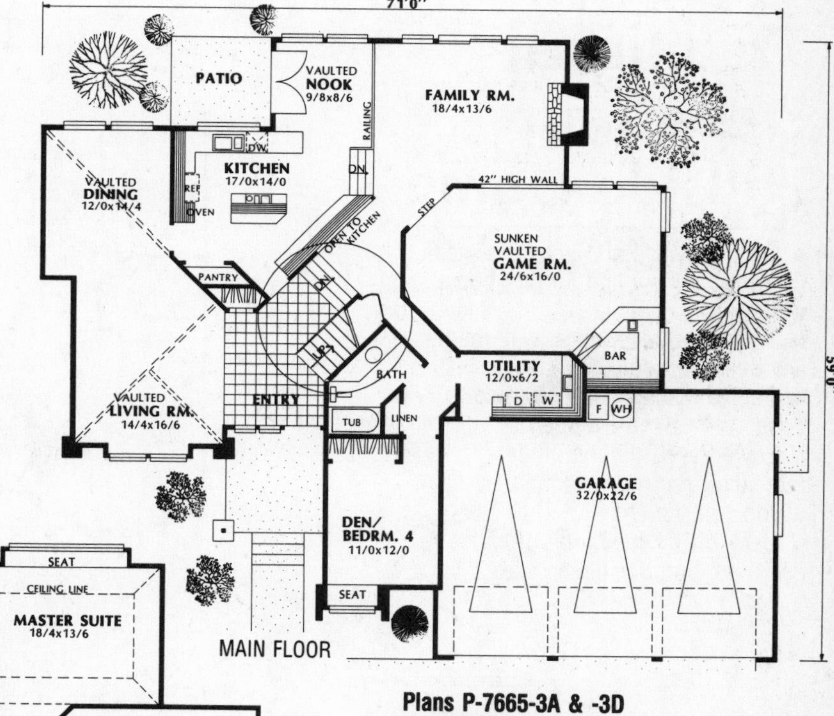

WITH DAYLIGHT BASEMENT

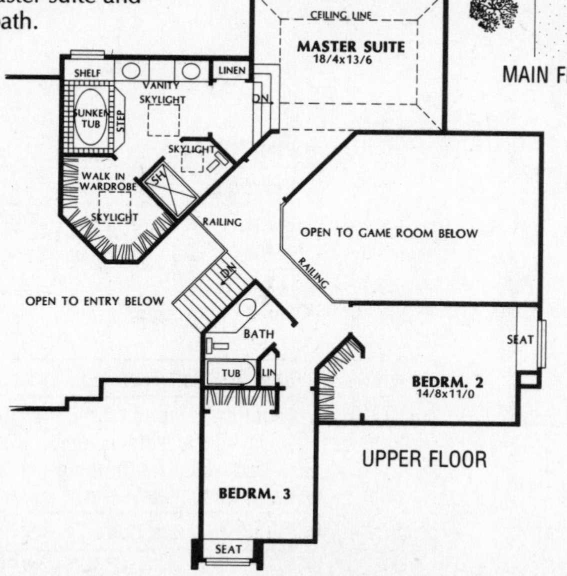

Plans P-7665-3A & -3D

Bedrooms: 3-4	**Baths:** 3
Space:	
Upper floor	1,160 sq. ft.
Main floor	2,124 sq. ft.
Total Living Area	**3,284 sq. ft.**
Basement	2,104 sq. ft.
Garage	720 sq. ft.
Exterior Wall Framing	2x4
Foundation options:	Plan #
Daylight Basement	P-7665-3D
Crawlspace	P-7665-3A
(Foundation & framing conversion diagram available—see order form.)	
Blueprint Price Code	E

Traditional Design for Hillside Home

- Window walls and solarium glass capture the view and fill this home with light.
- Traditional exterior is at home in any neighborhood.
- Deluxe master bedroom suite opens onto private deck.
- Lower level features huge recreation room with abundant window space.
- Deck off kitchen/nook provides delightful outdoor dining area.

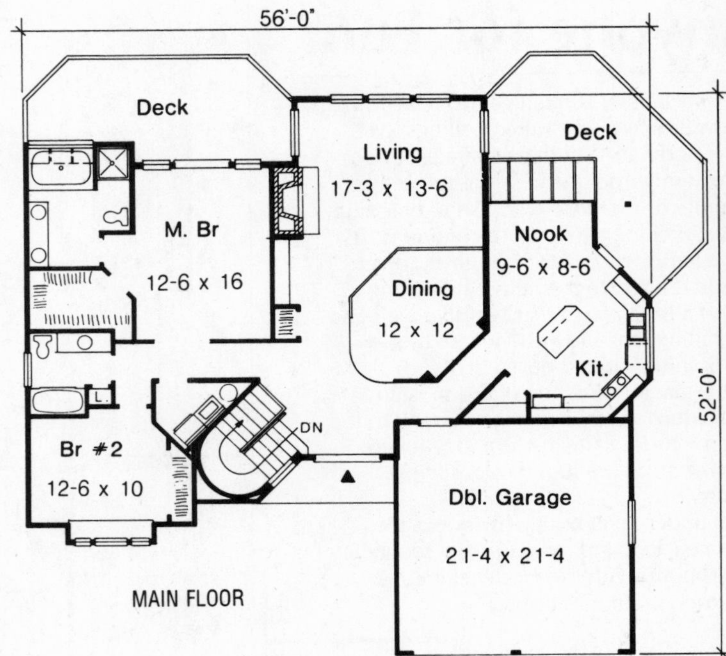

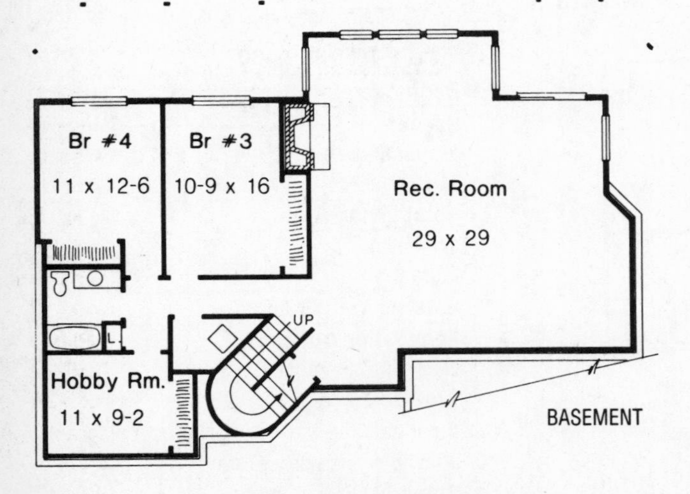

Plan NW-812	
Bedrooms: 4	**Baths:** 3
Space:	
Main floor:	1,685 sq. ft.
Lower floor:	1,611 sq. ft.
Total living area:	3,296 sq. ft.
Garage:	460 sq. ft.
Exterior Wall Framing:	2x6
Foundation options: Daylight basement only. (Foundation & framing conversion diagram available — see order form.)	
Blueprint Price Code:	E

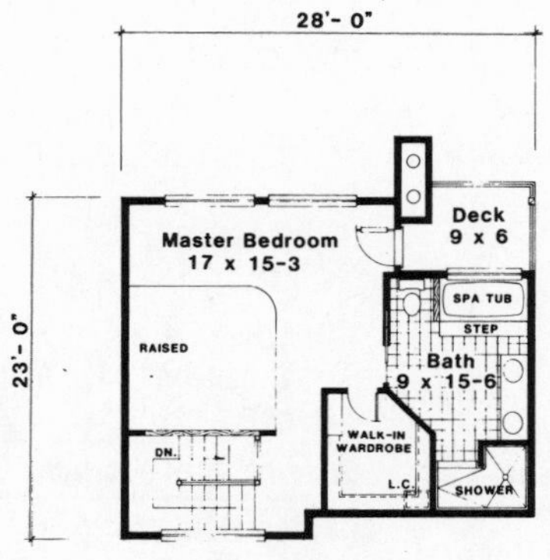

UPPER FLOOR

Tri-Level Living

- Upper level provides spectacular private master retreat with deluxe bath, private deck, raised bed area, large walk-in closet and large windows to the rear.
- Main floor includes spacious living room, library and formal dining room.
- Large kitchen adjoins sunny nook. Utility area also on main floor.
- Lower level features large family room, game room, wine cellar, two bedrooms and bath.

Plan NW-855

Bedrooms: 3	**Baths:** 2½
Space:	
Upper floor:	549 sq. ft.
Main floor:	1,388 sq. ft.
Lower floor:	1,371 sq. ft.
Total living area:	3,308 sq. ft.
Garage:	573 sq. ft.
Exterior Wall Framing:	2x6

Foundation options:
Daylight basement only.
(Foundation & framing conversion diagram available — see order form.)

Blueprint Price Code: E

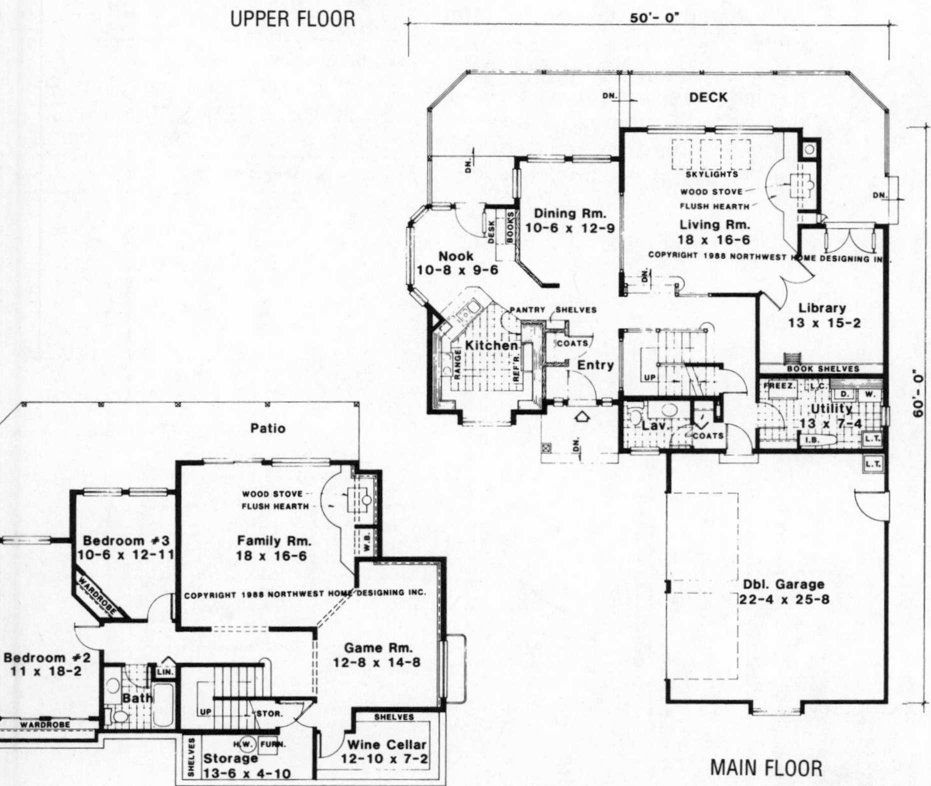

MAIN FLOOR

LOWER FLOOR

Sun Room Surprise

- A dramatic arched entry accented in brick and an angled garage characterize the exterior of this spacious home.
- A graceful arch leads visitors into the sunken living room, which is highlighted by an 11′ vaulted ceiling and handsome fireplace.
- Pillars mark the entrance into the adjoining dining room, which features a coffered ceiling and French doors that open to a deck outdoors.
- The kitchen features an angled center island and opens to the alcove nook and family room.
- Built-in cabinetry flanks the fireplace in the family room and French doors open into the adjoining sun room.
- Upstairs, the master bedroom includes a quiet sitting area nestled into an alcove and a luxurious private bath with two walk-in closets.
- A skylight brightens the continental bath shared by bedrooms two and three.
- Abundant space is provided in the daylight basement for expansion now or in the future. A fourth bedroom, study, rec room, bath, and reading alcove are all possible.

Plan CDG-2018

Bedrooms: 3-4	**Baths:** 2½
Space:	
Upper floor:	1,494 sq. ft.
Main floor:	1,822 sq. ft.
Total living area:	3,316 sq. ft.
Partial daylight basement:	1,306 sq. ft.
Garage:	836 sq. ft.
Exterior Wall Framing:	2x6
Ceiling Heights:	
Upper floor:	8′
Main floor:	9′
Foundation options:	
Partial daylight basement. (Foundation & framing conversion diagram available — see order form.)	
Blueprint Price Code:	E

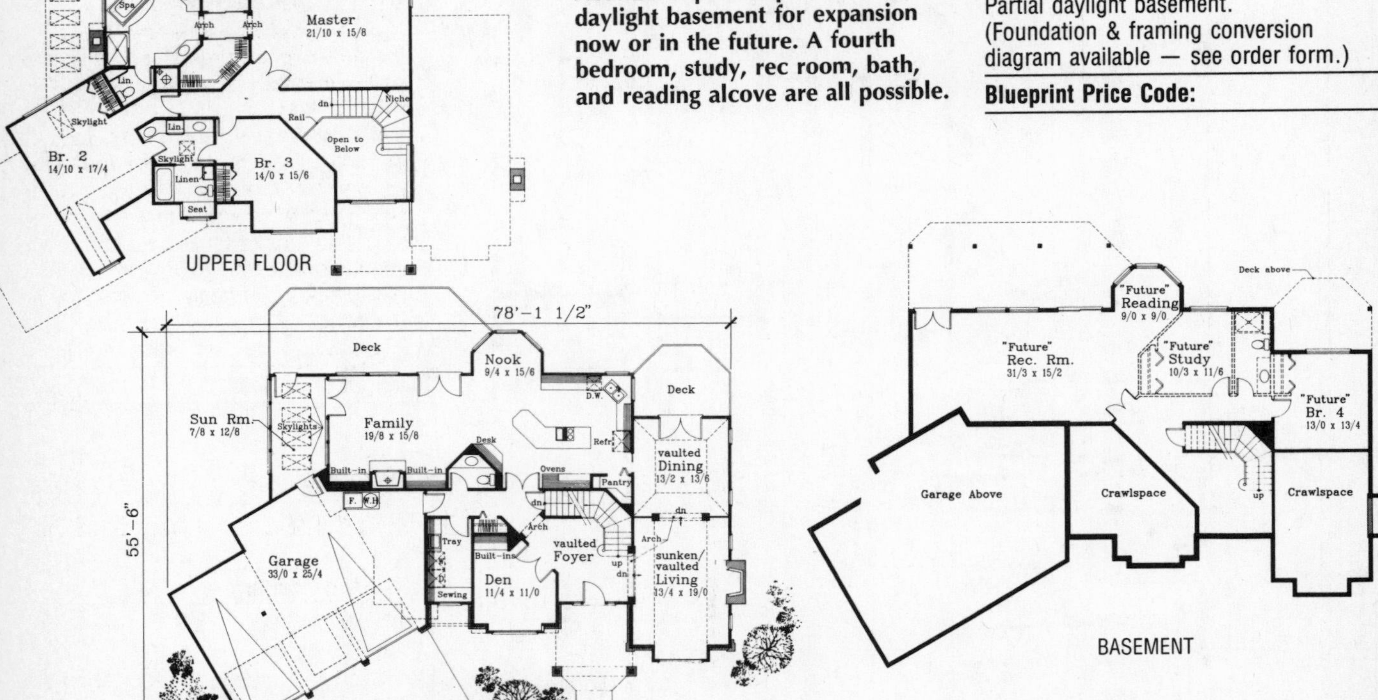

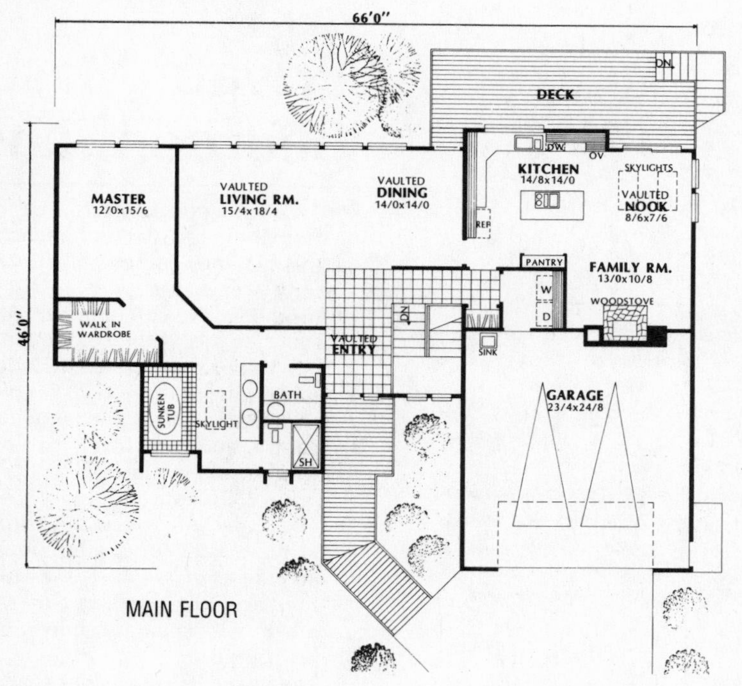

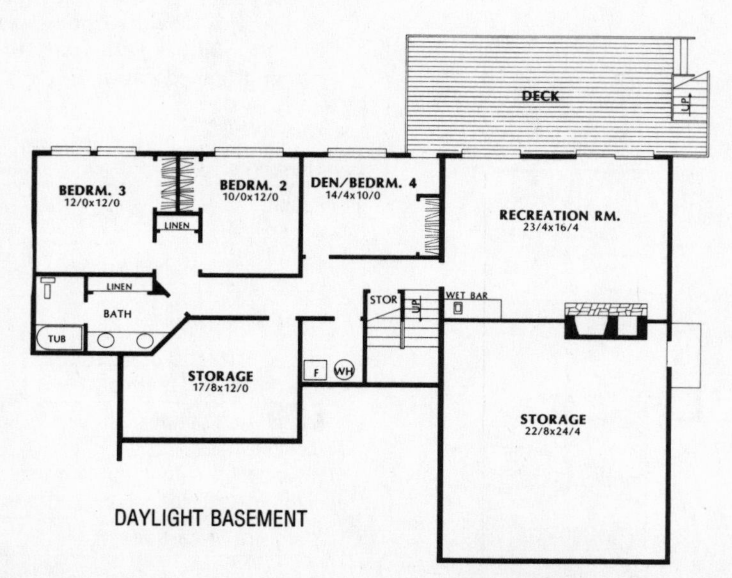

Spacious Home for Sloping Scenic Site

- Designed to gain full advantage of a sloping site with a view to the rear, this plan looks great from either side.
- The front view offers strong, horizontal lines and a series of stepped-up gable roofs. The rear offers eye-catching decks and abundant windows.
- Virtually every part of the interior offers a view to the backyard. The garage, storage areas and bathrooms face the street, to buffer the living areas.
- The island kitchen, nook and family room flow together for a great informal living space with a full window wall facing the view.
- The family room provides for a cozy wood stove, and the rec room offers an impressive fireplace as well as a wet bar.
- Huge "storage" areas on the lower level are available for many other uses, such as woodworking, exercise, play rooms or for a "cottage industry" of some type.

Plan P-7637-2D

Bedrooms: 4	**Baths:** 2½
Space:	
Main floor	1,691 sq. ft.
Daylight basement	2,023 sq. ft.
Total Living Area	**3,714 sq. ft.**
Garage	575 sq. ft.
Exterior Wall Framing	2x4

Foundation options:
Daylight Basement
(Foundation & framing conversion diagram available—see order form.)

Blueprint Price Code	**F**

Private Master Bedroom Loft

- An exciting deck wraps around the formal living areas and kitchen of this spacious contemporary, perfect for a scenic site.
- Inside, an eye-catching curved staircase lies at the center of the open floor plan, which includes a sunken living room with fireplace, an updated island kitchen with pantry, nook and lovely corner window above the sink, and a private library.
- The upper loft is devoted entirely to the master suite; attractions include a private deck and study, fireplace, huge walk-in closet, and a bath with separate shower and luxury tub.
- The lower level provides space for two additional bedrooms, a rec room, full bar with wine storage and attached patio.

Deck
DN.
Kit.
Nook
11 x 12-6
Dining
14 x 14
UP
UP
PANT.
L.C.
Util.
DN.
DN
UP
Foyer
Living
14 x 20
Deck
Garage
38 x 24
BOOKS
Library
12-4 x 11
BOOKS
Porch
MAIN FLOOR

90'10" x 57'2"

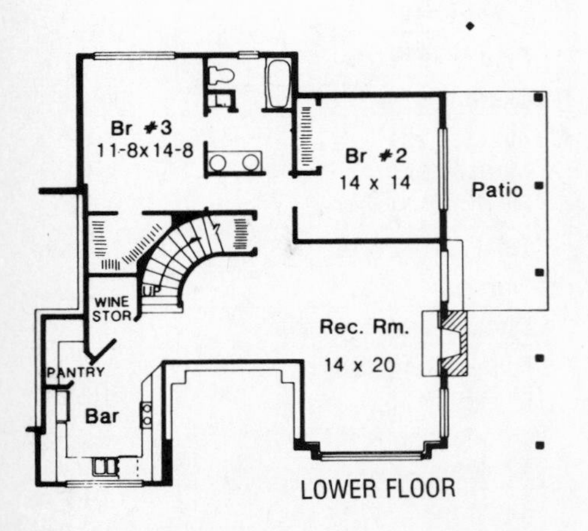

LOWER FLOOR

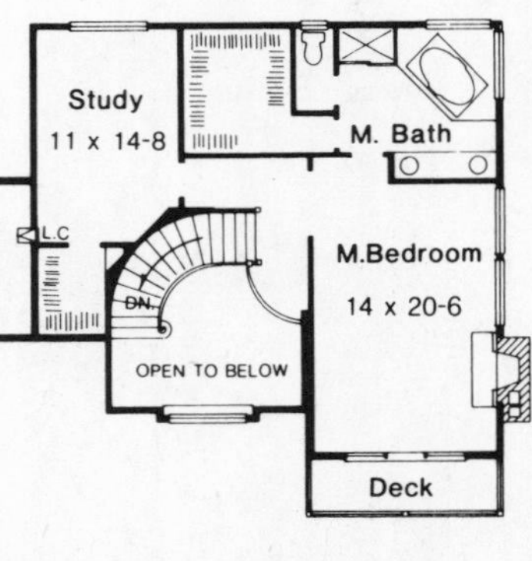

UPPER FLOOR

Plan NW-917	
Bedrooms: 3-4	**Baths:** 3½
Space:	
Upper floor:	905 sq. ft.
Main floor:	1,587 sq. ft.
Lower floor:	1,289 sq. ft.
Total living area:	3,781 sq. ft.
Garage:	912 sq. ft.
Exterior Wall Framing:	2x6
Foundation options:	
Daylight basement.	
(Foundation & framing conversion diagram available — see order form.)	
Blueprint Price Code:	F

An Array Of Luxuries

- This luxury home would ideally be built into a hill to allow full use of the home's basement.
- A panoramic view is captured from every primary room, including a deck that stretches along the rear of the home.
- Luxurious amenities inside include an island kitchen with separate walk-in pantry, window-enclosed nook, a huge family room with wood stove and rear window wall, a formal dining room with window seat, and a formal sunken living room.
- Other extras are the master bedroom with step-down onto the deck, roomy walk-in closet and a private bath with bayed step-up spa tub, separate shower and work area.
- Downstairs you'll find an exciting recreation room with wood stove and eye-catching bar, plus room for two additional bedrooms, a full bath and storage space.

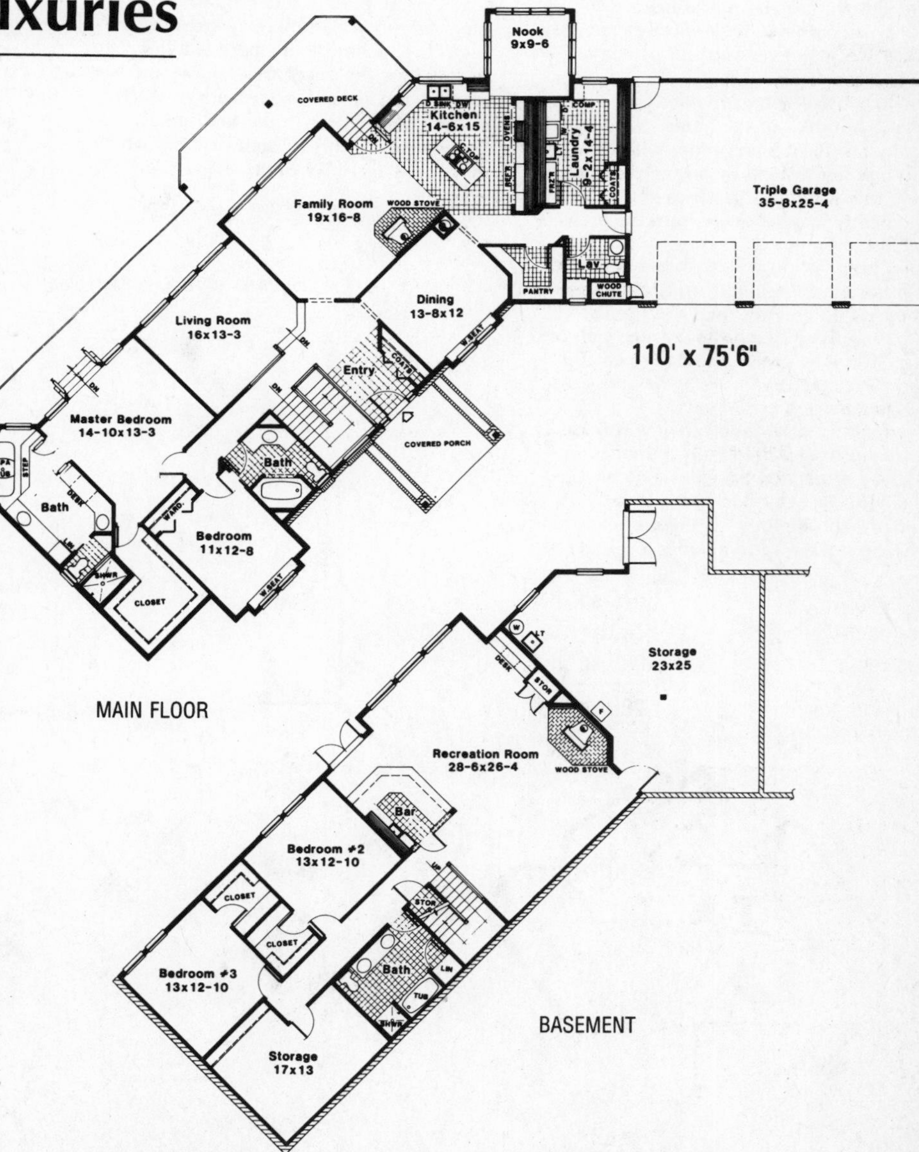

Plan NW-744

Bedrooms: 4	**Baths:** 3½
Space:	
Main floor:	2,539 sq. ft.
Daylight basement:	1,461 sq. ft.
Total living area:	4,000 sq. ft.
Storage rooms:	948 sq. ft.
Garage:	904 sq. ft.
Exterior Wall Framing:	2x6

Foundation options:
Daylight basement.
(Foundation & framing conversion diagram available — see order form.)

Blueprint Price Code:	G

Elegance at Every Turn

In this design, the warmth of brick masonry is combined with small-paned window treatment reminiscent of coastal New England styles.

The expansive entry provides easy access to all areas of the home. Note the octagonal, sunken living room with its multi-directional window arrangement. Also in this wing, is a spacious study conveniently located away from the active areas of the home.

Food preparation will be a dream in this kitchen of more than 250 sq. ft. Built-ins abound, as do counter tops and prep areas. A cooktop island range is the hub of this section. The breakfast nook opens up to the patio, extending the living and entertainment opportunities.

The master bedroom on the main floor is secluded from daily family activities, and a bay projection provides a quiet alcove. The French door opens to a secluded patio directly off the master suite. The master bath includes a raised soaking tub, private toilet, dual vanity, separate shower and large wardrobe.

On the second floor, there is a loft overlooking the entry area below, and two ample-sized secondary bedrooms which share a bath. There is also additional storage space, and a "bonus room" which may serve as a play room or for many other uses.

Main floor:	3,075 sq. ft.
Upper floor:	740 sq. ft.
Bonus room:	390 sq. ft.
Total living area: (Not counting garage)	4,205 sq. ft.

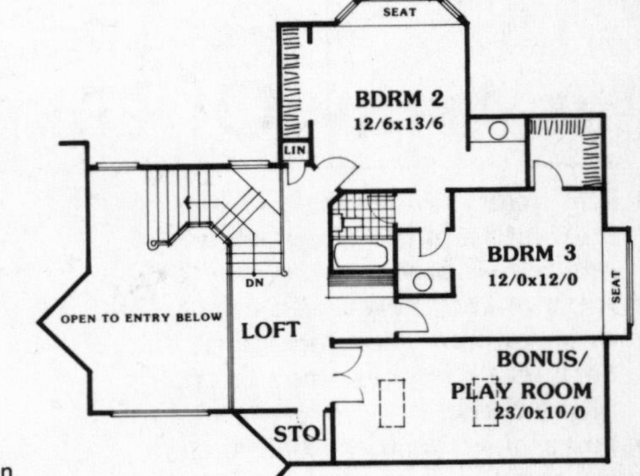

Exterior walls are 2x6 construction.

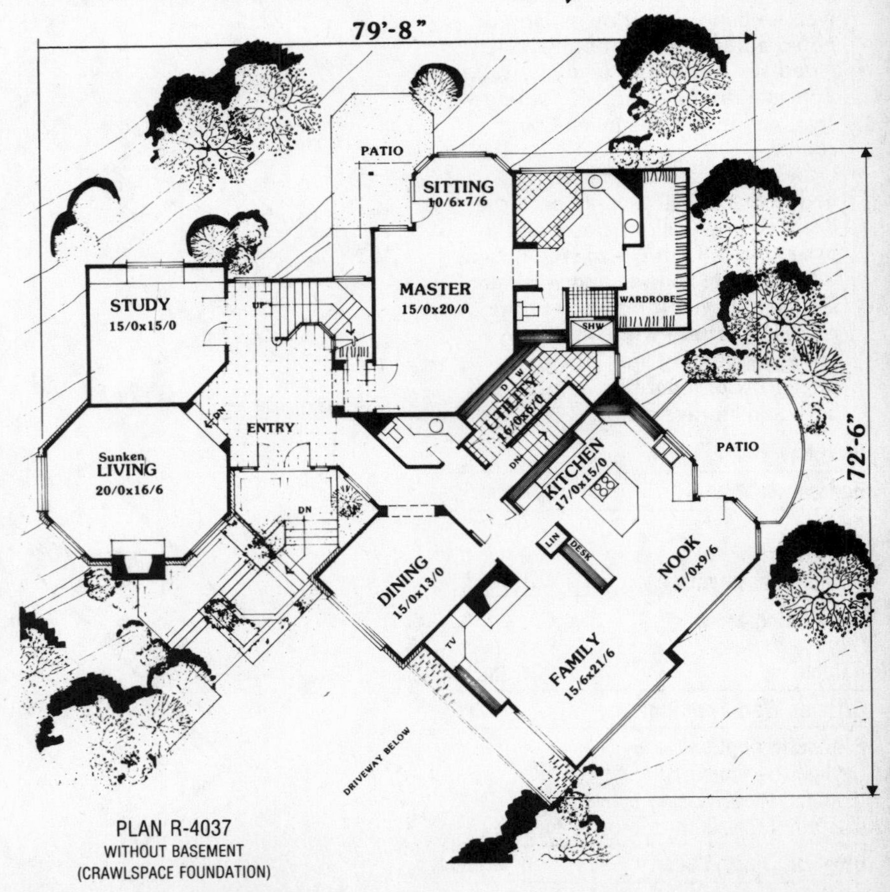

PLAN R-4037
WITHOUT BASEMENT
(CRAWLSPACE FOUNDATION)

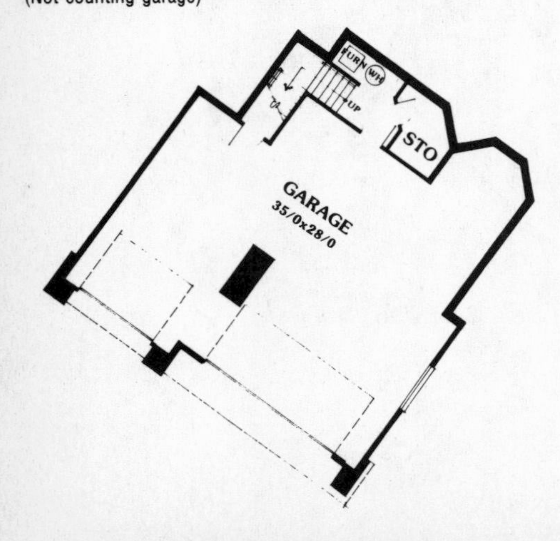

Blueprint Price Code G

Plan R-4037

PRICES AND DETAILS ON PAGES 12-15

Dramatic Interior Makes a Best-Seller

- **An incredible master suite takes up the entire 705 sq. ft. second floor, and includes deluxe bath, huge closet and skylighted balcony.**
- **Main floor design utilizes angles and shapes to create dramatic interior.**
- **Extra-spacious kitchen features large island, sunny windows and plenty of counter space.**
- **Sunken living room focuses on massive fireplace and stone hearth.**
- **Impressive two-level foyer is lit by skylights high above.**
- **Third bedroom or den with an adjacent bathroom makes an ideal home office or hobby room.**

Photo by Karlis Grants

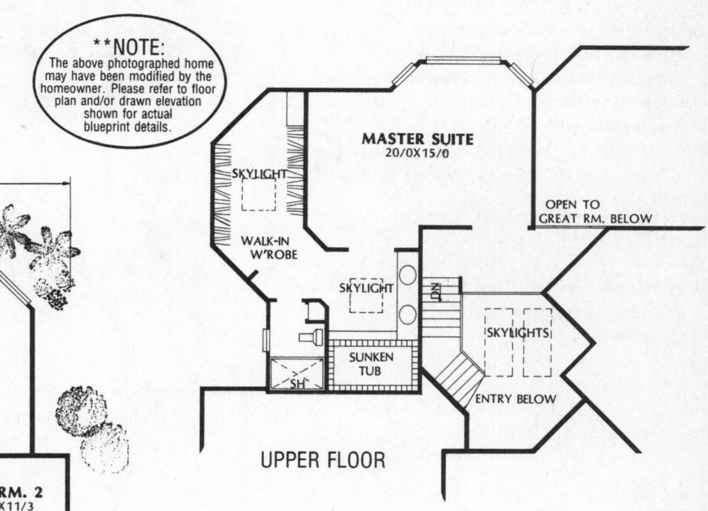

UPPER FLOOR

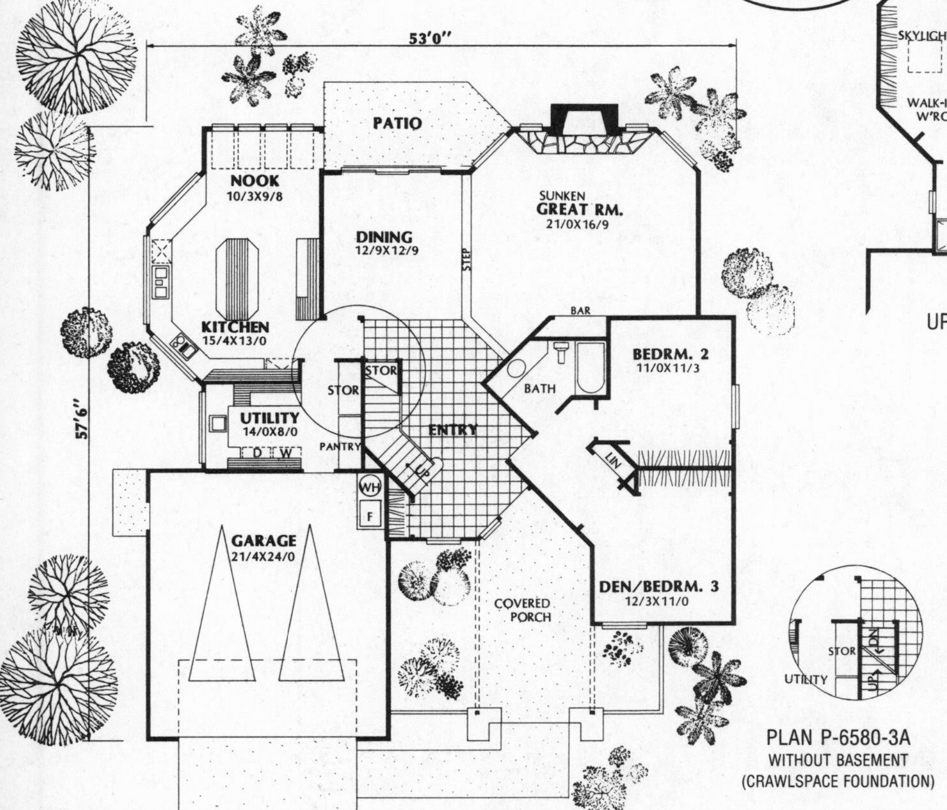

MAIN FLOOR

PLAN P-6580-3A
WITHOUT BASEMENT
(CRAWLSPACE FOUNDATION)

Plans P-6580-3A & -3D

Bedrooms: 2-3	**Baths:** 2
Space:	
Upper floor:	705 sq. ft.
Main floor:	1,738 sq. ft.
Total living area:	2,443 sq. ft.
Basement:	1,738 sq. ft.
Garage:	512 sq. ft.
Exterior Wall Framing:	2x4

Foundation options:
Daylight basement (Plan P-6580-3D).
Crawlspace (Plan P-6580-3A).
(Foundation & framing conversion diagram available — see order form.)

Blueprint Price Code: C

Luxury Home with Outdoor Orientation

Photo courtesy of Piercy & Barclay Designers, Inc.

- Courtyards, patios and a sun room orient this multi-level home to the outdoors.
- Interior design is carefully zoned for informal family living and formal entertaining.
- Expansive kitchen includes large island and plenty of counter space, and a sunny nook adjoins the kitchen.
- Soaring entry area leads visitors to the vaulted living room with fireplace, or to the more casual family room.
- An optional fourth bedroom off the foyer would make an ideal home office.
- Upstairs master suite includes luxury bath and big walk-in closet.
- Daylight basement version adds nearly 1,500 more square feet of space.

Plans P-7659-3A & -3D

Bedrooms: 3-4	**Baths:** 3
Space:	
Upper floor:	1,050 sq. ft.
Main floor:	1,498 sq. ft.
Total living area:	2,548 sq. ft.
Basement:	1,490 sq. ft.
Garage:	583 sq. ft.
Exterior Wall Framing:	2x4

Foundation options:
Daylight basement, Plan P-7659-3D.
Crawlspace, Plan P-7659-3A.
(Foundation & framing conversion diagram available — see order form.)

Blueprint Price Code: D

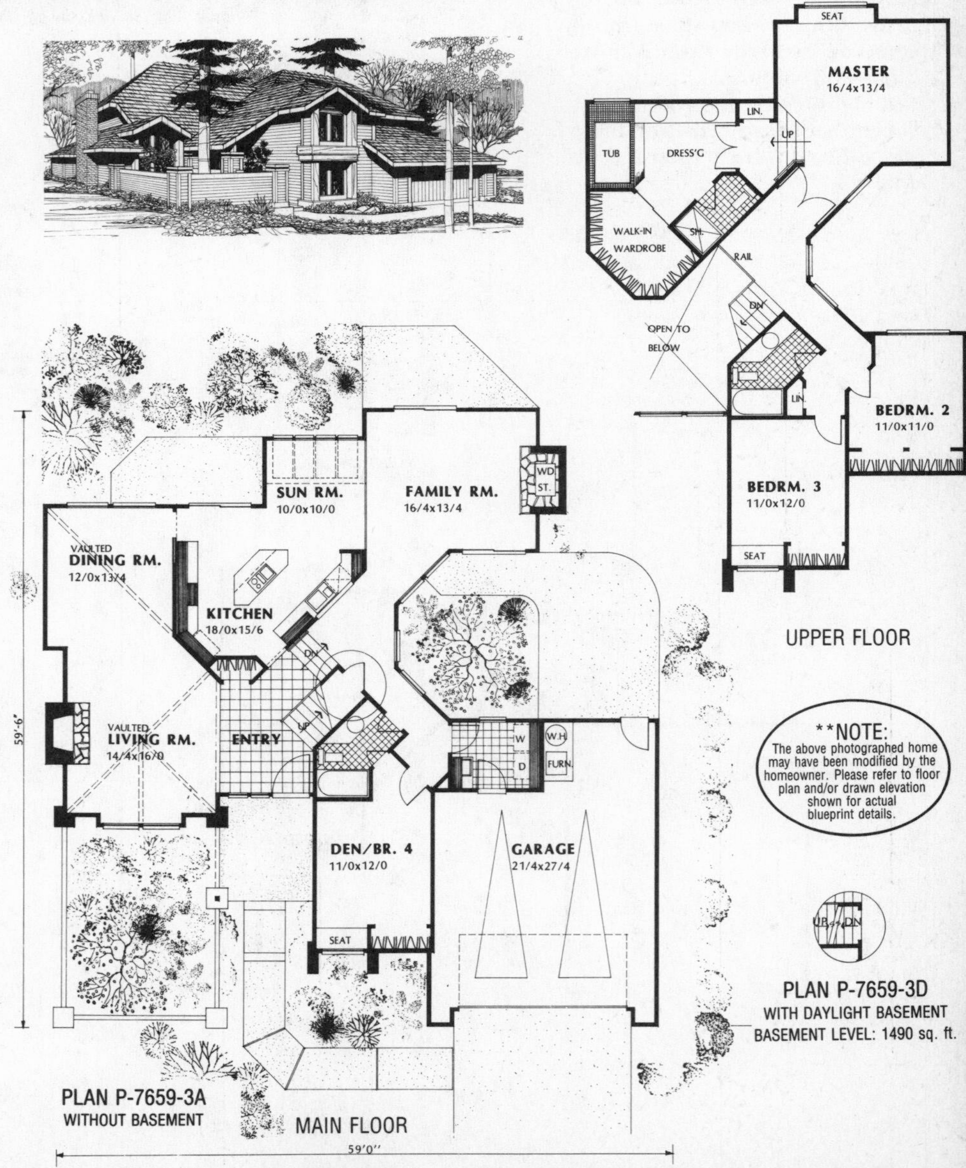

Gracious Open-Concept Floor Plan

- A striking and luxurious contemporary, this home offers great space and modern styling.
- A covered entry leads to a spacious foyer, which flows into the sunken dining and Great Room area.
- The vaulted Great Room boasts a spectacular two-story-high fireplace, dramatic window walls and access to a rear deck or patio.
- A bright nook adjoins the open kitchen, which includes a corner window above the sink.
- The den, which could be a guest bedroom, features a bay window overlooking the deck.
- The majestic master bedroom on the second floor offers a 10-ft.-high coved ceiling, a splendid bath, a large closet and a private deck.
- Two other upstairs bedrooms share a second bath and a balcony hallway overlooking the Great Room and entry below.

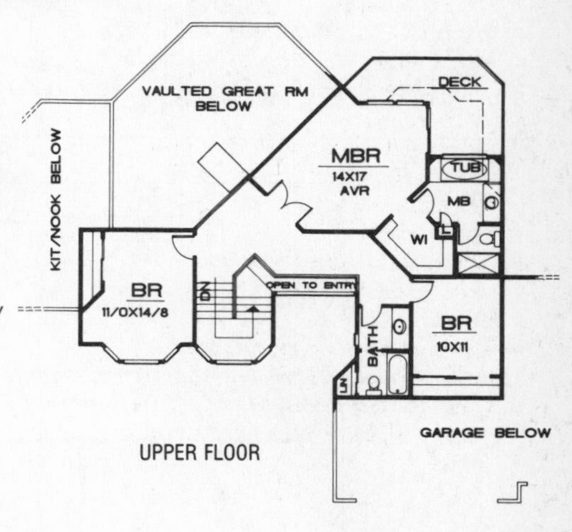

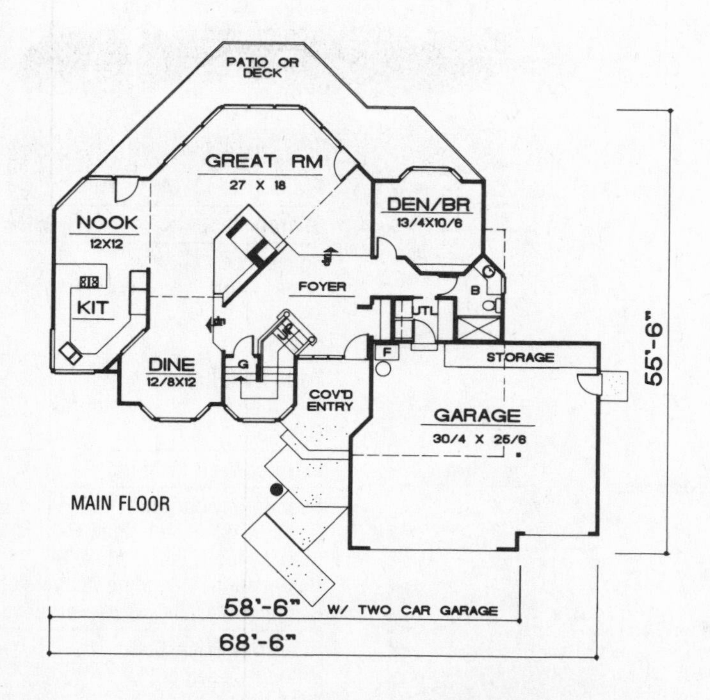

Plan S-41587	
Bedrooms: 3-4	**Baths:** 3
Living Area:	
Upper floor:	1,001 sq. ft.
Main floor	1,550 sq. ft.
Total Living Area:	**2,551 sq. ft.**
Basement	1,550 sq. ft.
Garage (three-car)	773 sq. ft.
Exterior Wall Framing:	2x6
Foundation Options:	
Daylight basement	
Standard basement	
Crawlspace	
Slab	
(Typical foundation & framing conversion diagram available—see order form.)	
BLUEPRINT PRICE CODE:	**D**

PLAN H-2114-1B REAR VIEW

Designed for Outdoor Living

- Dining room, living room, and spa are oriented toward the full-width deck extending across the rear of the home.
- Floor-to-ceiling windows, vaulted ceilings, and a fireplace are featured in the living room.
- Spa room has tile floor, operable skylights, and private access through connecting master suite.
- Upper level offers two bedrooms, spacious bathroom, and a balcony view of the living room and scenery beyond.

MAIN FLOOR

PLAN H-2114-1A
WITHOUT BASEMENT

PLAN H-2114-1B
WITH DAYLIGHT BASEMENT

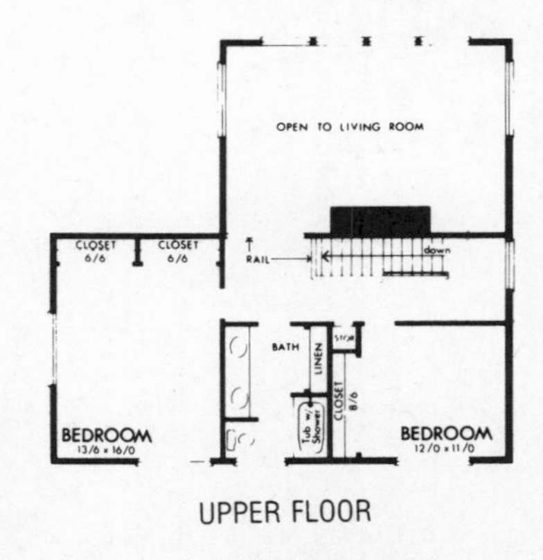

UPPER FLOOR

Plans H-2114-1A & -1B

Bedrooms: 3-4	**Baths:** 2½-3½
Space:	
Upper floor:	732 sq. ft.
Main floor:	1,682 sq. ft.
Spa room:	147 sq. ft.
Total living area:	2,561 sq. ft.
Basement:	approx. 1,386 sq. ft.
Garage:	547 sq. ft.
Exterior Wall Framing:	2x6

Foundation options:
Daylight basement (Plan H-2114-1B).
Crawlspace (Plan H-2114-1A).
(Foundation & framing conversion diagram available — see order form.)

Blueprint Price Code:	
Without basement:	D
With basement:	F

   PRICES AND DETAILS ON PAGES 12-15

Photo by Kevin Haslip

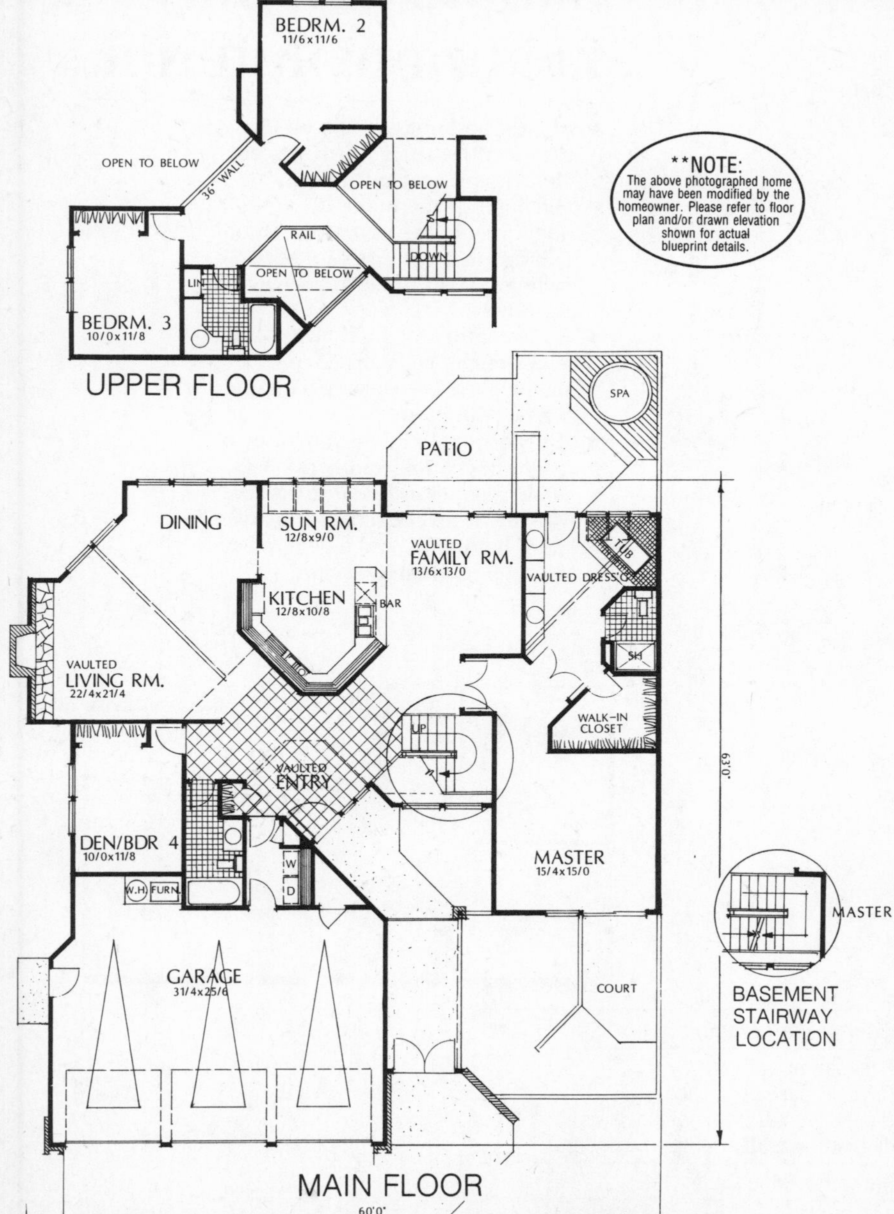

Privacy and Luxury

- This home's large roof planes and privacy fences enclose a thoroughly modern, open floor plan.
- A beautiful courtyard greets guests on their way to the secluded entrance. Inside, a vaulted entry area leads directly into the living and dining rooms, which also boast a vaulted ceiling, plus floor-to-ceiling windows, a fireplace and a wall-length stone hearth.
- A sun room next to the spacious, angular kitchen offers passive solar heating and natural brightness.
- The vaulted family room features access to a rear patio through sliding glass doors.
- The main-floor master bedroom boasts sliders to a secluded portion of the front courtyard. The vaulted master bath includes a walk-in closet, a raised tub, a separate shower and access to a private sun deck with a hot tub.
- Upstairs, two bedrooms are separated by a bridge hallway that overlooks the rooms below.

Plans P-7663-3A & -3D

Bedrooms: 3+	**Baths:** 3
Living Area:	
Upper floor	569 sq. ft.
Main floor	2,039 sq. ft.
Total Living Area:	**2,608 sq. ft.**
Daylight basement	2,039 sq. ft.
Garage	799 sq. ft.
Exterior Wall Framing:	2x4
Foundation Options:	**Plan #**
Daylight basement	P-7663-3D
Crawlspace	P-7663-3A
(Typical foundation & framing conversion diagram available—see order form.)	
BLUEPRINT PRICE CODE:	**D**

MAIN FLOOR

Simple Exterior, Luxurious Interior

- Modest and unassuming on the exterior, this design provides an elegant and spacious interior.
- Highlight of the home is undoubtedly the vast Great Room/ Dining area, with its vaulted ceiling, massive hearth and big bay windows.
- An exceptionally fine master suite is also included, with a large sleeping area, luxurious bath and big walk-in closet.
- A beautiful kitchen is joined by a bright bay-windowed breakfast nook; also note the large pantry.
- The lower level encompasses two more bedrooms and a generously sized game room and bar.

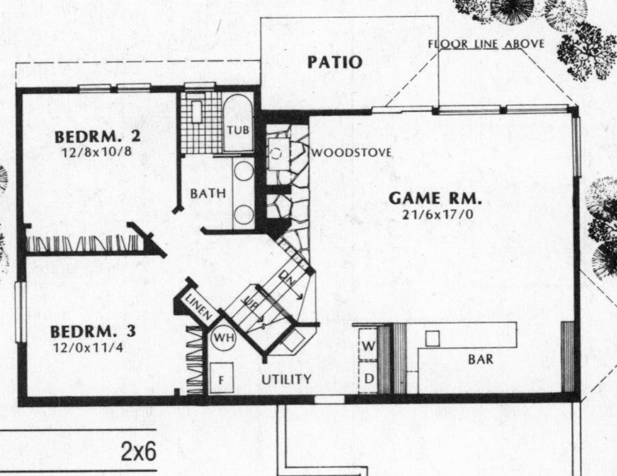

BASEMENT

Plan P-6595-3D

Bedrooms: 3	**Baths:** 2½
Space:	
Main floor:	1,530 sq. ft.
Lower level:	1,145 sq. ft.
Total living area:	2,675 sq. ft.
Garage:	462 sq. ft.

Exterior Wall Framing:	2x6
Foundation options:	
Daylight basement only. (Foundation & framing conversion diagram available — see order form.)	
Blueprint Price Code:	D

Classic Cape Cod

- Six eye-catching dormer windows and a charming front porch create a stately, dignified look for this handsome home.
- An elegant open staircase is the focal point of the inviting foyer, which is set off from the formal dining room by decorative wood columns.
- A swinging door leads to the exciting kitchen, which includes an angled counter overlooking the breakfast room.
- The spectacular skylighted family room boasts a soaring 17-ft.-high ceiling. A cozy fireplace is flanked by tall windows and a set of French doors to the backyard.
- The deluxe master bedroom offers a 13-ft. vaulted ceiling and a charming bay window. The skylighted master bath has a gaden spa tub, a separate shower, two walk-in closets and a dual-sink vanity.
- Upstairs, a railed balcony overlooks the family room and foyer. Three bright bedrooms share a hallway bath.

Plan CH-445-A

Bedrooms: 4	**Baths:** 2½
Living Area:	
Upper floor	988 sq. ft.
Main floor	1,707 sq. ft.
Total Living Area:	**2,695 sq. ft.**
Partial basement	1,118 sq. ft.
Garage	802 sq. ft.
Exterior Wall Framing:	2x4

Foundation Options:

Partial daylight basement
Partial basement
Crawlspace
(All plans can be built with your choice of foundation and framing. A generic conversion diagram is available. See order form.)

BLUEPRINT PRICE CODE: D

STORAGE
OPEN TO BELOW
BEDROOM #4
12'0" x 10'2"
DN
BEDROOM #2
12'0" x 16'0"
BEDROOM #3
12'5" x 14'6"

UPPER FLOOR

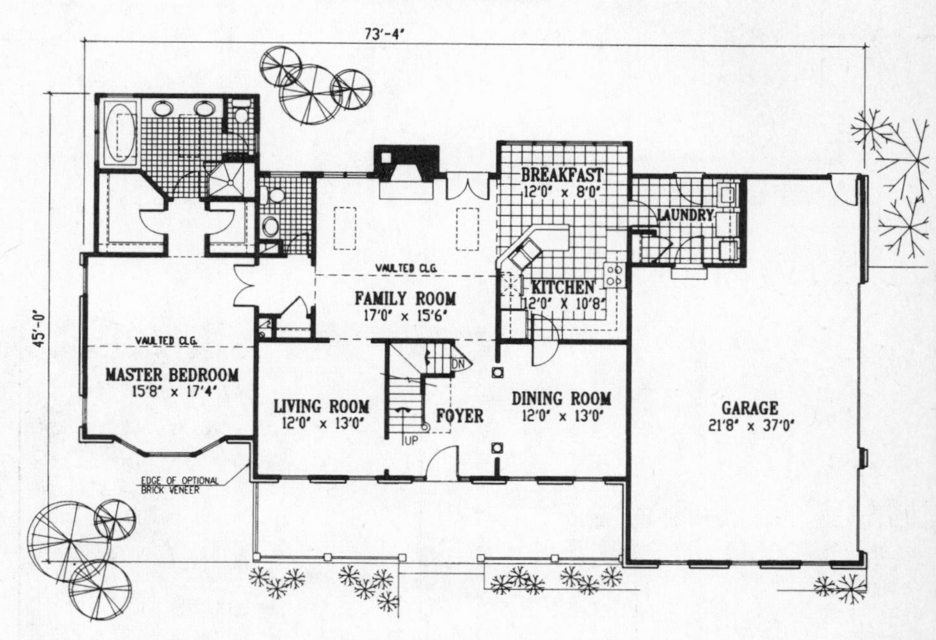

MAIN FLOOR

Dramatic Contemporary Takes Advantage of Slope

- Popular plan puts problem building site to work by taking advantage of the slope to create a dramatic and pleasant home.
- Spacious vaulted living/dining area is bathed in natural light from cathedral windows facing the front and clerestory windows at the peak.
- Big kitchen includes pantry and abundant counter space.
- Three main-level bedrooms are isolated for more peace and quiet.
- Lower level includes large recreation room, a fourth bedroom, third bath, laundry area and extra space for a multitude of other uses.

Photo by Kevin Robinson

**NOTE:
The above photographed home may have been modified by the homeowner. Please refer to floor plan and/or drawn elevation shown for actual blueprint details.

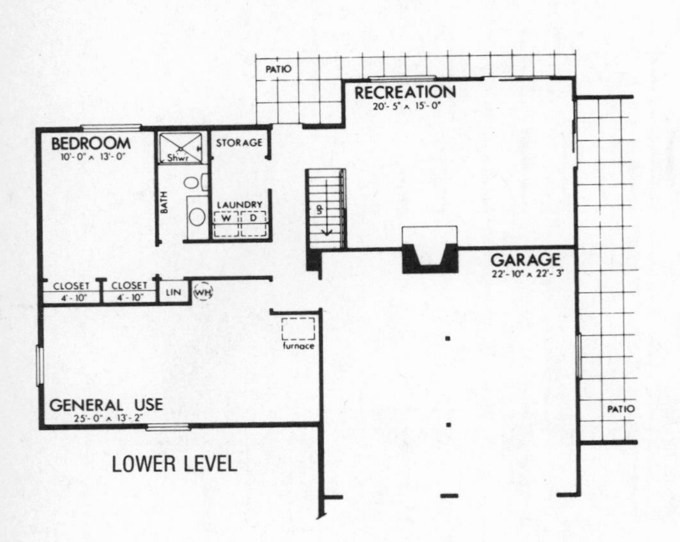

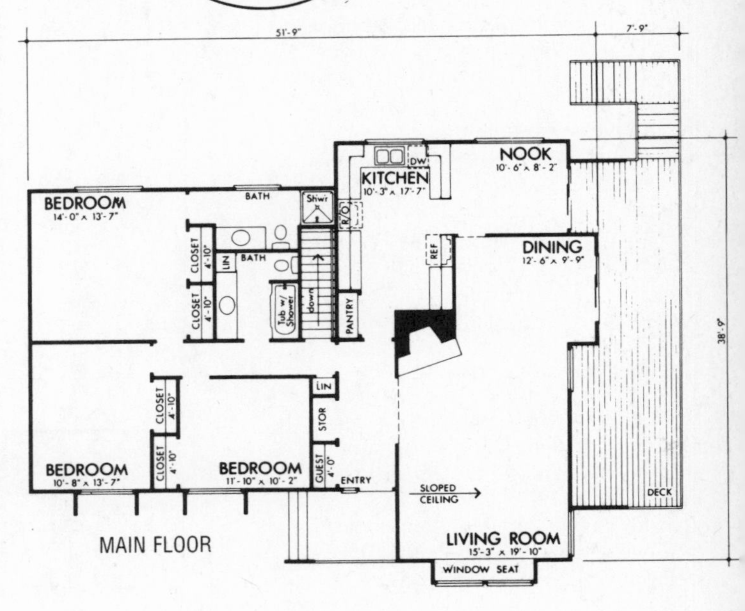

Plan H-2045-5

Bedrooms: 4	**Baths:** 3
Space:	
Main floor:	1,602 sq. ft.
Lower floor:	1,133 sq. ft.
Total living area:	2,735 sq. ft.
Garage:	508 sq. ft.
Exterior Wall Framing:	2x4

Foundation options:
Daylight basement only.
(Foundation & framing conversion diagram available — see order form.)

Blueprint Price Code: D

Photo by Mark Englund/HomeStyles

Soaring Entry

- A tall column at the forefront of this stylish home sets off a soaring two-story entry, where sidelights and a window above brighten a built-in art niche.
- The raised entry steps down to the living room, which features a striking fireplace and merges with the formal dining room. To the right of the entry, double doors open to a study with a boxed-out window.
- The casual areas flow together at the back of the home. The open kitchen offers easy service to the dining room and an island cooktop/snack bar to the breakfast nook. The sunny nook has a built-in desk and opens to a back patio. The adjoining family room has another fireplace and views to the backyard.
- An open-railed stairway leads to a balcony that overlooks the living room and the entry. The master suite features 9-ft. ceilings in the sleeping area and a luxurious garden bath.
- Each of the two secondary bedrooms has private access to another full bath. A large bonus room provides ample space for a play room, a guest room or a home studio.

NOTE:
The above photographed home may have been modified by the homeowner. Please refer to floor plan and/or drawn elevation shown for actual blueprint details.

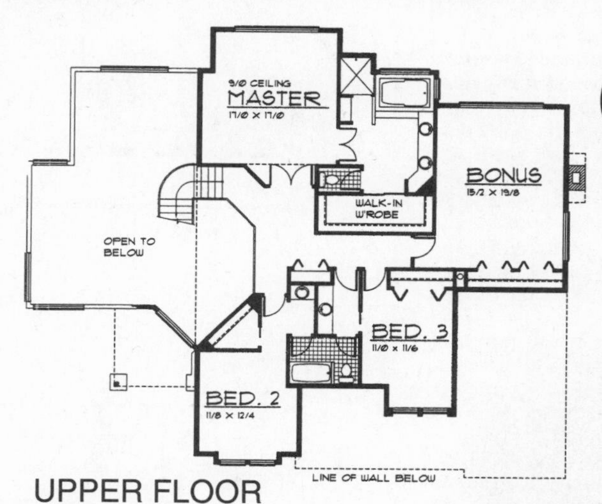

UPPER FLOOR

DINING
15/0 x 11/6
NOOK
10/6 x 11/6
FAMILY
15/0 x 17/0
PANTRY
LIVING
15/0 x 17/0
RAISED ENTRY
UTIL.
GARAGE
31/0 x 25/8
STUDY
11/6 x 14/0

MAIN FLOOR

Plan R-2167-D	
Bedrooms: 3+	**Baths:** 2½
Living Area:	
Upper floor	1275 sq. ft.
Main floor	1875 sq. ft.
Bonus room	355 sq. ft.
Total Living Area:	**3,505 sq. ft.**
Garage	765 sq. ft.
Exterior Wall Framing:	2x6
Foundation Options:	
Crawlspace	

(All plans can be built with your choice of foundation and framing. A generic conversion diagram is available. See order form.)

BLUEPRINT PRICE CODE: F

Attractive Hillside Home

This three-level recreation home is designed to fit comfortably on a slope of approximately 20 degrees, with a fall of 15 to 17 feet for the depth of the building. Naturally the stability of the ground must be taken into consideration, and local professional advice should be sought. Otherwise, this home is designed to meet the requirements of the Uniform Building Code.

The pleasing contemporary nature of the exterior is calculated to blend into the surroundings as unobtrusively as possible, following the natural contours.

The modest roadside facade consisting of garage doors and a wooden entrance deck conceals the spacious luxury that lies beyond. Proceeding from the rustic deck into the skylighted entry hall, one is struck by the immensity of the living-dining room and the huge deck extending beyond. A massive masonry backdrop provides a setting for the pre-fab fireplace of your choice (this same structure incorporates the flue for a similar unit on the lower level).

Before descending from the entry hall, one must take notice of the balcony-type den, library, hobby or office room on this level — a private retreat from the activities below.

The efficient U-shaped kitchen has an adjoining attached breakfast bar for casual dining whenever the roomy dining room facilities are not required. A convenient laundry room is an important part of this housekeeping section.

The master bedroom suite occupies the remainder of the 1,256 sq. ft. contained on this level. The room itself, 12' x 16' in size, is served by a private full bathroom and two huge wardrobe closets. Direct access to the large deck provides opportunity for morning sit-ups or evening conversation under the stars. A final convenience on this level is the small lavatory for general use.

The focal point of the lower level is the spacious recreation room which is a duplicate size of the living room above. Flanking this room at either end are additional large bedrooms, one having a walk-in closet and the other a huge wall-spanning wardrobe. Another full bathroom serves this level. A small work shop or storage room completes this arrangement.

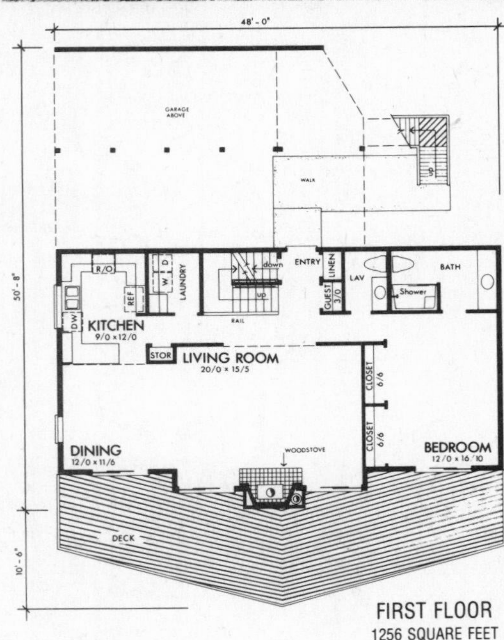

FIRST FLOOR
1256 SQUARE FEET

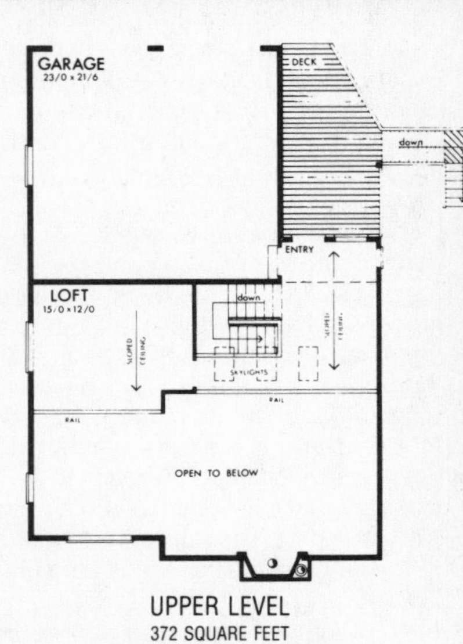

UPPER LEVEL
372 SQUARE FEET
528 SQUARE FEET - GARAGE

PLAN H-966-1B
WITH DAYLIGHT BASEMENT

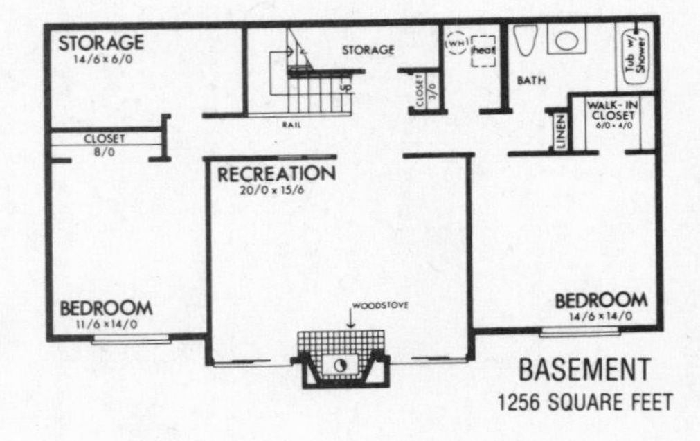

BASEMENT
1256 SQUARE FEET

(Exterior walls framed in 2x6 studs)

Upper level:	372 sq. ft.
Main floor:	1,256 sq. ft.
Basement:	1,256 sq. ft.
Total living area: (Not counting garage)	2,884 sq. ft.

Blueprint Price Code D

Plan H-966-1B

PRICES AND DETAILS ON PAGES 12-15

Dramatic Western Contemporary

- Dramatic and functional building features contribute to the comfort and desire of this family home.
- Master suite offers a spacious private bath and luxurious hydro spa.
- Open, efficient kitchen accommodates modern appliances, a large pantry, and a snack bar.
- Skylights shed light on the entryway, open staircase, and balcony.
- Upper level balcony area has private covered deck, and may be used as a guest room or den.

REAR VIEW

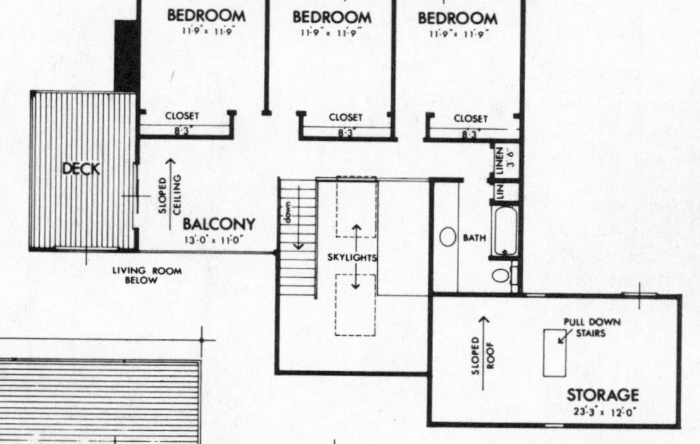

UPPER FLOOR

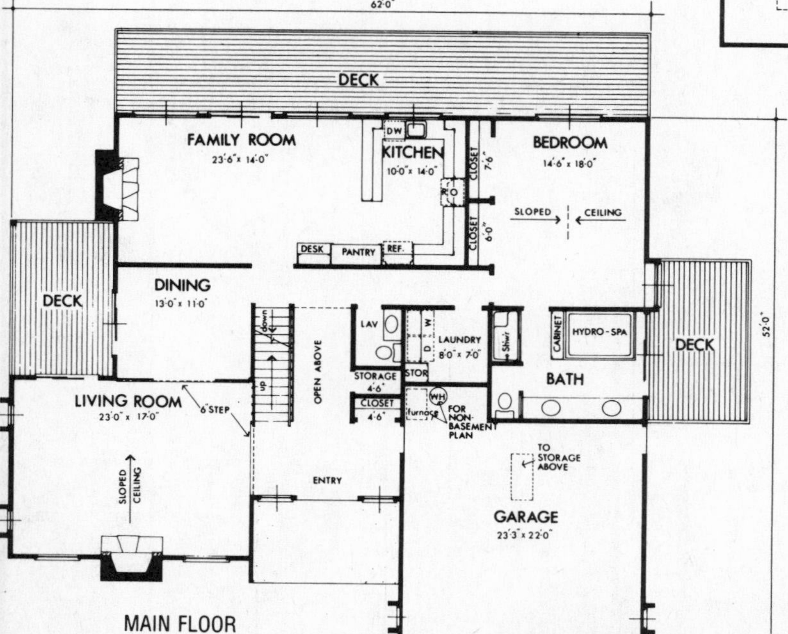

MAIN FLOOR

Plans H-3708-1 & -1A

Bedrooms: 4	**Baths:** 2½
Space:	
Upper floor:	893 sq. ft.
Main floor:	2,006 sq. ft.
Total living area:	2,899 sq. ft.
Basement:	approx. 2,006 sq. ft.
Garage:	512 sq. ft.
Exterior Wall Framing:	2x6

Foundation options:
Daylight basement (Plan H-3708-1).
Crawlspace (Plan H-3708-1A).
(Foundation & framing conversion diagram available — see order form.)

Blueprint Price Code:	D

Photo courtesy of Barclay Home Designs.

Tudor-Inspired Hillside Design

- The vaulted entry opens to a stunning living room with a high ceiling and massive fireplace.
- The dining room, five steps higher, overlooks the living room for a dramatic effect.
- Double doors lead into the informal family area, which consists of a beautifully integrated kitchen, nook and family room.
- The magnificent master suite, isolated downstairs, includes a sumptuous bath, enormous wardrobe and double-door entry.
- The upstairs consists of three more bedrooms, a bath and balcony hallway open to the entry below.
- Three-car garage is tucked under the family room/dining room area.

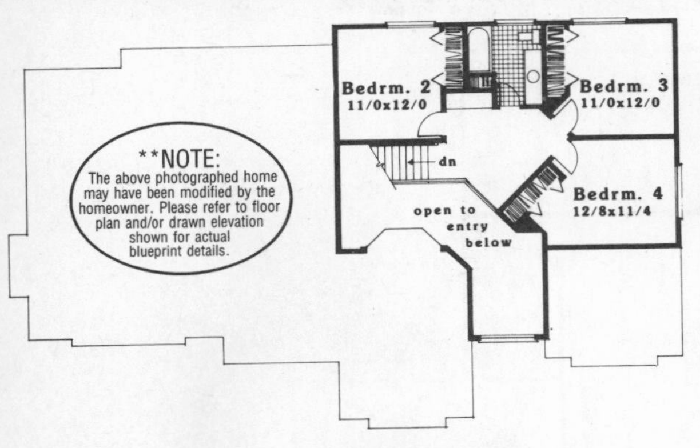

UPPER FLOOR

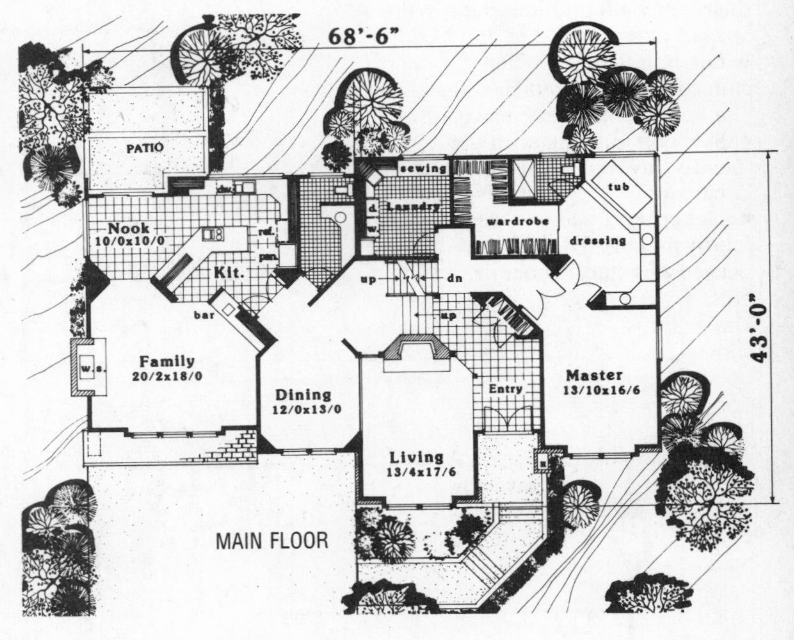

MAIN FLOOR

Plan R-4001	
Bedrooms: 4	**Baths:** 2½
Living Area:	
Upper floor	709 sq. ft.
Main floor	2,388 sq. ft.
Total Living Area:	**3,097 sq. ft.**
Garage	906 sq. ft.
Exterior Wall Framing:	2x6

Foundation Options:
Crawlspace
(Typical foundation & framing conversion diagram available—see order form.)

BLUEPRINT PRICE CODE: E

Photo by Jon Speck

Luxuries Abound

- This design is filled with luxuries, beginning with the front door. Sidelights and a large transom flood the vaulted, raised entry hall with light.
- Straight ahead, French doors and windows in the living room provide a stunning view of the backyard.
- The formal dining room is elegantly capped with an arched ceiling.
- Vaulted ceilings further expand the combination kitchen, eating nook and family room. This entire area opens to a four-season porch, which gives way to a deck for even more space for outdoor entertainment.
- The fabulous main-floor master suite showcases a bath with a tray ceiling, a luxurious whirlpool tub and double-door access to the backyard.
- Upstairs, a versatile loft and a balcony hall lead to three bedrooms and a compartmentalized bath.
- The home features 9-ft. ceilings throughout the main floor, unless otherwise noted.

Plan AH-3230	
Bedrooms: 4	**Baths:** 2½
Living Area:	
Upper floor	890 sq. ft.
Main floor	2,340 sq. ft.
Total Living Area:	**3,230 sq. ft.**
Daylight basement	2,214 sq. ft.
Garage	693 sq. ft.
Exterior Wall Framing:	2x6
Foundation Options:	
Daylight basement	

(All plans can be built with your choice of foundation and framing. A generic conversion diagram is available. See order form.)

BLUEPRINT PRICE CODE: E

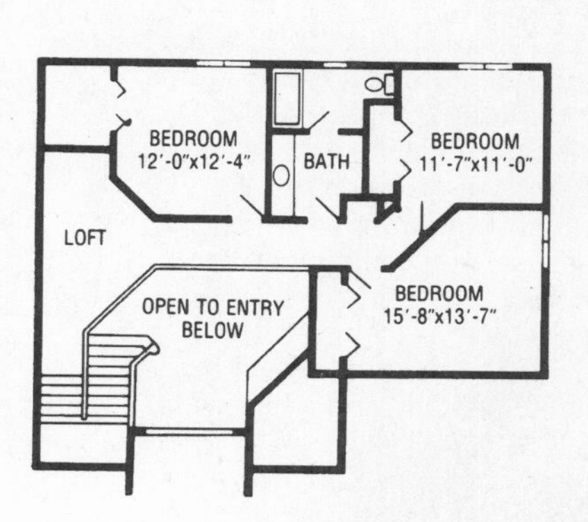

UPPER FLOOR

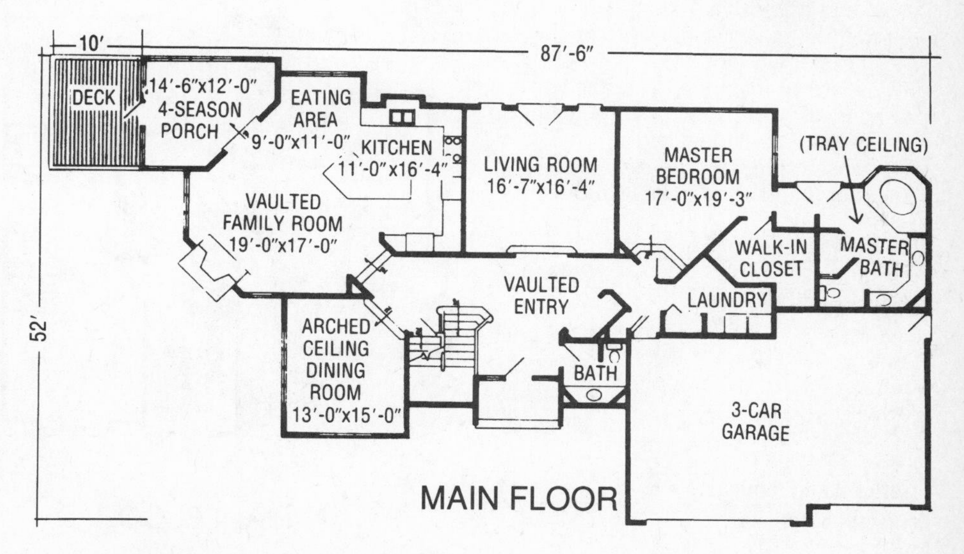

MAIN FLOOR

Photo by Mark Englund/HomeStyles

Step Up To Luxury

- This luxurious home is ideal for a sloping lot, with steps that rise to the two-story-high front entry.
- A column to the left of the entry introduces the living room, which is crowned by a stepped ceiling that rises to nearly 15 feet.
- Five steps up, columns embrace the entrance to the dining room, which has a 17½-ft. vaulted ceiling and a half-wall overlooking the living room.
- The roomy kitchen offers a bright corner sink and an island cooktop. French doors open from the bayed nook to the backyard patio. The adjoining family room features a 14-ft. vaulted ceiling and a focal-point fireplace.
- The luxurious master suite includes an opulent bath with a step-up garden tub, a separate shower and a walk-in closet. A quiet study is close by.
- The spacious main floor is further enhanced by 9-ft. ceilings throughout, unless otherwise indicated.
- Upstairs, a split bath serves two bedrooms and a large bonus room.

Plan R-4043

Bedrooms: 3+	**Baths:** 2-
Living Area:	
Upper floor	625 sq. ft.
Main floor	2,330 sq. ft.
Bonus room	425 sq. ft.
Total Living Area:	**3,380 sq. ft.**
Tuck-under garage	752 sq. ft.
Exterior Wall Framing:	2x4

Foundation Options:

Slab

(All plans can be built with your choice of foundation and framing. A generic conversion diagram is available. See order form.)

BLUEPRINT PRICE CODE: E

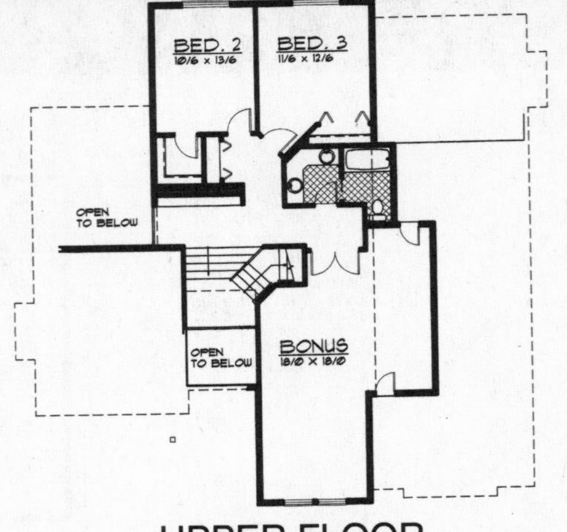

UPPER FLOOR

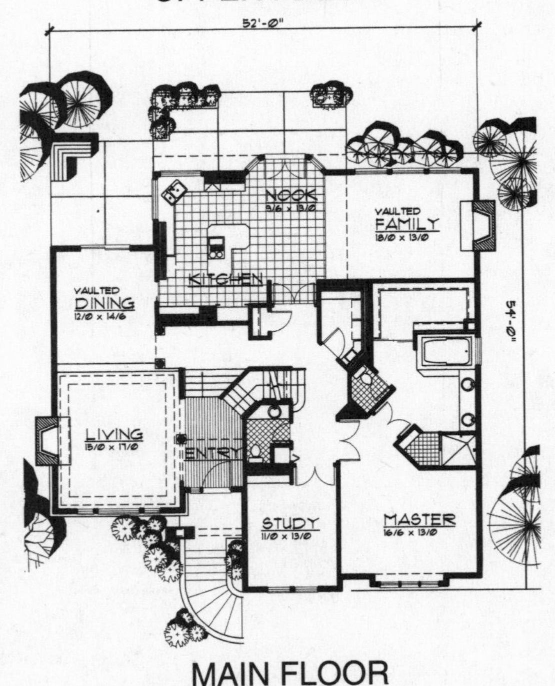

MAIN FLOOR

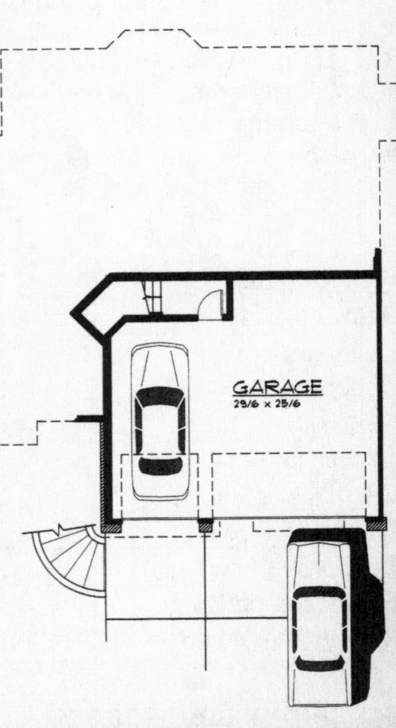

TUCK-UNDER GARAGE

TO ORDER THIS BLUEPRINT, CALL TOLL-FREE 1-800-547-5570

Plan R-4043

PRICES AND DETAILS ON PAGES 12-15

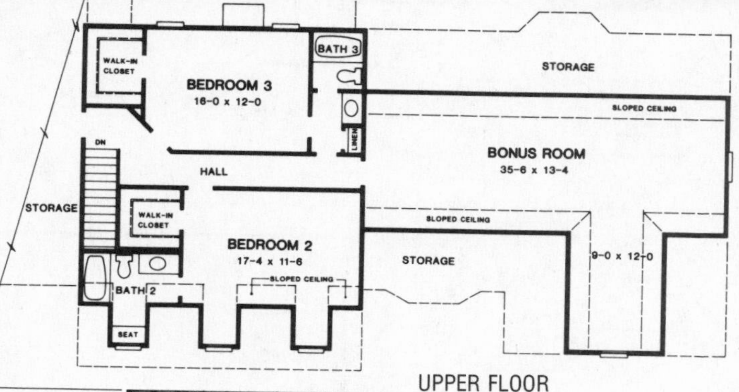

UPPER FLOOR

Deluxe Main-Floor Master Suite

- Traditional-style exterior with modern floor plan. Dormers and stone add curb appeal to this home.
- Formal entry with staircase leads to formal living or large family room.
- Large kitchen is conveniently located between formal dining room and secluded breakfast nook with bay window.
- Private master suite has tray ceiling and walk-in closet. Master bath has corner tub, shower, and dual vanities.
- Large screened porch off family room is perfect for outdoor living.
- Large utility room with pantry and toilet are conveniently located off the garage.
- Second floor features two large bedrooms with walk-in closets and two full baths.
- Optional bonus room (624 sq. ft.) can be finished as a large game room, bedroom, office, etc.

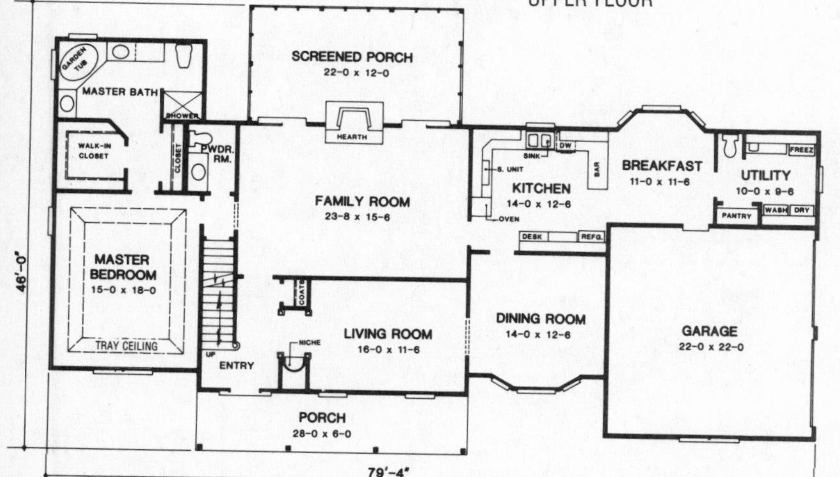

MAIN FLOOR

Plan C-8915

Bedrooms: 3	**Baths:** 3½
Space:	
Upper floor:	832 sq. ft.
Main floor:	1,927 sq. ft.
Bonus area:	624 sq. ft.
Total living area:	3,383 sq. ft.
Basement:	1,674 sq. ft.
Garage:	484 sq. ft.
Exterior Wall Framing:	2x4

Ceiling Heights:	
First floor:	9′
Second floor:	8′

Foundation options:
Daylight basement.
Crawlspace.
(Foundation & framing conversion diagram available — see order form.)

Blueprint Price Code: E

Superb Views

- This superb multi-level home is designed to take full advantage of spectacular surrounding views.
- The two-story-high entry welcomes guests in from the covered front porch. An open-railed stairway and a 23-ft. domed ceiling are highlights here.
- The sunken living and dining rooms are defined by archways and face out to a large wraparound deck. The living room has a 13-ft. cathedral ceiling and a nice fireplace. The dining room offers a 9½-ft. domed ceiling and a wet bar.
- The octagonal island kitchen hosts a Jenn-Aire range, a sunny sink and a bayed breakfast nook. Nearby, the utility room reveals a walk-in pantry, laundry facilities and garage access.
- The quiet den boasts a second fireplace, a cozy window seat and deck access.
- The entire upper floor is occupied by the master bedroom suite, which has a spacious bayed sleeping room with a 12½-ft. cathedral ceiling. Other features include a huge walk-in closet, separate dressing areas and a private bath with a curved shower and a Jacuzzi tub.
- The exciting daylight basement has a recreation room, an exercise room and another bedroom, plus a sauna and a hot tub surrounded by windows!

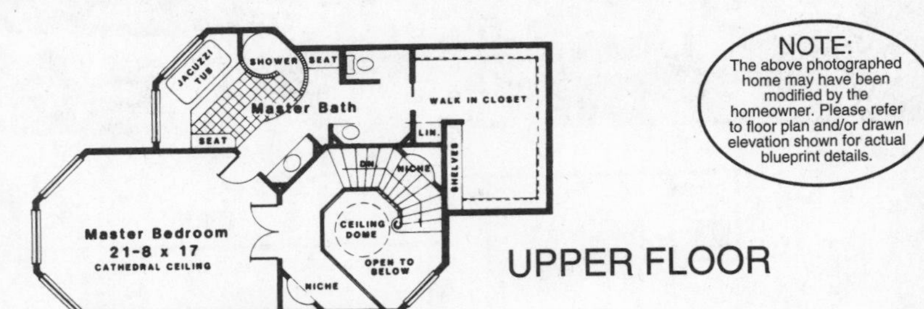

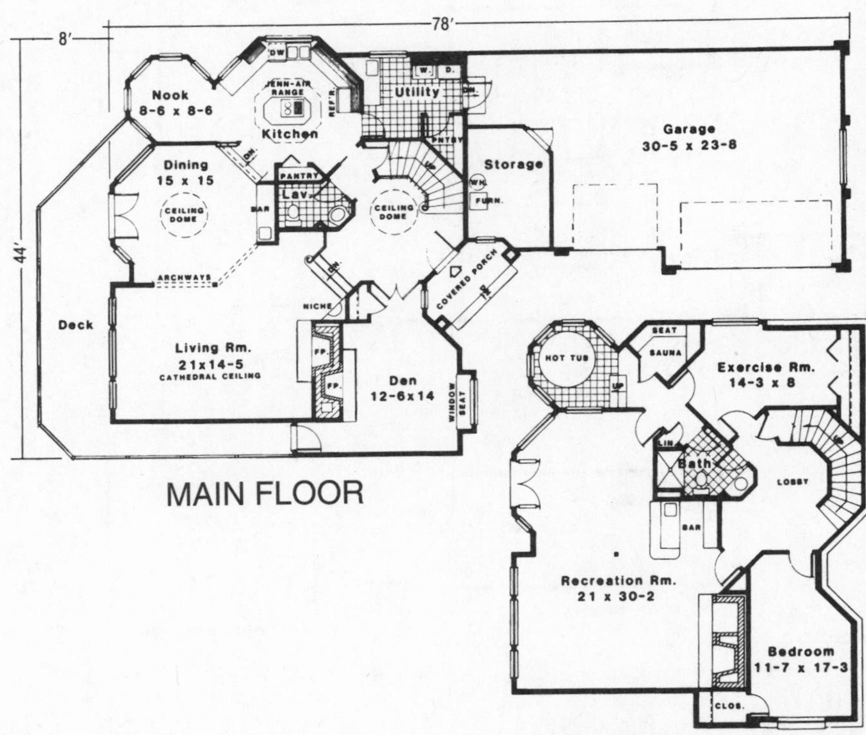

Plan NW-229	
Bedrooms: 2+	**Baths:** 2½
Living Area:	
Upper floor	815 sq. ft.
Main floor	1,446 sq. ft.
Daylight basement	1,330 sq. ft.
Total Living Area:	**3,591 sq. ft.**
Garage	720 sq. ft.
Exterior Wall Framing:	2x6

Foundation Options:

Daylight basement

(All plans can be built with your choice of foundation and framing. A generic conversion diagram is available. See order form.)

BLUEPRINT PRICE CODE: **F**

TO ORDER THIS BLUEPRINT, CALL TOLL-FREE 1-800-547-5570

Plan NW-229

PRICES AND DETAILS ON PAGES 12-15